The European Tour
Yearbook 2000

Lennard
Queen Anne Press

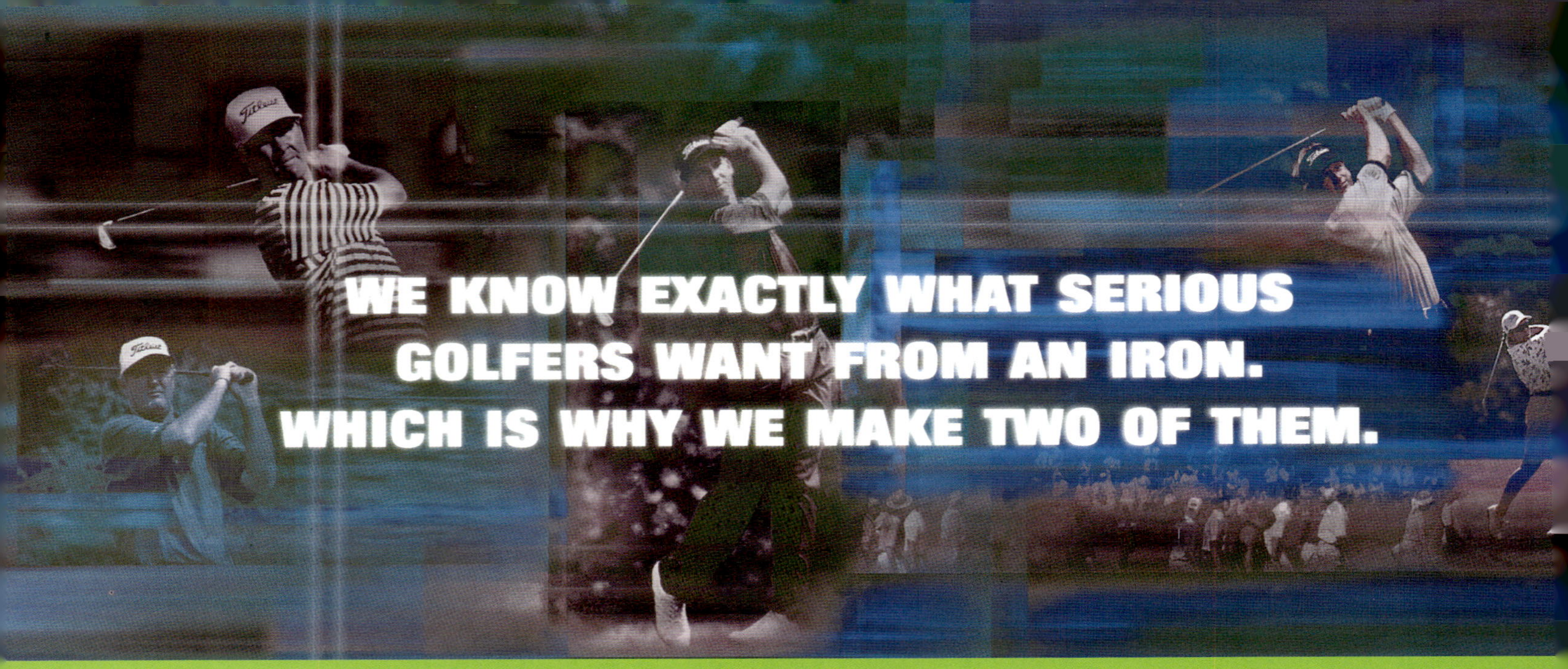

DCI 990 IRONS

The choice of Sergio Garcia, Davis Love III and other leading professionals, DCI 990 is the newest tour-proven iron from Titleist's industry-leading development team. A high performance blade design, the DCI 990 offers solid feel, shot-shaping control, playability and clean, classic looks. With a progressive muscleback cavity design, the long irons are easier to hit without sacrificing shot workability. The short irons promote a flatter trajectory and more controllable ball flight.

DCI 981 IRONS

The tour-proven DCI 981 is designed for both skilled and aspiring players who want high performance, great looks and solid feel in a progressive offset blade iron. DCI 981 offers a higher, straighter ball flight with the playability and forgiveness of an oversize iron. And with Titleist's renowned development prowess, it's easy to see why serious golfers rely on Titleist for the ultimate in high performance. For more information, visit your local golf shop, www.titleist.com or call Titleist free on 0800 616198.

Titleist, St. Ives, Cambs PE17 4LS www.titleist.com

Introduction from the European Tour

Executive Editor
Mitchell Platts

Editor in Chief
Mark Wilson

Editor
Chris Plumridge

Picture Editors
David Cannon
Stephen Munday
Andrew Redington

Art Director
Harpers of Northampton

Production
Denise Thurling
Vanessa O'Brien
Valerie Steele

The European Tour Yearbook 2000
is published by
the PGA European Tour,
Wentworth Drive, Virginia Water,
Surrey GU25 4LX.

Distributed through Lennard Queen Anne Press.

Colour reproduction and printing by
The Manson Group, St Albans

© PGA European Tour.

ISBN 1 85291 612 5

Colin Montgomerie's success in retaining his leadership of the Volvo Order of Merit for a record seventh successive time was among European golf's most outstanding achievements during 1999. The others included José Maria Olazábal's magnificent second triumph at Augusta National in the Masters Tournament, Paul Lawrie's superb victory in the 128th Open Championship, and the emergence of Sergio Garcia on the eve of a new millennium.

Colin won five times on the European Tour, including a successful defence of the Volvo PGA Championship at Wentworth Club, in addition to capturing the Cisco World Match Play Championship. His dominance of the Volvo Order of Merit during the last decade has set standards of the highest calibre, and we share with many observers the view that he has been the most consistent golfer in the world in this time.

José Maria's recovery from an illness which threatened his career continued with his outstanding win in the Masters Tournament. Paul demonstrated in capturing the Open Championship that he has the skill and the character possessed by all true champions of the game. Sergio won twice on the European Tour,

winning Rookie of the Year honours, and in addition finished runner-up in the US PGA Championship and partnered Miguel Angel Jiménez and José Maria Olazábal to win the Alfred Dunhill Cup for Spain.

There were many other moments to savour. Miguel Angel, Jarmo Sandelin and Lee Westwood, in addition to Colin, Paul and Sergio, were all multiple winners on the Tour. Tommy Horton led the European Seniors Tour Order of Merit for the fourth time in succession, and the fifth time in seven years, and Carl Suneson won three times on his way to finishing number one in the European Challenge Tour Rankings.

I know that the Members and the staff of the European Tour will agree that all these achievements were overshadowed in 1999 by the loss of Payne Stewart. This edition of the European Tour Yearbook includes a chapter on Payne's superb triumph in the 1999 US Open which appears as a tribute to the life and memory of a man who, above all, was devoted to his family and, unquestionably, was one of the finest sportsmen in the history of the game.

Kenneth D Schofield CBE
Executive Director • PGA European Tour

Contents

opposite: De Vere Slaley Hall, Northumberland

A Golden Decade

by Colin Montgomerie MBE

Vardon Trophy Winner 1993-94-95-96-97-98-99

It will always be a source of great pride to me and my family that I have been the number one golfer in Europe for the best part of the last decade of the millenium. Since the birth of the European Tour in 1971, only ten players have held the number one position, and not only to be one of them, but to have remained there from 1993 to 1999, is of great significance to me. It has given me the satisfaction of knowing I have carried the baton for European golf for that time. In keeping that position, I have enjoyed many fierce battles over the last seven years with worthy competitors, and that makes my achievements all the sweeter because I have "crossed swords" with some of Europe's finest in that time, Nick Faldo, Severiano Ballesteros, José Maria Olazábal, Bernhard Langer, Ian Woosnam, Sam Torrance and others. I will never forget the extraordinary pressure of the final day at the Volvo Masters in 1995 when the whole of the season came down to my last putt on the 18th green at Valderrama. Sam, you are some competitor!

In recent years, a new challenge has come from a younger generation. I relish all new challenges, and while I continue to improve each year, as I have strived to do over the last seven years, then I know that I can be competitive. What strikes me most clearly is how standards have improved over my years of experience. After my college years in the States and my amateur years in the UK, I went to La Manga, to the European Tour Qualifying School, in 1987. I returned to La Manga for the 1999 Lexus European Golf Cup and it made me realise how much had changed in those 12 years, for me and for the Tour. From a personal perspective, I have, thankfully, not had to return to the Tour School. However, in a broader sense, despite our great champions of the past, there is now strength in depth on the European Tour as never before. As the Tour travels further afield, to find suitable courses and climate in our year-round schedule, so the truly international nature of our player force has grown, producing golfers of extraordinary talent and with a diversity of cultural backgrounds. This will make the European Tour of the new millennium the genuinely cosmopolitan Tour that it will need to be to stand beside the US Tour, as it does at present, in the increasingly commercial world where sponsorship monies and TV rights revenues must be earned on merit and not

COLIN MONTGOMERIE: "The European Tour is a shop window internationally."

COLIN MONTGOMERIE and MEL PYATT, President and CEO of Volvo Event Management: another Volvo Order of Merit success to celebrate

simply guaranteed as of right.

I have always believed in meritocracy and have felt that I could achieve what I want if I put in sufficient effort and commitment. So must it be for the Tour and for all its members. It has often been speculated as to why I have not gone to play on the PGA Tour in the United States full-time. I have been completely consistent on this and that is because my family comes first, and always will, and Eimear and I want to bring up and educate our wonderful children in the UK. I want to be a 'hands-on' father to see them grow up. However, if we nurture the Tour, and with the advent of the World Golf Championship events, world-class golfers will have the choice of where they want to live and yet be able to compete at the highest level on a global basis. Such a prospect means that by the end of each year I will have accumulated a few air miles and put a few miles on the "Flying Scotsman" which British Aerospace kindly supply me to pursue that goal. This goal is, however, achievable if you have the determination, the right priorities and the

support and understanding of a great family behind you.

With all of this talk of the new millennium, we must not forget that the game owes a great deal to the founders of the European Tour; to the likes of Neil Coles, Tony Jacklin, Bernard Gallacher

and Peter Oosterhuis, whose play ignited a popular interest in the game so that John Jacobs, followed by Ken Schofield, could mastermind the progress achieved. Their performances, especially those of Jacklin in winning the Open and the US Open within 11 months, provided John

"Physically and mentally I am very strong."

"Ambition, drive and a will to succeed are highly motivating factors for me."

with the critical mass to take the professional Tour to the Continent of Europe. Subsequently, the growth of European golf can be measured not only by the success enjoyed by our players, but also by the strength of the Tour itself. We have a flourishing circuit, which visits approximately 20 countries each year. On other fronts, much progress has been made with the birth of both the European Challenge Tour for aspiring golfers and the European Seniors Tour.

In the year 2000, the total prize funds for the three Tours will be in excess of £50,000,000. Compare that to the few thousand pounds that Neil Coles earned for being the leading player in the Order of Merit in 1963 – the year I was born in Troon, one mile from the Open Championship venue.

There is no question that the Americans were then the dominant force in golf with Jack Nicklaus arriving on the scene to challenge Arnold Palmer, followed in time by the likes of Lee Trevino, Johnny Miller and Tom Watson. But at the same time the seeds had been sown that would transform the shape of the game in Europe.

Five Europeans – Seve Ballesteros, Nick Faldo, Bernhard Langer, Sandy Lyle and Ian Woosnam – had been born within months of each other and together they led a revolution in European golf. Their achievement in winning 16 major championships between them was remarkable, and also responsible for an upsurge in the game's popularity. We must not forget the likes of Greg Norman and Nick Price, who cut their teeth on the European Tour, or all the other fine players of these times. With the inspirational Ballesteros galvanising all others and leading Europe by example, a clear message was sent to the American nation that European and international golf was on the rise.

Initially I considered that I might have a part to play in all of this – by working as part of a management company and thereby utilising some of my legal and business qualifications acquired at Houston Baptist University. I could play the game well enough, but to turn professional seemed a risk at that time – something I don't trade in too often, on the course or off it. I enquired about job opportunities with the International Management Group and was called for interview over a few holes of golf. I played the front nine with a group of senior IMG executives on Turnberry's Ailsa course in 29 and we stopped at the halfway house. They told me: "This is ridiculous, we should be working for you, not the other way round." And they have been ever since. Ironically, that and my victory in the Scottish Amateur Championship at Nairn were the turning points because they gave me the confidence to move from amateur to professional status. I had played in two Walker Cup matches, but winning the Scottish Amateur – that was a pivotal week for me – not only because of the manner of my win, but more importantly because I met my future wife, Eimear, beside the clubhouse and life changed on many fronts.

My mother (who sadly passed away in 1991) and my father had always been supportive of my desire to play the game. My father passed on to me a passion for golf, my mother taught me that whatever you do, then you must give 110 per cent. I have never forgotten that and never will - it is an in-built and ingrained ambition. Not just on the course, but off it, whether as a husband, father or son, or more recently, as a businessman. Ambition, drive and a will to succeed are highly motivating factors for me. I want to be the best that I can in whatever I do, and expect the same high standards of those around me as I do of myself.

I am delighted to have played a role in the progress of the European Tour from those early days. The last ten years represent what you could call a golden decade for me. There have been individual highlights to savour among my thirty-odd wins around the world, from my first professional victory at the Portuguese Open in 1989, to winning the Volvo Masters in 1993 to secure the Volvo Order of Merit for the first time, and winning my first

ALASTAIR McLEAN (right): "Through thick and thin … a wonderful caddie."

Volvo PGA Championship title in 1998. I am proud to have been the 1998 Andersen World Champion and the 1999 Cisco World Match Play Champion. My first win on Scottish soil, at Loch Lomond in 1999, was also very moving. There have been moments to share the glory of winning as I did at St Andrews as a member of the Scottish team for the 1995 Alfred Dunhill Cup, and at Oak Hill in 1995 by winning the Ryder Cup on American soil and again at Valderrama in 1997 when Europe made a successful defence of the Cup with Seve at the helm, and I found myself in the final match of the singles with the whole match in the balance. There have been other times when my family, and especially my wife, Eimear, could share the fruits of what success brings. We were thrilled when the Board of Directors of the PGA European Tour unanimously accorded me Honorary Life Membership of the European Tour in 1997, after I had finished number one on the Volvo Order of Merit for a fifth successive time. We were together again, with our elder daughter, Olivia, at Buckingham Palace in November 1998, when I received the MBE from The Queen at the investiture ceremony. This year, 1999, has been my best year to date, so I am optimistic enough to believe there will be many more such moments to enjoy that our younger daughter, Venetia, and our son, Cameron, will have their chance to share in.

The year of 1999 was particularly rewarding for me for many reasons. I was delighted to retain the Volvo PGA Championship title, and for the first time in my career won five tournaments on the European Tour in addition to the

COLIN and NICK FALDO: Ryder Cup comrades in arms

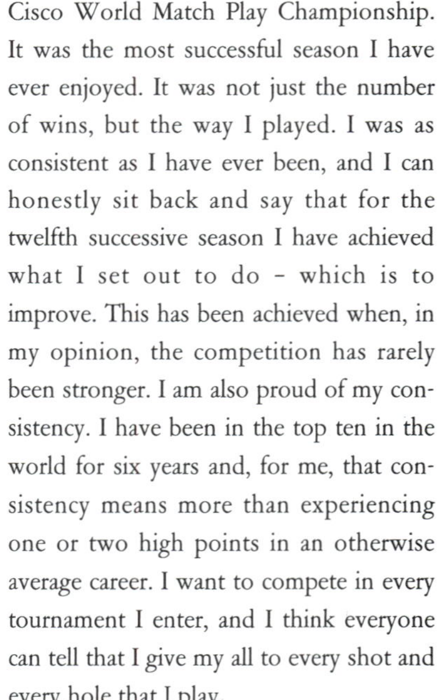

EIMEAR and COLIN

Vardon Trophy winner for a record seventh successive time

Cisco World Match Play Championship. It was the most successful season I have ever enjoyed. It was not just the number of wins, but the way I played. I was as consistent as I have ever been, and I can honestly sit back and say that for the twelfth successive season I have achieved what I set out to do – which is to improve. This has been achieved when, in my opinion, the competition has rarely been stronger. I am also proud of my consistency. I have been in the top ten in the world for six years and, for me, that consistency means more than experiencing one or two high points in an otherwise average career. I want to compete in every tournament I enter, and I think everyone can tell that I give my all to every shot and every hole that I play.

I could hardly discuss 1999 without mentioning The Country Club, Brookline. I would like to say that Mark James was a wonderful captain. He handled everything with good humour and great diplomacy. There was also a wonderful team atmosphere amongst what was a very young, and some may have felt, inexperienced side. It came as something of a surprise to be the oldest player on the team, since I feel that I have still so much to achieve. Yet the efforts of that side just showed some of the growing strength in depth on the European Tour and some of the talent that is emerging. It was a team effort, but I shall always be proud of how I played and conducted myself. Contrary to what many may think, I enjoyed the experience and learned a lot about myself. All my efforts in the past have been geared to being able to cope with and raise my game in such circumstances and I relish that sort of a situation. I was delighted when, following the match, the Members of the Association of Golf Writers voted me the Asprey and Garrard Golfer of the Month for September. Although I won the September Award, I feel that the whole team, including Mark James, should have won the Award since the Ryder Cup is, after all, a team game and not an individual one. Anyone who knows me will realise that the circumstances found in Boston would always bring the best out in me, and I would very much prefer to be seen to be leading by example than being a passive observer. The Brookline atmosphere made me all the more determined to get the job done. Although we lost the Ryder Cup, we can still look back with great pride on how well such a young team performed and we can all look forward to the 2001 match at The Belfry with great optimism. The Ryder Cup is the most special event in golf, and I am sure that I speak for every player that has played in saying that it is a

**ANGEL GALLARDO, PGA European Tour Vice-Chairman, and COLIN MONTGOMERIE:
another Golfer of the Month Award to celebrate**

privilege to be part of it.

I believe that the year 2000 will start another great decade for European golf. At the age of 36, and after little more than ten years in the game as a professional, there is so much for me to look forward to beyond winning tournaments and team successes. There are golf courses and Starwood Teaching Academies opening globally, bearing my name, and many junior and amateur initiatives which I am keen to see developed. I also passionately hope that I can, in some way, help to bring the Ryder Cup to Scotland in 2009 and in the meantime, I am keen to be actively involved in the development of golf in Scotland, the UK and across Europe.

I have been lucky to have a good team behind me – not just my family and my friends but also others. Alastair McLean has been with me through thick and thin and is a wonderful caddie, as well as a good friend; Guy Kinnings is my personal manager at the International Management Group, and he and I share many of the same values, not just our age. We co-ordi-nate a global team of loyal staff working within IMG and my Nairn Group of Companies on the different aspects of my businesses. I have also been wonderfully supported in my golfing efforts by many companies within the game that assist me in my career. I am grateful to all of these.

As for the future, everyone wants to go out at the top and that is my aim. Not many athletes make the right choice at the right time. Michael Jordan and Jackie Stewart are two of the rarities. I am 36, so hopefully I have a good few years left. Physically and mentally I am very strong. I will, however, know when it is time to go. Then I will carry my bag at Royal Troon, as I still all too rarely do with my father. I play golf because it has given me the opportunity of competitive success, but also because I simply enjoy the game, and although I would never push my children into the game, I look forward to a few fun rounds of golf with my family.

Golf is a great game. One that is available to most. It has been good to me and I hope that I have put something back into it and its growth. The European Tour, under the guidance of Ken Schofield and his team, is a shop window internationally – and as a player I believe that we can encourage more and more people around the world to enjoy the Royal and Ancient game, by striving for ever higher standards in every aspect of the European Tour.

I have so much going on in my life, with my golf and my developing business interests, and I look forward to progressing this area of my life both while I play professionally and after. I have laid the foundations to numerous global businesses and thoroughly enjoy this role, although it will never get in the way of my golf and family goals. The tragedy that befell Payne Stewart, a man for whom I had the utmost personal respect and admiration and who was obviously such a devoted family man, makes one realise just how fragile one's existence can be. So we must all treasure the time that we spend with our families – and that must come before anything else.

"I believe the year 2000 will start another great decade for European golf."

Fate rewards a believer

For two momentous days Europe ruled
at The Country Club, then America
produced the greatest comeback ever

*I*nevitably in a sporting world where coming second is increasingly, and ludicrously, regarded as falling somewhere between useless and irrelevant, there will be those who dismiss Europe's performance during the 33rd Ryder Cup as failure, clear and simple. Yet to do so is to miss the point – as Europe so narrowly, and frustratingly, did towards the end of their epic defeat by the United States of America – not just of this particular match but of the Ryder Cup. Here, whatever happens, is the game's most glorious showpiece. Here is honour, valour, commitment and, yes, hard-nosed endeavour, a grand game played out for no apparent reward by 24 of the world's outstanding golfers during a week filled with intensity and honest competition. Sadly, Brookline was filled with something else as well, but of this more later. So, although one must first salute an American side that came back from the wrong side of hopeless to rewrite the history books on a pulsating final day at The Country Club, there must also be genuine approval for a European team which all but clipped the wings of the bald eagle in its home lair.

Colin Montgomerie, whose attitude and form never deviated from the extraordinary throughout the match, caught the

TOUCHING EXPERIENCE: US Captain Ben Crenshaw and team united in joy of victory

defiant mood of the Europeans when he leaned towards his microphone in the post-match interview to suggest that: "We Europeans take great heart from this match. Okay, the Americans played better than us today, and good luck to them, but everybody made us overwhelming underdogs coming into this match, everybody, and yet we have managed to give the Americans a hell of a fright. This is what we shall be taking with us into 2001 at The Belfry."

And, of course, Montgomerie is correct. Few, if any, critics gave Europe much chance against an American team studded with champions of one kind or another from World No.1 Tiger Woods through to their only rookie David Duval, who happens to be the World No.2. Europe, on the other hand, is going through a transitional period prompted by the decline of that generation of great players who turned this match into a vital and

compelling contest once more in the mid-1980s.

While only a fool would dismiss totally the chances of Nick Faldo, Severiano Ballesteros, Bernhard Langer or Ian Woosnam reclaiming the Ryder Cup high ground they once occupied so relentlessly, it does appear that it is now up to a fresh generation of players to establish themselves as worthy successors. In this sense there is indeed much for Europe to take from this match. While Montgomerie, José Maria Olazábal, Jesper Parnevik and Lee Westwood are recognised world-wide, the continuing rise in confidence and play of Open champion Paul Lawrie was heartening, the forward momentum of Padraig Harrington impressive and the debut of teenager Sergio Garcia simply sensational.

Paired alongside Parnevik, with whom he has practised on the US Tour, the young Spaniard was not so much a revela-

tion as a confirmation that here is a very special talent indeed and one upon which European golf may feed for some considerable time. To suggest that Garcia is Ballesteros Born Again is a nonsense. There will never be another Seve, but there is much in Garcia's play to suggest that the same swashbuckling attitude prevails, that adventure and challenge are the names of this prodigy's game, and that there is an awful lot of fun and games to come.

With Parnevik happily and impressively playing the role of "older brother", the duo proved unbeatable, taking three and a half points from their four fourball and foursomes matches. "Jesper is terrific for me to play alongside. He gives me confidence. Every time I need him he is there," a wild-eyed Garcia admitted. Parnevik, for his part, said: "Sergio has so much energy that when I felt a bit tired I just plugged into him and I was fine again."

The European Team

Back row left to right: Sergio Garcia, Miguel Angel Jiménez, Padraig Harrington, Darren Clarke, Jarmo Sandelin, Andrew Coltart, Jesper Parnevik, Jean Van de Velde. Front row left to right: Sam Torrance (vice-captain), Lee Westwood, José Maria Olazábal, Mark James (captain), Colin Montgomerie, Paul Lawrie, Ken Brown (vice-captain)

The United States Team

Back row left to right: Steve Pate, Payne Stewart, Tom Lehman, Jim Furyk, Davis Love III, Hal Sutton, Mark O'Meara,
Front row left to right: Justin Leonard, Phil Mickelson, Jeff Maggert, Ben Crenshaw (captain), David Duval, Tiger Woods

JARMO SANDELIN (left), ANDREW COLTART (centre), JEAN VAN DE VELDE (right): rookie threesome

SERGIO GARCIA: Ryder Cup debut was "simply sensational"

TIGER WOODS: World No. 1 amassed two points

Meanwhile, Montgomerie and Lawrie were forming their own impressive team within a team. If there is anything more frightening than a Scot coming at you with raw determination glinting in his eyes, then it is a couple of them rearing up at the same time. Montgomerie, despite suffering a disgraceful litany of abuse from a small, but not insignificant, and certainly brutally vociferous, section of the American gallery, played probably the most brilliantly sustained golf of his life, while Lawrie rose magnificently to the occasion alongside the big man.

Words of praise too for Miguel Angel Jiménez, a latecomer to the Ryder Cup table but a man who seems destined to reserve a place for some time to come. He, Westwood, Darren Clarke and Ireland's Harrington could hardly have played better over the first two days as Europe shocked America by opening up a four points lead. On Saturday evening, with just the singles to come, this appeared impregnable. It was easy over a glass of wine to begin to feel the warm, reassuring glow of complacency.

COLIN MONTGOMERIE: putt holed, then a restrained rebuke for another heckler

Ireland

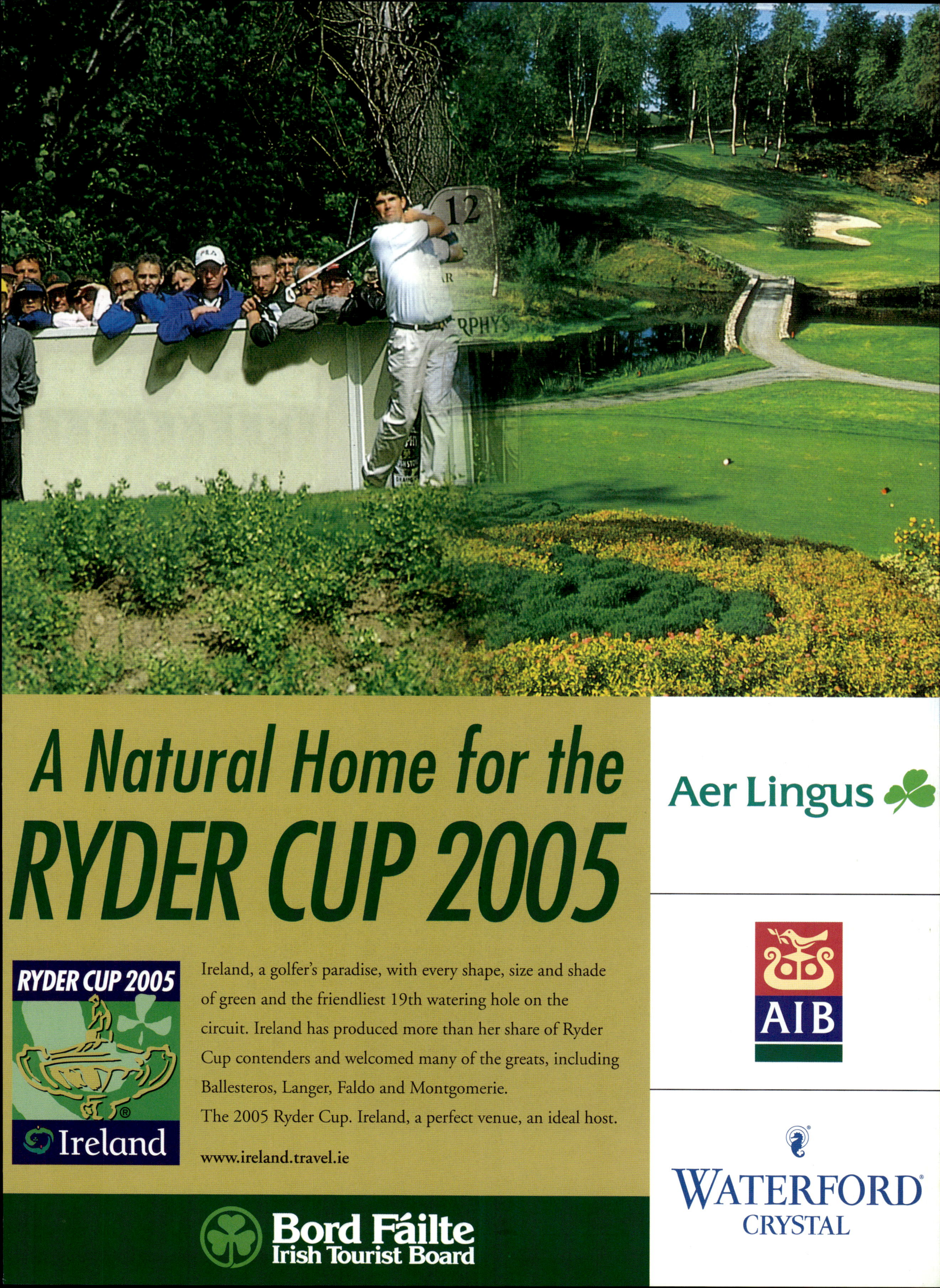

A Natural Home for the
RYDER CUP 2005

Ireland, a golfer's paradise, with every shape, size and shade of green and the friendliest 19th watering hole on the circuit. Ireland has produced more than her share of Ryder Cup contenders and welcomed many of the greats, including Ballesteros, Langer, Faldo and Montgomerie.

The 2005 Ryder Cup. Ireland, a perfect venue, an ideal host.

www.ireland.travel.ie

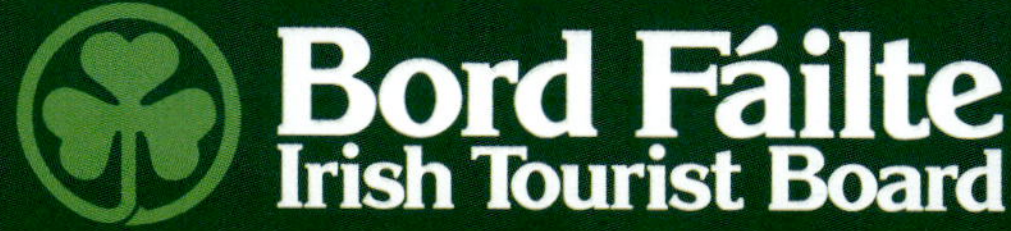

TOM LEHMAN: he led USA comeback on final day

DAVID DUVAL: one-time quiet American turns cheer leader

The United States might have had the world ranking points but Europe had a four-point advantage and, mark this, no-one has ever recovered from such a position. Ho hum. What was underestimated, of course, was that this was the Ryder Cup where records are set only to tumble swiftly, that this was a competition that encourages the unlikely, the improbable and sometimes even the downright, absolutely unbelievable.

On Saturday night while Europe's skipper Mark James was maintaining that wonderful poker face of his and rebutting every attempt by journalists to have him crow over apparently defeated opponents, Ben Crenshaw was doing what he does best which is to say he went all over-emotional on us. After beating back a barrage of criticism from American journalists frustrated at the USA team's apparent lack of cohesion and commitment, Crenshaw told us that he had a dream.

Well, perhaps not quite a dream but certainly a premonition of sorts. "I'll tell you this," he said, wagging a finger, the lump in his throat clearly visible. "I'm a

JESPER PARNEVIK and **SERGIO GARCIA**: high-stepping unbeatable duo

VICE-CAPTAIN SAM TORRANCE: a shoulder to weep on

SHOT OF THE WEEK

Although Justin Leonard's birdie putt of 45 feet on the 17th green contained more than an element of luck about it, the stroke was so momentous in the context of this Ryder Cup that it still has to be the shot of the weekend at Brookline. Leonard looked to be hard pressed to halve the hole against José Maria Olazábal when he hit his approach on this 370-yard dog-leg on to the lower tier of a frighteningly tilted green. Even when he hit his putt he misjudged the pace, and his ball seemed destined to finish high above the hole from where it would be difficult to make par. Instead Leonard's line was perfect, his ball thumping into the back of the hole and dropping to make history.

JUSTIN LEONARD: the putt that proved all decisive …

… then had him appealing for law and order …

… after his mobbing on the 17th green by USA team-mates

PADRAIG HARRINGTON: won his singles

MIGUEL ANGEL JIMÉNEZ: outstanding latecomer

great believer in fate and I have a good feeling about tomorrow. That's all I'm going to say."

What was certain about Sunday was that James finally had to play his remaining three rookies. Andrew Coltart, a captain's pick, had been left on the sidelines as had France's first Ryder Cup player, Jean Van de Velde, and Sweden's Jarmo Sandelin. Now in the safe knowledge that Crenshaw had no option but to front-load his singles squad with his strongest players, James sent Sandelin out third, Van de Velde out fourth and Coltart fifth.

Their opponents were Phil Mickelson, Davis Love III and Woods. To be fair, it is difficult to see what else James could have done. While the final decision on who plays with whom and when is his, his captaincy was based on democracy and it was the team who decided to keep this rookie trio on the sidelines.

Would it have made any difference if he had played them earlier? Well maybe, but then again the James way meant that Europe had that apparently decisive four points lead on Saturday evening. "The decisions we took were as a team and I think they were right. I'd do exactly the same if I were in that position again," he said.

What James had to hope was that his first two men out, Westwood and Clarke, would gain at least a point for Europe's cause. When the Englishman and the Irishman were swept away by Tom Lehman and Hal Sutton the plan began to go seriously pear-shaped. Yet in the end it was Justin Leonard's comeback against Olazábal that won this match for the USA. Two years ago in Spain, Leonard was four up against Thomas Björn and ended with a half point. This time he was four down to Olazábal and crumbling before everyone's eyes after a week in which it seemed he could do little right.

Suddenly, however, the tide turned in his favour. Olazábal played two poor shots at the 12th and 13th holes for bogeys and then Leonard birdied the 14th and 15th to square the game. It sounds simple enough

JOSÉ MARIA OLAZÁBAL: fate singled him out for special attention

KEN BROWN: shared vice-captain role with Sam Torrance

HAL SUTTON: most successful American

when put like this, but it was an immense effort by Leonard in the circumstances. For him, however, fate, as identified by Crenshaw, was about to single him out for special attention.

With America on 14 points and needing just a half from one of three remaining matches on the course, Leonard surveyed an improbable birdie putt of 45 feet on the severely angled 17th green. Olazábal, it

should be pointed out, was half as near again. Leonard, who had struggled to hole any putt for three days, banged his putter into his ball and into the hole it went. Such was the pace of this putt that had it missed the return would, to say the very least, have been of a severely testing length.

What then happened is now well documented. Some American players, wives and caddies going wild, running on

the green and over Olazábal's line to embrace their man. It was an ill-conceived celebration that pumped up an already wild crowd on the other side of the ropes. This was pandemonium which has no place on a golf course.

Crenshaw's apology afterwards – he himself was not involved – was sincere and unambiguous, but the damage had been done, not by unruly spectators but

For further information please contact: ESCADA AG, Germany 0049 / 89 / 9944 - 0 · UK 0044 / 171 / 580 6066
www.escada.com

MARK JAMES: a dignified and inspiring captain for Europe

JEFF MAGGERT: on song

PHIL MICKELSON: singles winner

PAYNE STEWART: touch of grace

DARREN CLARKE and LEE WESTWOOD: beat World No. 1 and No. 2 combination

THE COURSE

The Country Club at Brookline is woven inextricably into the fabric of American golf history. The game was first played here by enthusiastic Bostonians in 1893 and the Club became one of the five charter members of the group that subsequently founded the United States Golf Association.

This 7,033 par 71 course – 35 out, 36 in – is as a traditional layout as it is possible to play in the United States. Similar in character, look and feel to the great English inland courses such as Sunningdale and Wentworth, there is no fake trickery here. Trees stand sentinel alongside every fairway with bunkers strategically placed everywhere but especially to guard greens that are smaller, more intimidating targets than is usual in America these days. Presented in immaculate condition and with the rough sensibly constructed rather than encouraged into the now all too familiar jungle, The Country Club was a superb Ryder Cup venue, encouraging shot-making and occasional adventure, but always willing to punish the errant drive or miss-hit approach. "Our players are delighted with the course and how it is playing," was Mark James's comment after the first practice day, and their contentment was understandable.

PAUL LAWRIE: rose magnificently to the occasion

LET THE CELEBRATIONS BEGIN: America's fans take to the 18th fairway

by unruly players. Olazábal, meanwhile, was clearly shocked as he waited an age to strike his own birdie effort. The fact is that Leonard's putt had not won America the match for if Olazábal had holed his attempt then Europe might well have retained the trophy.

Of course, his putt trickled inches wide of the hole but, while no-one can say what would have happened if the Spaniard had been allowed to play normally, there can be no doubt that the shot doubled in difficulty because of those disgraceful antics. "As a player you expect to be shown respect and that did not happen for me in this moment. It was an ugly picture to see," he was to say.

So a Ryder Cup that had begun so well ended in a most unfortunate manner, although it must be added that Payne Stewart's concession to Montgomerie on the 18th green displayed a much needed touch of grace. There was indeed much for the Europeans to take away from Boston, but perhaps the more important point is that there remains much for some spectators and players to learn about this great game. One can only hope that the lesson will have been digested properly by 2001 and that the Ryder Cup seamlessly reaffirms its hard-won reputation as a wonderfully fierce but relentlessly sporting contest.

Bill Elliott

JOLLY GOOD SHOW: stylish European supporters

THE COUNTRY CLUB, BROOKLINE, MASSACHUSETTS, USA, SEPTEMBER 24–26, 1999 • PAR 71 • YARDS 7033

• CAPTAINS: MARK JAMES (EUROPE), BEN CRENSHAW (USA) •

EUROPE		USA	
DAY ONE			
Foursomes: Morning			
C Montgomerie & P Lawrie (3&2)	1	D Duval & P Mickelson	0
J Parnevik & S Garcia (2&1)	1	T Lehman & T Woods	0
M A Jiménez & P Harrington (halved)	½	D Love III & P Stewart (halved)	½
D Clarke & L Westwood	0	H Sutton & J Maggert (3&2)	1
Europe 2½		USA 1½	
Fourballs: Afternoon			
C Montgomerie & P Lawrie (halved)	½	D Love III & J Leonard (halved)	½
J Parnevik & S Garcia (1 hole)	1	P Mickelson & J Furyk	0
M A Jiménez & J M Olazábal (2&1)	1	H Sutton & J Maggert	0
D Clarke & L Westwood (1 hole)	1	D Duval & T Woods	0
Europe 6		USA 2	
DAY TWO			
Foursomes: Morning			
C Montgomerie & P Lawrie	0	H Sutton & J Maggert (1 hole)	1
D Clarke & L Westwood (3&2)	1	J Furyk & M O'Meara	0
M A Jiménez & P Harrington	0	S Pate & T Woods (1 hole)	1
J Parnevik & S Garcia (3&2)	1	P Stewart & J Leonard	0
Europe 8		USA 4	

EUROPE		USA	
DAY TWO (continued)			
Fourballs: Afternoon			
D Clarke & L Westwood	0	P Mickelson & T Lehman (2&1)	1
J Parnevik & S Garcia (halved)	½	D Love III & D Duval (halved)	½
M A Jiménez & J M Olazábal (halved)	½	J Leonard & H Sutton (halved)	½
C Montgomerie & P Lawrie (2&1)	1	S Pate & T Woods	0
Europe 10		USA 6	
DAY THREE			
Singles			
L Westwood	0	T Lehman (3&2)	1
D Clarke	0	H Sutton (4&2)	1
J Sandelin	0	P Mickelson (4&3)	1
J Van de Velde	0	D Love III (6&5)	1
A Coltart	0	T Woods (3&2)	1
J Parnevik	0	D Duval (5&4)	1
P Harrington (1 hole)	1	M O'Meara	0
M A Jiménez	0	S Pate (2&1)	1
J M Olazábal (halved)	½	J Leonard (halved)	½
C Montgomerie (1 hole)	1	P Stewart	0
S Garcia	0	J Furyk (4&3)	1
P Lawrie (4&3)	1	J Maggert	0
Final Score	**EUROPE 13½**		**USA 14½**

Individual Performances
Europe

	P	W	L	H	Pts
S Garcia	5	3	1	1	3½
P Lawrie	5	3	1	1	3½
C Montgomerie	5	3	1	1	3½
J Parnevik	5	3	1	1	3½
D Clarke	5	2	3	0	2
M A Jiménez	5	1	2	2	2
J M Olazábal	3	1	0	2	2
L Westwood	5	2	3	0	2
P Harrington	3	1	1	1	1½
A Coltart	1	0	1	0	0
J Sandelin	1	0	1	0	0
J Van de Velde	1	0	1	0	0

Individual Performances
USA

	P	W	L	H	Pts
H Sutton	5	3	1	1	3½
D Love III	4	1	0	3	2½
T Lehman	3	2	1	0	2
J Maggert	4	2	2	0	2
P Mickelson	4	2	2	0	2
S Pate	3	2	1	0	2
T Woods	5	2	3	0	2
D Duval	4	1	2	1	1½
J Leonard	4	0	1	3	1½
J Furyk	3	1	2	0	1
P Stewart	3	0	2	1	½
M O'Meara	2	0	2	0	0

New Order sets fast pace

'It is now clear the world of golf

is judged on how it measures

up against European standards'

The New Age of European golf is truly upon us, and those inspiring standards that graced the latter part of the 20th century are clearly destined to continue into the next Millennium as a fresh generation of heroes uphold the traditions handed on by their predecessors.

The evidence is indisputable. Old myths and preconceptions have been brushed aside in an exhilarating gallop for success by a breed of ambitious campaigners for whom only one axiom now applies: "If you are good enough, you are old enough to be a winner."

It is a doctrine that has brought an exuberance to the European game as this New Order of talented performers eagerly pursues the limitless opportunities for global achievement that now beckon, and in so doing feeds on its own success and sets the pattern for others.

The season of 1999 glitters with shining examples of this new philoso-

COLIN MONTGOMERIE: another vintage year

phy. A new Open champion springs from the ranks as Paul Lawrie sweeps past the established superstars in commanding style at Carnoustie. A European Ryder Cup squad, virtually written off because of so-called inexperience, comes within a single point of victory against the United States.

A Spanish teenager turns professional, wins two tournaments in his first season, very nearly captures a major championship, and earns an inspiring and pivotal place in the Ryder Cup team. Such are the statistics of Sergio Garcia's phenomenal debut.

And, as if to illustrate the full breadth of this wave of confidence now sweeping through the European game, 12 campaigners seized their moment and became winners for the first time in 1999. Moreover, the scope of the European Tour was further underlined by the fact that these new champions represented nine different countries.

In truth, Garcia himself epitomises the excitement this new breed brings to the game. He is a genius who follows his own high standards and is satisfied with nothing less. He began the season as an amateur, winning the medal in the Masters Tournament, and ended it as a highly successful professional with two titles – the

WARREN BENNETT (left), **VAN PHILLIPS** (centre), **DAVID PARK** (right): winning graduates

Murphy's Irish Open at Druids Glen and the Linde German Masters in Cologne – to his credit. In addition, he captained Spain and partners Miguel Angel Jiménez and José Maria Olazábal to victory in the Alfred Dunhill Cup.

Above all, he demonstrated that golf at the highest level can still be fun and his last-day pursuit of eventual winner Tiger Woods in the US PGA Championship, as well as the wonder strokes he produced at Medinah, earned him a huge following of admirers on both sides of the Atlantic who suspect they have seen the next great influence on the game.

But the new breed had started to make an impact in 1999 long before Garcia joined their ranks. Indeed, one first-time winner, David Howell, led the Volvo Order of Merit for 12 weeks after his Dubai Desert Classic win and, in fact, the merit table top spot changed hands seven times - although with only four players involved - until taking on a familiar look with Colin Montgomerie assuming what has become a customary role as the most dominant figure in Europe.

What gives the European Tour such immense appeal, and almost certainly accounts for its healthy state, is the diverse manner in which so many winners have found their way to the top and in so

doing proved that there is no prescribed pattern for success. Sweden's Pierre Fulke won the Trophée Lancôme against a distinguished field after serving a solid apprenticeship on the European Challenge Tour, where aspirants acquire the basic skills of competitive golf before graduating on merit to the main Tour.

English professional Warren Bennett, winner of the Scottish PGA Championship at the Gleneagles Hotel, emerged via the same route after taking top honours in the 1998 European Challenge Tour with five victories. Frenchman Jean-Francois Remsey made twelve attempts to qualify for the Tour

before finding a secure place and then capturing the Estoril Open.

Australian Jarrod Moseley had been a professional for only eighteen months when he took on Ernie Els and other world-class performers to score his first win with the Heineken Classic at The Vines Resort in Perth.

Welshman David Park came very close to making history in his first European Tour event when he found himself in a play-off for the Moroccan Open with Miguel Angel Martin, but lost at the sixth extra hole in Agadir. A week later he equalled Greg Norman's 22-year-old record of winning at only his second

PAUL LAWRIE: defeated the world's strongest field

SERGIO GARCIA: looking to a bright future

Tour until his winning chance came and he snapped up the Victor Chandler British Masters at Woburn, his first-ever win as a professional. Van Phillips, another European Challenge Tour graduate, showed the benefit of his apprenticeship when he won the Algarve Portuguese Open at Le Meridien Penina Golf and Resort in a play-off from John Bickerton, who also came up though those ranks.

The collective presence of all these performers marked one of the most exciting developments in modern times. It was not, however, a complete coup in which existing favourites were displaced unceremoniously and banished to a dark corner. Montgomerie, Europe's most forceful figure, allowed his rivals the best part of a three-month start at the beginning of the season before he moved into gear and by late autumn had not only acquired six titles – the Benson and Hedges International Open at The Oxfordshire, a successful title defence of the Volvo PGA Championship at Wentworth Club, The Standard Life Loch Lomond, the Volvo Scandinavian Masters in Malmo, the BMW International Open in Munich and the Cisco World Match Play Championship at Wentworth Club, but had set himself towards an unprecedented seventh successive Volvo Order of Merit title.

Lee Westwood's form followed a similar pattern after a somewhat dormant first half to the season until he erupted to win the TNT Dutch Open at Hilversumsche, followed by the Smurfit European Open at The K Club, south of Dublin, and the Canon European Masters at Crans-sur-Sierre in Switzerland. It meant that the

attempt when he captured the Compaq European Grand Prix at Slaley Hall.

American Gerry Norquist campaigned all over the world for five years after a failed attempt to join the European Tour, but signed up after winning the Benson and Hedges Malaysian Open in Kuala Lumpur. Spaniard Pedro Linhart, who first attempted to join the European Tour in 1986, had to toil for 13 years before his breakthrough came at the age of 36 when he won the Madeira Island Open.

Former Scottish amateur champion Dean Robertson, in his sixth year on Tour, made an impressive entrance into the winners' circle when he held off the collective challenge of reigning Masters champion José Maria Olazábal, as well as

former US Open champion Lee Janzen and Bernhard Langer, to take the Fiat and Fila Italian Open in Turin.

Bob May, the former American Walker Cup player, had been waiting patiently for eight years on the European

LEE WESTWOOD: erupted to win three in a row

BOB MAY: patience rewarded after eight years

Worksop professional had won in three consecutive appearances on the European Tour and faced the real prospect of equalling the four-in-a-row record set by Nick Faldo (1989) until Bob May thwarted his effort by taking the Victor Chandler British Masters title.

To describe Lawrie simply as a multiple winner in 1999 - the Qatar Masters and the Open Championship - is to do little justice to the enormity of his achievements and the fact that he conquered all self-doubt to face and defeat the strongest field in the world over the toughest golf course in the world to take the coveted silver claret jug. His exhilarating success also endorsed the priceless working ethic that has developed on the European Tour, directly as a result of the globe-trotting policies laid down by its architects, in that each week you "play what you find" and stop grumbling about the difference. Thus, while the superstars were disgruntled at the challenge set by Carnoustie, two European campaigners - Jean Van de Velde and Lawrie himself - held centre stage, to be joined eventually by former champion Justin Leonard in the play-off.

The incredible drama of Van de Velde's 72nd hole, when victory slipped from his grasp, cannot mask the fact that Lawrie produced a brilliant last round 67 that erased a ten-stroke deficit with the leader, and that he then birdied the last two holes of the play-off to become rightful champion with the best golf of the day.

And Van de Velde made his own unique contribution to the game's ethos with his disarming acceptance of what fate had dealt him and offered a timely reminder that for all the wealth and glory the royal and ancient pursuit may bring, it remains at heart simply a game to be savoured and enjoyed. For that alone he has earned a special place in the game's history, and also given the lie to the old adage: "Nobody remembers who came second." This time, nobody will ever forget.

It is a measure of Jarmo Sandelin's multiple success in 1999 - Peugeot Open de España in Barcelona and German Open in Berlin - that the Swedish professional maintained a high level of consistency to remain in the top ten automatic qualifiers for Europe's 12-man Ryder Cup squad. Sandelin had to beat Retief Goosen - winner of the Novotel Perrier Open de France in Bordeaux - in a play-off for the German title and had earlier been involved in a notable Swedish double when compatriot Jesper Parnevik (his subsequent Ryder Cup teammate) won on the US PGA Tour on the same day that he took the Spanish title. Another Swedish player, Robert Karlsson, struck winning form late in the year by capturing the Belgacom Open one week after Denmark's Thomas Björn had triumphed in The Sarazen World Open.

Another measure of the European Tour's success was that it could claim two current major champions among its ranks. A few months before Lawrie's historic moment, José Maria Olazábal - perhaps the most inspirational figure in golf - marked an emphatic triumph over the physical problems that had threatened to wreck his life when he bounced back to become the winner of the Masters Tournament for a second time. No words sum up the poignancy of that moment better than his own: "Two years ago there were doubts not just about my golf career but the quality of my life. I am proud of my achievement."

He has quietly assumed the role hitherto performed by Severiano Ballesteros, serving - as it were - as the heart and soul of European golf. Moreover, he brought

JEAN VAN DE VELDE: disarming acceptance of fate

Romero reaching the quarter-finals from a 13-strong European contingent. Miguel Angel Jiménez enhanced his growing reputation by making a successful defence of the Turespaña Masters-Open Andalucia at the Parador Malaga del Golf where he learned to play, and some seven months later he completed a notable double by becoming the first Spaniard to win the Volvo Masters. Moreover, he achieved this famous win at Montecastillo, little more than 120 miles from his home in Malaga, with an outstanding closing round of 65. Darren Clarke touched peak form to win The Compass Group English Open at Hanbury Manor and Tiger Woods gained his second and third European Tour victories by capturing the Deutsche Bank – SAP Open TPC of Europe and the WGC – American Express Championship. But Costantino Rocca left his return to form which earned him the West of Ireland Golf Classic in Galway a little too late to secure a Ryder Cup place.

It was a season of hope, too, for those great stars who initially transformed the European Tour into a world force. Nick Faldo began to regain some of the old magic. Bernhard Langer toiled manfully knowing that success is but part of the equation that always involves hard work, and was rewarded with a tie for second place in the Volvo Masters. Seve Ballesteros worked diligently at his game. Ian Woosnam persistently showed flashes of his traditional brilliance and Sandy Lyle found signs of the consistency that had been so elusive. All offer living proof that while form may vary, class is permanent.

One final point. The season of 1999 marked a decisive transition in the game itself. It is now clear the world of golf is judged on how it measures up against European standards. It is the real reason for such unprecedented American jubilation at their Ryder Cup success. It is also the highest compliment the American players and public could have paid to the European Tour.

Michael McDonnell

JOSÉ MARIA OLAZÁBAL: dignity and poise

both dignity and poise to the task – sometimes in the most difficult circumstances.

Other familiar figures also provided the occasional reminder that the New Order did not quite have things all its own way. Ernie Els set the pace early in the season by winning the Alfred Dunhill South African PGA Championship in Johannesburg, and David Frost followed a week later by taking the Mercedes-Benz - Vodacom South African Open in Cape Province.

The WGC – Andersen Consulting Match Play was won by Jeff Maggert in California, with Olazábal and Eduardo

Pro-Golf – Winning streak for 29 years

The end of every successful European Tour season still leaves one major challenge to be met. **Pro-Golf**, the European Tour Media Guide respected throughout the golf world as an essential work of reference, has to be produced to the exacting, high standards that have made it a winner for 29 successive years.

Doing full justice to the Tour's 1999 achievements isn't easy. The records and revealing statistics behind Colin Montgomerie's fantastic defence of his marathon command of the Volvo Order of Merit title need to be meticulously chronicled.

So do the Open Championship victory of Scotsman Paul Lawrie and the Masters Tournament triumph of Spain's José Maria Olazábal, along with all the other outstanding feats of the European Tour's many world-class players.

Has any Tour rookie made a greater impact than young Sergio Garcia? Who shared the accolade of first-time winner with him in 1999? The answers and thousands more facts are in the illustrated **Pro-Golf 2000**.

More than 400 pages contain detailed biographies, the Tour history, tournament scores, prize money, everything worth knowing about the ever-expanding European Tour and the challengers who make it the most concentrated international examination of great golf talent in the world.

It's a must for all followers of golf who want to keep fully informed.

Ordering a copy of Pro-Golf 2000 is simple: send a cheque for £15 (which includes postage and packing), made payable to the PGA European Tour, to Frances Jennings, Communications Division, European Tour, Wentworth Drive, Virginia Water, Surrey GU25 4LX, or telephone 01344 840446 with credit card details.

Canon Shot of the Year 1999

S ergio Garcia arrived on the professional scene with the impact of a hurricane. As an amateur of immense promise, he was reputed to be touched by the same sort of magic which characterised the play of the Spaniard to whom he had been so often compared, Severiano Ballesteros.

On a warm Sunday afternoon at Medinah Country Club, Chicago, Illinois, in August, 1999, Garcia delivered the conclusive proof that he is, indeed, a special talent by hitting the stunning stroke which has been named as the Canon Shot of the Year.

Going into the final round of the US PGA Championship, Garcia – then still just 19 – was in joint third place, level with American Stewart Cink and two strokes behind leaders Tiger Woods and Mike Weir, of Canada.

After an absorbing tussle, Garcia still trailed Woods by two shots when he reached the tee at the 452-yard 16th hole. The scene was set for one of the greatest single strokes in the illustrious history of the US PGA Championship. Here, in Garcia's own words, is how he executed the 1999 Canon Shot of the Year.

The Shot by Sergio Garcia

"I hit a three wood off the tee, thinking if I hit it with a big draw it would be something from a seven to a nine iron to the hole. I hit it a little thin, and it went high and straight instead of drawing, and probably went to the driest spot on the golf course.

"It took a big kick and went straight at the tree and I said 'oh no, get down.' I walked there thinking 'please give me a shot' because I was only two behind and still had a chance.

"When I got to the ball I thought 'oh no' again, but then I started to see the shot I wanted to hit and how the ball was lying. The lie was pretty good but I had a little twig beside the ball so I removed it carefully and focused on the shot.

"It was between a five and six iron and I had to aim about 60-70 yards left of the hole because the pin was on the right as well. I had 189 yards to the hole and had two roots near the ball. I had to slice it, go from the outside to the inside, and I couldn't afford to hit the first root. Then I had to make sure not to start it too far right or I might have hit the second root and the ball could have come back and hit me.

"I assessed all those options. I asked Jerry, my caddie: 'What do you think?' He said I should lay up, but I said : 'I feel comfortable, I can do it, give me the six iron.'

"I opened the face as much as I could and hit a big cut and tried to get out of the way in case it hit the tree. I had to go for it. It is probably the greatest shot I've played so far in my life.

"I can tell you, the ball emerged amid an explosion of roots and dirt. I closed my eyes and moved quickly from the scene in case of a ricochet off the tree. You could say that the exuberance of youth paid off, but I knew the shot was on.

"I took off up the hill after the ball because I was excited to see the result. The ball landed on the green and from there I made my par four. In the end it was not good enough to catch Tiger, but I did finish runner-up in my first US PGA Championship with the help of that shot, which I'm delighted has been named Canon Shot of the Year for 1999."

Who else but Els

Tour's latest Honorary Life Member

starts new season with a win

and a call from President Mandela

As Ernie Els lined up a putt of some 20 feet on Houghton Golf Club's 16th green, a group of children from a school over the boundary fence suddenly burst into a falsetto chorus of "For He's a Jolly Good Fellow". Ernie backed off, smiled and waved, and then shaved the cup.

That was in the second round of the first European Tour event of the year, where he was a dominant presence from beginning to end, and became the "jolly good fellow" who held the Alfred Dunhill South African PGA Championship trophy in one hand and took a call from President Mandela on a mobile phone held in the other.

Instead the pace was set by the professional from the Silver Lakes club, near Pretoria, Nico van Rensburg, with a first round, seven under par 65, two ahead of his "old pal" Els. While van Rensburg was rattling in six birdies and an eagle, Els was falling victim of the kikuyu-grass rough.

It was as much a feature of the scenic, yet suburban course as the jacaranda, hibiscus, oleander, plovers, geese and ibises that decorated the fairways and ponds. Rarely has a course been blessed with such attractive flora and fauna.

Els, the European Tour's newest Honorary Life Member in recognition of his two US Open and unprecedented three successive World Match-Play Championship wins, was a giant stalking those fairways, and it was only a matter of time before he began to show the touches that have made him one of the best players in the world. As van Rensburg went into retreat on the second day it was another South African who emerged to throw down a challenge, Richard Kaplan, former lawyer and long-time member of Houghton before turning professional.

Altogether, the week was a marvellous wedding present for Els who had married his long-time girl friend, Liezl Wehmeyer on New Year's Eve and came into Houghton after showing her the joys of cray-fishing on the coast. He won with rounds of 67, 69, 69, 68, four strokes ahead of fellow South African Richard Kaplan. The Northern Hemisphere's most successful player was Steve Webster, who was tied third with David Frost, Stephen Leaney and Jeev Milkha Singh, three behind Kaplan and seven behind Els.

There had been hopes that the tournament might become a gripping head to head between Els and Nick Faldo, another imposing competitor. It was not to be. Faldo was having problems and missed the cut, quickly taking off to polish where rust had gathered over the short winter break.

SHOT OF THE WEEK

Wimpie Botha, a popular local golfer, was struggling and on his way to a high score when he came to the short 12th, a tricky 160 yards over water. He reached for his four iron and saw the ball land on the green, but short and wide of the flagstick. To his and everyone else's astonishment, the ball then set off on an anti-clockwise roll and into the hole for an ace.

Tragically, Wimpie was killed soon after in a car crash.

While Els was shooting the only bogey-free round of the tournament for his 69 to take over the lead, Kaplan came leap-frogging his way up the scoreboard and a 70 put him two shots off the pace. The third round on Saturday was supposed to be the time for Els to stroll away from the field.

It didn't happen because Kaplan hung in. Playing with Els, he matched the big man's 69 and revealed the human side of golf. He had gone home after his Friday round to find his answering machine crammed with messages of support. All evening the phone kept ringing and the advice was invariably: be your own man.

ERNIE ELS: *thumb up for victory*

He was. Early in the round Els stretched his two-stroke lead to five and it seemed the trophy engraver would be able to start work early. But Kaplan stuck in and as Els dropped shots, the home-club player nipped in with birdies. It was impressive stuff and afterwards he could say: "I was not intimidated by Ernie, but I am always in awe of what he has achieved and the ease and grace with which he hits the ball.

"I can't drive it past him and I can't hit the ball as high, but I was pleased the way I hung in. There were a lot of Houghton members out there shouting for me but the biggest cheers were still for Ernie."

They came to the sunny Sunday with Els on 205, Kaplan on 207, Peter Lonard

RICHARD KAPLAN: "Be your own man" messages

of Australia on 209 and Webster and Singh on 210. Would there be a gripping climax? Could Kaplan complete his marvellous weekend in style?

In the build-up to the tournament, Els had talked about ridding himself of the disappointments of the latter half of 1998 when his ailing back had been affecting his swing. He needed a return to the winner's circle. He made three birdies in the first five holes and Kaplan could not recover from that, although the spirit that existed between them as they played together in front of an enormous gallery was commendable.

After returning 70 to Els's 68, Kaplan said: "Ernie is great to be paired with. He doesn't impose his stature or his super-stardom on you. You always feel you can share a joke with him or talk about the cricket, which we did today. He doesn't brush you off. In fact, the easy way he swings the club rubs off on you and makes you play well."

For Els, it was the perfect beginning to his season as he talked about his plans for the majors and his decision to base himself at Wentworth for much of the year. On this early January day he was already talking of arriving at No. 1 in the world, a position he held for two months early in 1998. He is the ultimate competitor who manages to smile a lot and fully justifies the soubriquet "Big Easy".

As he relaxed with a beer after taking that call from his President, he was saying: "I know there are a lot of other good players in the world but the fact is that for the first five months of 1998 I played like the No. 1 in the world and for two months I was the No. 1. Then I got my back injury and the rest of the year was very frustrating because I lost form as a result. I dropped to No. 5 but I firmly believe I have the talent to get back to No. 1." Who wants to argue.

James Mossop

STEVE WEBSTER: anyone seen my ball?

Houghton GC, Johannesburg, January 14–17, 1999 • Par 72 • Yards 7309

Pos	Name & Country	Rnd 1	Rnd 2	Rnd 3	Rnd 4	Total	Prize Money €	£
1	Ernie ELS (SA)	67	69	69	68	273	83564.96	59689.26
2	Richard KAPLAN (SA)	68	70	69	70	277	60851.35	43465.25
3	Jeev Milkha SINGH (Ind)	73	69	68	70	280	25803.72	18431.23
	David FROST (SA)	70	73	71	66	280	25803.72	18431.23
	Stephen LEANEY (Aus)	73	68	70	69	280	25803.72	18431.23
	Steve WEBSTER (Eng)	69	73	68	70	280	25803.72	18431.23
7	Mark MCNULTY (Zim)	69	70	72	70	281	14341.27	10243.76
	Francis QUINN (USA)	69	72	72	68	281	14341.27	10243.76
9	Peter BAKER (Eng)	69	72	71	70	282	11462.44	8187.46
10	Peter LONARD (Aus)	73	70	66	74	283	9283.53	6631.09
	Patrik SJÖLAND (Swe)	72	74	68	69	283	9283.53	6631.09
	Justin HOBDAY (SA)	71	75	67	70	283	9283.53	6631.09
	Nico VAN RENSBURG (SA)	65	74	76	68	283	9283.53	6631.09
14	Marc CAYEUX (Eng)	73	68	71	72	284	7606.42	5433.16
	Desvonde BOTES (SA)	74	72	68	70	284	7606.42	5433.16
	Nic HENNING (SA)	71	74	72	67	284	7606.42	5433.16
17	Steve VAN VUUREN (SA)	72	73	71	69	285	6998.96	4999.26
	Andrew MCLARDY (SA)	73	70	69	73	285	6998.96	4999.26
19	Tjaart VAN DER WALT (SA)	72	75	68	71	286	6356.29	4540.21
	Steen TINNING (Den)	72	71	74	69	286	6356.29	4540.21
	Marco GORTANA (It)	74	70	71	71	286	6356.29	4540.21
22	Mathias GRÖNBERG (Swe)	70	75	70	72	287	5718.03	4084.31
	John MELLOR (Eng)	71	73	72	71	287	5718.03	4084.31
	Sven STRÜVER (Ger)	74	71	70	72	287	5718.03	4084.31
	Massimo SCARPA (It)	72	71	74	70	287	5718.03	4084.31
26	Paul BROADHURST (Eng)	70	75	71	72	288	5097.35	3640.96
	Ignacio GARRIDO (Sp)	69	75	71	73	288	5097.35	3640.96
	Gary ORR (Scot)	71	75	72	70	288	5097.35	3640.96
	Roger WESSELS (SA)	71	76	68	73	288	5097.35	3640.96
30	Wimpie BOTHA (SA)	78	69	67	75	289	4595.54	3282.53
	Anders HANSEN (Den)	75	72	71	71	289	4595.54	3282.53
	Chris WILLIAMS (SA)	72	75	69	73	289	4595.54	3282.53
33	Francis VALERA (Sp)	73	69	75	73	290	4172.97	2980.69
	Massimo FLORIOLI (It)	73	73	70	74	290	4172.97	2980.69
	Christopher HANELL (Swe)	72	74	70	74	290	4172.97	2980.69
	Mark MOULAND (Wal)	71	70	73	76	290	4172.97	2980.69
	Darren FICHARDT (SA)	76	71	73	70	290	4172.97	2980.69
38	Per HAUGSRUD (Nor)	72	72	74	73	291	3591.92	2565.66
	Hennie WALTERS (SA)	74	72	72	73	291	3591.92	2565.66
	Bruce VAUGHAN (USA)	71	69	74	77	291	3591.92	2565.66
	Ian GARBUTT (Eng)	76	69	71	75	291	3591.92	2565.66
	Paul MCGINLEY (Ire)	77	69	69	76	291	3591.92	2565.66
	Ashley ROESTOFF (SA)	74	70	71	76	291	3591.92	2565.66
44	Rolf MUNTZ (Hol)	68	75	73	76	292	3169.34	2263.81
	Andrew SHERBORNE (Eng)	73	74	75	70	292	3169.34	2263.81
46	Chris DAVISON (SA)	76	71	71	75	293	2799.58	1999.70
	Clinton WHITELAW (SA)	69	75	76	73	293	2799.58	1999.70
	John BICKERTON (Eng)	74	73	73	73	293	2799.58	1999.70
	Jamie SPENCE (Eng)	73	72	75	73	293	2799.58	1999.70
	Gavin LEVENSON (SA)	71	76	73	73	293	2799.58	1999.70
51	Ian HUTCHINGS (Eng)	73	72	75	74	294	2271.36	1622.40
	Warren ABERY (SA)	70	75	75	74	294	2271.36	1622.40
	Marc FARRY (Fr)	72	72	74	76	294	2271.36	1622.40
	David CARTER (Eng)	70	74	73	77	294	2271.36	1622.40
	Bob MAY (USA)	80	67	74	73	294	2271.36	1622.40
56	Olivier EDMOND (Fr)	72	71	76	76	295	1901.61	1358.29
	Andrew BEAL (Eng)	73	73	75	74	295	1901.61	1358.29
58	Scott DUNLAP (USA)	71	75	73	77	296	1716.73	1226.24
	Paolo QUIRICI (Swi)	73	74	76	73	296	1716.73	1226.24
60	Michael ARCHER (Eng)	76	71	76	74	297	1637.50	1169.64
61	Anthony WALL (Eng)	71	74	76	78	299	1584.67	1131.91
62	Fredrik LINDGREN (Swe)	70	75	79	76	300	1531.85	1094.18
63	Patrick O'BRIEN (SA)	72	72	78	80	302	1452.62	1037.59
	Bafana HLOPHE (SA)	69	76	81	76	302	1452.62	1037.59
65	Desmond TERBLANCHE (SA)	73	73	78	W/D	224	1373.39	980.99

DAVID FROST: a hot 66 finish

Scotts products are chosen by professionals looking for the very best results: the PGA European Tour recommend Greenmaster turfcare products such as those used at the Wentworth Club. The All England Lawn Tennis and Croquet Club, Wimbledon, also uses Scotts products on its famous courts. Scotts is dedicated to producing the best for the gardener too, with leading brands such as Levington compost, Evergreen lawncare products, Miracle-Gro and Tomorite plant foods and Weedol and Pathclear weedkillers. We are so confident of their performance that we will offer you your money back if you use our products as recommended and are not completely satisfied. And if you want help or advice about any of our products just phone our garden advice line on 0870 5301010.

Scotts

The Scotts Difference®

Salisbury House, Weyside Park, Catteshall Lane, Godalming, Surrey, GU7 1XE. Tel: (0) 1483 410210 Fax: (0) 1483 410220

Always read the label. Use pesticides safely Pathclear contains amitrole, diquat, paraquat and simazine. Weedol contains diquet and paraquat.
® ™ Trade Marks of the Scotts Company or its affiliates © The Scotts Company (UK) Ltd. 05-99

"The Scotts Company is the leader in research, manufacturing and marketing of products for domestic lawn care and gardening, professional turf care, ornamental horticulture and field and vegetable production. From bases in the U.S.A. and Europe, Scotts sells its products in more than 50 countries worldwide."

Frost warms to welcome

Emotional victory for the local hero

inspired by a homecoming

vision in scenic Stellenbosch

A flourish of old-fashioned sporting romance decorated the Mercedes-Benz - Vodacom South African Open Championship in the heart of the breath-taking Cape Winelands. David Frost, local hero and club member, won in a manner that ensured there was hardly a dry eye in the Stellenbosch clubhouse.

It was a story of dreams coming true over four days of enthralling golf for one of the world's oldest Open titles that has been won by players from outside South Africa only five times in almost a century. For much of the time it appeared that Sven Strüver of Germany would make that tally six. But any vision of victory he had turned into a third day nightmare, though he endeared himself to many with his easy-going charm amid the adversity of an eight at the par five 12th when his five-shot lead began to crumble.

For much of the four days, the wind was up in late afternoon. The greens became increasingly difficult and the heat on them was so intense that watering teams were out during play. The course played long with players often hitting their longest irons into some of the par fours. With the fairways narrow and tall trees encroaching, there were pitfalls aplenty. No time, then, to take in the pleasing backdrop of the towering Nederburg Mountains, the flowering gum trees and the rolling vineyards bordering the course.

David Frost had grown up with all of that and all week he lurked in the pack just behind the leaders, finally coming through on the Sunday with a solid 68 for a total of 279 (five under par) that put him one ahead of the Indian Jeev Milkha Singh and American Scott Dunlap.

For Frost it was an emotional time with all the local support urging him on and afterwards, before heading back to celebrate at the 120-hectare St. Clement winery he owns near Paarl, about 15 miles from the course, he recounted the joy of winning and the memories it rekindled.

He said: "I had a vision I would win this week. The one problem I had was keeping my concentration because guys I hadn't seen for years were calling to me from behind the ropes. I ended up playing with my head between my legs. This win brings me back to where it all began. My dad would sit in the bar here and I would play holes seven, eight and nine. He told me he would buy me a set of clubs the first time I broke 80.

DAVID FROST: home for a family celebration

My first set cost R30 from a member in 1975. I remember needing pars on 17 and 18 to break 80 but I double-bogeyed both."

On the final day in this, the 1999 Mercedes-Benz - Vodacom SA Open, he needed all the cool maturity of his 39 years as he was trailing by two with five to play and it seemed that any chance had disappeared when he hit his second shot into the water at the 12th. He took a drop, chipped the ball dead and tapped it in for a par five. He birdied the 13th and 17th and was on his way while Strüver, who won everyone's sympathy, was back in third after hitting into the water at

the last, after his tee-shot had landed in a divot.

Overall, it was one of those tournaments that held the attention of everyone from start to finish. There was the added attraction of Ernie Els going for a second successive win and Nick Faldo determined to prove the previous week's missed cut had been an aberration. Els finished tied sixth and Faldo survived all four days for 290 but, Frost apart, some unusual names were frequently at the head of the action.

At the end of the long, hot, sunny, opening day, the three men locked together at the head of the leaderboard were Yorkshireman Ian Garbutt, Strüver

SCOTT DUNLAP: 65 for joint runner-up

SVEN STRÜVER: five-shot lead vanished

and Ronnie McCann, a South African who has spent the last 19 years in the United States where he has no Tour card and has won nothing bigger than a few local events around Orlando, where he lives, in Florida.

All of them shot 67 on the par 71 course after a 6.50am tee off. Garbutt revealed that he had gone to bed at 9pm and rose at 4.30 and was extremely pleased with his position. Could he keep it up? Sadly not, for the second day belonged to Strüver, the man from Hamburg, who put together another 67 and that was good enough to give him a three-shot lead.

Playing alongside Strüver was John Bickerton, who was going out in the last group in a European Tour event for the first time in his career. Bickerton had opened his year among the rookies at MacGregor Week (The European Tour

ERNIE ELS: shared sixth place

THE COURSE

Stellenbosch Golf Club is in the heart of the Cape Winelands, 40 minutes' drive from Cape Town, and is a par 71 course stretching over 7,112 yards of parkland amid spectacular scenery and flowering gum trees. The 466 yards tenth hole, until recently a par five, proved particularly testing.

JEEV MILKHA SINGH: tied second

Training School) in San Roque, Spain, and was keen to say that the advice of such legends as John Jacobs and Tommy Horton had helped him. His bogey-free, Friday 66 helped him to a decent cheque and ensured that his two-week trip to South Africa had been well worthwhile.

Still Strüver appeared to be controlling things and seven holes from home on the third day, when the cream usually begins to rise to the top, he stood on the 12th tee with a five-shot lead. By the time he had collected his ball from the hole 21 other players were back in real contention. Strüver's eight was a severe blow. He had driven poorly into the thick, club-grabbing, kikuyu-grass rough and failed to get back on the fairway with his second.

He had around 140 yards to the flag, chose his wedge and saw the ball come up short, slipping into the water. He dropped out for a one-shot penalty, pitched up short and three-putted. His anguish was clear as he sighed: "It didn't fly. It just didn't fly," he said of his third shot. After his first three-putt of the tournament he committed two more on the run-in until a birdie at the last sent him into the final round one shot ahead of Spain's Ignacio Garrido. Frost, at this stage, was four off the pace.

But the South African was a man inspired, moving up through the field as Garrido fell away with a closing 81. Singh (70) and Dunlap (71) were steady enough without generating true brilliance. Like Strüver, they needed birdies at the last to catch Frost. None of them made it and the championship went to a popular and worthy winner.

James Mossop

Stellenbosch GC, Cape Province, January 21–24, 1999 · Par 71 · Yards 7112

Pos	Name & Country	Rnd 1	Rnd 2	Rnd 3	Rnd 4	Total	Prize Money €	£
1	David FROST (SA)	69	69	73	68	279	127505.69	91075.49
2	Jeev Milkha SINGH (Ind)	71	71	68	70	280	74324.52	53088.94
	Scott DUNLAP (USA)	73	65	71	71	280	74324.52	53088.94
4	Sven STRÜVER (Ger)	67	67	73	74	281	39623.60	28302.57
5	Hennie OTTO (SA)	72	67	72	71	282	33329.02	23806.44
6	Bob MAY (USA)	70	70	70	73	283	24075.44	17196.74
	Thomas BJÖRN (Den)	72	73	68	70	283	24075.44	17196.74
	Ernie ELS (SA)	71	70	70	72	283	24075.44	17196.74
9	John BICKERTON (Eng)	71	66	74	73	284	17431.16	12450.83
	Jean HUGO (AM) (SA)	74	69	71	70	284		
10	Alex CEJKA (Ger)	68	71	74	72	285	14102.29	10073.06
	Wallie COETSEE (SA)	71	73	74	67	285	14102.29	10073.06
	Jonathan LOMAS (Eng)	73	73	68	71	285	14102.29	10073.06
	Francisco CEA (Sp)	74	70	73	68	285	14102.29	10073.06
14	Ashley ROESTOFF (SA)	69	72	72	73	286	10854.12	7752.94
	Peter BAKER (Eng)	72	71	69	74	286	10854.12	7752.94
	Sammy DANIELS (SA)	71	69	76	70	286	10854.12	7752.94
	Steve WEBSTER (Eng)	73	68	75	70	286	10854.12	7752.94
	Nico VAN RENSBURG (SA)	73	71	70	72	286	10854.12	7752.94
	Mark ROE (Eng)	71	67	72	76	286	10854.12	7752.94
20	Van PHILLIPS (Eng)	74	68	75	70	287	8850.08	6321.49
	Stephen ALLAN (Aus)	71	73	70	73	287	8850.08	6321.49
	Phillip PRICE (Wal)	73	70	71	73	287	8850.08	6321.49
	Paul MCGINLEY (Ire)	69	69	73	76	287	8850.08	6321.49
	James KINGSTON (SA)	68	72	76	71	287	8850.08	6321.49
	Chris DAVISON (SA)	74	72	71	70	287	8850.08	6321.49
26	Michael JONZON (Swe)	72	71	70	75	288	7202.46	5144.61
	Miguel Angel MARTIN (Sp)	71	73	70	74	288	7202.46	5144.61
	Bernhard LANGER (Ger)	72	71	71	74	288	7202.46	5144.61
	Patrik SJÖLAND (Swe)	71	72	76	69	288	7202.46	5144.61
	Jarmo SANDELIN (Swe)	72	73	71	72	288	7202.46	5144.61
	Michael LONG (NZ)	73	72	68	75	288	7202.46	5144.61
	Greg OWEN (Eng)	71	71	75	71	288	7202.46	5144.61
	Gordon BRAND JNR. (Scot)	77	67	69	75	288	7202.46	5144.61
34	Ricardo GONZALEZ (Arg)	71	75	72	71	289	5729.69	4092.64
	Ian GARBUTT (Eng)	67	72	75	75	289	5729.69	4092.64
	Desvonde BOTES (SA)	71	74	73	71	289	5729.69	4092.64
	Mark MCNULTY (Zim)	71	73	73	72	289	5729.69	4092.64
	Ian HUTCHINGS (Eng)	71	71	76	71	289	5729.69	4092.64
	Ignacio GARRIDO (Sp)	70	69	69	81	289	5729.69	4092.64
	Donald GAMMON (SA)	71	71	69	78	289	5729.69	4092.64
	Jamie SPENCE (Eng)	75	70	72	72	289	5729.69	4092.64
	Dean VAN STADEN (SA)	73	73	72	71	289	5729.69	4092.64
43	Ronnie MCCANN (USA)	67	75	76	72	290	4438.49	3170.35
	Alan MCLEAN (Scot)	75	70	70	75	290	4438.49	3170.35
	Søren KJELDSEN (Den)	73	69	75	73	290	4438.49	3170.35
	Nick FALDO (Eng)	70	71	75	74	290	4438.49	3170.35
	Clinton WHITELAW (SA)	70	68	71	81	290	4438.49	3170.35
	Marco GORTANA (It)	70	71	75	74	290	4438.49	3170.35
	Derrick COOPER (Eng)	75	70	69	76	290	4438.49	3170.35
50	Justin HOBDAY (SA)	70	72	74	75	291	3308.69	2363.35
	Andrew PITTS (USA)	71	73	73	74	291	3308.69	2363.35
	Ian WOOSNAM (Wal)	72	70	74	75	291	3308.69	2363.35
	Pierre FULKE (Swe)	75	67	77	72	291	3308.69	2363.35
	Massimo FLORIOLI (It)	75	70	69	77	291	3308.69	2363.35
	Andrew BEAL (Eng)	72	71	75	73	291	3308.69	2363.35
	Kevin STONE (SA)	74	72	71	74	291	3308.69	2363.35
57	Mark MOULAND (Wal)	69	70	78	75	292	2582.39	1844.56
	Paul BROADHURST (Eng)	72	74	79	67	292	2582.39	1844.56
	David CARTER (Eng)	74	70	77	71	292	2582.39	1844.56
60	Richard KAPLAN (SA)	69	72	73	79	293	2219.25	1585.18
	Steen TINNING (Den)	71	73	73	76	293	2219.25	1585.18
	Robbie STEWART (SA)	72	74	77	70	293	2219.25	1585.18
	David FAUGHT (SA)	69	77	71	76	293	2219.25	1585.18
	Craig HAINLINE (USA)	70	74	74	75	293	2219.25	1585.18
	Thomas GÖGELE (Ger)	77	69	73	74	293	2219.25	1585.18
66	Per NYMAN (Swe)	71	75	71	77	294	1191.00	850.71
	Wayne WESTNER (SA)	73	73	76	72	294	1191.00	850.71
	Brenden PAPPAS (SA)	71	73	79	71	294	1191.00	850.71
	Michael ARCHER (Eng)	73	73	73	75	294	1191.00	850.71
	Ronald WHITTACKER (USA)	71	74	75	74	294	1191.00	850.71
71	Mark WILTSHIRE (SA)	72	74	71	78	295	1179.00	842.14
	Greg PETERSEN (USA)	75	71	77	72	295	1179.00	842.14
	Anthony WALL (Eng)	73	69	74	79	295	1179.00	842.14
	Henk ALBERTS (AM) (SA)	69	74	78	75	296		
74	Sean PAPPAS (SA)	69	75	81	83	308	1173.00	837.86

JOHN BICKERTON: *trip well worthwhile*

53

Moseley makes his name

Late call-up leads to nerve-testing

success in Australia's

richest tournament of the year

Ernie Els had never heard of Jarrod Moseley. Nor, if truth be told, had most European Tour players as the Tour moved on from South Africa to the splendid Vines Resort in Perth for the Heineken Classic, Australia's richest tournament.

There was no shame in their ignorance. Sure, the 26-year-old had been part of the Australian side which won the World Amateur Eisenhower Trophy title in 1996, but in 18 months as a professional his best finishes were two seconds – in the Fijian and Samoan Opens. They do not quite compare to the two US Opens on Els's curriculum vitae.

Ten days before the tournament Moseley was not even in it. But then came a telephone call to tell him he was. It was to prove one of the most important calls of his life. Not that Els had any need to pay special attention to him for the first three rounds of the Classic. For while Moseley opened impressively with two 68s and a 69, the first of them left him three shots behind the world number five, the second five back and the third made no difference.

Arriving for the final 18 holes, the man from Mandurah admitted he was not thinking about the possibility of winning. How could he when the player in whose slipstream he trailed was one of the game's undoubted superstars? No, the player in Moseley's sights was not Els, but Sweden's Jarmo Sandelin, two ahead of him in second place. If he could overtake him and be runner-up to Els his career would take a big leap forward.

It had been Sandelin who set off the fastest on day one, nine birdies coming in an eight under par 64 – one outside the

JARROD MOSELEY: salute to a birdie

ERNIE ELS and JARMO SANDELIN: crowded company for final day troubles

course record, yet good enough only for a one-stroke advantage over both Els and Devon's Roger Winchester, making a welcome return to the Tour after losing his card in 1993 and having such a struggle that he was forced to sell his home in Wimbledon.

Els came into his own in the second round, despite being out on the course as the famous "Freemantle Doctor" wind picked up strength after lunch. While Sandelin took 71 and Winchester 74, he shot 66. It included four successive birdies around the turn, another on the 12th and another on the downwind 517-yard last,

Lee Trevino, Gary Player and course designer Graham Marsh (above) provided an added attraction for the crowds during the week by playing three separate Seniors challenge matches. Thrilling and entertaining the fans in equal measure, Trevino won twice and Marsh once.

THE COURSE

A mini-tornado – known locally as a 'willy-willy' – caused devastation to two of the hospitality marquees two days before the championship, but thankfully it left this masterpiece of a course undamaged. Graham Marsh designed the wonderful test of golf in the Swan Valley wine-growing region just outside Perth. It rewards power and accuracy and with its huge greens, undulating and slick, good putters prosper as well.

There is as much joy to be found in the wildlife around as in playing the course. Families of kangaroos roam and it is a bird-spotter's delight.

SHOT OF THE WEEK

A gleaming red Jaguar car sat behind the tee at the 170-yard 13th, unclaimed all week. Over 50,000 euro (£38,000) in casino chips were on offer for a hole-in-one at the 196-yard 16th, but nobody could grab them either. There were no prizes at the 208-yard fourth, much the toughest par three on the course, so the least Norwegian Per Haugsrud deserves for this third-round ace there with a four iron is to have it named 'Shot of the Week'.

where his enormous drive knocked off 365 of those yards. He had opened up a four-shot lead.

Sandelin came back to narrow that margin by one in the third round, but Els still looked odds-on to make it two wins from three starts in 1999. At 16 under par he was already eight ahead of the mark which gave Thomas Björn the title 12 months earlier. In short, he seemed a class apart and it appeared that only if he fell apart would the chasing pack have a chance.

Instead, Els birdied the second and Sandelin took a double-bogey seven on the third. Six strokes clear, tournament over. Or so everybody thought. Then came the 413-yard seventh. Els went right off the tee, left with his second. After taking a penalty drop away from a bush he could only chip onto the front of the green and from there three-putted.

It added up to a triple-bogey seven and suddenly, with Moseley having birdied the sixth and seventh and Peter Lonard having gone to the turn in 32, the two Australians were only one behind. Moseley then birdied the long ninth and Els, "shell-shocked" he confessed afterwards, three-putted again there for a bogey six. Now, though hardly able to believe it himself, Moseley led – first by

ERNIE ELS: why me?

57

one, then by two when he made a birdie putt of 12 feet on the 14th and then by three when Els – or at least the unsure character who had taken over his skin – missed from three feet to bogey the short 13th.

Lonard's birdie at the difficult 17th and Moseley's subsequent bogey on it reduced the gap to one again as the tension mounted. After driving into sand, however, Lonard was unable to birdie the par five last and while Moseley found the same bunker he knew a five would leave Els having to eagle the hole to force a play-off.

Aware of all that was at stake, Moseley admitted later he was shaking like a leaf as he played his eight iron third over the lake, but it was as good a shot as he had struck all week. It pulled up 12 feet from the flag and after playing companion Bernhard Langer, finishing strongly, had holed from ten feet to join Lonard on 13 under par, Moseley two-putted for his par and 14 under.

Now he could only stand and watch as Els tried to repair the earlier damage. Another big drive was followed by an approach to 25 feet, but the eagle attempt was never on line. Moseley was champion, and Els, for one, would never forget the name.

Mark Garrod

JARMO SANDELIN: nine birdies for first day lead

BERNHARD LANGER: finished strongly for second place tie

The Vines Resort, Perth, Australia, January 28–31, 1999 • Par 72 • Yards 7101

Pos	Name & Country	Rnd 1	Rnd 2	Rnd 3	Rnd 4	Total	Prize Money €	£
1	Jarrod MOSELEY (Aus)	68	68	69	69	274	152447.12	108890.80
2	Bernhard LANGER (Ger)	70	68	68	69	275	61404.21	43860.15
	Ernie ELS (SA)	65	66	69	75	275	61404.21	43860.15
	Peter LONARD (Aus)	68	67	72	68	275	61404.21	43860.15
5	Bob MAY (USA)	71	69	70	67	277	33881.61	24201.15
6	Craig PARRY (Aus)	72	71	68	67	278	30494.25	24201.15
7	Pierre FULKE (Swe)	69	70	69	71	279	24843.29	17745.21
	Paul DEVENPORT (NZ)	69	70	68	72	279	24843.29	17745.21
	Jarmo SANDELIN (Swe)	64	71	68	76	279	24843.29	17745.21
10	John SENDEN (Aus)	69	69	71	71	280	18916.09	13511.49
	Tim ELLIOTT (Aus)	70	71	70	69	280	18916.09	13511.49
	Jean Louis GUEPY (Fr)	70	70	68	72	280	18916.09	13511.49
13	Alex CEJKA (Ger)	71	70	68	72	281	12760.92	9114.94
	Per HAUGSRUD (Nor)	72	69	68	72	281	12760.92	9114.94
	Christopher HANELL (Swe)	70	71	68	72	281	12760.92	9114.94
	Andrew COLTART (Scot)	66	76	68	71	281	12760.92	9114.94
	Henrik BJORNSTAD (Nor)	68	73	71	69	281	12760.92	9114.94
	Craig HAINLINE (USA)	67	69	72	73	281	12760.92	9114.94
19	Kyoung-Ju CHOI (Kor)	69	74	70	69	282	8621.84	6158.46
	Raymond RUSSELL (Scot)	70	69	72	71	282	8621.84	6158.46
	Gary ORR (Scot)	70	71	70	71	282	8621.84	6158.46
	Wayne SMITH (Aus)	68	72	72	70	282	8621.84	6158.46
	Roger WINCHESTER (Eng)	65	74	73	70	282	8621.84	6158.46
	Peter O'MALLEY (Aus)	71	71	69	71	282	8621.84	6158.46
	Robert Jan DERKSEN (Hol)	70	70	70	72	282	8621.84	6158.46
26	Scott LAYCOCK (Aus)	69	71	74	69	283	6521.26	4658.04
	Thomas BJÖRN (Den)	73	66	74	70	283	6521.26	4658.04
	Lucas PARSONS (Aus)	71	73	69	70	283	6521.26	4658.04
	Bradley KING (Aus)	71	70	71	71	283	6521.26	4658.04
30	Peter FOWLER (Aus)	72	70	74	68	284	5211.11	3722.22
	Daniel CHOPRA (Swe)	72	72	70	70	284	5211.11	3722.22
	Gavin COLES (Aus)	69	72	71	72	284	5211.11	3722.22
	Wayne RILEY (Aus)	70	71	70	73	284	5211.11	3722.22
	Jeremy ROBINSON (Eng)	72	71	74	67	284	5211.11	3722.22
	Matthew LANE (NZ)	71	73	73	67	284	5211.11	3722.22
36	Ian GARBUTT (Eng)	71	72	70	72	285	3894.25	2781.61
	Anders HANSEN (Den)	69	71	74	71	285	3894.25	2781.61
	Steve CONRAN (Aus)	68	74	70	73	285	3894.25	2781.61
	Peter SENIOR (Aus)	72	70	77	66	285	3894.25	2781.61
	Nick O'HERN (Aus)	69	70	72	74	285	3894.25	2781.61
	Sven STRÜVER (Ger)	70	68	69	78	285	3894.25	2781.61
	Andrew RAITT (Eng)	69	74	74	68	285	3894.25	2781.61
	Eiji MIZOGUCHI (Jpn)	69	74	70	72	285	3894.25	2781.61
	Van PHILLIPS (Eng)	71	73	70	71	285	3894.25	2781.61
45	Andrew SHERBORNE (Eng)	72	70	70	74	286	2627.01	1876.44
	Mats LANNER (Swe)	71	69	72	74	286	2627.01	1876.44
	Craig SPENCE (Aus)	67	73	73	73	286	2627.01	1876.44
	John BICKERTON (Eng)	73	71	73	69	286	2627.01	1876.44
	Andrew MCLARDY (SA)	68	72	75	71	286	2627.01	1876.44
	David SMAIL (NZ)	69	74	71	72	286	2627.01	1876.44
51	Thomas LEVET (Fr)	71	72	72	72	287	2023.56	1445.40
	Padraig HARRINGTON (Ire)	71	73	74	69	287	2023.56	1445.40
53	Christopher D GRAY (Aus)	72	71	74	71	288	1862.65	1330.46
	Neil KERRY (Aus)	66	76	73	73	288	1862.65	1330.46
	Wayne GRADY (Aus)	75	68	71	74	288	1862.65	1330.46
	Anthony PAINTER (Aus)	72	72	69	75	288	1862.65	1330.46
57	Grant KENNY (Aus)	72	71	72	74	289	1770.11	1264.36
	Anthony WALL (Eng)	74	70	72	73	289	1770.11	1264.36
	Mike CLAYTON (Aus)	73	68	74	74	289	1770.11	1264.36
	Craig JONES (Aus)	71	71	72	75	289	1770.11	1264.36
	Gary EMERSON (Eng)	74	70	72	73	289	1770.11	1264.36
	Stephen ALLAN (Aus)	73	69	75	72	289	1770.11	1264.36
63	Gary EVANS (Eng)	70	72	75	73	290	1713.80	1224.14
64	Justin COOPER (Aus)	72	70	75	75	292	1685.63	1204.02
	Anthony EDWARDS (Zim)	73	70	73	76	292	1685.63	1204.02
66	Paul GOW (Aus)	71	72	72	79	294	1207.00	862.14
67	Robert STEPHENS (Aus)	68	74	77	76	295	1204.00	860.00
68	Fredrik JACOBSON (Swe)	72	70	76	79	297	1201.00	857.86

PETER LONARD: it goes thataway

Never say never

Gerry Norquist did, then a class

victory made him think again

on a journey down Memory Lane

There is so much wildlife to be seen at the Saujana Golf and Country Club, any visitor to the Benson & Hedges Malaysian Open, presented by Carlsberg, would not have been surprised to have seen the name of David Attenborough on top of the leaderboard.

There are reputed to be 18 different species of cobra in residence, initially introduced when the course was a palm plantation to control the vermin population. Only one person has ever been bitten and recovered quickly, but locals delight in telling visitors that they have serum to counteract every type of snake, just as long as you can identify the culprit. Otherwise you may be asleep inside 20 minutes. Time for just one more hole then.

GERRY NORQUIST: the crowds cheered and the chimps chattered

Cut through a one-time palm plantation, the 6,947 yards, par 72 Saujana Golf and Country Club course is not only one of Malaysia's finest, but also most demanding.

It meanders majestically through tough terrain. Champions here have not only to be shot makers, but also athletes as the ground rises and falls in roller-coaster fashion.

Drives on the par fours and fives require just one swing thought – hit the fairway. The par threes are equally demanding – the tee shot has to stay below the hole. It is a true test.

The snakes, a threat only when threatened, were nowhere to be seen during a particularly memorable and pleasant first European Tour visit to Malaysia, but monkeys were an altogether different species. Several families delighted in screeching and swinging their way through the dense jungle oblivious to the calls of "Stand still please" aimed by marshals at the galleries.

Monkeys may be comparatively harmless, but they are certainly mischievous. One club golfer enjoying a round with business associates returned to his buggy after putting out to discover his mobile phone missing. Believing he may have dropped it close by, he asked his playing partner to ring the number. The phone rang out – 20 yards up a tree where it was being passed around by its new owners. Serves him right for taking his phone on the course.

The only bells ringing for some of Europe's best golfers were alarm ones. With this class of field, this was no forgiving stretch of 18 holes on which to be emerging from winter hibernation. Unlike some other courses in this neck of

BOB MAY: the gallery and Saujana monkey appreciate a good swing

Snake alert

the jungle – transplanted pieces of Florida – Saujana stays loyal to its palm tree roots and is all the better for it.

Newlywed Lee Westwood, a course winner and runner-up, quickly discovered his honeymoon was over. At four over par after two rounds, he was far from dissatisfied and confident he would be able to shake away more winter cobwebs at the weekend. He was mistaken. Plus fours were not required weekend attire. Close friend Darren Clarke , winner of the 1998 Volvo Masters, also left early after returning rounds of 76 and 79.

So the two pre-tournament favourites were out of the contest at halfway, leaving room for others to challenge for the last

DARREN CLARKE: early exit for 1998 Volvo Masters Champion

ALEX CEJKA: grim determination

two rounds. It was a trip into the unknown for the European Tour, but a journey down Memory Lane for American Gerry Norquist. The 36-year-old is an Asian Tour specialist and a lover of warm climes. He was hot for four days. That's more than can be said for his first and only visit to Europe.

Unaware that late autumn in Montpellier can be tourist season for eskimos, Norquist arrived at the 1991 European Tour Qualifying School ill equipped to deal with a wind which attacked his ribs with the subtlety of a crazed acupuncturist.

Norquist succumbed, spent the two days immediately before the event cocooned in bed, emerged to shoot 80-81

and caught the first plane home. He never returned, not until this year that is. For just as soon as the ink was dry on his 103,223.16 euro (£73,730) cheque, Norquist was taking up his European options that came with first prize. "I know I said I'd never go back, but now I can't wait," said Norquist, following a win he had to grind out after faltering in the third round.

This co-sanctioned event – a first liaison between the two Tours – was an unmitigated success even though the golfing gods were at odds with their own weathermen. Kuala Lumpur in monsoon season is nothing if not spectacular. One minute humidity and heat, the next explosions and Niagara-style waterfalls.

But the washouts prevented neither the tournament coming to a full conclusion nor the emergence of a class champion.

The Stars and Stripes flew proudest – Norquist winning by three strokes from fellow American Bob May and Germany's Alex Cejka. Two Thais also made the top ten – another indication of the growing strength of Asian golfers.

But it was Norquist, who found no quest too difficult in returning a record fifth Asian Tour triumph and first on the European Tour. The crowds cheered and the chimps chattered. They saluted a true champion, and a new dawn in golf.

Martin Hardy

Saujana G. & C.C., Kuala Lumpur, Malaysia, February 4–7, 1999 · Par 72 · Yards 6947

Pos	Name & Country	Rnd 1	Rnd 2	Rnd 3	Rnd 4	Total	Prize Money €	£
1	Gerry NORQUIST (USA)	67	67	75	71	280	103223.16	73730.83
2	Bob MAY (USA)	72	69	70	72	283	55382.58	39558.99
	Alex CEJKA (Ger)	70	73	69	71	283	55382.58	39558.99
4	Andrew COLTART (Scot)	70	71	73	70	284	23009.50	16435.36
	Tse-Peng CHANG (Tai)	77	64	73	70	284	23009.50	16435.36
	Padraig HARRINGTON (Ire)	70	73	70	71	284	23009.50	16435.36
	Chawalit PLAPHOL (Thai)	76	71	69	68	284	23009.50	16435.36
	Shaun MICHEEL (USA)	69	71	70	74	284	23009.50	16435.36
9	Prayad MARKSAENG (Thai)	72	72	72	69	285	13518.08	9655.77
	Ed FRYATT (Eng)	70	69	71	75	285	13518.08	9655.77
11	Craig HAINLINE (USA)	70	71	72	73	286	9363.59	6688.28
	Jong-Duk KIM (Kor)	73	71	71	71	286	9363.59	6688.28
	Kyoung-Ju CHOI (Kor)	68	71	73	74	286	9363.59	6688.28
	Christopher HANELL (Swe)	75	67	72	72	286	9363.59	6688.28
	Scott ROWE (HK)	74	70	72	70	286	9363.59	6688.28
	Christian CHERNOCK (USA)	70	71	70	75	286	9363.59	6688.28
	Frankie MINOZA (Phil)	67	74	73	72	286	9363.59	6688.28
	WANG TER-CHANG (Tai)	69	72	71	74	286	9363.59	6688.28
	Andrew BONHOMME (Aus)	70	74	70	72	286	9363.59	6688.28
	Nick O'HERN (Aus)	74	71	70	71	286	9363.59	6688.28
21	Gary EVANS (Eng)	75	67	72	73	287	6998.72	4999.09
	Anders HANSEN (Den)	70	71	73	73	287	6998.72	4999.09
	Jarmo SANDELIN (Swe)	74	71	68	74	287	6998.72	4999.09
	Paul MCGINLEY (Ire)	74	71	68	74	287	6998.72	4999.09
	Jim RUTLEDGE (Can)	70	74	74	69	287	6998.72	4999.09
	Thomas LEVET (Fr)	72	73	70	72	287	6998.72	4999.09
27	Robert KARLSSON (Swe)	74	70	74	70	288	5848.25	4177.32
	Dean WILSON (USA)	71	68	75	74	288	5848.25	4177.32
	Geoff OGILVY (Aus)	74	73	68	73	288	5848.25	4177.32
	John BICKERTON (Eng)	73	72	73	70	288	5848.25	4177.32
	David HOWELL (Eng)	70	75	74	69	288	5848.25	4177.32
	Simon YATES (Eng)	77	69	68	74	288	5848.25	4177.32
33	Pierre FULKE (Swe)	73	69	72	75	289	4665.82	3332.73
	Gilberto MORALES (Ven)	71	72	74	72	289	4665.82	3332.73
	Andrew MCLARDY (SA)	78	67	73	71	289	4665.82	3332.73
	Lian-Wei ZHANG (Chi)	66	75	75	73	289	4665.82	3332.73
	Chris WILLIAMS (Eng)	73	71	74	71	289	4665.82	3332.73
	Eric MEEKS (USA)	71	73	73	72	289	4665.82	3332.73
	John MELLOR (Eng)	72	73	72	72	289	4665.82	3332.73
	Katsuyoshi TOMORI (Jpn)	72	73	71	73	289	4665.82	3332.73
	Daniel CHOPRA (Swe)	71	74	71	73	289	4665.82	3332.73
	Per HAUGSRUD (Nor)	74	70	74	71	289	4665.82	3332.73
43	Greg OWEN (Eng)	71	72	70	77	290	3771.00	2693.57
	Brad ANDREWS (Aus)	73	74	73	70	290	3771.00	2693.57
	Ali KADIR (Mal)	75	71	70	74	290	3771.00	2693.57
	Angel CABRERA (Arg)	76	70	71	73	290	3771.00	2693.57
47	Christian PENA (USA)	66	75	74	76	291	3323.59	2373.99
	José COCERES (Arg)	75	69	76	71	291	3323.59	2373.99
	Jyoti RANDHAWA (Ind)	71	72	70	78	291	3323.59	2373.99
50	Rolf MUNTZ (Hol)	73	74	74	71	292	3004.02	2145.73
	Keng-Chi LIN (Tai)	72	72	70	78	292	3004.02	2145.73
52	Marcello SANTI (It)	70	71	74	78	293	2620.53	1871.81
	Tomas Jesus MUÑOZ (Sp)	68	71	80	74	293	2620.53	1871.81
	Eric RUSTAND (USA)	70	76	73	74	293	2620.53	1871.81
	Robert HUXTABLE (USA)	75	70	75	73	293	2620.53	1871.81
56	Jerry SMITH (USA)	71	73	75	75	294	2237.04	1597.89
	S MURTHY (Mal)	76	70	74	74	294	2237.04	1597.89
58	Jonathan LOMAS (Eng)	73	74	77	72	296	1949.42	1392.44
	Kyi Hla HAN (Bur)	72	73	73	78	296	1949.42	1392.44
	Gwang-Soo CHOI (Kor)	73	72	73	78	296	1949.42	1392.44
	Stephen BENNETT (Eng)	71	76	73	76	296	1949.42	1392.44
62	Robin BYRD (USA)	75	72	75	75	297	1789.63	1278.31
63	Robert Jan DERKSEN (Hol)	74	71	73	80	298	1725.71	1232.65
64	Charlie WI (Kor)	73	71	80	75	299	1661.80	1187.00
65	Marimuthu RAMAYAH (Mal)	73	74	72	82	301	1597.88	1141.34

LEE WESTWOOD: hot and bothered

Sands of time

David Howell recovers from
injury for impressive
triumph in the desert

If someone had entered a room where David Howell was sitting a month before the tenth Dubai Desert Classic and asked: "Anyone for tennis?" the 23-year-old from Swindon would have had to respond in the negative.

Howell would not have been able to accept an invitation to play golf either. He was still having treatment on the right ankle he badly damaged playing tennis the week after winning the Australian PGA Championship in Sydney.

"When I injured the ankle it flashed through my mind how bad it might be," he admitted, conveying the awful feeling he had while being carted to hospital that he might have jeopardised his chosen career in golf.

The damage turned out to be a sprain, albeit a nasty one, and in mid-February he turned up in the Gulf physically restored and mentally refreshed. Six days later he was clutching the magnificent trophy and celebrating number one spot in the Volvo Order of Merit after a four-shot victory at the Dubai Creek Golf and Yacht Club course, where the rough was of US Open standard.

On the eve of the tournament Colin Montgomerie, a man whose predictions are rarely wrong, indicated that four rounds of 70 – eight under par – might suffice. But even with the added complication of an intermittent wind, Howell posted a 13 under par aggregate of 275, four better than Lee Westwood, five better than Ryder Cup captain Mark James and Paul McGinley and seven ahead of Montgomerie, Wayne Riley and Ed Fryatt.

After the first round Mark O'Meara named Westwood, Darren Clarke and Andrew Coltart among a rapidly growing number of young British golfing lions. By the Sunday evening he had added Howell.

It was an outstanding week for world class sport in Dubai, with the ATP Tennis Tour event staged only a John Daly-drive away, and a major horse race meeting at the famous Nad al Shiba track. It had not been a good week for England, however. The cricket team were demolished in Australia and over the road at the tennis Greg Rusedski lost early on before Tim Henman went out in the quarter-finals to 61st ranked player, Jerome Golmard.

Rusedski had the honour of throwing up the balls to decide the teams for the Challenge Match at the Jebel Ali Hotel

DAVID HOWELL: the line is the left edge of the furthest skyscraper …

THE COURSE

After nine years at the magnificent Emirates course, the event was switched to the Dubai Creek Golf and Yacht Club.

The soaring clubhouse has to be one of the most spectacular in the world, a towering monument to the traditional ocean-going Arab dhows. The course, designed by Karl Litten and opened in 1993, is a masterpiece too, considering it was built on such a compact piece of land alongside the creek and close to the international airport and new shopping mall.

Accuracy, not length, was the key here, especially as the rough for the Classic was ferocious. Indeed, Colin Montgomerie did not have a driver in his bag all week.

on the Tuesday. Thereafter there was a regular cross-flow of talent. One morning, four handicap Henman confirmed his ability with a club in his hand by shooting a 73 over the Emirates course while most evenings many golfers and their caddies were spotted at the tennis or the racing.

Once again there was no joy for the older generation, Nick Faldo, Ian Woosnam and Severiano Ballesteros all missing the cut. Although Justin Rose again failed to prosper, there was a heightening feeling that a changing-of-the-guard was taking place on Tour, stimulated by the fact that Howell, Alex Cejka, Warren Bennett, Jarmo Sandelin and the hugely talented Spanish amateur, Sergio Garcia, all broke 70 in the first round on a course set up for the experienced player.

Mind you, one player who broke 70 on the first day and again on the second was no fledgling. Peter Downie is the Creek's 36-year-old head professional, and before each round he had to check that the marshals had turned up and the caddie's bibs changed from the previous day.

Yet, while greater exponents toiled, the Longniddry-born club professional – who never has been a member of any major Tour – had a ball. By halfway he was only one off the lead, and early in the third round his name was actually on top of the leaderboard.

For a player with no experience at the highest level, the dream had to end sometime, and it did in the final hour when Howell showed his coolness under pressure, denying Westwood, McGinley,

COLIN MONTGOMERIE: reflective mood

DAVID HOWELL: dhow ahoy

James and Montgomerie even a glimmer of hope.

Having taken the lead in the second round with a 68 and holding it jointly with Riley after a third round of 71, he accelerated away from them all on Sunday by going to the turn in 31.

By then he was five in front and when he also birdied the long tenth his lead was six. For the remainder of the round his progress was as tranquil as that of the old trading dhows which used to sail gently up the Creek to the sheltered harbour.

In David Howell, the Tour had found another potential superstar. He could play, he could lead and he revelled in being in that situation. But he had one confession to make.

"I didn't look at a leaderboard until the 14th," he said. "I concentrated on the next shot." It was American sports psychologist Bob Rotella's book, "Golf is not a Game of Perfect", which taught him to remain in the present, and it was Peter Cowen's coaching which did the rest.

For a lad, who in the winters, made £10 a day cladding and guttering, fitting windows and packing books for Reader's Digest, a vivid new chapter had been written.

Jock MacVicar

PETER DOWNIE: dream had to end

SHOT OF THE WEEK

Mark O'Meara did not enjoy one of his best tournaments, but the 1998 Open Champion's two iron second shot at the 487-yard fifth hole in the second round was the stroke of a master.

The hole is dog-legged right-to-left, with only water between the fairway and the edge of the green.

O'Meara's ball from his tee shot lay in the semi-rough just short of the water and he was standing slightly below it – a frightening prospect. From there, however, he rifled his ball to ten feet and holed the putt for an eagle three.

Dubai Creek Golf and Yacht Club, Dubai, February 11–14, 1999 • Par 72 • Yards 6843

Pos	Name & Country	Rnd 1	Rnd 2	Rnd 3	Rnd 4	Total	Prize Money €	£
1	David HOWELL (Eng)	69	68	71	67	275	198324.00	141660.00
2	Lee WESTWOOD (Eng)	72	71	69	67	279	132216.00	94440.00
3	Paul MCGINLEY (Ire)	67	71	75	67	280	66997.00	47855.00
	Mark JAMES (Eng)	73	69	69	69	280	66997.00	47855.00
5	Wayne RILEY (Aus)	68	70	70	74	282	42583.33	30416.66
	Colin MONTGOMERIE (Scot)	70	70	72	70	282	42583.33	30416.66
	Ed FRYATT (Eng)	70	70	70	72	282	42583.33	30416.66
8	Miguel Angel JIMÉNEZ (Sp)	73	67	70	73	283	26702.67	19073.34
	Jyoti RANDHAWA (Ind)	73	69	70	71	283	26702.67	19073.34
	Anthony WALL (Eng)	70	70	72	71	283	26702.67	19073.34
11	Michael JONZON (Swe)	71	68	76	69	284	19929.00	14235.00
	Phillip PRICE (Wal)	67	73	73	71	284	19929.00	14235.00
	Alex CEJKA (Ger)	68	73	75	68	284	19929.00	14235.00
	Michael CAMPBELL (NZ)	71	71	71	71	284	19929.00	14235.00
15	Warren BENNETT (Eng)	69	70	71	75	285	15517.00	11083.57
	Steen TINNING (Den)	69	71	72	73	285	15517.00	11083.57
	Dean ROBERTSON (Scot)	71	73	72	69	285	15517.00	11083.57
	Jarmo SANDELIN (Swe)	69	70	75	71	285	15517.00	11083.57
	John BICKERTON (Eng)	73	73	71	68	285	15517.00	11083.57
	Gary EVANS (Eng)	72	70	75	68	285	15517.00	11083.57
	Paul AFFLECK (Wal)	69	72	74	70	285	15517.00	11083.57
22	Bob MAY (USA)	69	74	71	72	286	13209.00	9435.00
	Steve WEBSTER (Eng)	70	70	74	72	286	13209.00	9435.00
	Pierre FULKE (Swe)	73	72	74	67	286	13209.00	9435.00
25	Angel CABRERA (Arg)	73	71	76	67	287	11602.50	8287.50
	Per NYMAN (Swe)	71	72	72	72	287	11602.50	8287.50
	Per-Ulrik JOHANSSON (Swe)	72	74	70	71	287	11602.50	8287.50
	José Maria OLAZABAL (Sp)	69	73	73	72	287	11602.50	8287.50
	Mark O'MEARA (USA)	72	67	77	71	287	11602.50	8287.50
	Francisco CEA (Sp)	69	73	72	73	287	11602.50	8287.50
31	Jamie SPENCE (Eng)	70	69	73	76	288	9906.75	7076.25
	Russell CLAYDON (Eng)	75	71	73	69	288	9906.75	7076.25
	Thomas LEVET (Fr)	69	73	72	74	288	9906.75	7076.25
	José RIVERO (Sp)	72	71	73	72	288	9906.75	7076.25
	Sergio GARCIA (AM) (Sp)	68	73	75	72	288		
35	Jonathan LOMAS (Eng)	74	66	77	72	289	8687.00	6205.00
	Gary ORR (Scot)	72	70	73	74	289	8687.00	6205.00
	Peter BAKER (Eng)	73	73	71	72	289	8687.00	6205.00
	Eduardo ROMERO (Arg)	70	75	72	72	289	8687.00	6205.00
	Ricardo GONZALEZ (Arg)	74	72	74	69	289	8687.00	6205.00
	Shaun MICHEEL (USA)	71	75	71	72	289	8687.00	6205.00
41	Andrew OLDCORN (Scot)	76	69	72	73	290	7378.00	5270.00
	Ross MCFARLANE (Eng)	72	72	75	71	290	7378.00	5270.00
	Andrew SHERBORNE (Eng)	75	68	75	72	290	7378.00	5270.00
	Andrew COLTART (Scot)	71	70	74	75	290	7378.00	5270.00
	Raymond RUSSELL (Scot)	70	73	77	70	290	7378.00	5270.00
	Trevor IMMELMAN (AM) (SA)	70	72	72	76	290		
46	Peter DOWNIE (Scot)	69	69	75	78	291	6069.00	4335.00
	Mark MOULAND (Wal)	71	74	71	75	291	6069.00	4335.00
	Richard GREEN (Aus)	72	67	75	77	291	6069.00	4335.00
	Costantino ROCCA (It)	72	74	69	76	291	6069.00	4335.00
	Sven STRÜVER (Ger)	70	71	77	73	291	6069.00	4335.00
	Jean VAN DE VELDE (Fr)	77	69	76	69	291	6069.00	4335.00
52	Barry LANE (Eng)	69	74	72	77	292	5236.00	3740.00
53	Thomas BJÖRN (Den)	72	73	74	74	293	4879.00	3485.00
	Domingo HOSPITAL (Sp)	75	71	73	74	293	4879.00	3485.00
55	Joakim HAEGGMAN (Swe)	72	69	77	76	294	4165.00	2975.00
	Ian GARBUTT (Eng)	73	72	75	74	294	4165.00	2975.00
	Eamonn DARCY (Ire)	71	74	74	75	294	4165.00	2975.00
	Fredrik LINDGREN (Swe)	70	70	77	77	294	4165.00	2975.00
59	Santiago LUNA (Sp)	75	70	81	69	295	3570.00	2550.00
	David GILFORD (Eng)	71	75	76	73	295	3570.00	2550.00
	Van PHILLIPS (Eng)	72	72	80	71	295	3570.00	2550.00
62	Derrick COOPER (Eng)	73	72	79	73	297	3213.00	2295.00
	Darren CLARKE (N.Ire)	70	73	77	77	297	3213.00	2295.00
	Jim PAYNE (Eng)	73	73	76	75	297	3213.00	2295.00
65	Mark PILKINGTON (Wal)	73	71	79	75	298	2380.00	1700.00
	Søren KJELDSEN (Den)	72	74	78	74	298	2380.00	1700.00

When it comes to sports results, you could say we really know the score.

In sports - just like business - results are everything. And not just to the millions worldwide who depend on our systems to deliver real-time scores and analysis of premier sporting events on the Web and on TV - but to the networks and press that cover them. Events like the Volvo PGA Championship, the Trophée Lancôme, the Volvo Scandinavian Masters and others on the PGA European Tour, the Open Championship, the US Open, U.S. Seniors Open, U.S. Women's Open, Australian Open, Rugby World Cup, Macau Grand Prix and many more. We ensure the results keep pouring in thanks to the powerful teaming of Unisys software, Windows NT servers and our dedicated people. It's the same combination our customers around the world rely on to solve their real-time business problems and get them results. Which is why we take sports very seriously - it's what keeps us ahead of the game. www.unisys.com.

©1999 Unisys Corporation.

We eat, sleep and drink this stuff.

Lawrie of Arabia

Scot charges to seven-shot win

with 23 birdies in Doha

for second European Tour title

*I*t is just a one-hour flight from Dubai to Doha, but from Paul Lawrie's viewpoint they must seem worlds apart.

In the Dubai Desert Classic the 30-year-old Scot played 36 holes in ten over par with 13 bogeys and a mere three birdies. He had missed the halfway cut by eight strokes and, for a first appearance of the season, it was not quite the advertisement for his new coach, Adam Hunter, the former Portuguese Open champion, that he had in mind.

At the Qatar Masters a week later it was different. Very different. Seventy-two holes produced 23 birdies, just three bogeys – and, not surprisingly, a handsome cheque and a handsome trophy. Lawrie of Arabia was a story that went from the ridiculous to the sublime.

The inaugural staging of the event in 1998 had brought fellow countryman Andrew Coltart his

PAUL LAWRIE : champion again

Peter Harradine designed the lavish facility that is Doha Golf Club using all the naturally existing features and adding some of his own. Sixty-five giant cacti were imported from Arizona to contrast with the ancient limestone rocks scattering the area, most notably at the signature 319-yard 16th, where the direct route to the green is blocked by a massive rock some 30 yards wide and 15 feet high. Eight artificial lakes add to the obstacles and also provide a source of irrigation for the grasses, which after the first Qatar Masters underwent a massive overseeding programme to produce a stunning improvement.

maiden European Tour victory. Lawrie's win, by a runaway seven-stroke margin, was his second, but in every sense more satisfying than the first. It was not his fault that the 1996 Open Catalonia was ruined by near gale-force winds and reduced to 36 holes. He had won and he resented the fact that there was a hint from some of it not being regarded as a "proper" success.

He wanted to show that he could last the full distance – and when he did it was with real style on a far from easy course in far from easy, windy conditions. Nobody could live with him once he got his nose in front. Lawrie's opening 68 left him two shots off the lead, set by Frenchman Marc Farry and matched by another Scot, Raymond Russell. One behind were American Bob May, fast becoming the Mr Consistency of the Tour, and 45-year-old Ryder Cup captain Mark James, continu-

EDUARDO ROMERO: hole-in-one wins ace BMW car

ALEX CEJKA: the desert can be a lonely experience

ing his form of Dubai, but insistent that however long it lasted he would not be playing against the Americans in September. "It's hard enough to be captain and keep breathing, let alone play as well," he said.

Farry, Russell, James and May did not have the spotlight to themselves. Three players had the excitement of holes-in-one. Eduardo Romero at the 161-yard 17th (the Argentinean won a BMW Roadster car for that) and on the second day John Bickerton at the 206-yard 13th and Patrik Sjöland also at the 17th.

Lawrie could not manage an ace, but he did just about everything else right. He added a 65 to move two in front at halfway and when a 67 was tagged on to that he was already five clear. His one previous experience of such an advantage was the UAP European Under-25s Championship in 1992. He had led by six there after three rounds and went on to win by eight.

The memory of that did not put his mind at rest, though, He suffered a near-sleepless night before the final round. It was

JOHN BICKERTON: sign language

the tenth and birdies at the 17th and 18th, were the ones to benefit from a last-hole nightmare by Russell. Hoping for a birdie on the 592-yard hole, which would give him the runners-up position outright, Russell was twice in water. It cost him a triple bogey eight and he tumbled to fifth spot.

Kjeldsen had held on to his Tour card by the skin of his teeth at the end of 1998, but even before February was out 1999 was shaping up to be a much better year.

It is hard to argue against any one of the three holes-in-one during the week, but Jean Van de Velde did not have the luxury of a tee-peg or grass beneath his feet once he had blocked his drive down the 470-yard 15th – Doha's toughest hole – in the third round. He was not so much in trouble, as in rubble.

The ball came to rest in amongst rocks, boulders and stones and perched on a footprint of dried earth. A lake was in front of him, but Van de Velde chose to take the shot on, hit a crisp two iron over the water and on the green. His boldness was rewarded with a birdie putt from 50 feet.

so bad he even found himself watching television cricket coverage of India playing Pakistan in Calcutta. His practice session did not go well and his first three holes went even worse. Scrambled pars at the opening two holes were followed by only his second bogey of the week on the short third.

Then, however, a pitch to two feet on the 391-yard fourth led to his first birdie of the day and as challengers were blown away he went into overdrive again with four more birdies in a row around the turn. That, effectively, was that and by the time he arrived on the final tee Lawrie knew he could take 11 and still win. Just six weeks earlier in a North-East of Scotland Alliance he had blasted three balls out of bounds on one hole at Buckpool for a ten (yet amazingly still shot 66 and won the £100 first prize), but here a five completed the best week's work of his life.

In the battle for second place Søren Kjeldsen – not so much a great Dane as a pocket-sized marathon-running one – and Welshman Phillip Price, with an eagle on

Doha Golf Club, Qatar, February 17–20, 1999 · Par 72 · Yards 7268

Pos	Name & Country	Rnd 1	Rnd 2	Rnd 3	Rnd 4	Total	Prize Money €	£
1	Paul LAWRIE (Scot)	68	65	67	68	268	143196.27	102283.05
2	Phillip PRICE (Wal)	70	68	69	68	275	74622.56	53301.83
	Søren KJELDSEN (Den)	70	65	72	68	275	74622.56	53301.83
4	John BICKERTON (Eng)	68	67	71	71	277	42960.60	30686.14
5	Christopher HANELL (Swe)	71	67	70	70	278	30759.79	21971.28
	Jean VAN DE VELDE (Fr)	69	66	70	73	278	30759.79	21971.28
	Raymond RUSSELL (Scot)	66	70	70	72	278	30759.79	21971.28
8	Ian WOOSNAM (Wal)	68	70	70	71	279	19274.99	13767.85
	Bob MAY (USA)	67	70	72	70	279	19274.99	13767.85
	Jamie SPENCE (Eng)	71	67	72	69	279	19274.99	13767.85
11	Alex CEJKA (Ger)	69	69	69	73	280	14378.91	10270.65
	Mathias GRÖNBERG (Swe)	72	67	71	70	280	14378.91	10270.65
	Patrik SJÖLAND (Swe)	74	69	72	65	280	14378.91	10270.65
	Wook-Soon KANG (S.Kor)	71	67	69	73	280	14378.91	10270.65
15	Stephen GALLACHER (Scot)	69	68	69	76	282	12630.42	9021.73
16	Katsuyoshi TOMORI (Jpn)	69	70	72	72	283	11363.08	8116.49
	Paul MCGINLEY (Ire)	72	69	72	70	283	11363.08	8116.49
	Anders HANSEN (Den)	72	70	70	71	283	11363.08	8116.49
	Fredrik LINDGREN (Swe)	72	68	74	69	283	11363.08	8116.49
20	Retief GOOSEN (SA)	70	71	72	71	284	9923.90	7088.50
	Mark JAMES (Eng)	67	71	72	74	284	9923.90	7088.50
	Wayne RILEY (Aus)	69	70	71	74	284	9923.90	7088.50
	Peter MITCHELL (Eng)	75	67	69	73	284	9923.90	7088.50
24	Padraig HARRINGTON (Ire)	71	70	72	72	285	8892.85	6352.04
	Michael JONZON (Swe)	71	71	73	70	285	8892.85	6352.04
	Andrew MCLARDY (SA)	73	69	69	74	285	8892.85	6352.04
	José RIVERO (Sp)	72	70	71	72	285	8892.85	6352.04
28	Iain PYMAN (Eng)	74	70	70	72	286	7312.85	5223.46
	David HOWELL (Eng)	72	72	70	72	286	7312.85	5223.46
	Miguel Angel MARTIN (Sp)	70	72	68	76	286	7312.85	5223.46
	Andrew COLTART (Scot)	71	69	74	72	286	7312.85	5223.46
	Gerry NORQUIST (USA)	74	67	72	73	286	7312.85	5223.46
	Steve WEBSTER (Eng)	75	67	71	73	286	7312.85	5223.46
	Mark ROE (Eng)	72	68	72	74	286	7312.85	5223.46
	Paul BROADHURST (Eng)	72	72	72	70	286	7312.85	5223.46
	Gary EVANS (Eng)	69	70	71	76	286	7312.85	5223.46
37	Van PHILLIPS (Eng)	70	72	72	73	287	6186.33	4418.81
	Fabrice TARNAUD (Fr)	72	71	72	72	287	6186.33	4418.81
	Ian GARBUTT (Eng)	71	71	73	72	287	6186.33	4418.81
40	Per NYMAN (Swe)	68	70	74	76	288	5241.19	3743.71
	Marc FARRY (Fr)	66	75	71	76	288	5241.19	3743.71
	Mark MOULAND (Wal)	72	70	71	75	288	5241.19	3743.71
	Paolo QUIRICI (Swi)	72	72	72	72	288	5241.19	3743.71
	Eduardo ROMERO (Arg)	69	71	72	76	288	5241.19	3743.71
	Lian-Wei ZHANG (Chi)	71	73	72	72	288	5241.19	3743.71
	Angel CABRERA (Arg)	74	69	70	75	288	5241.19	3743.71
	Costantino ROCCA (It)	73	69	73	73	288	5241.19	3743.71
48	Mats LANNER (Swe)	75	69	70	75	289	4124.22	2945.87
	Per-Ulrik JOHANSSON (Swe)	72	72	69	76	289	4124.22	2945.87
	Warren BENNETT (Eng)	71	69	78	71	289	4124.22	2945.87
	Henrik NYSTROM (Swe)	75	69	73	72	289	4124.22	2945.87
	Ricardo GONZALEZ (Arg)	72	72	75	70	289	4124.22	2945.87
53	Paul AFFLECK (Wal)	70	74	67	79	290	3179.09	2270.78
	Jim PAYNE (Eng)	75	68	74	73	290	3179.09	2270.78
	Malcolm MACKENZIE (Eng)	72	70	74	74	290	3179.09	2270.78
	Soren HANSEN (Den)	74	69	75	72	290	3179.09	2270.78
	Richard GREEN (Aus)	72	71	73	74	290	3179.09	2270.78
	Brian DAVIS (Eng)	73	71	75	71	290	3179.09	2270.78
59	Philip WALTON (Ire)	72	71	76	72	291	2534.68	1810.49
	Miles TUNNICLIFF (Eng)	71	72	74	74	291	2534.68	1810.49
	Andrew OLDCORN (Scot)	73	71	68	79	291	2534.68	1810.49
	Thomas GÖGELE (Ger)	73	70	76	72	291	2534.68	1810.49
63	Robert Jan DERKSEN (Hol)	71	72	77	72	292	1639.61	1171.15
	Santiago LUNA (Sp)	72	72	72	76	292	1639.61	1171.15
	Roger CHAPMAN (Eng)	72	68	77	75	292	1639.61	1171.15
	Paul EALES (Eng)	71	72	77	72	292	1639.61	1171.15
	Gordon BRAND JNR. (Scot)	72	72	75	73	292	1639.61	1171.15
	Greg OWEN (Eng)	73	71	74	74	292	1639.61	1171.15
	Marcello SANTI (It)	74	70	75	73	292	1639.61	1171.15
	Stephen FIELD (Eng)	71	73	75	73	292	1639.61	1171.15
	Trevor IMMELMAN (AM) (SA)	75	69	78	70	292		
71	Ross MCFARLANE (Eng)	68	75	79	71	293	1271.00	907.86
	Barry LANE (Eng)	75	68	78	72	293	1271.00	907.86
	Steen TINNING (Den)	72	68	75	78	293	1271.00	907.86
74	Massimo FLORIOLI (It)	73	70	78	77	298	1265.00	903.57

PHILLIP PRICE: birdie, birdie, finish

Thanks a million

Jeff Maggert stretches the incredible drama
of the first World Golf Championship
to two extra holes and a $1,000,000 victory

"This time," advised the slogan, "it's for the world." And so it was, the first tournament uniting the five leading professional Tours, an event to celebrate the global significance of the old Scottish game.

The Andersen Consulting Match Play championship had a $5 million purse (4,295,796 euro – £3,068,425) and a field so deep in talent that after two days only the number one seed, Tiger Woods, remained from the top ten and after three days not even he was left.

That the unexpected turned out to be the norm, with Jeff Maggert chipping in for a birdie on the second extra hole of Sunday's scheduled 36-hole final to defeat Andrew Magee and earn $1 million (859,158 euro – £613,684), would not have been surprising had we listened to young Mr Woods.

"This isn't like tennis," said Woods, even before he lost to Maggert in the quarter-finals. "People can't really fathom the quality of the field. The players ranked 63 and 64 are great players." It turned out the players ranked 24th, Maggert, and 50th, Magee, were the greatest of the lot at

the inaugural World Golf Championship organised by the International Federation of PGA Tours, dramatically staged at La Costa resort on the California coast some 30 miles north of San Diego. While Woods and David Duval, Colin Montgomerie and Nick Price all went tumbling out, some earlier than others, we once more became aware of the vagaries and drama of head-to-head competition. "Between two good professionals on their day," said Woods, "it's anybody's game."

Good doesn't begin to describe the contestants in the championship which brought together players from the Japan Tour, European Tour, the US PGA Tour, the Southern Africa PGA Tour and the PGA Tour of Australasia. All were champions of one sort or another.

Some people will tell you the best thing about match-play golf, rarely seen in America beyond the Ryder Cup, is that it is entirely unpredictable. Some people will tell you the worst thing about match-play golf is that it is entirely unpredictable.

Or, in the immortal words of Eduardo Romero of Argentina, the 60th seed, who merely knocked out Lee Westwood (5), Greg Norman (28) and Phil Mickelson (12) in the first three rounds: "You never know." What the lords of golf knew was this was the start of something special, and the whimsical daily results provided the theatre that kept everyone from contestants to journalists as fascinated as they were bewildered.

Observed US PGA Tour Commissioner Tim Finchem: "It couldn't have been a better start." And after the upsets along the way, it couldn't have been a better finish, Maggert coming back from three down in the final to win at the 38th hole.

It was Norman who several years before had suggested a world golf tour, an idea seen as worthy but requiring the combined authoritative administration of the major international Tours to achieve a successful globalisation of the game at the very highest level. In 1999, the World Golf Championships were reality, the NEC

JEFF MAGGERT: Asked for pin to be pulled, and chipped in

TIGER WOODS AND NICK FALDO: This isn't like tennis

GREG NORMAN: match-play is the purest form of golf

THE COURSE

The championship course at La Costa Resort and Spa is actually a merging of the best holes of two courses open to the public. About a mile inland from the Pacific Ocean, at the edge of Batiquitos Lagoon, La Costa's championship course plays to a length of 7,022 yards (or 6,423 metres) and par of 36-36-72. For many years it was the site of the event that was the Tournament of Champions that then became known as the Mercedes Championships.

Jeff Maggert's chip in from 20 feet at the 180-yard 11th, the 38th hole of the final, may have been the shot of the year, since it gave him the championship and a $1 million first prize. "I had pulled an eight iron to about the same spot in the morning round," said Maggert. "I hit the chip a little firmer than I wanted. I had the pin out. If I had left it in, the ball might have hit the stick and bounced five feet away."

PATRIK SJÖLAND: putting on the style

Invitational in August at Akron, Ohio; the American Express Championship in November at Valderrama and the starter, the Andersen Consulting Match Play at La Costa.

"Match-play," insisted Norman, "is the purest form of golf." But the purists rarely have their way because one bad round by a star or one great round by an opponent eliminates an attraction for the fans and the television audience. "But this event," said Finchem, "is not only historic it's good for golf." It was different. "This was cut-throat," said Phil Mickelson, who grew up half an hour away in San Diego. "Usually in golf, you play well and have a top ten finish and guys come up and say: 'Hey, great playing.' And you say, 'Thanks.' But here it was win or lose, and we're not used to that. It was difficult for some players to deal with."

The dramas came swiftly. All five British challengers who made the field of 64, decided on the two-year Official World Golf Ranking system, lost opening-round matches. Overall, lower seeds won 17 of the 32 matches on day one. By the end of the second round, Duval was out. So was Norman. And Price. It was match-play golf at its best. "Who," asked Mickelson rhetorically, "expected 90 percent of the top seeds to lose by the third round. I didn't." All Duval would say was: "You get what you deserve when you don't play well. I'm not a proponent of match-play golf. It's not indicative of who is the best player." That was one man's opinion. His colleagues enjoyed the change from the usual stroke-play events. "The ebb and

DAVID DUVAL: You get what you deserve …

flow of match-play," said Woods, "is amazing."

So for a long while was Romero of Argentina. He beat Westwood, 3 and 2, then Norman on the third extra hole, then Mickelson, 2 and 1. Norman was three up with four to play, but Romero won the 15th with a birdie, the 16th with a par and the 18th with a birdie after hitting a seven iron to a foot of the cup. On the 21st hole, Romero ran in a putt of 25 feet, and all Norman could do was sigh: "This is what match-play is all about." The original plan was to hold the quarter-finals and semi-finals on the fourth day, Saturday. A change was made to allow for the possibility of inclement weather, rare as that might be in southern California the last week of February, and the third round and quarter-finals were held Friday.

When Maggert, on his inexorable march, rallied in the quarters to defeat Woods 2 and 1 (the only one of his six matches that ended before the 18th hole) nobody higher than a 24th seed, Maggert, was left for the week-end. Maggert came from three down to overcome Steve Pate in one Saturday semi-final, while Magee also came from behind to defeat John Huston, 3 and 1. Jack Graham, producing the championship for ABC-TV had reason to be content. The ratings, so important in America, were quite impressive.

The ending couldn't have been more stunning. The 35-year-old Maggert, who had finished second eight times since his only US victory in December 1993, came up short of the green with his tee shot on the 38th hole, the 180 yards 11th. He asked for the pin to be pulled, and chipped in for a birdie two. Magee, 36, whose consolation was the $500,000 second prize, said: "I thought it was kind of neat, even though he beat me. What a great way to win." Magee, as some of the others, had come to La Costa from the preceding week's Nissan Open in Los Angeles some 100 miles away, and by the semi-finals was out of clean clothes. "I thought I'd be going home by now," he said. Instead, he went to the pro shop and bought two pairs of socks.

Maggert didn't need to buy anything. But he gained a great deal, including that

LEE WESTWOOD (left) and EDUARDO ROMERO: You never know …

$1 million, not to mention the Walter Hagen Trophy, designed and produced by Wedgewood of England, a sister company of Waterford Crystal, and named after a man recognised as one of the most successful match-play golfers in history.

A mountain had been climbed. "I've been waiting five and a half years for this," said Maggert. "Now I can finish second and it will be okay."

Although maybe not for his 11-year-old son, Matt. "He's been giving me a hard time about finishing second," Maggert said, referring to the boy. "I'm going straight home to call him and give him a hard time."

Art Spander

SHIGEKI MARUYAMA: thirsty work

ANDREW MAGEE: $500,000 consolation

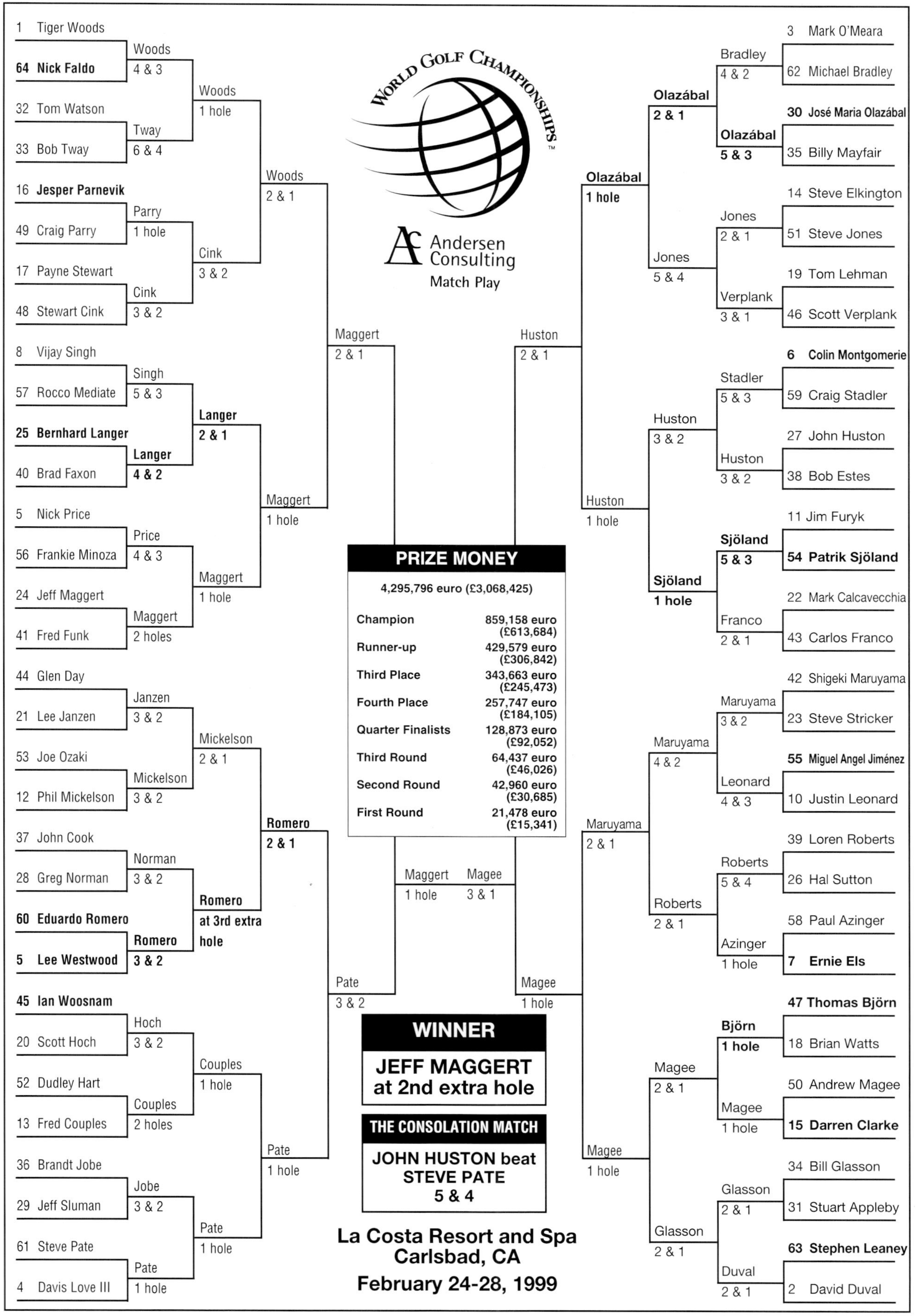
WORLD GOLF CHAMPIONSHIPS
Andersen Consulting
Match Play

1 Tiger Woods
Woods 4 & 3
64 Nick Faldo
Woods 1 hole
32 Tom Watson
Tway 6 & 4
33 Bob Tway
Woods 2 & 1
16 Jesper Parnevik
Parry 1 hole
49 Craig Parry
Cink 3 & 2
17 Payne Stewart
Cink 3 & 2
48 Stewart Cink

8 Vijay Singh
Singh 5 & 3
57 Rocco Mediate
Langer 2 & 1
25 Bernhard Langer
Langer 4 & 2
40 Brad Faxon
Maggert 1 hole
5 Nick Price
Price 4 & 3
56 Frankie Minoza
Maggert 1 hole
24 Jeff Maggert
Maggert 2 holes
41 Fred Funk

44 Glen Day
Janzen 3 & 2
21 Lee Janzen
Mickelson 2 & 1
53 Joe Ozaki
Mickelson 3 & 2
12 Phil Mickelson
Romero 2 & 1
37 John Cook
Norman 3 & 2
28 Greg Norman
Romero at 3rd extra hole
60 Eduardo Romero
Romero 3 & 2
5 Lee Westwood

45 Ian Woosnam
Hoch 3 & 2
20 Scott Hoch
Couples 1 hole
52 Dudley Hart
Couples 2 holes
13 Fred Couples
Pate 1 hole
36 Brandt Jobe
Jobe 3 & 2
29 Jeff Sluman
Pate 1 hole
61 Steve Pate
Pate 1 hole
4 Davis Love III

Maggert 2 & 1
Maggert 1 hole
Pate 3 & 2

Maggert 1 hole   Magee 3 & 1

Huston 2 & 1
Huston 1 hole
Magee 1 hole

3 Mark O'Meara
Bradley 4 & 2
62 Michael Bradley
Olazábal 2 & 1
30 José Maria Olazábal
Olazábal 5 & 3
35 Billy Mayfair
Olazábal 1 hole
14 Steve Elkington
Jones 2 & 1
51 Steve Jones
Jones 5 & 4
19 Tom Lehman
Verplank 3 & 1
46 Scott Verplank

6 Colin Montgomerie
Stadler 5 & 3
59 Craig Stadler
Huston 3 & 2
27 John Huston
Huston 3 & 2
38 Bob Estes
Huston 1 hole
11 Jim Furyk
Sjöland 5 & 3
54 Patrik Sjöland
Sjöland 1 hole
22 Mark Calcavecchia
Franco 2 & 1
43 Carlos Franco

42 Shigeki Maruyama
Maruyama 3 & 2
23 Steve Stricker
Maruyama 4 & 2
55 Miguel Angel Jiménez
Leonard 4 & 3
10 Justin Leonard
Maruyama 2 & 1
39 Loren Roberts
Roberts 5 & 4
26 Hal Sutton
Roberts 2 & 1
58 Paul Azinger
Azinger 1 hole
7 Ernie Els

47 Thomas Björn
Björn 1 hole
18 Brian Watts
Magee 2 & 1
50 Andrew Magee
Magee 1 hole
15 Darren Clarke
Magee 1 hole
34 Bill Glasson
Glasson 2 & 1
31 Stuart Appleby
Glasson 2 & 1
63 Stephen Leaney
Duval 2 & 1
2 David Duval

PRIZE MONEY
4,295,796 euro (£3,068,425)
Champion   859,158 euro (£613,684)
Runner-up   429,579 euro (£306,842)
Third Place   343,663 euro (£245,473)
Fourth Place   257,747 euro (£184,105)
Quarter Finalists 128,873 euro (£92,052)
Third Round   64,437 euro (£46,026)
Second Round   42,960 euro (£30,685)
First Round   21,478 euro (£15,341)

WINNER
JEFF MAGGERT at 2nd extra hole

THE CONSOLATION MATCH
JOHN HUSTON beat STEVE PATE 5 & 4

La Costa Resort and Spa
Carlsbad, CA
February 24-28, 1999

Sir Henry would approve

Van Phillips collars title after a tie

and a sudden-death finish

on the Maestro's course at Penina

Van Phillips's earlier sporting life spent on the judo mat may have provided the determination for him to finish on top at Le Meridien Penina. A dogged refusal to lose his grip on a tournament where a fellow Englishman always looked to have the upper hand, earned the former Walker Cup player from Maidenhead his maiden European Tour title.

Ironically for a player who had shed his male model image, elegant Phillips, supported by a neckwear company in past seasons, collared his debut victory after a tie at the Algarve Portuguese Open.

Compatriot John Bickerton, stretching a great run of consistency, provided the other half of the tense finale at the home of the late Sir Henry Cotton. Henry, the *Maestro*, would have been delighted to see two Englishmen battling it out down the closing stretch and then testing each other in sudden-death play-off at the course he designed lovingly on the Algarve.

For most of the weekend and right until he missed the first extra green in the play-off, however, it looked as though Bickerton would be the one to take his maiden title. A rousing 64 on Saturday in which he ran in ten birdies in the first 15 holes, was only marred by two late bogeys – bogeys which would eventually cost him dearly.

When Bickerton wrested the lead early on from Italy's Massimo Scarpa on Sunday afternoon and held it until the fateful 17th hole, it seemed sure that the West Midlander would prevail. But chillingly for the man twice hit by lightning in his career, that 17th hole would strike three times at him to deny him success. The 17th provided him with one of his late bogeys on Saturday, he bogeyed it again the next day to allow Phillips to draw level going to the 72nd hole. And the 17th was the first extra hole.

It was not just by Bickerton's own hand, though, that Phillips followed Peter Mitchell into the Portuguese Open record book. He had never allowed his arch-rival to get away from him by more than a shot. And when Phillips holed a crucial putt of ten feet to save par on that same 17th hole in the final round, fate smiled his way. Producing the shot of the week at the last hole, fading his approach around trees and finding the par-five green with his second, after his only rival had hit the fairway and made the green for an eagle chance, Phillips marched to his destiny.

Both protagonists had to settle for closing birdies and 68s for 12-under-par,

VAN PHILLIPS and CADDIE: two in winning harmony

After months of heavy rain preferred lies became a necessity. But Sir Henry Cotton's design still provided a stern and worthy challenge with severe punishment for the wayward shot. One major change was the shortening of the course (6,875 yards from 6,903) from a par 73 to a 72, with the watershed 17th reduced by 28 yards to a par four which crucially influenced the sudden-death outcome of the tournament.

three shots better than a trio of experienced past winners, Alex Cejka, Robert Karlsson and Santiago Luna.

Then Phillips held his nerve best, found the play-off hole's green in two and sank the two putts, after his opponent had floundered into a bunker with his third shot, to earn the 93,320 euro (£66,657) first prize.

Long before the tournament turned into a two-horse race, however, two veterans with combined experience of more than 1,000 European Tour events and 45 world-wide victories, were attracting attention. Sam Torrance returned from an injury lay-off to shoot a 69 in the opening round. He would take four of those, said the Scot, and then prepare for the

MASSIMO SCARPA: trouble attracts a crowd

SHOT OF THE WEEK

A candidate for easiest choice of the year. When Van Phillips drove behind trees on the 72nd hole and, spurning a free-drop in Ground Under Repair that would take him further behind them, he opted to stand on the concrete cart-path to fade a four iron 30 yards from 200 yards out, and hit the final green in two. "I'd normally use a seven-iron to play a shot like that," said Phillips. "In the circumstances it has to be the best shot I've ever hit."

JOHN BICKERTON and VAN PHILLIPS: thanks for the game

ALEXANDER CEJKA: stoops to conquer

prize-giving. Well, Torrance got the target absolutely right. Trouble was, he did not even make the weekend after crashing to an 80 and out the next day.

A player who has always admired Torrance's ability to stay on top in 28 years on Tour, is Des Smyth. The genial Irishman has played for a quarter of a century himself, but had to scramble in 1998 to retain his full playing-rights in 114th place. Could he win his eighth title at the age of 46, the third-oldest man in the field behind senior Antonio Garrido and Smyth's great friend and peer by just a few months, Eamonn Darcy? A 66 in the first round for a two-shot lead begged that question. When he kept that lead, cut to one stroke after two rounds, as young Swede Fredrik Jacobson faltered at the tough finish, the question was still being asked on Friday night. On Saturday, though, the answer came with a pair of double-bogeys which plummeted Ireland's perennial Mr Nice Guy off the leaderboard.

The young bloods took over. By Saturday night, Phillips, Bickerton and Scarpa had taken over. By Sunday night, Phillips had turned the screw. "I always felt I had the temperament to win," said the winner, playing in only his third full Tour year, but four years after running Ernie Els close in the South African PGA Championship. "It had been a frustrating time when the win didn't come along and I wondered then if I'd ever do it. But I always had confidence in myself."

Norman Dabell

89

LE MERIDIEN, PENINA, PORTUGAL, MARCH 4–7, 1999 • PAR 72 • YARDS 6875

Pos	Name & Country	Rnd 1	Rnd 2	Rnd 3	Rnd 4	Total	Prize Money €	£
1	Van PHILLIPS (Eng)	72	68	68	68	276	93320.00	66657.14
2	John BICKERTON (Eng)	71	73	64	68	276	62210.00	44435.71
3	Robert KARLSSON (Swe)	69	72	71	67	279	28916.67	20654.76
	Alex CEJKA (Ger)	71	70	70	68	279	28916.67	20654.76
	Santiago LUNA (Sp)	68	72	70	69	279	28916.67	20654.76
6	Anthony WALL (Eng)	71	69	71	69	280	19600.00	14000.00
7	Daren LEE (Eng)	75	70	69	67	281	15400.00	11000.00
	Craig HAINLINE (USA)	71	73	69	68	281	15400.00	11000.00
9	Paul BROADHURST (Eng)	76	68	71	67	282	9924.57	7088.98
	Ricardo GONZALEZ (Arg)	72	74	68	68	282	9924.57	7088.98
	Mark ROE (Eng)	72	69	70	71	282	9924.57	7088.98
	Bob MAY (USA)	70	69	71	72	282	9924.57	7088.98
	Fredrik JACOBSON (Swe)	68	71	71	72	282	9924.57	7088.98
	Paul LAWRIE (Scot)	71	69	69	73	282	9924.57	7088.98
	Massimo SCARPA (It)	69	71	68	74	282	9924.57	7088.98
16	Ian GARBUTT (Eng)	70	71	72	70	283	7560.00	5400.00
	Gerry NORQUIST (USA)	74	73	66	70	283	7560.00	5400.00
	Angel CABRERA (Arg)	72	70	69	72	283	7560.00	5400.00
19	Iain PYMAN (Eng)	72	70	72	70	284	6650.00	4750.00
	David HOWELL (Eng)	74	72	68	70	284	6650.00	4750.00
	Peter MITCHELL (Eng)	71	71	71	71	284	6650.00	4750.00
	Richard BOXALL (Eng)	71	70	71	72	284	6650.00	4750.00
23	Roger WINCHESTER (Eng)	70	76	72	67	285	6132.00	4380.00
	Roger WESSELS (SA)	71	75	66	73	285	6132.00	4380.00
25	Marc FARRY (Fr)	76	67	72	71	286	5376.00	3840.00
	Jeev Milkha SINGH (Ind)	73	69	73	71	286	5376.00	3840.00
	Raphaël JACQUELIN (Fr)	72	70	75	69	286	5376.00	3840.00
	Des SMYTH (Ire)	66	72	76	72	286	5376.00	3840.00
	Andrew OLDCORN (Scot)	71	74	69	72	286	5376.00	3840.00
	Francis VALERA (Sp)	69	72	71	74	286	5376.00	3840.00
	Wayne RILEY (Aus)	72	71	66	77	286	5376.00	3840.00
32	Peter BAKER (Eng)	73	72	71	71	287	4424.00	3160.00
	Barry LANE (Eng)	72	75	70	70	287	4424.00	3160.00
	Miles TUNNICLIFF (Eng)	72	69	76	70	287	4424.00	3160.00
	Gary EVANS (Eng)	72	69	73	73	287	4424.00	3160.00
	Jean VAN DE VELDE (Fr)	68	73	72	74	287	4424.00	3160.00
	Miguel Angel JIMÉNEZ (Sp)	68	73	70	76	287	4424.00	3160.00
38	Tony JOHNSTONE (Zim)	71	71	75	71	288	3752.00	2680.00
	Thomas LEVET (Fr)	73	70	72	73	288	3752.00	2680.00
	José RIVERO (Sp)	70	74	71	73	288	3752.00	2680.00
	Anders HANSEN (Den)	73	72	70	73	288	3752.00	2680.00
	Gary ORR (Scot)	73	73	69	73	288	3752.00	2680.00
	Katsuyoshi TOMORI (Jpn)	68	79	68	73	288	3752.00	2680.00
44	José COCERES (Arg)	74	72	70	73	289	3136.00	2240.00
	David GILFORD (Eng)	69	76	72	72	289	3136.00	2240.00
	John MELLOR (Eng)	72	73	73	71	289	3136.00	2240.00
	Stephen GALLACHER (Scot)	73	72	70	74	289	3136.00	2240.00
	Warren BENNETT (Eng)	75	69	70	75	289	3136.00	2240.00
49	Pedro LINHART (Sp)	71	69	75	75	290	2520.00	1800.00
	Steve WEBSTER (Eng)	70	77	70	73	290	2520.00	1800.00
	Soren HANSEN (Den)	74	73	70	73	290	2520.00	1800.00
	Robert Jan DERKSEN (Hol)	73	74	71	72	290	2520.00	1800.00
	Andrew COLTART (Scot)	71	75	72	72	290	2520.00	1800.00
	Henrik NYSTROM (Swe)	73	73	75	69	290	2520.00	1800.00
55	Emanuele CANONICA (It)	72	70	73	76	291	1806.00	1290.00
	Stephen BENNETT (Eng)	72	70	73	76	291	1806.00	1290.00
	Philip WALTON (Ire)	76	68	72	75	291	1806.00	1290.00
	Jesus Maria ARRUTI (Sp)	72	71	74	74	291	1806.00	1290.00
	Eamonn DARCY (Ire)	76	70	72	73	291	1806.00	1290.00
	Peter HEDBLOM (Swe)	72	75	74	70	291	1806.00	1290.00
	Diego BORREGO (Sp)	72	71	71	77	291	1806.00	1290.00
	Domingo HOSPITAL (Sp)	73	73	68	77	291	1806.00	1290.00
63	Fabrice TARNAUD (Fr)	74	72	71	75	292	1484.00	1060.00
	Max ANGLERT (Swe)	74	71	74	73	292	1484.00	1060.00
65	Francisco CEA (Sp)	71	72	75	75	293	1400.00	1000.00
66	Jamie SPENCE (Eng)	74	73	71	76	294	838.50	598.83
	Retief GOOSEN (SA)	68	78	73	75	294	838.50	598.83
68	Paul EALES (Eng)	73	72	71	79	295	829.50	592.50
	Scott HENDERSON (Scot)	72	74	73	76	295	829.50	592.50
	Roger CHAPMAN (Eng)	78	65	76	76	295	829.50	592.50
	Thomas GÖGELE (Ger)	74	71	75	75	295	829.50	592.50
72	Pierre FULKE (Swe)	71	76	74	75	296	822.00	587.14
73	Jorge BERENDT (Arg)	73	74	77	73	297	819.00	585.00
74	Padraig HARRINGTON (Ire)	74	73	77	75	299	816.00	582.86
75	Paul AFFLECK (Wal)	71	76	76	77	300	813.00	580.71
76	Tomas Jesus MUÑOZ (Sp)	73	74	77	78	302	810.00	578.57
77	Tom GILLIS (USA)	73	73	78	79	303	807.00	576.43
	Nuno CAMPINO (AM) (Port)	73	72	76	85	306		

ROBERT KARLSSON:

high finish, deep thoughts

Golf INDUSTRY NEWS EUROPE Awards 98
Best Waterproof Suit 1998 Voted by the PGA Professionals

Golf WEEKLY Awards 99
Best Waterproof Suit 1999 Voted by the UK golfing public

MASTERS OF PROQUIP WEATHERWEAR

RYDER CUP 1927 1999 THE COUNTRY CLUB

The 1999 European Ryder Cup team has found ENLITENMENT.

In the opinion of team captain, Mark James, and the 1999 European Ryder Cup committee, there's nothing to beat the new UltraLite playing top.

Worn with UltraLite trousers, it's their official team waterproof. Slip one on, and you'll understand why.

As the name suggests, it's ultra-lightweight. Come the rain, you'll discover it's ultra-waterproof. Its ultra-breathability is enough to take your breath away. And the new half-zip pullover design gives you ultimate freedom of movement.

Whatever challenges lie ahead for the European Ryder Cup team, the weather won't be one of them.

PROQUIP

ULTRALITE
by
PROQUIP
MASTERS OF WEATHERWEAR

The new UltraLite playing top is part of the award-winning UltraLite family of products. For details of your nearest stockists, call ProQuip on 01620 892 219.

ProQuip Limited, 1 Tantallon Road, North Berwick, East Lothian, EH39 5NF, Scotland. Part of the Caledonian Golf Group.

Local hero does it again

Family, neighbours and friends
see Miguel Angel Jiménez
keep title for a second year

Miguel Angel Jiménez did not have far to go to work in the second week of March: not 15 minutes' drive from his home in his regular, runabout saloon and barely ten in his Ferrari Marinello (bright red, of course). Luxury, sheer luxury, for a man accustomed to travelling countless thousands of air miles a year in the pursuit of his craft.

Jiménez's home is in Benalmadena Pueblo, a picturesque and fashionable village on the Costa del Sol, not more than a par-72 away from his office for the week, the Parador Malaga del Golf just outside the bustling and fashionable holiday resort that lends the course part of its name. This was home territory for the native Malagueno and he made it count, with drums beating and castanets clacking.

Jiménez had more than one reason for wanting to do well in the Turespaña Masters-Open Andalucía. First, he was playing in front of family, friends and many more who would

Life on Tour can be all sunshine

claim him as their neighbour. Second, he was the defending champion. And third, on the evening of the second day of the tournament he had been extended a late invitation to play in the Masters tournament at Augusta National, so he had to celebrate somehow. The manner in which he chose to do it was simple – he won.

The quiet Andalucian has always preferred to let his golf be his most powerful spokesperson. Deeds rather than words are his speciality, and this time they were more than enough as he won the tournament in his own backyard with a total of 264, 24 under par. It was a winning aggregate that had been beaten only twice in the history of the European Tour. But the victory meant much more to him than that as he prevailed by four strokes from Steve Webster with Raphaël Jacquelin a further shot adrift.

Much was expected of Jiménez when he embarked on his campaign on a course that was as familiar to him as the nose on his weather-beaten face. He had played the Parador layout scores of time before and, in a region that is re-inventing itself as the Costa del Golf, far from the Blackpool-with-sun image of Torremelinos and Fuengirola, he had a civic duty that went far beyond the desire for personal fulfilment. With his triumph, Malaga and its environs were left handsomely in his debt.

Jiménez played hard to get during the first 36 holes of the tournament. He was

SVEN STRÜVER: woodman, spare that tree

SHOT OF THE WEEK

Miguel Angel Jiménez had recovered from a bad patch at the end of the front nine in the final round, but was still only a shot ahead of Steve Webster when he missed the green and plunged into a greenside bunker in two on the long 14th. A bogey loomed – instead, Jiménez pulled out his trusty sand-wedge and splashed out. The ball dropped cleanly into the hole on the second bounce. Jiménez had four holes to play, but it was this shot that effectively won him the tournament.

only just in touch with the leader after the first round and got marginally closer following the second, but the round that made his fifth European Tour victory possible was the third, when he produced a coruscating 62, at the time the lowest score on Tour thus far in 1999, to take a five-shot advantage into the final day. His 54-hole total of 197, also a seasonal European low to date, was achieved with two competent rounds and one outstanding one. He had a 69 on the first day to trail leader Paulo Quirici by four and followed it with a 66 on the second to be two off the pace that had been set by Fredrik Lindgren. His performance on the third, however, was on a different plane altogether.

A 62 it was, and it broke, by a single stroke, the course record that had been set

the day before by his compatriot, Ignacio Garrido. There were two eagles and six birdies in a flawless round; to describe it as brilliant would be to understate the case by a factor of about ten. Per-Ulrik Johansson, he of the flat cap worn with the peak pointing down his neck, summed it up after that third day after finishing five strokes behind Jiménez. "If Miguel plays in the last round like he did today, nobody has a chance of living with him," said the pragmatic Swede. Well, he didn't, quite, but it was a pretty darned close-run thing.

Jiménez saved the scariest moments of his final round for the latter stages of the front nine. He was leading by the length of a medium-sized street when he dropped three shots to par in the three holes heading to the turn, including a double-bogey

THE COURSE

This was the second time that the Parador course had been used for a European Tour event, but the difference in its condition between 1992, when Vijay Singh won the inaugural Turespaña Masters, and 1999, was striking. Now, markedly improved with skill and dedication to match, it was gratefully recognised by players as a worthy place for a European Tour event to be held. If you are wayward on this course, you will pay a heavy price; if you are straight and accurate, it will produce a proper reward. A successful venue, by any criterion.

STEVE WEBSTER: high-flying finish

after a drive out-of-bounds on the seventh. It left the pursuing pack, led by 20-somethings Webster and Jacquelin, now only one behind and seeing the glimmerings of an opening.

In the event, it never transpired, but Jiménez, who saved at least one shot when a foot belonging to a member of the gallery inadvertently stopped his ball from going into water on the 11th, had to rely on two outrageous strokes to re-establish himself as the man most likely to walk away with the 83,330 euro (£59,521) top prize.

First he chipped in from greenside sand with a sand-wedge on the tenth for an unlikely birdie, then repeated the trick on the 14th with the greatest escape act of

IGNACIO GARRIDO: short-lived record

PER-ULRIK JOHANSSON: prophesy proved right

the lot. Again he was in a bunker by the green, again he was looking at something nasty on his card. It was time for the trusty sand-wedge again. Out it came from his bag and, seconds later, out the ball came, too. Had the flag-stick not got in the way, it was heading for the next parish. Instead, like a heat-seeking missile, it looked for its target, found it, locked on it and dropped into the hole on the second bounce for an eagle three.

It was, effectively, the final act of the tournament. He had another birdie on the 16th that was at once satisfying and totally irrelevent. The tournament, and the first prize, and the glory, and the satisfaction of producing something special for his people, was much more precious. Whatever he achieves in the rest of his career, it will not come much better than this. And now all that remained after his inquisition by the media corps was to dance an impromptu fandango, with appropriate chants, with a young female member of the press office team. It could only happen in Spain .

Mel Webb

Parador Malaga del Golf, Spain, March 11–14, 1999 • Par 72 • Yards 6743

Pos	Name & Country	Rnd 1	Rnd 2	Rnd 3	Rnd 4	Total	Prize Money €	£
1	Miguel Angel JIMÉNEZ (Sp)	69	66	62	67	264	83330.00	59521.43
2	Steve WEBSTER (Eng)	69	66	67	66	268	55550.00	39678.57
3	Raphaël JACQUELIN (Fr)	71	67	66	65	269	31300.00	22357.14
4	Marc FARRY (Fr)	69	67	66	69	271	25000.00	17857.14
5	Alex CEJKA (Ger)	71	65	67	69	272	17900.00	12785.71
	Per-Ulrik JOHANSSON (Swe)	67	67	68	70	272	17900.00	12785.71
	Fredrik LINDGREN (Swe)	67	66	75	64	272	17900.00	12785.71
8	Thomas GÖGELE (Ger)	68	69	68	68	273	11825.00	8446.43
	Gary ORR (Scot)	67	67	69	70	273	11825.00	8446.43
10	Bob MAY (USA)	73	65	68	68	274	8694.00	6210.00
	Roger WINCHESTER (Eng)	67	67	70	70	274	8694.00	6210.00
	John BICKERTON (Eng)	68	68	69	69	274	8694.00	6210.00
	Ian GARBUTT (Eng)	67	67	69	71	274	8694.00	6210.00
	Richard BOXALL (Eng)	70	69	67	68	274	8694.00	6210.00
15	Christopher HANELL (Swe)	67	72	71	65	275	6760.00	4828.57
	Rolf MUNTZ (Hol)	70	70	68	67	275	6760.00	4828.57
	Ignacio GARRIDO (Sp)	73	63	66	73	275	6760.00	4828.57
	Ricardo GONZALEZ (Arg)	67	68	68	72	275	6760.00	4828.57
	Roger CHAPMAN (Eng)	70	69	65	71	275	6760.00	4828.57
20	Barry LANE (Eng)	72	68	69	67	276	5775.00	4125.00
	Jeev Milkha SINGH (Ind)	70	68	71	67	276	5775.00	4125.00
	Greg OWEN (Eng)	68	68	68	72	276	5775.00	4125.00
	Anthony WALL (Eng)	70	70	68	68	276	5775.00	4125.00
24	Miguel Angel MARTIN (Sp)	69	72	69	67	277	5100.00	3642.86
	Katsuyoshi TOMORI (Jpn)	68	68	70	71	277	5100.00	3642.86
	Miles TUNNICLIFF (Eng)	68	71	71	67	277	5100.00	3642.86
	Soren HANSEN (Den)	71	68	69	69	277	5100.00	3642.86
	Massimo FLORIOLI (It)	69	69	70	69	277	5100.00	3642.86
29	Angel CABRERA (Arg)	67	72	69	70	278	4360.00	3114.29
	Derrick COOPER (Eng)	69	71	69	69	278	4360.00	3114.29
	Fredrik JACOBSON (Swe)	67	74	71	66	278	4360.00	3114.29
	Jorge BERENDT (Arg)	71	69	69	69	278	4360.00	3114.29
	Craig HAINLINE (USA)	70	69	71	68	278	4360.00	3114.29
34	Paolo QUIRICI (Swi)	65	72	71	71	279	3900.00	2785.71
	Massimo SCARPA (It)	69	71	69	70	279	3900.00	2785.71
	Andrew RAITT (Eng)	70	71	69	69	279	3900.00	2785.71
37	David GILFORD (Eng)	69	72	70	69	280	3600.00	2571.43
	Costantino ROCCA (It)	70	71	70	69	280	3600.00	2571.43
	Jamie SPENCE (Eng)	72	68	70	70	280	3600.00	2571.43
40	Diego BORREGO (Sp)	67	73	69	72	281	3300.00	2357.14
	Per NYMAN (Swe)	72	66	68	75	281	3300.00	2357.14
	Francisco CEA (Sp)	71	69	68	73	281	3300.00	2357.14
43	Alberto BINAGHI (It)	70	71	73	68	282	2850.00	2035.71
	Emanuele CANONICA (It)	71	69	71	71	282	2850.00	2035.71
	John MELLOR (Eng)	70	71	71	70	282	2850.00	2035.71
	Carlos RODILES (Sp)	70	71	72	69	282	2850.00	2035.71
	Robert KARLSSON (Swe)	70	71	70	71	282	2850.00	2035.71
	John SENDEN (Aus)	72	67	72	71	282	2850.00	2035.71
	Raul QUIROS (AM) (Sp)	71	70	68	73	282		
49	Gary EVANS (Eng)	71	70	71	71	283	2300.00	1642.86
	Mark JAMES (Eng)	67	73	70	73	283	2300.00	1642.86
	Padraig HARRINGTON (Ire)	71	69	71	72	283	2300.00	1642.86
	Anders HANSEN (Den)	68	73	73	69	283	2300.00	1642.86
	Jose Manuel LARA (Sp)	74	67	71	71	283	2300.00	1642.86
54	Pierre FULKE (Swe)	69	71	72	72	284	1900.00	1357.14
	Paul AFFLECK (Wal)	72	69	73	70	284	1900.00	1357.14
	Stephen FIELD (Eng)	70	69	77	68	284	1900.00	1357.14
57	Yago BEAMONTE (Sp)	71	70	71	73	285	1700.00	1214.29
58	Peter MITCHELL (Eng)	73	68	71	74	286	1600.00	1142.86
59	Jesus Maria ARRUTI (Sp)	72	69	74	72	287	1525.00	1089.29
	Sam TORRANCE (Scot)	69	72	72	74	287	1525.00	1089.29
61	Des SMYTH (Ire)	69	71	76	72	288	1425.00	1017.86
	Mark PILKINGTON (Wal)	69	70	75	74	288	1425.00	1017.86
63	Juan Carlos AGUERO (Sp)	72	69	74	75	290	1350.00	964.29
64	José SOTA (Sp)	70	71	74	78	293	1300.00	928.57
65	Manuel PIÑERO (Sp)	69	72	78	79	298	1250.00	892.86

Island of Dreams

Pedro Linhart thwarts Ryder Cup

captain for his first

victory on the European Tour

When Pedro Linhart served as an assistant professional in New Jersey, his mind would often wander back to Europe, to the place of his birth, Las Palmas, in the Canary Islands. While going through his numerous duties, he would picture himself lifting his first trophy on the European Tour. Linhart, the son of a Brooklyner, reckoned he had the 'right stuff'. He knew he could be a winner.

When the dream came true, though, could the ambitious Spaniard, who took out naturalisation a decade before his memorable victory, have imagined its where-abouts and the circumstances in which it would be achieved? Given a choice of venue for his maiden success, Linhart might well have chosen Las Palmas. Madeira, though, just up the Atlantic, is near enough. Different country, but not far from home.

But to beat the Ryder Cup captain on the Santo da Serra course for your first win? That would be too much to ask before stepping into the winner's enclosure for the first time. And to relegate the current European number one to third place? Dream on! By Sunday late afternoon, though, something of a fairytale came true for Linhart, play-ing in his sixth year on the

European Tour, having had to qualify for the last two years of that spell. The disappointments of runner-up spot in Lyon five years previously and letting a golden chance go in last year's Peugeot Open de France, were forgotten.

A valiant birdie on the penultimate hole of a pulsating Sunday finally separated Linhart from the man who would lead Europe into battle at Brookline later in the year, Mark James. Before the denouement, however, there was a battle of attrition to be won, not with players but with the weather as the spectacular holiday island's tournament was to be cursed by the vagaries of fog caused by low cloud, and heavy rain. The opening round was only half-done when play had

The view can sometimes make even the earliest of morning starts a pleasure

DIEGO BORREGO: dusk patrol

SHOT OF THE WEEK

Any one of Pedro Linhart's five stunning nine irons in his 64 , the nearest to six inches, furthest four feet, and another nine iron in to just three inches on the first in the final round, might qualify. But Mark James's remarkable pitch over the mounds to 15 feet for a birdie on the third hole in the final round deserves the vote.

PEDRO LINHART: Hail the winner

to be abandoned, with two Britons, the recent Algarve Portuguese Open winner Van Phillips showing further liking for Portugal, and the Tour Qualifying School champion Ross Drummond sharing an early lead on 68 with the confident young Swedish rookie Christopher Hanell.

By the time the first round closed next day, they had been joined by the Volvo Order of Merit leader David Howell. When play ended in gathering gloom and extremity-stiffening cold on Friday night, one man stood out from the rest. A 64 by Linhart, equalling his career-best and containing six birdies in eight holes coming home, took the 36-year-old Canary Islander four strokes clear on ten under par. No man is an island, but Linhart is certainly a man for an island. His previous 64s were achieved on Tenerife and Majorca. This was an omen not to be ignored.

His fellow-countryman Diego Borrego was his nearest challenger on Friday night, four behind. When Saturday lunchtime came, Stephen Field of England and the young Frenchman Raphaël Jacquelin were also in second place. It would always be a scramble to get a whole third round in before the light went and it finished with Linhart and Borrego putting out in near darkness. Linhart's birdie on the short 17th separated the Spaniards to give the man from Las Palmas a one-stroke advantage on 11 under par.

In the gaggle of players five strokes off the lead in third place was James, demonstrating his skills at 45 and showing, too, that the pressures of Ryder Cup team captaincy were not yet a burden. When Linhart birdied the first hole on Sunday, the strains of a church congregation singing somewhere along the mountain, seemed to strike up in celebration. His nearest rival Borrego double-bogeyed it, and it seemed it would be a stroll to victory.

THE COURSE

Forget the fog and rain, it just helps make the course greener say the agronomists, just drink in the views. Nine month's course-improvement with a new greenkeeper and a decision to spend £30,000 a month permanently on upkeep, reaped rich dividends and brought glowing accolades from the Tour Members who found Santo da Serra in its best condition yet.

That was reckoning without a brilliant, swashbuckling round from James as he wiped out the five strokes and drew level, nearly falling off the edge of the mountain with an audacious pitch on the third, and chipping in for a sixth birdie on the 17th. His only blemish was a three-putt bogey on the 13th, his first dropped shot since the 13th in the second round. It was to cost him his chance of a second Madeira Open win in six years.

With two holes to go the pair were locked together. James saved par from six feet on the last for a 67 to keep it that way. It needed something special to win this one. Linhart found it on the penultimate hole. A courageous putt of 15 feet went to ground for a final birdie on the way to a 71 and 12 under par for a one-shot victory. Instead of Gran Canaria, Madeira became the island of dreams for Pedro Linhart.

MARK JAMES: swashbuckling finish

STEPHEN FIELD: early threat

Norman Dabell

Santo da Serra, Madeira, March 25–28, 1999 · Par 72 · Yards 6606

Pos	Name & Country	Rnd 1	Rnd 2	Rnd 3	Rnd 4	Total	Prize Money €	£
1	Pedro LINHART (Sp)	70	64	71	71	276	81660.00	58328.57
2	Mark JAMES (Eng)	70	71	69	67	277	54430.00	38878.57
3	David HOWELL (Eng)	68	72	70	69	279	30670.00	21907.14
4	John BICKERTON (Eng)	69	71	72	69	281	16719.67	11942.62
	Retief GOOSEN (SA)	71	69	71	70	281	16719.67	11942.62
	Andrew COLTART (Scot)	72	70	68	71	281	16719.67	11942.62
	Alberto BINAGHI (It)	71	73	66	71	281	16719.67	11942.62
	Padraig HARRINGTON (Ire)	73	71	66	71	281	16719.67	11942.62
	Diego BORREGO (Sp)	71	67	68	75	281	16719.67	11942.62
10	Fredrik JACOBSON (Swe)	71	73	71	67	282	9081.33	6486.66
	Ross DRUMMOND (Scot)	68	71	73	70	282	9081.33	6486.66
	Andrew MCLARDY (SA)	69	73	69	71	282	9081.33	6486.66
13	Dean ROBERTSON (Scot)	72	70	75	66	283	7367.50	5262.50
	Niclas FASTH (Swe)	70	71	72	70	283	7367.50	5262.50
	Peter BAKER (Eng)	70	72	69	72	283	7367.50	5262.50
	Santiago LUNA (Sp)	74	70	67	72	283	7367.50	5262.50
17	Nick O'HERN (Aus)	75	72	72	65	284	5867.75	4191.25
	Anders HANSEN (Den)	73	72	70	69	284	5867.75	4191.25
	Paul AFFLECK (Wal)	73	69	72	70	284	5867.75	4191.25
	Richard BOXALL (Eng)	71	71	72	70	284	5867.75	4191.25
	Ian GARBUTT (Eng)	71	72	71	70	284	5867.75	4191.25
	Wayne RILEY (Aus)	72	74	68	70	284	5867.75	4191.25
	Gary EMERSON (Eng)	72	70	71	71	284	5867.75	4191.25
	Roger CHAPMAN (Eng)	75	70	68	71	284	5867.75	4191.25
25	Paul LAWRIE (Scot)	72	73	70	70	285	4924.50	3517.50
	Miles TUNNICLIFF (Eng)	71	75	68	71	285	4924.50	3517.50
	Fredrik LINDGREN (Swe)	69	73	71	72	285	4924.50	3517.50
	Lucas PARSONS (Aus)	74	67	70	74	285	4924.50	3517.50
29	David CARTER (Eng)	74	72	72	68	286	4272.80	3052.00
	Raimo SJÖBERG (Swe)	76	68	71	71	286	4272.80	3052.00
	Jose Manuel LARA (Sp)	74	68	72	72	286	4272.80	3052.00
	Roger WINCHESTER (Eng)	69	71	73	73	286	4272.80	3052.00
	Stephen FIELD (Eng)	70	68	72	76	286	4272.80	3052.00
34	Steen TINNING (Den)	71	72	74	70	287	3724.00	2660.00
	Van PHILLIPS (Eng)	68	77	74	68	287	3724.00	2660.00
	Paul EALES (Eng)	69	75	71	72	287	3724.00	2660.00
	Johan RYSTRÖM (Swe)	71	73	70	73	287	3724.00	2660.00
	Thomas LEVET (Fr)	71	71	71	74	287	3724.00	2660.00
39	Carlos LARRAIN (Ven)	74	71	71	72	288	3087.00	2205.00
	Costantino ROCCA (It)	73	74	70	71	288	3087.00	2205.00
	Stephen BENNETT (Eng)	71	75	72	70	288	3087.00	2205.00
	Raymond RUSSELL (Scot)	74	73	71	70	288	3087.00	2205.00
	Mark MOULAND (Wal)	75	66	77	70	288	3087.00	2205.00
	Massimo SCARPA (It)	74	71	74	69	288	3087.00	2205.00
	Daren LEE (Eng)	73	74	72	69	288	3087.00	2205.00
	Raphaël JACQUELIN (Fr)	71	67	76	74	288	3087.00	2205.00
47	António SOBRINHO (Port)	73	74	71	71	289	2401.00	1715.00
	Stephen GALLACHER (Scot)	72	69	77	71	289	2401.00	1715.00
	John SENDEN (Aus)	73	72	74	70	289	2401.00	1715.00
	Kalle BRINK (Swe)	72	75	72	70	289	2401.00	1715.00
	Jesus Maria ARRUTI (Sp)	71	74	70	74	289	2401.00	1715.00
	Thomas GÖGELE (Ger)	69	75	68	77	289	2401.00	1715.00
53	Gordon J BRAND (Eng)	71	74	73	72	290	1813.00	1295.00
	Alex CEJKA (Ger)	73	72	74	71	290	1813.00	1295.00
	Des SMYTH (Ire)	72	75	72	71	290	1813.00	1295.00
	Dennis EDLUND (Swe)	72	72	71	75	290	1813.00	1295.00
	Christopher HANELL (Swe)	68	71	74	77	290	1813.00	1295.00
	Geoff OGILVY (Aus)	71	71	70	78	290	1813.00	1295.00
59	Andrew SHERBORNE (Eng)	73	74	70	74	291	1470.00	1050.00
	Francisco DE PABLO (Sp)	75	72	71	73	291	1470.00	1050.00
	Gary ORR (Scot)	72	75	73	71	291	1470.00	1050.00
62	Max ANGLERT (Swe)	73	74	69	76	292	1298.50	927.50
	Tom GILLIS (USA)	73	74	71	74	292	1298.50	927.50
	Andrew SANDYWELL (Eng)	76	70	75	71	292	1298.50	927.50
	Steven BOTTOMLEY (Eng)	70	76	76	70	292	1298.50	927.50
66	Peter MITCHELL (Eng)	74	67	75	77	293	732.00	522.86
	Andrew CLAPP (Eng)	73	72	73	75	293	732.00	522.86
	Jorge BERENDT (Arg)	73	73	72	75	293	732.00	522.86
69	Marcello SANTI (It)	72	75	72	75	294	724.50	517.50
	Ian HUTCHINGS (SA)	72	73	76	73	294	724.50	517.50
71	Jeff REMESY (Fr)	72	72	74	77	295	718.50	513.21
	Gary EVANS (Eng)	71	75	73	76	295	718.50	513.21
73	Mark ROE (Eng)	74	73	73	76	296	709.50	506.79
	Søren KJELDSEN (Den)	72	75	74	75	296	709.50	506.79
	Nigel PRESTON (Eng)	72	75	73	76	296	709.50	506.79
	Morten BACKHAUSEN (Den)	75	72	74	75	296	709.50	506.79
77	Clinton WHITELAW (SA)	73	74	75	76	298	702.00	501.43
78	Jean Pierre CIXOUS (Fr)	76	71	83	71	301	699.00	499.29

DAVID HOWELL: third place all wrapped up

Victory over injustice

José Maria Olazábal first had to win

a two-year fight for health before

sealing his second success at Augusta

There was not a dry eye in the house, and nor should there have been, when at Augusta National the redoubtable José Maria Olazábal won the Masters Tournament for the second time in six years.

When Olazábal won the Masters Tournament for the first time in 1994 there was good reason to believe that he was on the threshold of developing a winning relationship with the major championships similar to that enjoyed by his compatriot Severiano Ballesteros.

What happened soon after rendered examination of Olazábal's record as irrelevant. Instead, the world of golf lived in hope that the Spaniard would recover his health following the cruel injustice of being forced to withdraw to his home in the beautiful countryside 11 miles from San Sebastian.

Indeed, as Olazábal wrestled with coming to terms with being incapacitated by what was first diagnosed as a foot injury, so his thoughts swung from no longer wondering about his career on the fairways to considering what it might be like to end his life in a wheelchair.

"In those days when I woke up in the morning I knew my first move would be to the bathroom," he recalled. "It was only nine feet from my bedroom, but I could not get there on my feet. I had to crawl. At that point I thought I would end my life in a wheelchair. I did not think that I would ever play golf again."

Olazábal had become a prisoner in his own home. He could not walk to the sink to pour himself a glass of water. He could not drive. He could not venture out. He could not stand upright for more than ten minutes. And, of course, he could not play golf. Since the age of two, Olazábal had hit golf balls. His kindergarten was the driving range at the Real Golf Club de San Sebastian. Often he would spend half a day rehearsing his putting on the practice green. His sheer talent, coupled to dedication, was rewarded. He became a world-class golfer on the sporting stage. Then, suddenly, out of nowhere, for reasons apparent neither to those doctors

treating him nor to himself, he was in pain. Real, excruciating pain.

Olazábal had been told it was rheumatoid arthritis. He did not want to hear that, but he needed to be told something. He was now at home. He had not struck a competitive shot since the Trophée Lancôme in September 1995. He had withdrawn from the 1995 European Ryder Cup Team. Nine months had passed. The postman was now the most regular visitor to the home he shared with his parents and younger sister, Sabina. He received

one communication after another. Most people wrote to wish him well. Some felt obliged to suggest what he might do to counter the 'illness'. And it was because of one of those suggestions that, miraculously, he was cured.

Adidas, the sports company, felt that they could build for him a pair of shoes that might assist his return to the fairways. So Olazábal flew to Munich. At the airport to greet him was Ulrich Schulte. They were old friends from amateur days. Schulte suggested that Olazábal should

JOSÉ MARIA OLAZÁBAL and GREG NORMAN: joined by sportsmanship

visit Dr Hans-Wilhelm Muller-Wohlfahrt during his stay in Munich. Olazábal had gone to the German city for two days; he stayed three weeks.

Dr Muller-Wohlfahrt, well known by German Olympic athletes and many sporting icons, cringed in shock when he first looked at Olazábal.

"His feet were emaciated," he said. "There was no padding, the muscles were atrophied, there was one toe completely out of joint and another pointing up in the air. The symptoms were similar to rheumatoid arthritis, but I felt the swelling in the toes could have another origin."

He determined following an MRI (Magnetic Resonance Imaging) scan, that Olazábal had a hernia between the fifth lumbar and the first sacral spinal bones. Olazábal was sent to a neurologist. Dr Muller-Wohlfahrt devised an exercise programme and the curing process began.

Olazábal returned to the fairways in February, 1997, and the rest, as they say, is history.

You could be forgiven, however, on the eve of the Masters Tournament for examining Colin Montgomerie or Lee Westwood, David Duval or Tiger Woods, as potential winners, and excluding Olazábal from all calculations. Olazábal went into the tournament as an outsider because from the tee he was struggling to keep the ball on the straight and narrow, and that failing had been compounded by the knowledge that for the first time in more than two decades the players would be confronted by rough at Augusta National.

Initially, Davis Love III and Nick Price, two seriously considered contenders, climbed to the top of the leader-board alongside two lesser known players in the Americans Brandel Chamblee and Scott McCarron. They shot 69, but

SERGIO GARCIA and VICTOR, his father and caddie: united family challenge

Olazábal was on their heels after a 70. The Spaniard was ahead with a superb second round of 66 and still one in front after a third round of 73. Greg Norman, like Olazábal, had been suitably inspired by Augusta. The Australian held second place; Love and Steve Pate were tied third.

The final round would provide further evidence that the last nine holes at the Masters provides an annual feast of golf so compelling that you immediately start looking forward to next year.

This time Duval charged; Woods did not. Lee Westwood came out of the pack, finished tied sixth, and Sergio Garcia, aged

DAVIS LOVE III: shadowing Olazábal into second place

LEADERS

THRU 14

OLAZABAL	6
GLASSON	1
CHAMBLEE	2

PRIOR	HOLE	1	2	3	4	5	6	7	8	9	10	11	12	13	14	15	16	17	18
	PAR	4	5	4	3	4	3	4	5	4	4	4	3	5	4	5	3	4	4
1	ESTES	1	2	2	1	0	1	1	1	1	1	1	1	0	1	2	3	2	2
3	LOVE	3	4	4	3	4	3	4	4	4	4	4	4	5	4				
3	McCARRON	4	4	4	5	5	5	5	5	5	5	5	4						
3	PRICE	3	3	3	2	3	2	2	2	3	2	2	2	3	4	3	3	3	3
2	JANZEN	2	3	4	3	3	3	4	4	4	3	3	3	3	4	4	4	4	5
2	OLAZABAL	2	3	3	3	3	4	4	4	4	4	5	5	6	6				
1	NORMAN	0	1	2	2	3	3	3	3	3	3	3	4	5	5	5	5	5	5
2	LEONARD	2	3	2	1	1	1	1	2	1	2	2	2	2					
1	ELS	1	1	1	0	0	0	0	1	1	0	0	1	3	3				
2	SLUMAN	1	1	2	2	2	2	3	3	2									

LANGER	66	2

JOSÉ MARIA OLAZÁBAL: heading for a 66 and half-way lead

19, claimed much honour in finishing the leading amateur prior to turning professional. Those last nine holes, however, eventually belonged to Olazábal, Love, Norman and Pate. First Olazábal edged ahead with a birdie putt of 20 feet at the tenth, and held his lead at the short 12th with a wonderful shot from the back bunker to save par.

There was more drama at the long 13th where Norman holed from 20 feet for an eagle, and Olazábal followed him in from slightly shorter length for a birdie. The two exchanged a glance that told the world how much respect they held for each other. Yet ahead of them Love was to hole such an audacious chip at the 16th for a two that, suddenly, it seemed the American might advance to a famous win. Olazábal was in no

SERGIO GARCIA and TIGER WOODS: trust me, it's a simple game

THE COURSE

Some years the changes to the Augusta National course are no more than subtle, other times they can be drastic enough to force a re-think of strategy. Rarely, however, is so much debate provoked as the toughening of the 17th hole for the 1999 action. The tee went back 25 yards to lengthen the par four to 425 yards, so calling for a long iron second shot into a tight green. But the major added-difficulty factor came with the planting of 30-foot pine trees on the right of the fairway to put a greater premium on driving accuracy. What never changes is the condition of the course – again it was immaculate.

mood to open the door. He came to the 16th himself, struck a magnificent shot to three feet, holed the putt, extended his lead to two and finished with two pars for a 71. His winning total of 280 was two better than that of Love and three ahead of Norman. More importantly Olazábal had won another major championship, confirming his wonderful recovery from illness.

So unquestionably, there was more emotion in Olazábal's voice as he spoke following his second win in the Masters Tournament. He recalled those days, weeks, months at home when not even the comforting words of his devoted parents could soothe the pain and frustration he felt from being divorced from the fairways he loved. He thanked Dr Muller-Wohlfahrt. He searched for words to describe his feelings. They came, though not as easily as the shots that had made him a true champion. His emotions were being stretched.

Throughout his wretched months at home Olazábal was helped not only by his family but also by Sergio Gomez. The two met on the practice ground at the Real Golf de San Sebastian, set in the lush foothills of the Pyrenees, in 1979. Since then Gomez has become manager, confidant, mentor and friend to the young man who was born in the hamlet of Fuenterrubia, on February 6, 1966, and where, by a stroke of good timing, a golf course had been opened adjacent to the hippodrome.

Gomez, like the other members of the Real Golf de San Sebastian, was simply mesmerised by the artistry of Olazábal's game. The young Olazábal had been drawn to the golf course because that is where his father, Gaspar, worked as the greenkeeper and his mother, Julia, as wardrobe mistress. Olazábal's life, from the moment he held a golf club when less than two feet tall, revolved around the game. Aged seven, he won the Spanish Championship for under nines. Soon afterwards, Ballesteros would entrance the sporting world by leading the 1976 Open Championship and Olazábal, although committed to studying at the public school in Fuenterrubia, knew that he wanted to aspire to such heights especially when three years later Ballesteros returned to his home further along the Spanish coast with the famous silver claret jug won at Royal Lytham & St Annes.

Jesus Arruti, the club professional who spent marathon session after marathon session with Olazábal on the practice range, and Gomez were soon

SHOT OF THE WEEK

Winner José Maria Olazábal thought his putt of 20 feet for a charge-launching birdie at the tenth hole, his nerve-testing bunker recovery from the back of the 12th green, and his putt for another birdie at the par five 13th were all critical. But the vote for the most critical of all must go to the putt of 20 feet he made at the 13th after Greg Norman had holed from 25 feet for an eagle. If Olazábal had missed then the Australian would have taken over the lead.

aware of the fire that burned within the young pupil. He was innately shy, true, but he could not mask his desire to succeed. Moreover, he was supremely talented.

Olazábal's meteoric amateur career, during which he won the 'triple crown' of British Boys' Championship, British Amateur Championship and British Youths' Championship, provided ample evidence of that talent, so it was no surprise to Gomez or Arruti when their protégé graduated to Sir Henry Cotton European Tour Rookie of the Year in 1986 when he finished runner-up to Ballesteros in the Volvo Order of Merit.

Olazábal, who advanced the following year to represent Europe and to partner Ballesteros in the Ryder Cup, was consumed by the game and at times he found it hard to camouflage his disappointment. There were to be times when Gomez was compelled to make it clear to Olazábal that he must not always be so hard on himself and times when others chastised him. On one occasion his intensity showed when on leaving the practice

DAVID DUVAL: on a charge

range he collapsed and was taken to hospital. Tests revealed he had an ulcer, and the specialist informed him that as a professional sportsman it was imperative that he learned to relax.

Even so one disappointment left a scar that he needed to erase. In 1991 at Augusta National he walked to the 18th tee on the final day tied for the lead. He bogeyed the hole. Ian Woosnam slipped into the coveted green jacket; Olazábal slipped away to console himself. He returned and won the Masters in 1994, exorcising the demons of 1991, but there was to be a more daunting mountain to scale.

Olazábal achieved that when he walked without pain from the Munich clinic back to the fairways. He knew then that he had regained his life. The craving to win remained, of course, but it was no longer a matter of life and death. Yet the streets around his home that were packed with people when he returned from Augusta National also told a story. "It became clear to me that it had been a very special victory," he said. The world of sport echoes those words.

LEE WESTWOOD: out of the pack

Mitchell Platts

Augusta National, Georgia, USA, April 8–11, 1999 · Par 72 · Yards 6985

Pos	Name & Country	Rnd 1	Rnd 2	Rnd 3	Rnd 4	Total	€	£
1	José Maria OLAZÁBAL (Spn)	70	66	73	71	280	628037.00	448597.85
2	Davis LOVE III (USA)	69	72	70	71	282	376822.00	269158.57
3	Greg NORMAN (Aus)	71	68	71	73	283	237259.00	169470.71
4	Bob ESTES (USA)	71	72	69	72	284	153520.00	109657.14
	Steve PATE (USA)	71	75	65	73	284	153520.00	109657.14
6	David DUVAL (USA)	71	74	70	70	285	109209.00	78006.43
	Carlos FRANCO (Par)	72	72	68	73	285	109209.00	78006.43
	Phil MICKELSON (USA)	74	69	71	71	285	109209.00	78006.43
	Nick PRICE (Zim)	69	72	72	72	285	109209.00	78006.43
	Lee WESTWOOD (Eng)	75	71	68	71	285	109209.00	78006.43
11	Steve ELKINGTON (Aus)	72	70	71	74	287	80249.00	57320.71
	Bernhard LANGER (Ger)	76	66	72	73	287	80249.00	57320.71
	Colin MONTGOMERIE (Scot)	70	72	71	74	287	80249.00	57320.71
14	Jim FURYK (USA)	72	73	70	73	288	61059.00	43613.57
	Lee JANZEN (USA)	70	69	73	76	288	61059.00	43613.57
	Brandt JOBE (USA)	72	71	74	71	288	61059.00	43613.57
	Ian WOOSNAM (Wal)	71	74	71	72	288	61059.00	43613.57
18	Brandel CHAMBLEE (USA)	69	73	75	72	289	45498.00	32498.57
	Bill GLASSON (USA)	72	70	73	74	289	45498.00	32498.57
	Justin LEONARD (USA)	70	72	73	74	289	45498.00	32498.57
	Scott McCARRON (USA)	69	68	76	76	289	45498.00	32498.57
	Tiger WOODS (USA)	72	72	70	75	289	45498.00	32498.57
23	Larry MIZE (USA)	76	70	72	72	290	36286.00	25918.57
24	Brad FAXON (USA)	74	73	68	76	291	30704.00	21931.43
	Per-Ulrik JOHANSSON (Swe)	75	72	71	73	291	30704.00	21931.43
	Vijay SINGH (Fij)	72	76	71	72	291	30704.00	21931.43
27	Stewart CINK (USA)	74	70	71	77	292	25296.00	18068.57
	Fred COUPLES (USA)	74	71	76	71	292	25296.00	18068.57
	Ernie ELS (SA)	71	72	69	80	292	25296.00	18068.57
	Rocco MEDIATE (USA)	73	74	69	76	292	25296.00	18068.57
31	Tom LEHMAN (USA)	73	72	73	75	293	20690.00	18068.57
	Shigeki MARUYAMA (Jpn)	78	70	71	74	293	20690.00	18068.57
	Mark O'MEARA (USA)	70	76	69	78	293	20690.00	18068.57
	Jeff SLUMAN (USA)	70	75	70	78	293	20690.00	18068.57
	Brian WATTS (USA)	73	73	70	77	293	20690.00	18068.57
36	John HUSTON (USA)	74	72	71	77	294	17533.00	12523.57
	Andrew MAGEE (USA)	70	77	72	75	294	17533.00	12523.57
38	Billy ANDRADE (USA)	76	72	72	75	295	15003.00	10716.43
	Mark BROOKS (USA)	76	72	75	72	295	15003.00	10716.43
	Ray FLOYD (USA)	74	73	72	76	295	15003.00	10716.43
	Craig STADLER (USA)	72	76	70	77	295	15003.00	10716.43
	Steve STRICKER (USA)	75	72	69	79	295	15003.00	10716.43
	Sergio GARCIA (AM) (Sp)	72	75	75	73	295		
44	Jay HAAS (USA)	74	69	79	75	297	12212.00	8722.86
	Tim HERRON (USA)	75	69	74	79	297	12212.00	8722.86
	Scott HOCH (USA)	75	73	70	79	297	12212.00	8722.86
	Tom McKNIGHT (AM) (USA)	73	74	73	77	297		
48	Sandy LYLE (Scot)	71	77	70	80	298	10467.00	7476.43
	Craig PARRY (Aus)	75	73	73	77	298	10467.00	7476.43
50	Chris PERRY (USA)	73	72	74	80	299	9560.00	6828.57
	Matt KUCHAR (AM) (USA)	77	71	73	78	299		
52	Olin BROWNE (USA)	74	74	72	80	300	8705.00	6217.86
	John DALY (USA)	72	76	71	81	300	8705.00	6217.86
	Payne STEWART (USA)	73	75	77	75	300	8705.00	6217.86
	Bob TWAY (USA)	75	73	78	74	300	8705.00	6217.86
56	Trevor IMMELMAN (AM) (SA)	72	76	78	79	305		
57	Thomas BJÖRN (Den)	76	73			149	4361.00	3115.00
	Fred FUNK (USA)	76	73			149	4361.00	3115.00
	Miguel Angel JIMÉNEZ (Sp)	72	77			149	4361.00	3115.00
	Frank LICKLITER (USA)	72	77			149	4361.00	3115.00
	Fuzzy ZOELLER (USA)	72	77			149	4361.00	3115.00
62	Stuart APPLEBY (Aus)	73	77			150	4361.00	3115.00
	John COOK (USA)	76	74			150	4361.00	3115.00
	J.P. HAYES (USA)	76	74			150	4361.00	3115.00
	Jumbo OZAKI (Jpn)	71	79			150	4361.00	3115.00
66	Charles COODY (USA)	77	74			151	4361.00	3115.00
	Jesper PARNEVIK (Swe)	74	77			151	4361.00	3115.00
	Patrik SJÖLAND (Swe)	76	75			151	4361.00	3115.00
	Tom WATSON (USA)	74	77			151	4361.00	3115.00
	Willie WOOD (USA)	79	72			151	4361.00	3115.00
71	Paul AZINGER (USA)	74	78			152	4361.00	3115.00
	Mark CALCAVECCHIA (USA)	75	77			152	4361.00	3115.00
	Gabriel HJERTSTEDT (Swe)	74	78			152	4361.00	3115.00
	Hank KUEHNE (AM) (USA)	74	78			152		
	Loren ROBERTS (USA)	76	76			152	4361.00	3115.00
76	Darren CLARKE (N Ire)	75	78			153	4361.00	3115.00
	Ben CRENSHAW (USA)	74	79			153	4361.00	3115.00
	Nick FALDO (Eng)	80	73			153	4361.00	3115.00
	Billy MAYFAIR (USA)	78	75			153	4361.00	3115.00
	Corey PAVIN (USA)	75	78			153	4361.00	3115.00
81	Jeff MAGGERT (USA)	78	76			154	4361.00	3115.00
	David TOMS (USA)	78	76			154	4361.00	3115.00
	Scott VERPLANK (USA)	78	76			154	4361.00	3115.00
84	Glen DAY (USA)	78	77			155	4361.00	3115.00
	Trevor DODDS (Nam)	78	77			155	4361.00	3115.00
	Hal SUTTON (USA	79	76			155	4361.00	3115.00
87	Seve BALLESTEROS (Sp)	78	78			156	4361.00	3115.00
	Steve JONES (USA)	77	79			156	4361.00	3115.00
89	Gary PLAYER (SA)	79	79			158	4361.00	3115.00
90	Tommy AARON (USA)	77	82			159	4361.00	3115.00
91	Arnold PALMER (USA)	83	78			161	4361.00	3115.00
92	John "Spider" MILLER (USA)	81	81			162	4361.00	3115.00
93	Joe DURANT (USA)	87	79			166	4361.00	3115.00

SERGIO GARCIA and JOSÉ MARIA OLAZÁBAL:
the new Spanish Armada

Top of the class

After 12 Q-School visits, Jean-Francois Remesy

completes his education

with a masterly win at Penha Longa

He started out as plain Jeff, but by the time he had finished he had been outed as a fully-fledged Jean-Francois. Losers don't always mind what they're called, but winners can be much more particular.

Jeff – sorry, Jean-Francois – Remesy came to the inaugural Estoril Open in April like a storm-tossed ship in search of a safe haven. Just how appropriate the analogy is will soon become clear, but it is a fact that before he pitched up in Portugal, Remesy was a golfer viewed on Tour as being guided more by hope than expectation.

Prior to this tournament, Remesy was known in European golf for not very much, quite honestly, but if a scintilla of celebrity did stick to him, it was that he was a serial persister. He attended his first European Tour Qualifying School in 1987 and, quite clearly lacking nothing in determination, had been back for more pressure every year since. The School of 1998 had been no more successful for him than a host of others, in that he had failed to win his card back after just losing it at the end of the season.

There were various shades of luminosity present at Penha Longa. The likes of Mark James, Sam Torrance and Costantino Rocca were the long-life arclamps, a few others shone only slightly less brightly and there were plenty of standard-issue 100-watt jobs around. By comparison, Remesy was a career night-light.

He was, in short, the sort of chap who looked to have little, if any, chance of becoming Estoril Open champion. But he did it, splendidly and resolutely, with a score of 286, two under par. Against par, it was the highest winning score of the European Tour season to date, by three strokes, but the measure of Remesy's achievement can be gained by the revelation that after four days of hard labour he was the only man in the field to complete the 72 holes under par.

The weather at this time of year in the environs of Lisbon, 15 miles north of Penha Longa, is usually balmy. At this time of this year, you had to be barmy to step outside the club-house. It was cold and, above all, it was windy. Oh my, was it windy.

The pro-am was cancelled because of the wind, the first round was ruined because of it and the second lap was no better. Now, wind is no particular problem to professional golfers. A capriciously gusting gale is. Consider the following statistics; they don't lie. After the first round, there were only 13 players under par, following the second a mere eight, at the conclusion of the third just two remained and by the finish on Sunday afternoon Remesy was left in glorious isolation. The prosecution rests, your honour.

Remesy came into the tournament having beaten Raphaël Jacquelin in a play-off for the French PGA title the week before, so he was in good heart when he

SHOT OF THE WEEK

It was just a normal little eight-iron, the sort that professional golfers hit for fun. It was Jean-Francois Remesy's third shot at the last hole of the last round, and he was looking down the barrel of a play-off with Andrew Coltart. He was precisely 150 yards from the flag and, needing desperately to get it close, he put his ball five feet from the pin. No, not a stroke of genius – but in the context of the piece, it was absolutely priceless.

embarked on his challenge. He was in touch but threatening nobody after a first round that was transformed from the simple playing of a game to a battle for survival and sanity. All things considered, the scores of 69 produced by Van Phillips and Phillip Price deserved a house mark from teacher. The highest round was suffered

DAVID CARTER: a putt agonisingly missed but still a brilliant 67 to finish

VAN PHILLIPS: deserved a house mark

by one Antonio Dantas da Silva, who was 19 over par. Not so surprising, perhaps – it was a 19-over-par sort of a day – except that da Silva's regular job is as an assistant at Penha Longa. So much for local knowledge.

The wind still cast its malign influence over proceedings in the second round, but Remesy was up to the challenge, moving into a one-stroke lead after a 69. A calamitous 77 in the third round left him toiling in joint eleventh place, apparently out of it as Spanish veteran José Rivero moved into the lead. Remesy played well enough for the first 15 holes, which he covered in one over par, and appallingly for the last three, dropping four strokes to leave him four off the pace.

There seemed no way back for the 34-year-old Frenchman. Nobody turns round a four-stroke deficit behind an old hustler like Rivero, right? Wrong.

It was clear that if he was to win, no matter how well Remesy played, he would still need some high-scoring help from those above him and, generously, they came to his assistance. Rivero had a 77, Søren Kjeldsen and Sean Corte-Real, the other two players in the final group, scored

SØREN KJELDSEN: humanitarian aid on a grand scale

THE COURSE

Like all celebrated artists, Robert Trent Jones has his critics, but the great American designer got it absolutely right at Penha Longa. This is a beautiful course whose looks are matched by its splendour as a test of golf as it meanders its way through the hills of Sintra. It is tough at the best of times – the winds that tormented it on this week made it considerably more so.

ANDREW COLTART: on the verge of a problem

78 and 76 respectively and Mark Mouland, Gary Emerson and Paul Lawrie took a dart at the lead and just as quickly faded. This was humanitarian aid on a grand scale.

David Carter had a brilliant 67 from way down the field and eventually finished second alongside Andrew Coltart and Massimo Florioli, with Coltart providing the strongest and most sustained attack on Remesy's aspirations.

Playing alongside Remesy, Coltart was with the Frenchman until the 17th, then met his Waterloo when he put his tee shot into a bunker. The consequence was that the rangy Scot thinned the ball into thick rough on the other side of the green and, although he escaped well enough, he then two-putted for a double-bogey five.

It was still not over. If Coltart could birdie the last and Remesy somehow dropped a shot, there would be a play-off. It did not happen. Remesy, exactly 150 yards from the flag in two, hit an eight-iron to five feet. Coltart had a putt of 12 feet for birdie but missed it, and Remesy pushed the knife in a little deeper by holing his own birdie putt. Contest over – and, perhaps, a new life for Jean-Francois Remesy, born-again golfer and newly christened winner.

Mel Webb

PENHA LONGA, ESTORIL, PORTUGAL, APRIL 15–18, 1999 · PAR 72 · YARDS 6879

Pos	Name & Country	Rnd 1	Rnd 2	Rnd 3	Rnd 4	Total	Prize Money €	£
1	Jean-Francois REMESY (Fr)	72	69	77	68	286	93320.00	66657.14
2	Massimo FLORIOLI (It)	72	75	70	71	288	41753.33	29823.81
	David CARTER (Eng)	70	72	79	67	288	41753.33	29823.81
	Andrew COLTART (Scot)	77	72	70	69	288	41753.33	29823.81
5	Geoff OGILVY (Aus)	73	75	71	70	289	20033.33	14309.52
	Van PHILLIPS (Eng)	69	77	73	70	289	20033.33	14309.52
	Peter MITCHELL (Eng)	74	71	72	72	289	20033.33	14309.52
8	Gary EMERSON (Eng)	72	72	72	74	290	12006.00	8575.71
	Emanuele CANONICA (It)	74	71	73	72	290	12006.00	8575.71
	Peter BAKER (Eng)	73	74	73	70	290	12006.00	8575.71
	Niclas FASTH (Swe)	73	69	74	74	290	12006.00	8575.71
12	Daniel CHOPRA (Swe)	72	77	70	72	291	7578.67	5413.34
	José RIVERO (Sp)	72	72	70	77	291	7578.67	5413.34
	Retief GOOSEN (SA)	70	74	76	71	291	7578.67	5413.34
	Jamie SPENCE (Eng)	72	75	71	73	291	7578.67	5413.34
	Andrew RAITT (Eng)	72	70	77	72	291	7578.67	5413.34
	Robert COLES (Eng)	72	74	73	72	291	7578.67	5413.34
	Thomas LEVET (Fr)	79	69	70	73	291	7578.67	5413.34
	Phillip PRICE (Wal)	69	77	76	69	291	7578.67	5413.34
	Ignacio GARRIDO (Sp)	76	73	73	69	291	7578.67	5413.34
	Nick O'HERN (Aus)	73	73	72	73	291	7578.67	5413.34
	Mark MOULAND (Wal)	73	75	69	74	291	7578.67	5413.34
	Anthony WALL (Eng)	72	72	73	74	291	7578.67	5413.34
24	Tom GILLIS (USA)	71	77	73	71	292	5297.60	3784.00
	Dennis EDLUND (Swe)	72	75	76	69	292	5297.60	3784.00
	John SENDEN (Aus)	72	75	75	70	292	5297.60	3784.00
	Paul EALES (Eng)	76	72	75	69	292	5297.60	3784.00
	Gary ORR (Scot)	77	69	73	73	292	5297.60	3784.00
	Paul LAWRIE (Scot)	72	74	71	75	292	5297.60	3784.00
	Raphaël JACQUELIN (Fr)	76	71	72	73	292	5297.60	3784.00
	Des SMYTH (Ire)	76	73	75	68	292	5297.60	3784.00
	Paul AFFLECK (Wal)	76	72	70	74	292	5297.60	3784.00
	Sean CORTE-REAL (Port)	75	72	69	76	292	5297.60	3784.00
34	Søren KJELDSEN (Den)	74	69	72	78	293	3976.00	2840.00
	John BICKERTON (Eng)	73	75	74	71	293	3976.00	2840.00
	Paul MCGINLEY (Ire)	70	75	74	74	293	3976.00	2840.00
	Carl WATTS (Eng)	73	75	73	72	293	3976.00	2840.00
	Santiago LUNA (Sp)	74	73	71	75	293	3976.00	2840.00
	Ian HUTCHINGS (SA)	71	78	74	70	293	3976.00	2840.00
	Jonathan LOMAS (Eng)	70	73	77	73	293	3976.00	2840.00
	Massimo SCARPA (It)	72	77	70	74	293	3976.00	2840.00
	Jeremy ROBINSON (Eng)	76	73	73	71	293	3976.00	2840.00
	Ian GARBUTT (Eng)	75	70	73	75	293	3976.00	2840.00
44	Stephen BENNETT (Eng)	73	75	74	72	294	2968.00	2120.00
	Jesus Maria ARRUTI (Sp)	72	71	77	74	294	2968.00	2120.00
	Juan QUIROS (Sp)	73	76	75	70	294	2968.00	2120.00
	David HOWELL (Eng)	78	70	72	74	294	2968.00	2120.00
	Francis VALERA (Sp)	77	71	76	70	294	2968.00	2120.00
	Francisco CEA (Sp)	73	74	73	74	294	2968.00	2120.00
	Michael LONG (NZ)	75	73	73	73	294	2968.00	2120.00
	Scott HENDERSON (Scot)	75	70	74	75	294	2968.00	2120.00
52	Johan RYSTRÖM (Swe)	71	77	73	74	295	2296.00	1640.00
	Mark JAMES (Eng)	76	73	71	75	295	2296.00	1640.00
	Derrick COOPER (Eng)	72	76	77	70	295	2296.00	1640.00
	Jean VAN DE VELDE (Fr)	73	73	73	76	295	2296.00	1640.00
56	Roger CHAPMAN (Eng)	73	75	70	78	296	1904.00	1360.00
	Paolo QUIRICI (Swi)	71	72	80	73	296	1904.00	1360.00
	Christian CÉVAER (Fr)	74	72	73	77	296	1904.00	1360.00
59	Andrew OLDCORN (Scot)	71	74	78	74	297	1680.00	1200.00
	Anders HANSEN (Den)	71	73	77	76	297	1680.00	1200.00
	Gordon SHERRY (Scot)	76	73	75	73	297	1680.00	1200.00
62	Costantino ROCCA (It)	76	73	74	75	298	1540.00	1100.00
	Carl SUNESON (Sp)	75	72	78	73	298	1540.00	1100.00
64	Warren BENNETT (Eng)	79	70	79	71	299	1428.00	1020.00
	Marc FARRY (Fr)	72	75	77	75	299	1428.00	1020.00
66	Alberto BINAGHI (It)	75	71	75	79	300	840.00	600.00
67	Ivo GINER (Sp)	78	71	78	74	301	835.50	596.79
	Pedro LINHART (Sp)	73	75	78	75	301	835.50	596.79
69	Fabrice TARNAUD (Fr)	72	75	76	79	302	829.50	592.50
	Miles TUNNICLIFF (Eng)	72	77	77	76	302	829.50	592.50
71	Philip WALTON (Ire)	77	72	77	77	303	825.00	589.29
72	Eamonn DARCY (Ire)	73	76	79	78	306	820.50	586.07
	Ricardo GONZALEZ (Arg)	74	75	81	76	306	820.50	586.07

Double Swedish rhapsody

Jarmo Sandelin claims title

in Barcelona with style,

a smile and a putting record

The debt that the European professional game owes to Spanish golf is already enormous. It is likely to reach astronomical proportions if the final Peugeot Open de España of the 20th Century proves a reliable guide to the game's future prospects in the Iberian peninsula.

This sporting version of the Festival of the Three Kings at the Real Club de Golf 'El Prat' in Barcelona featured the incomparable Severiano Ballesteros; the indomitable José Maria Olazábal, and the incredible Sergio Garcia; making triumphant homecomings from Augusta, the latter embarking on a professional career that promises to do so much for his country and Europe in the new millennium.

It also starred Ignacio Garrido and Miguel Angel Jiménez who have already played significant roles in one momentous Ryder Cup victory; Juan Carlos Aguero, a 23-year-old from Seve's home club of Pedrena; and Alvaro Salto, from Madrid, twice a World Universities champion, whose second round 63 equalled the course record that has stood for 28 years.

Also in the field were Masters champions Nick Faldo and Bernhard Langer, yet they and this enviable array of Spanish talent were all eclipsed by an extraordinary Swedish golfer, Jarmo Sandelin, who rivals

PEUGEOT
OPEN
PEUGEOT
OPEN
16
17
22

Mark Roe achieved the first ace of his career with an eight iron at the 156 yards third hole in the second round, and Ignacio Garrido scored his second at the same hole with a seven iron the following day. But they took second place to the long bunker shot under pressure that underlined the strength of Jarmo Sandelin's short game. From 35 yards at the first in the final round he splashed his ball to within a few inches.

IGNACIO GARRIDO: up and under to tied second

fellow countryman Jesper Parnevik, coincidentally a winner on the same day in the United States, for the title of European golf's number one extrovert.

Sandelin would never pass unnoticed in a crowd. He wears psychedelic shirts, crocodile skin golf shoes, studded leather belts, and smites a golf ball almost out of sight with a 52 inch driver. He used to have five wedges in the tournament bag carried by his fianceé Linda Lundgren until he decided so many options were a recipe for confusion.

His putting is also sensational. Sandelin's total of 98 putts for his three opening rounds of 66 and his closing 69 for a 21 under par total of 267, produced an average of 24.5 putts per round which set the benchmark for the innovative Axa Performance Data programme. And he did it with style and a smile.

Born in Finland, Sandelin moved to Sweden with his parents at the age of seven, and spent seven years on the European Challenge Tour before he established himself at senior level with a

swashbuckling victory over Ballesteros in the 1995 Turespaña Open Canarias. The following year he won the Madeira Island Open while in the process of making an abortive attempt to establish himself in the United States.

Since adding discretion to his undoubted valour, the strapping Sandelin has set his heart on scaling the peaks of the game. After dedicating his victory to his mother Sinikka, who died two months previously, he nominated a Ryder Cup place, ascent in the Official World Golf Ranking, and naturally success in a major, as his principal ambitions.

The ability to chip and putt like a dream was one of the principal reasons Olazábal won his second Masters title the previous weekend, and with the 19-year-old Garcia from Castellon becoming the first European to win the amateur award, hopes that they would continue in the same vein were high among Catalan fans.

THE COURSE

The renowned 'El Prat' seaside course at Llobregat, designed by Javier Arana, and opened in 1956, will disappear when work begins in 2000 on extending the runways at the adjacent airport. But the Real Club de Golf, whose original course was at Pedralbes in the centre of the city, will have a new home on a 260 hectares inland site in Tarrasa on the west side of Barcelona ready by March 2002. Jack Nicklaus, Greg Norman, and Robert Von Hagge are the contenders to design two 18 hole courses, with a third to be added later.

SERGIO GARCIA: stylish professional debut

Both were hailed as heroes, but Olazábal, who had given his all in conquering Augusta, had to find more to cope with the avalanche of attention his achievement rightly merited. Like Ballesteros before him, he discovered that mind and body were unable to summon another supreme effort. Scores of 72 and 71 saw him fail to make the cut by one stroke.

Garcia, who donned a designer suit to announce his switch to the professional ranks, accompanied by his father Victor and manager José Marquina, proceeded to make a stylish debut, exhibiting the full range of talents that had stamped him as the world's best amateur in returning a nine under par total of 279. The teenager finished tied 25th, his first cheque being worth almost 8000 euro (£5,670). He hardly noticed the burden of expectation, and if anyone can convince the football-crazy Spaniards that golf is a game to be ranked alongside their second loves of cycling and basketball, then Garcia is the man.

England's Jamie Spence was cruelly unfortunate when his drive at one hole went under a parked car, and his ball could not be found. He had to deem it lost and return to the tee. The result, a double-bogey seven halted a spirited charge in pursuit of Sandelin, who held off the challenges of Ireland's Paul McGinley, Garrido, and Jiménez whose closing 64 made it a three-way tie for second place, by four strokes.

Mike Britten

REAL CLUB DE GOLF 'EL PRAT', BARCELONA, SPAIN, APRIL 22–25, 1999 · PAR 72 · YARDS 6639

Pos	Name & Country	Rnd 1	Rnd 2	Rnd 3	Rnd 4	Total	Prize Money €	Prize Money £
1	Jarmo SANDELIN (Swe)	66	66	66	69	267	140000.00	100000.00
2	Ignacio GARRIDO (Sp)	65	71	67	68	271	62633.33	44738.09
	Miguel Angel JIMÉNEZ (Sp)	72	68	67	64	271	62633.33	44738.09
	Paul MCGINLEY (Ire)	67	68	66	70	271	62633.33	44738.09
5	Juan Carlos AGUERO (Sp)	65	70	67	70	272	32480.00	23200.00
	Jamie SPENCE (Eng)	65	68	70	69	272	32480.00	23200.00
7	Anthony WALL (Eng)	65	72	69	67	273	23100.00	16500.00
	Paul LAWRIE (Scot)	66	66	73	68	273	23100.00	16500.00
9	Alex CEJKA (Ger)	68	69	68	70	275	17810.00	12721.43
	Peter O'MALLEY (Aus)	71	67	69	68	275	17810.00	12721.43
11	Paul AFFLECK (Wal)	68	74	68	66	276	14050.00	10035.71
	Alvaro SALTO (Sp)	73	63	69	71	276	14050.00	10035.71
	Gary EVANS (Eng)	72	64	69	71	276	14050.00	10035.71
	Diego BORREGO (Sp)	68	70	72	66	276	14050.00	10035.71
15	John MELLOR (Eng)	70	69	73	65	277	12096.00	8640.00
	Ian GARBUTT (Eng)	72	67	71	67	277	12096.00	8640.00
17	Massimo SCARPA (It)	70	69	70	69	278	10059.00	7185.00
	Peter MITCHELL (Eng)	71	71	68	68	278	10059.00	7185.00
	Van PHILLIPS (Eng)	69	69	71	69	278	10059.00	7185.00
	Santiago LUNA (Sp)	71	67	71	69	278	10059.00	7185.00
	Paul EALES (Eng)	69	67	73	69	278	10059.00	7185.00
	Pierre FULKE (Swe)	70	70	70	68	278	10059.00	7185.00
	Michael JONZON (Swe)	67	69	71	71	278	10059.00	7185.00
	Des SMYTH (Ire)	74	64	69	71	278	10059.00	7185.00
25	Michael LONG (NZ)	73	69	70	67	279	7938.00	5670.00
	Christopher HANELL (Swe)	71	70	67	71	279	7938.00	5670.00
	Michael CAMPBELL (NZ)	67	71	73	68	279	7938.00	5670.00
	Miguel Angel MARTIN (Sp)	71	67	71	70	279	7938.00	5670.00
	Sergio GARCIA (Sp)	67	73	70	69	279	7938.00	5670.00
	Peter BAKER (Eng)	68	73	69	69	279	7938.00	5670.00
	David CARTER (Eng)	69	72	70	68	279	7938.00	5670.00
	Soren HANSEN (Den)	71	68	69	71	279	7938.00	5670.00
33	Jean VAN DE VELDE (Fr)	67	75	69	69	280	6384.00	4560.00
	Dean ROBERTSON (Scot)	69	73	71	67	280	6384.00	4560.00
	Phillip PRICE (Wal)	70	69	72	69	280	6384.00	4560.00
	Gerry NORQUIST (USA)	74	68	71	67	280	6384.00	4560.00
	Thomas LEVET (Fr)	69	69	73	69	280	6384.00	4560.00
	José ROZADILLA (Sp)	73	69	73	65	280	6384.00	4560.00
	Emanuele CANONICA (It)	72	64	71	73	280	6384.00	4560.00
40	Max ANGLERT (Swe)	65	76	71	69	281	5292.00	3780.00
	Gary ORR (Scot)	68	70	73	70	281	5292.00	3780.00
	Alberto BINAGHI (It)	66	76	69	70	281	5292.00	3780.00
	Joakim HAEGGMAN (Swe)	68	72	73	68	281	5292.00	3780.00
	Robert KARLSSON (Swe)	70	70	72	69	281	5292.00	3780.00
	Costantino ROCCA (It)	69	70	72	70	281	5292.00	3780.00
46	Brian DAVIS (Eng)	69	72	70	71	282	4116.00	2940.00
	Andrew OLDCORN (Scot)	71	71	69	71	282	4116.00	2940.00
	Ivo GINER (Sp)	68	74	71	69	282	4116.00	2940.00
	Mark MCNULTY (Zim)	68	73	73	68	282	4116.00	2940.00
	David HOWELL (Eng)	68	74	68	72	282	4116.00	2940.00
	Retief GOOSEN (SA)	71	70	74	67	282	4116.00	2940.00
	Angel CABRERA (Arg)	70	72	74	66	282	4116.00	2940.00
	Søren KJELDSEN (Den)	69	71	71	71	282	4116.00	2940.00
54	Gary EMERSON (Eng)	68	74	71	70	283	3108.00	2220.00
	Domingo HOSPITAL (Sp)	67	73	74	69	283	3108.00	2220.00
	Padraig HARRINGTON (Ire)	71	68	75	69	283	3108.00	2220.00
	Andrew BEAL (Eng)	71	68	74	70	283	3108.00	2220.00
58	Mathias GRÖNBERG (Swe)	72	70	74	68	284	2604.00	1860.00
	Mark ROE (Eng)	73	64	76	71	284	2604.00	1860.00
	Warren BENNETT (Eng)	70	70	74	70	284	2604.00	1860.00
61	José RIVERO (Sp)	67	72	75	71	285	2394.00	1710.00
	Roger WINCHESTER (Eng)	71	67	73	74	285	2394.00	1710.00
63	Scott HENDERSON (Scot)	70	70	73	73	286	2184.00	1560.00
	José Manuel CARRILES (Sp)	68	72	71	75	286	2184.00	1560.00
	Seve BALLESTEROS (Sp)	73	69	73	71	286	2184.00	1560.00
66	Steve WEBSTER (Eng)	68	72	74	73	287	1260.00	900.00
67	Per HAUGSRUD (Nor)	69	71	77	73	290	1257.00	897.86
68	José Manuel LARA (Sp)	71	71	75	75	292	1254.00	895.71

SERGIO GARCIA: first day at the office

HEREDEROS DEL
MARQUES DE RISCAL

OFFICIAL WINE SUPPLIER
TO THE PGA EUROPEAN TOUR

*V*inos de los *H*erederos del *M*arqués de *R*iscal, S.A.

Laurent-Perrier (UK) Ltd
66-68 Chapel Street
Marlow
Buckinghamshire SL7 1DE
Tel: 01628 475 404
Fax: 01628 471 891

Confidence breeds success

Dean Robertson told friends

to back him, and his

first-time win rewarded them well

After becoming the 1999 European Tour's seventh first-time winner in the Fiat and Fila Italian Open at Turin's Circologolf, a jubilant, tongue-in-cheek Dean Robertson remarked: "Mr Janzen must have got a surprise at the quality of the European Tour here this week."

Robertson, the 28-year-old-Scot, former Walker Cup and Eisenhower Trophy amateur, felt 1993 and 1998 US Open champion Janzen might have expected his first outing on the Tour since the 1993 Dutch Open – excluding Open Championships and Ryder Cups – to be a less surprising experience than the eye-opener he received at the strength of the competition and the quality of the golf course and practice facilities.

To his credit "Mr Janzen", who ended tied 66th some 16 strokes behind Robertson, was fully aware of what he faced and had commented before the off: "It's very good for your c.v.

CHAMPION AND CADDIE: "Together we did it"

PADRAIG HARRINGTON: time to enjoy the view

to win outside the US but you can't go anywhere in the world and expect a field to be weak.

"The standard has gone up in Europe thanks to the big five – Sandy Lyle, Seve Ballesteros, Bernhard Langer, Ian Woosnam and Nick Faldo. Like Jack Nicklaus and Tom Watson they have influenced a lot of young players. There are so many good ones in Europe right now, like defending Italian Champion Patrik Sjöland. When he beat Jim Furyk in the Andersen Consulting Match Play Championship everyone took notice."

Janzen, with British caddie Dave Musgrove, who won three majors with Lyle and Ballesteros before helping the American to his second US Open crown, at his side, probably expected José Maria Olazábal, Bernhard Langer and on-form Swedes to prove the men to beat in the 56th Fiat & Fila Italian Open, which offered a record one million euro (£730,132) prize fund.

Mats Lanner, who dramatically regained his Tour "ticket" with victory in the 1998 Madeira Open, was certainly one

FRANCISCO CEA: leader at the half-way stage

SHOT OF THE WEEK

It earned Seve Ballesteros a two at the short 13th – his fourth – after his tee shot finished on a downslope in the rough with a deep bunker between him and the pin and only a few feet of green to work with. His 'parachute' recovery landed the ball so softly it would have stopped only inches past had it not rolled straight into the cup.

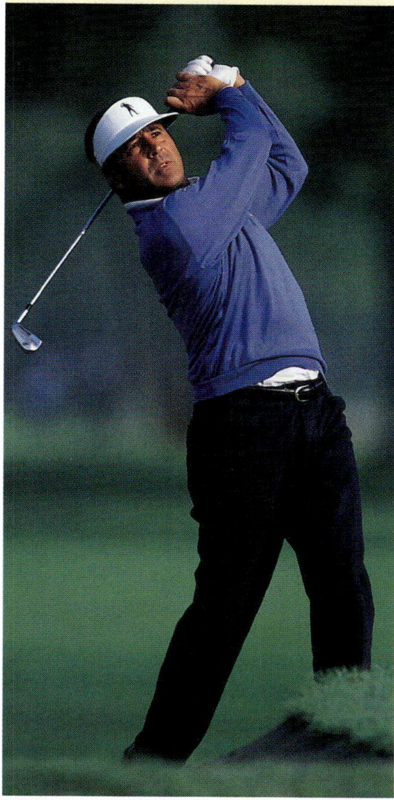

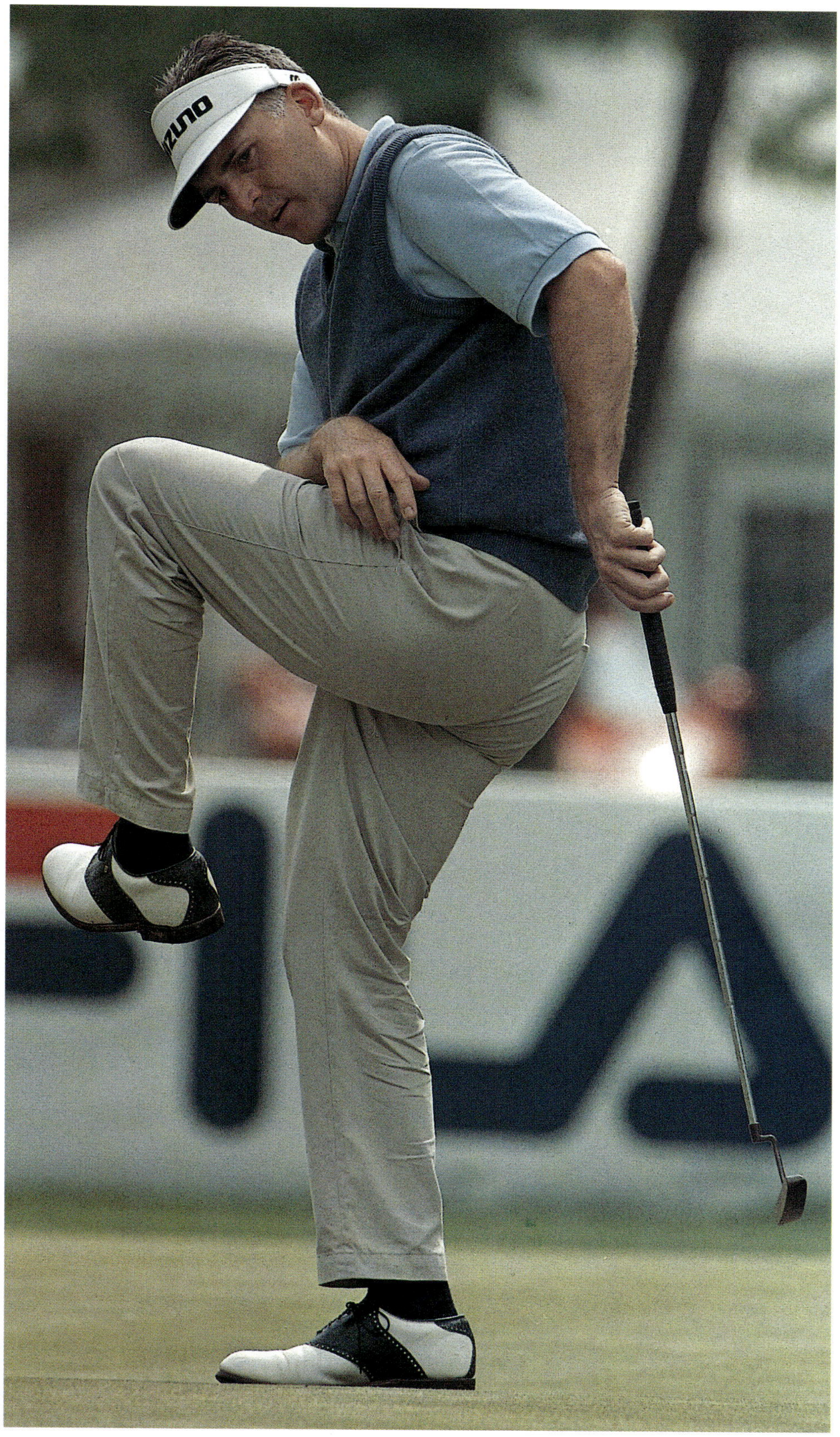

PHILLIP PRICE: Welshman tries "body English"

hot Scandinavian when he opened up with a career best 62, a record for the tree-lined 6,954 yards 'Blu' course, to snatch a three-stroke lead.

But the man from Gothenburg slipped back with 77s on days two and four and although Olazábal, runner-up in the previous two Italian championships to Sjöland and Langer, shrugged off his Masters hang-over with a Sunday 66 and 12 under par 276 to edge a stroke ahead of a resurgent Ballesteros, out in 31 to finish with a 67, he ended no better than third best Spaniard in joint sixth place behind Miguel Angel Jiménez and the young man he coaches on the Costa del Sol, Francisco Cea.

Cea, who pipped Sergio Garcia in a play-off for the 1995 Spanish Amateur title and won the Open de Dijon on the European Challenge Tour the following year, had high hopes of beating the much-vaunted Garcia to a first Tour victory when he opened up 67, 65 but never quite recovered from ending round three with a brace of bogey fives. And that let in Robertson, Padraig Harrington, Russell,

THE COURSE

Englishman John Morrison created the 'Blu' championship course in 1956 amid the rolling acres of the majestic Mandria Park, once the hunting estate of the Savoy royal family.

Against a snow-dropped alpine backdrop the mainly flat layout and its adjacent 'yellow' course wind among centuries-old woods, streams and lakes.

Claydon, Gary Evans and Phillip Price to make it a Britain and Ireland monopoly of the top five spots.

Welshman Price, who had spectacularly holed from 30 yards off the green to eagle the ninth (his 18th) and squeeze among the 80 qualifiers at two under par or better, was the target setter as he fired a career best closing 63.

Claydon finished the week as he had begun it with a 66 and Evans, who had shot 64 on day two of the previous week's Peugeot Open de España and launched his Italian challenge with a 65, wound up with a pair of 68's to match their 15 under par 273 scores.

Meanwhile, Robertson and Harrington, team-mates in the 1993 Walker Cup, were fighting a cliff-hanging duel for the top spot. The 166,660 euro (£119,043) victory cheque finally ended up in the Scotsman's pocket as he covered the first 15 holes in a magical five under par then kept his nerve down the home straight as the Irishman, following birdies at the 14th from 20 feet and 15th, stayed only one behind.

Harrington, 1996 Peugeot Open de España champion, crucially bogeyed the short 16th where Robertson bravely saved par from sand, but then saw his bold putt of five yards for a birdie three at the last nudge him clear of the trio at 13 under for a 111,100 euro runner-up (£79,357) prize. He was gracious in defeat, conceding: "Apart from three putts on the 17th, Dean never put a foot wrong and thoroughly deserved to win."

Despite eight missed cuts on his previous 11 Tour outings Robertson was far from surprised at his breakthrough, admitting: " I told my pals back home to put a few bob on me – they must have got good odds.

" I used to win a lot as an amateur but you win more from other people's mistakes at that level. As a European Tour player you have to win going forward. It's difficult to control the adrenaline and last year at Wentworth in the Volvo PGA Championship, when I had a putt to go two ahead with four to play but lost out to Colin Montgomerie, I didn't have what it took to go ahead and win.

"That was my reference point, more so than finishing second in the Jersey Open in 1995, and it stood me in great stead in Italy. At Wentworth I was fighting the pressure. Today I went with it. I felt nervous but knew that was natural and forced myself to keep going and enjoy it as much as possible. My legs were shaking over the last couple of holes but my caddie, Brian Byrne, kept me calm and I think I handled it all right.

"I've worked very hard with my coach David Whelan – its frightening, how much I've improved my swing. I also capitalised on a bit of advice from my pal Stephen Hendry". He is in the same Ian Doyle management stable and was busy winning a record seventh World Snooker title the same weekend.

"He told me the key to his success was to 'Practise like you play and you will play like you practise' – in other words hit every shot on the range as though it was your last shot in the Open and it becomes a habit."

Winning Tour titles could well become a habit for the confident Scot.

Gordon Richardson

CircoloGolf, Torino, Italy, April 29–May 2, 1999 · Par 72 · Yards 6954

Pos	Name & Country	Rnd 1	Rnd 2	Rnd 3	Rnd 4	Total	Prize Money €	£
1	Dean ROBERTSON (Scot)	70	65	68	68	271	166660.00	119042.86
2	Padraig HARRINGTON (Ire)	68	66	68	70	272	111100.00	79357.14
3	Russell CLAYDON (Eng)	66	68	73	66	273	51666.67	36904.76
	Phillip PRICE (Wal)	71	71	68	63	273	51666.67	36904.76
	Gary EVANS (Eng)	65	72	68	68	273	51666.67	36904.76
6	Miguel Angel JIMÉNEZ (Sp)	68	68	70	68	274	28075.00	20053.57
	Ricardo GONZALEZ (Arg)	71	65	68	70	274	28075.00	20053.57
	Retief GOOSEN (SA)	69	68	72	65	274	28075.00	20053.57
	Francisco CEA (Sp)	67	65	71	71	274	28075.00	20053.57
10	John SENDEN (Aus)	71	66	71	67	275	18520.00	13228.57
	Costantino ROCCA (It)	71	68	68	68	275	18520.00	13228.57
	Gary ORR (Scot)	70	65	72	68	275	18520.00	13228.57
13	Peter MITCHELL (Eng)	67	71	70	68	276	15045.00	10746.43
	Mark MCNULTY (Zim)	69	71	70	66	276	15045.00	10746.43
	José Maria OLAZÁBAL (Sp)	71	69	70	66	276	15045.00	10746.43
	David CARTER (Eng)	68	68	72	68	276	15045.00	10746.43
17	Seve BALLESTEROS (Sp)	70	71	69	67	277	13500.00	9642.86
18	Craig HAINLINE (USA)	71	67	69	71	278	12650.00	9035.71
	Rodger DAVIS (Aus)	69	68	72	69	278	12650.00	9035.71
20	Patrik SJÖLAND (Swe)	67	69	73	70	279	11700.00	8357.14
	Emanuele CANONICA (It)	71	68	70	70	279	11700.00	8357.14
	Olle KARLSSON (Swe)	71	69	69	70	279	11700.00	8357.14
23	Michael CAMPBELL (NZ)	69	70	70	71	280	10050.00	7178.57
	Raphaël JACQUELIN (Fr)	70	72	68	70	280	10050.00	7178.57
	Mathias GRÖNBERG (Swe)	72	70	69	69	280	10050.00	7178.57
	Jeev Milkha SINGH (Ind)	71	69	68	72	280	10050.00	7178.57
	Roger WESSELS (SA)	70	66	72	72	280	10050.00	7178.57
	Peter BAKER (Eng)	72	69	69	70	280	10050.00	7178.57
	Joakim HAEGGMAN (Swe)	71	71	68	70	280	10050.00	7178.57
	Paul EALES (Eng)	72	68	71	69	280	10050.00	7178.57
31	Derrick COOPER (Eng)	66	73	74	68	281	8014.29	5724.29
	Francis VALERA (Sp)	68	74	69	70	281	8014.29	5724.29
	Eduardo ROMERO (Arg)	69	70	70	72	281	8014.29	5724.29
	Jarmo SANDELIN (Swe)	71	67	71	72	281	8014.29	5724.29
	Søren KJELDSEN (Den)	71	69	68	73	281	8014.29	5724.29
	Massimo SCARPA (It)	71	71	65	74	281	8014.29	5724.29
	Roger WINCHESTER (Eng)	72	70	68	71	281	8014.29	5724.29
38	Andrew OLDCORN (Scot)	69	73	69	71	282	6400.00	4571.43
	Bernhard LANGER (Ger)	70	68	73	71	282	6400.00	4571.43
	Greg TURNER (NZ)	68	72	74	68	282	6400.00	4571.43
	Jorge BERENDT (Arg)	69	71	70	72	282	6400.00	4571.43
	Massimo FLORIOLI (It)	71	71	67	73	282	6400.00	4571.43
	Alex CEJKA (Ger)	71	71	68	72	282	6400.00	4571.43
	Mark ROE (Eng)	73	67	71	71	282	6400.00	4571.43
	Marc FARRY (Fr)	71	68	70	73	282	6400.00	4571.43
	David GILFORD (Eng)	71	71	68	72	282	6400.00	4571.43
47	Steen TINNING (Den)	72	70	70	71	283	4800.00	3428.57
	Marcello SANTI (It)	71	68	75	69	283	4800.00	3428.57
	Andrew COLTART (Scot)	69	71	74	69	283	4800.00	3428.57
	Jarrod MOSELEY (Aus)	69	67	75	72	283	4800.00	3428.57
	Mats LANNER (Swe)	62	77	67	77	283	4800.00	3428.57
	Thomas LEVET (Fr)	70	70	72	71	283	4800.00	3428.57
	Soren HANSEN (Den)	69	70	74	70	283	4800.00	3428.57
54	Barry LANE (Eng)	69	73	71	71	284	3600.00	2571.43
	Per NYMAN (Swe)	65	74	74	71	284	3600.00	2571.43
	Anthony WALL (Eng)	71	71	73	69	284	3600.00	2571.43
	António SOBRINHO (Port)	69	72	73	70	284	3600.00	2571.43
	Pierre FULKE (Swe)	71	68	75	70	284	3600.00	2571.43
59	Robert Jan DERKSEN (Hol)	71	71	72	71	285	3000.00	2571.43
	Stephen DODD (Wal)	72	70	73	70	285	3000.00	2571.43
	Daren LEE (Eng)	72	68	74	71	285	3000.00	2571.43
62	Miles TUNNICLIFF (Eng)	72	66	75	73	286	2650.00	1892.86
	Max ANGLERT (Swe)	69	71	75	71	286	2650.00	1892.86
	Jean VAN DE VELDE (Fr)	68	72	74	72	286	2650.00	1892.86
	Thomas GÖGELE (Ger)	72	70	73	71	286	2650.00	1892.86
66	Andrew SHERBORNE (Eng)	71	67	76	73	287	1492.50	1066.07
	Anders HANSEN (Den)	75	67	76	69	287	1492.50	1066.07
	Stephen GALLACHER (Scot)	67	75	74	71	287	1492.50	1066.07
	Robert KARLSSON (Swe)	71	70	73	73	287	1492.50	1066.07
	Lee JANZEN (USA)	72	68	73	74	287	1492.50	1066.07
	Paolo QUIRICI (Swi)	74	68	72	73	287	1492.50	1066.07
72	Steve WEBSTER (Eng)	70	70	76	72	288	1479.00	1056.43
	Clinton WHITELAW (SA)	73	69	74	72	288	1479.00	1056.43
	Diego BORREGO (Sp)	73	68	74	73	288	1479.00	1056.43
75	Scott HENDERSON (Scot)	72	70	77	70	289	1468.50	1048.93
	Pedro LINHART (Sp)	72	69	73	75	289	1468.50	1048.93
	Jim PAYNE (Eng)	70	72	74	73	289	1468.50	1048.93
	Alberto BINAGHI (It)	72	70	75	72	289	1468.50	1048.93
79	Tom GILLIS (USA)	70	72	79	69	290	1461.00	1043.57
80	John MCHENRY (Ire)	70	72	76	74	292	1458.00	1041.43

RUSSELL CLAYDON: impressive finish

Encore L'Entente Cordiale

A challenging new venue but the old

winning ways for South African

Retief Goosen on his return to France

It was a case of many happy returns for Retief Goosen, but not for injured Sam Torrance when the Novotel Perrier Open de France got under way at Golf du Médoc near Bordeaux.

South Africa's Goosen, who captured the title two years earlier at Le Golf National, near Paris, triumphed again after a sudden-death play-off against Greg Turner, of New Zealand. Scotland's Torrance, however, having arrived at Médoc as the defending champion, left for home without hitting a single shot.

Torrance, who led from start to finish to score his emotional 21st career victory in France the previous June, had been troubled by a rib problem most of the season to suffer one of his worst campaign openings in 29 years on the European Tour.

The Scot flew to Bordeaux with high hopes after "some heavy work" the day before with a leading osteopath who advised a programme of intensive

SHOT OF THE WEEK

It had to be Yorkshireman John Mellor's 124 yards wedge shot straight into the cup for a career first hole-in-one at the eighth hole on day one if you don't count Angel Cabrera's 312-yard hit to win his weight in Bordeaux – 76 bottles – in the long driving contest. Sadly Mellor missed out on a Renault Twingo on offer for an ace at the 17th.

JOHN MELLOR: first ace

exercise to strengthen his back. Next morning, however, he felt stiff and sore and was forced to withdraw and rest.

Goosen, too, had grappled with early season injury problems, which forced him to pull out of January's Mercedes Benz - Vodacom South African Open, which he won in 1995. He belatedly discovered he had broken an arm on a skiing holiday in Switzerland over the New Year.

He was out of action for a month and when he returned to the Tour at the Qatar Masters his confidence was at a low ebb. The man whose ten successive wins were the key to South Africa's Alfred Dunhill Cup successes in 1997 and 1998 explained: "I needed to build up my mental strength and I sought the help of Belgian sports psychologist Joss Vantisphout.

"He's walked with me in practice rounds and given me tips on how to stay focused and calm and I owe him a lot. I never got ahead of myself in Bordeaux."

Goosen, who suffered health problems for a time after being struck by lightning in his amateur days, twisted a knee two weeks before teeing off in France. But apart from causing him discomfort when

IAN WOOSNAM: out in 30

he bent to read putts it proved no serious handicap and rounds of 69, 65, 68 and 70 left him tied at 12 under par with Turner, one of the stars of the International Team's 1998 trouncing of the Americans after being called into the Presidents Cup as a "wild card" by captain Peter Thomson.

MARC FARRY: ten birdies for 63

With its wide fairways, fringed with broom and heather, and fast greens swept by the winds off the Atlantic, the Chateaux Course at Golf du Médoc is reminiscent of a Scottish links, with water often an additional hazard. Texan Bill Coore, who built it ten years ago, paid a flying visit to upgrade it for the Novotel Perrier Open de France.

Turner, playing in only his third European Tour event of the year after a two month winter break, led at halfway after rounds of 67 and 65. First day pacesetter Stephen Dodd, of Wales, followed a 65 with a 76, and the New Zealander looked a likely winner when Masters champion José Maria Olazábal and compatriot Severiano Ballesteros missed the cut. Ian Woosnam trailed seven behind after shooting 71, 68.

But Woosnam sped out in 30 next day en route to a 66 to close to within three strokes of leaders Turner, Goosen and Marc Farry, whose ten-birdie second day 63 raised his hopes of becoming the first Frenchman to take the title since Jean Garaialde 30 years before at Saint-Nom-La-Bretèche.

Beset by putting problems, however, Woosnam was unable to mount a

GREG TURNER: "I gave him a bit of a fright"

serious last day challenge and Farry's hopes were dashed by a quadruple bogey seven after two visits to the water at the short fifth.

Goosen, whose silky swing is admired as much as that of his great friend since boyhood, Ernie Els, looked to be comfortable when he moved three shots ahead with five holes to play. But Turner matched his birdie four at the 14th, then snapped up birdies at the 15th and 16th, where Goosen took five, and suddenly they were level.

Indeed, it took a brave up and down from sand at the 72nd to earn Goosen a play-off and another at the same hole in extra time to 'stay alive'. When they played the dog-leg 18th a third time it was Turner who missed the green and Goosen pounced to scoop top prize of 141,660 euro (£101,185).

Turner, who earned 94,440 euro (£67,457), admitted: "I struggled with the putter all day and at the end came up one putt short. Retief came back after I gave him a bit of a fright. Good on him."

The pair ended two ahead of Santiago Luna and José Coceres. One further back were Woosnam, Jorge Berendt and 46-year-old Irishman Eamonn Darcy, whose best finish since his fourth place in the 1995 Volvo Scandinavian Masters netted him a cheque for 30,416 euro (£21,726). He explained: "After experimenting with two different 'broomhandles' and Bernhard Langer's split handed grip I acquired a new 'Teardrop' putter from a rep in Bordeaux this week – I owe him a drink."

It was drinks all round on Retief Goosen among the Chateaux of Margaux, Saint-Julien, Paulliac and Saint-Estephe after a vintage third European Tour triumph.

Gordon Richardson

EAMONN DARCY: change of putter, change of fortune

GOLF DU MÉDOC, BORDEAUX, FRANCE, MAY 6–9 1999 · PAR 71 · YARDS 6909

Pos	Name & Country	Rnd 1	Rnd 2	Rnd 3	Rnd 4	Total	Prize Money €	Prize Money £
1	Retief GOOSEN (SA)	69	65	68	70	272	141660.00	101185.71
2	Greg TURNER (NZ)	67	65	70	70	272	94440.00	67457.14
3	Santiago LUNA (Sp)	67	72	67	69	275	47855.00	34182.14
	José COCERES (Arg)	69	69	66	71	275	47855.00	34182.14
5	Ian WOOSNAM (Wal)	71	68	66	71	276	30416.67	21726.19
	Eamonn DARCY (Ire)	66	70	72	68	276	30416.67	21726.19
	Jorge BERENDT (Arg)	69	67	68	72	276	30416.67	21726.19
8	Marc FARRY (Fr)	70	63	69	75	277	18215.00	13010.71
	Marc PENDARIES (Fr)	67	72	68	70	277	18215.00	13010.71
	Andrew SHERBORNE (Eng)	66	67	70	74	277	18215.00	13010.71
	Emanuele CANONICA (It)	73	69	66	69	277	18215.00	13010.71
12	Massimo SCARPA (It)	68	74	67	70	279	13152.00	9394.29
	Diego BORREGO (Sp)	71	70	67	71	279	13152.00	9394.29
	Jamie SPENCE (Eng)	68	72	66	73	279	13152.00	9394.29
	Eduardo ROMERO (Arg)	68	70	72	69	279	13152.00	9394.29
	Ross MCFARLANE (Eng)	71	68	67	73	279	13152.00	9394.29
17	Des SMYTH (Ire)	70	69	71	70	280	10625.00	7589.29
	Jean Francois REMESY (Fr)	66	68	75	71	280	10625.00	7589.29
	Wayne RILEY (Aus)	75	66	72	67	280	10625.00	7589.29
	Anders HANSEN (Den)	70	68	70	72	280	10625.00	7589.29
	Anders FORSBRAND (Swe)	68	74	70	68	280	10625.00	7589.29
22	Jarmo SANDELIN (Swe)	72	68	71	70	281	9307.50	6648.21
	Tomas Jesus MUÑOZ (Sp)	69	71	69	72	281	9307.50	6648.21
	Peter MITCHELL (Eng)	68	71	69	73	281	9307.50	6648.21
	Christian CÉVAER (Fr)	68	70	69	74	281	9307.50	6648.21
26	Alexandre BALICKI (Fr)	69	72	68	73	282	7788.13	5562.95
	Angel CABRERA (Arg)	70	66	70	76	282	7788.13	5562.95
	Jeremy ROBINSON (Eng)	67	68	71	76	282	7788.13	5562.95
	Gustavo ROJAS (Arg)	68	72	73	69	282	7788.13	5562.95
	Costantino ROCCA (It)	69	73	71	69	282	7788.13	5562.95
	Mark ROE (Eng)	69	69	70	74	282	7788.13	5562.95
	Bob MAY (USA)	66	72	71	73	282	7788.13	5562.95
	Daren LEE (Eng)	66	73	69	74	282	7788.13	5562.95
34	Roger CHAPMAN (Eng)	68	74	69	72	283	6630.00	4735.71
	Richard GREEN (Aus)	72	68	73	70	283	6630.00	4735.71
	Roger WESSELS (SA)	68	69	71	75	283	6630.00	4735.71
37	Stephen GALLACHER (Scot)	71	70	69	74	284	5440.00	3885.71
	Nick O'HERN (Aus)	69	68	75	72	284	5440.00	3885.71
	Jorgen AKER (Swe)	73	69	70	72	284	5440.00	3885.71
	Gregory HAVRET (AM) (Fr)	70	68	77	69	284		
	Simon WAKEFIELD (Eng)	69	68	72	75	284	5440.00	3885.71
	Jeev Milkha SINGH (Ind)	68	69	73	74	284	5440.00	3885.71
	Nicolas JOAKIMIDES (Fr)	70	69	71	74	284	5440.00	3885.71
	Kalle BRINK (Swe)	71	71	70	72	284	5440.00	3885.71
	Johan RYSTRÖM (Swe)	70	70	72	72	284	5440.00	3885.71
	Lucas PARSONS (Aus)	78	64	70	72	284	5440.00	3885.71
	Michele REALE (It)	72	68	70	74	284	5440.00	3885.71
	Brian NELSON (USA)	69	73	71	71	284	5440.00	3885.71
48	Carl SUNESON (Sp)	68	74	69	74	285	4080.00	2914.29
	Clinton WHITELAW (SA)	74	68	70	73	285	4080.00	2914.29
	Sebastien DELAGRANGE (Fr)	69	69	74	73	285	4080.00	2914.29
	Howard CLARK (Eng)	73	68	73	71	285	4080.00	2914.29
	Carl WATTS (Eng)	71	67	72	75	285	4080.00	2914.29
53	Fernando ROCA (Sp)	71	69	70	76	286	3006.88	2147.77
	Henrik NYSTROM (Swe)	69	71	70	76	286	3006.88	2147.77
	Jesus Maria ARRUTI (Sp)	68	74	74	70	286	3006.88	2147.77
	Andrew SANDYWELL (Eng)	68	70	74	74	286	3006.88	2147.77
	Morten BACKHAUSEN (Den)	71	68	71	76	286	3006.88	2147.77
	Frédéric CUPILLARD (Fr)	72	69	75	70	286	3006.88	2147.77
	Andrew RAITT (Eng)	70	69	74	73	286	3006.88	2147.77
	Richard BOXALL (Eng)	70	72	70	74	286	3006.88	2147.77
61	Stephen BENNETT (Eng)	67	71	74	75	287	2380.00	1700.00
	Pascal EDMOND (Fr)	70	72	69	76	287	2380.00	1700.00
	Ian HUTCHINGS (SA)	67	75	72	73	287	2380.00	1700.00
64	Jonathan LOMAS (Eng)	71	70	73	74	288	1630.20	1164.43
	Andrew BEAL (Eng)	69	72	72	75	288	1630.20	1164.43
	Brian DAVIS (Eng)	73	69	71	75	288	1630.20	1164.43
	Stephen DODD (Wal)	65	76	71	76	288	1630.20	1164.43
	Domingo HOSPITAL (Sp)	70	69	74	75	288	1630.20	1164.43
69	Steve ALKER (NZ)	71	71	72	75	289	1264.50	903.21
	Jim PAYNE (Eng)	70	72	73	74	289	1264.50	903.21
71	John MCHENRY (Ire)	67	70	75	78	290	1254.00	895.71
	Benoit TEILLERIA (Fr)	70	70	69	81	290	1254.00	895.71
	Nick LUDWELL (Eng)	76	66	75	73	290	1254.00	895.71
	Olle KARLSSON (Swe)	71	68	72	79	290	1254.00	895.71
	Carlos LARRAIN (Ven)	71	71	75	73	290	1254.00	895.71
76	Scott HENDERSON (Scot)	69	72	76	74	291	1245.00	889.29
	Oliver DAVID (AM) (Fr)	71	70	74	77	292		
77	Robert LEE (Eng)	70	68	76	81	295	1242.00	887.14

JOSÉ MARIA OLAZÁBAL: glum day at the office

Gifted and awesome

Colin Montgomerie brilliantly
lived up to the star billing
given him at The Oxfordshire

*B*efore he embarked on the final round of the Benson and Hedges International Open with Colin Montgomerie, José Maria Olazábal spoke for many of his fellow professionals when he said of his long-time friend and rival: "It looks like we are just average workers, and he's the one who's gifted." Eighteen holes later, after Montgomerie had won the 29-year-old title for the first time, Olazábal, the reigning Masters champion, described him as "awesome".

Montgomerie had been blown off course at The Oxfordshire in three of the previous four years when in contention, twice finishing with rounds in the 80s, but this time, he made no mistake. His trademark consistency was relentless. Three bogey-free rounds and an unerringly accurate driver created numerous birdie opportunities, and although his putter was not as well-behaved as he wanted it to be, Montgomerie still acknowledged that his performance over the four days was his most consistent ever.

Remarkably, it was achieved after a complete battery-charging break of three weeks, during which he never picked up a club, not even ten minutes practice putting on the carpet at home. "In that respect, I'm possibly unique," he admitted. "I don't give myself the opportunity to get stale, though I'm not saying what's right for me is right for everyone else."

Leading by one shot from Olazábal going into the final round, Montgomerie's

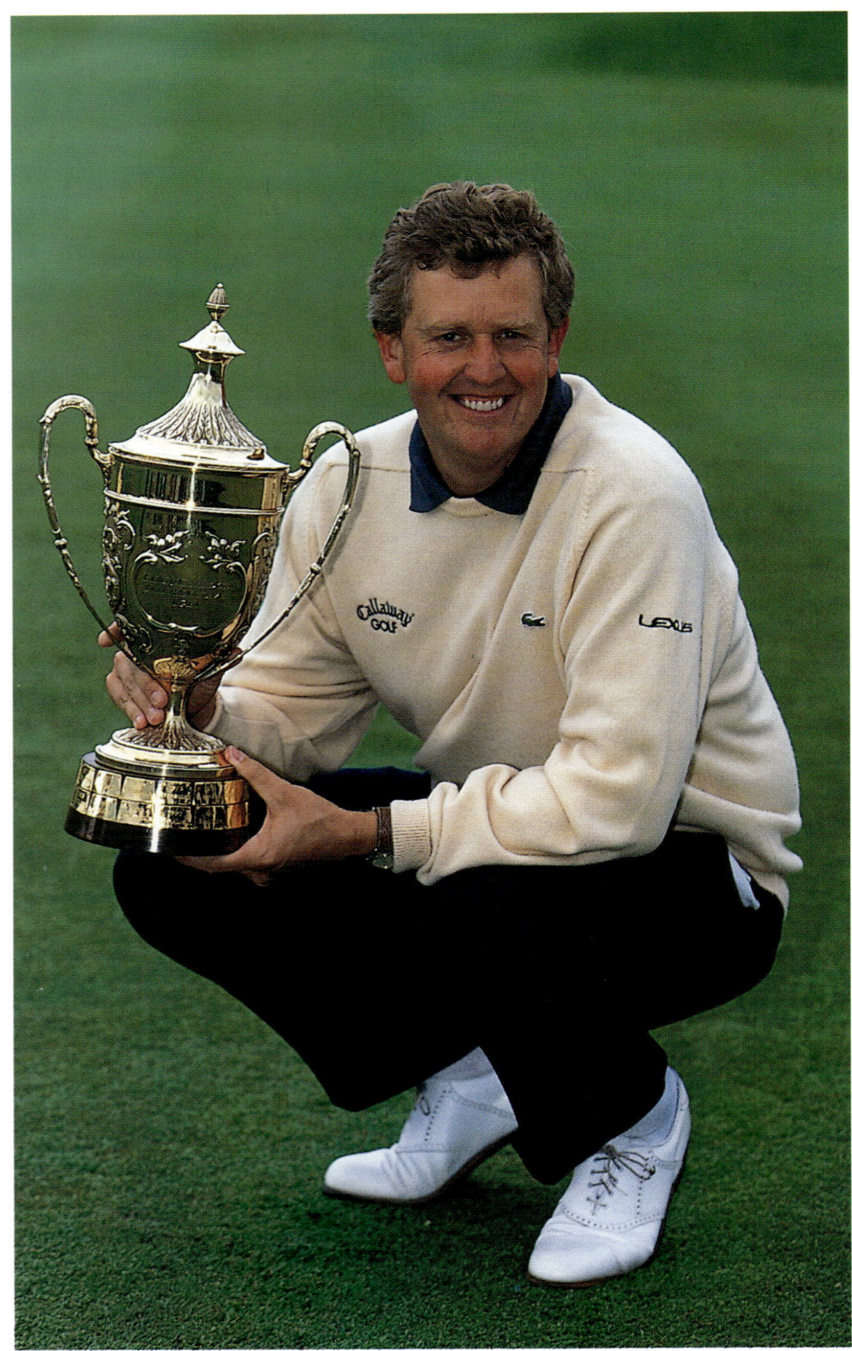

PER-ULRIK JOHANSSON: four birdies and an eagle in succession

three-stroke victory was sealed on the fairway at the pivotal par five 585-yard 17th.

Unaware that his closest challenger, Angel Cabrera, had bogeyed the 18th, Montgomerie believed he needed a birdie to provide him with a two-shot cushion up the last. With the lake yawning in front of him and the breeze at his back, Montgomerie had a carry of 252 yards from a slightly downhill lie. The three-wood "came right out of the middle of the bat", pitched 260 yards, set up a birdie, and increased the Scot's lead to three.

"I put it in the same category as my driver off the fairway to win in Dubai in 1996," said Montgomerie who, at that point, had amassed 18 European Tour victories.

Cabrera was certain he needed to birdie the last to give himself a chance of becoming the latest first-time winner on Tour, but his six iron from the fairway found the bunker to the right of the green. "Still, no worries," he said, with a cheery smile. "This is the best I've played and it's been a great week."

The powerful Argentine shared second place with the halfway leader Per-Ulrik Johansson. The strikingly-attired Swede had eclipsed his playing partner Montgomerie on the second day with a 65.

NICK FALDO: building on belief

ANGEL CABRERA: great week

THE COURSE

Colin Montgomerie described The Oxfordshire as "the best conditioned course in England at this time of year". Rees Jones's design, which offers some sweeping views across the county, is demanding off the tee, and requires the use of every club in the bag, especially when, as in this year's tournament, the wind changes direction. The par five 17th, with its intimidating second shot over water, if braved, once again had a crucial bearing on the outcome.

JOSÉ MARIA OLAZÁBAL: generous praise for Montgomerie

It included a run of four birdies and an eagle in five holes from the seventh. Such was his golden touch with the putter that when he was faced with a putt of ten feet for par on the 12th, Montgomerie suggested he need not bother putting. Sure enough, the ball disappeared – Johansson's sixth single putt in a row.

Miguel Angel Jiménez strengthened his challenge for Ryder Cup selection by finishing tied fourth. He had set the first round pace with a course record-equalling 65, along with Phillip Price. The Spaniard admitted that by playing at The Oxfordshire he had missed the chance of revving up his beloved red Ferrari 550 in a Ferrari Race Club day at Jerez. Another 500 Ryder Cup points were ample compensation.

The crowds at The Oxfordshire also enjoyed strong performances by three more of Europe's major championship winners. Severiano Ballesteros, Nick Faldo and Sandy Lyle were all well-placed at halfway, with Faldo buoyed by the belief that he was starting to hit the ball more solidly than for some time. Lyle, too, had noticed some green shoots of recovery after an arid spell.

The round of the week, though, belonged to Jeremy Robinson. He was a last-minute replacement for the injured Alex Cejka and his course record 64 in the final round lifted him into sixth place. Mind you, he had quite an incentive on the Sunday, as he had to miss his son Tom's christening. The ceremony, which had already been postponed three times, took place at 11.30am. Robinson confessed afterwards that he glanced at his watch just before he rolled in a putt of 15 feet to birdie the last. It was 11.30am.

Rob Nothman

THE OXFORDSHIRE G.C., THAME, ENGLAND, MAY 13–16, 1999 • PAR 72 • YARDS 7205

Pos	Name & Country	Rnd 1	Rnd 2	Rnd 3	Rnd 4	Total	Prize Money €	£
1	Colin MONTGOMERIE (Scot)	68	66	71	68	273	186670.00	133335.71
2	Angel CABRERA (Arg)	69	67	71	69	276	97200.00	69428.57
	Per-Ulrik JOHANSSON (Swe)	68	65	74	69	276	97200.00	69428.57
4	Miguel Angel JIMÉNEZ (Sp)	65	72	72	68	277	51800.00	37000.00
	Diego BORREGO (Sp)	74	67	66	70	277	51800.00	37000.00
6	Jeremy ROBINSON (Eng)	73	67	74	64	278	39200.00	28000.00
7	Jean VAN DE VELDE (Fr)	71	70	68	70	279	22276.89	15912.06
	Eamonn DARCY (Ire)	72	68	68	71	279	22276.89	15912.06
	Bob MAY (USA)	71	70	68	70	279	22276.89	15912.06
	Per NYMAN (Swe)	74	66	73	66	279	22276.89	15912.06
	Nick FALDO (Eng)	68	69	73	69	279	22276.89	15912.06
	Eduardo ROMERO (Arg)	71	68	73	67	279	22276.89	15912.06
	Bernhard LANGER (Ger)	68	72	68	71	279	22276.89	15912.06
	Patrik SJÖLAND (Swe)	69	70	71	69	279	22276.89	15912.06
	Richard GREEN (Aus)	72	69	70	68	279	22276.89	15912.06
16	Jonathan LOMAS (Eng)	71	67	71	71	280	14797.50	10569.64
	Ian WOOSNAM (Wal)	71	70	71	68	280	14797.50	10569.64
	Padraig HARRINGTON (Ire)	70	71	71	68	280	14797.50	10569.64
	José Maria OLAZÁBAL (Sp)	70	67	69	74	280	14797.50	10569.64
20	Paul MCGINLEY (Ire)	72	67	70	72	281	12096.00	8640.00
	Phillip PRICE (Wal)	65	70	72	74	281	12096.00	8640.00
	Emanuele CANONICA (It)	71	70	71	69	281	12096.00	8640.00
	Darren CLARKE (N.Ire)	70	71	71	69	281	12096.00	8640.00
	Dean ROBERTSON (Scot)	72	69	72	68	281	12096.00	8640.00
	Gary EVANS (Eng)	72	67	71	71	281	12096.00	8640.00
	Rodger DAVIS (Aus)	72	69	72	68	281	12096.00	8640.00
	Mathias GRÖNBERG (Swe)	72	69	68	72	281	12096.00	8640.00
	Anders FORSBRAND (Swe)	70	70	69	72	281	12096.00	8640.00
29	Peter O'MALLEY (Aus)	71	69	70	72	282	9912.00	7080.00
	Paul AFFLECK (Wal)	71	69	69	73	282	9912.00	7080.00
	Stephen LEANEY (Aus)	70	71	72	69	282	9912.00	7080.00
	Soren HANSEN (Den)	69	68	71	74	282	9912.00	7080.00
33	Andrew SHERBORNE (Eng)	69	72	66	76	283	8624.00	6160.00
	Roger WINCHESTER (Eng)	71	71	71	70	283	8624.00	6160.00
	Gary ORR (Scot)	70	70	72	71	283	8624.00	6160.00
	Seve BALLESTEROS (Sp)	70	71	69	73	283	8624.00	6160.00
	Marc FARRY (Fr)	68	72	74	69	283	8624.00	6160.00
	Barry LANE (Eng)	68	70	73	72	283	8624.00	6160.00
39	Peter MITCHELL (Eng)	69	71	67	77	284	7056.00	5040.00
	John SENDEN (Aus)	72	68	75	69	284	7056.00	5040.00
	Fredrik LINDGREN (Swe)	70	69	69	76	284	7056.00	5040.00
	Sandy LYLE (Scot)	69	70	72	73	284	7056.00	5040.00
	Andrew RAITT (Eng)	73	68	70	73	284	7056.00	5040.00
	Andrew COLTART (Scot)	72	66	72	74	284	7056.00	5040.00
	Santiago LUNA (Sp)	71	70	71	72	284	7056.00	5040.00
	Stephen ALLAN (Aus)	70	71	72	71	284	7056.00	5040.00
47	Andrew BEAL (Eng)	70	70	68	77	285	5712.00	4080.00
	Stephen FIELD (Eng)	70	71	72	72	285	5712.00	4080.00
	Richard BOXALL (Eng)	71	71	76	67	285	5712.00	4080.00
	Miguel Angel MARTIN (Sp)	70	70	71	74	285	5712.00	4080.00
51	Andrew OLDCORN (Scot)	70	72	70	74	286	4592.00	3280.00
	Søren KJELDSEN (Den)	71	70	74	71	286	4592.00	3280.00
	Ignacio GARRIDO (Sp)	70	72	71	73	286	4592.00	3280.00
	Robert KARLSSON (Swe)	70	69	72	75	286	4592.00	3280.00
	Russell CLAYDON (Eng)	69	73	73	71	286	4592.00	3280.00
	Christopher HANELL (Swe)	74	65	75	72	286	4592.00	3280.00
	Adam FRAYNE (AM) (Eng)	72	69	74	71	286		
57	Olle KARLSSON (Swe)	72	69	77	69	287	3556.00	2540.00
	Greg TURNER (NZ)	71	69	73	74	287	3556.00	2540.00
	Olivier EDMOND (Fr)	74	67	72	74	287	3556.00	2540.00
	Roger WESSELS (SA)	67	71	75	74	287	3556.00	2540.00
61	Tony JOHNSTONE (Zim)	69	72	72	75	288	3248.00	2320.00
62	Greg OWEN (Eng)	74	68	75	72	289	3136.00	2240.00
63	Francis VALERA (Sp)	69	70	73	78	290	3024.00	2160.00
64	Van PHILLIPS (Eng)	70	71	74	76	291	2912.00	2080.00
65	Roger CHAPMAN (Eng)	71	71	77	78	297	2800.00	2000.00

IF YOUR LONGEST DRIVE IS STILL NOT LONG ENOUGH...
YOU'RE READY.
INTRODUCING...
ADAMS™ SC SERIES™ TITANIUM DRIVERS
THE DRIVE REDEFINED™

ADAMS™ SC Series
FALDO
818 FC
TRANS-BETA FORGED TITANIUM

Four Models, Each Designed for a Specific Swing Type...
Introducing the Adams SC Series Titanium Drivers. Not one driver. Four incredible drivers. Each model finely tuned to dramatically reduce and control distance-robbing spin. The spin that creates your slice. The spin that creates your hook. Even straight hitters benefit from the SC Series. Not only will the SC Series redefine the driver category just like Adams Tight Lies® redefined fairway woods, it will redefine your perception of distance.

Superior Spin Control for More Distance...
With painstaking precision, we milled premium Trans-Beta Forged Titanium to exact tolerances...minutely varying the asymmetry across the face. By doing so, we discovered golf's version of the Holy Grail: the first and only series of high performance drivers delivering superior spin control resulting in longer drives. Much longer. An average of six to nineteen yards longer than the three leading drivers tested.

Only from Adams...
These intricate, patent-pending designs cannot be found in any other driver made. The Adams SC Series Titanium Drivers, not bigger, not smaller, redefined.

For more information call Adams Golf
0181 947 6555

Choose the Adams SC Series Driver designed to fit your swing...

824 FC+
818FC
808HC
814N
TRANS-BETA FORGED TITANIUM

SLICE CONTROL
824 FC+
FADE CONTROL
818 FC
HOOK CONTROL
808 HC
NEUTRAL
814 N

Adams Superior Spin Control Technology = Longer Drives

ADAMS®
LEADING BY DESIGN™

Tigermania bites deep

Heidelberg falls for the magic

and diplomacy of Tiger Woods

prowling to a three-shot victory

There was a magnificent cast for the Deutsche Bank - SAP Open TPC of Europe, but even the likes of Darren Clarke, Ernie Els, Bernhard Langer, Colin Montgomerie, Jesper Parnevik and Nick Price were compelled on this occasion to play supporting roles.

From the moment he landed in Germany aboard a 14-seater jet, loaned from the Orlando Magic basketball team, Tiger Woods was to produce a performance that smacked of such character that even those world-class stars assembled at St. Leon Rot could not halt him from moving centre stage and dominating the headlines.

For months leading up to the event, publicity had centred upon the 1997 Masters champion's first appearance in a stroke-play event in mainland Europe. "See Tiger Woods Live" was the exhortation to the residents of a region that had never before staged a professional golf tournament of comparable size.

But, as anyone who has followed the fickle fortunes of the royal and ancient game knows, there is no guarantee that any player will compete to his capability on a given occasion. No matter how big the star he cannot simply turn on the style like Luciano Pavarotti, Bruce Springsteen or Bette Midler to delight the adoring fans.

Yet somehow Woods did. Whatever the spectators, who filled the flat, testing course to capacity, were expecting they got in abundance on the outskirts of the university city of Heidelberg. Woods provided an educated performance for all, exciting as only he can, and revealed just what all the fuss has been about. What must he have done for the golf industry in Germany? Judging from the regular lapses in normal course etiquette many spectators were new to the sport and must have taken away the most favourable impression. It was good for the game, good for golf in Germany.

Not only did Woods give a memorable demonstration of what he does best, but he showed that he is also a mature 23-year-old off the course. Having successfully sidestepped a tricky question at the pre-tournament press conference on his impressions of Germany, he carefully avoided criticising the locals, who clicked cameras or made distracting noises, during his opening round 69. He explained: "The German public was very receptive and we had complimentary applause when we hit good shots. At least cell phones aren't a problem like they are in the States. Here it's just cameras."

Even so Woods, despite the fanfare arrival, was forced on day one to accept the supporting role himself as Scotland's Gary Orr, a gifted player running into form, and Els swept ahead with superb opening scores of 66. Els had taken five weeks off to recover from a final round of 80 at the Masters Tournament, settle into his new home at Wentworth and recharge his batteries. Having started as if bursting with energy, he was slowed by a second round 73 and eventually finished tied fifth, seven shots behind the winner.

The arrival of a swirling wind in Saturday's second round over the German Bank Holiday weekend proved to be just the challenge that Woods needed. While many faltered, the American's joint best-of-the-day 68 took him into a lead he was never to relinquish. Apart from the four birdie putts on the front nine which sent him surging to the head of the field Woods displayed an admirable capacity for escaping from trouble, repeatedly holing out single putts to save par and keep his score together. His only blemish came at the 18th, where he drove into the water, took a penalty drop and hit an excellent recovery to 15 feet but, for once, failed to hole out. With that he took a two-shot advantage into the third round ahead of Els, Parnevik and Jarmo Sandelin. Whenever his challengers closed the gap, he would pull away again and, like a tiger in the jungle, remain just out of reach.

Now Woods had to prove his front-running ability to the German spectators. On Sunday he began the third round by holing a putt of 30 feet for an eagle, proceeded to miss several shorter ones and then signed off in style by holing from 20 feet for birdie on the 18th, and another 68.

GARY ORR: running into form

RETIEF GOOSEN: snow-boarding break

ERNIE ELS: back from recharging batteries

Tiger Woods was in no doubt that the 464 yards 12th hole provided the key to his victory. Over the four rounds he played the testing par four in one under par. But it was his recovery on the final day which left the most indelible impression. After pulling his two iron tee shot into the rough, he hacked out with a nine iron leaving himself 50 yards from the pin and struck an immaculate pitch to two feet to save par. "It was a huge turning point," said Woods, who maintained his three-shot advantage to eventually cruise to victory.

By then two Englishmen, Brian Davis and Peter Baker, both with rounds of 66, had moved into contention. They were three shots back, sharing second place, but both were thirsty for the challenge.

What is more, Woods knew that either one could overhaul him and deny him the victory he also craved, and that behind him others had queued up to attack given the chance. Then there was Price. He had swept through the pack with a third round of 65, and would continue his grand prix-like charge with another 65 that took him with a phenomenal 14 under par score for the last 36 holes from the cut line to third place.

Woods might have been seriously challenged had it not been for a remarkable shot which demonstrated how his all-round game has developed in the past two years. After driving into the rough on the 464 yards 12th hole, he could only blast his recovery back on to the fairway. But from 50 yards he hit the perfect pitch to two feet to save par – and remain three ahead.

The St. Leon Rot course near Heidelberg won a vote of approval from most of the players. Built only two years ago, the flat, parkland layout of 7,236 yards with water hazards and numerous bunkers provided a creditable test. Length off the tee was an asset, as Woods showed by averaging 304 yards, but those who kept the ball in play and hit the greens were rewarded by some smooth putting surfaces that won high praise.

JESPER PARNEVIK: birdies, eagles, now a swan

In the end Retief Goosen, fully recovered from the broken arm he suffered snow-boarding in the winter, came closest to propelling Woods from centre stage with four birdies in the final six holes which gave him a 66 and a four-round total of 12 under par 276.

But there was no denying Woods his glory. A third successive 68 gave him a three-shot victory, his second of the year and his first on European soil. As expected he topped the driving statistics, averaging 304 yards over the four days. But it was his accuracy in hitting more greens in regulation – 81.9 per cent – which assured him of victory in a week when the stars of world golf shone, but one more brightly than the others.

Peter Higgs

St. Leon Rot, Heidelberg, Germany, May 21–24, 1999 · Par 72 · Yards 7236

Pos	Name & Country	Rnd 1	Rnd 2	Rnd 3	Rnd 4	Total	Prize Money €	Prize Money £
1	Tiger WOODS (USA)	69	68	68	68	273	280000.00	200000.00
2	Retief GOOSEN (SA)	73	69	68	66	276	186650.00	133321.43
3	Nick PRICE (Zim)	71	76	65	65	277	105160.00	75114.29
4	Peter BAKER (Eng)	69	73	66	71	279	84000.00	60000.00
5	Ernie ELS (SA)	66	73	70	71	280	64980.00	46414.29
	Brian DAVIS (Eng)	69	73	66	72	280	64980.00	46414.29
7	Miguel Angel JIMÉNEZ (Sp)	71	72	70	68	281	40875.00	29196.43
	Jarmo SANDELIN (Swe)	70	69	73	69	281	40875.00	29196.43
	Darren CLARKE (N.Ire)	70	73	69	69	281	40875.00	29196.43
	Barry LANE (Eng)	73	68	70	70	281	40875.00	29196.43
11	Peter SENIOR (Aus)	72	72	72	66	282	27440.60	19600.43
	Bernhard LANGER (Ger)	71	74	70	67	282	27440.60	19600.43
	Bob MAY (USA)	70	71	71	70	282	27440.60	19600.43
	Jesper PARNEVIK (Swe)	71	68	71	72	282	27440.60	19600.43
	Robert KARLSSON (Swe)	72	71	67	72	282	27440.60	19600.43
16	Gary ORR (Scot)	66	74	71	72	283	23671.00	16907.86
17	John MELLOR (Eng)	73	68	76	67	284	21728.00	15520.00
	John SENDEN (Aus)	72	69	74	69	284	21728.00	15520.00
	Jean VAN DE VELDE (Fr)	68	73	70	73	284	21728.00	15520.00
20	Marc FARRY (Fr)	69	73	73	70	285	19656.00	14040.00
	Colin MONTGOMERIE (Scot)	71	70	71	73	285	19656.00	14040.00
	Sergio GARCIA (Sp)	70	70	71	74	285	19656.00	14040.00
23	David GILFORD (Eng)	70	75	72	69	286	16884.00	12060.00
	Stephen ALLAN (Aus)	71	75	72	68	286	16884.00	12060.00
	Jeev Milkha SINGH (Ind)	74	73	73	66	286	16884.00	12060.00
	Peter O'MALLEY (Aus)	70	72	74	70	286	16884.00	12060.00
	Roger WINCHESTER (Eng)	72	70	74	70	286	16884.00	12060.00
	Stephen LEANEY (Aus)	71	73	72	70	286	16884.00	12060.00
	Diego BORREGO (Sp)	74	68	73	71	286	16884.00	12060.00
	Ian GARBUTT (Eng)	73	70	72	71	286	16884.00	12060.00
31	Steve WEBSTER (Eng)	72	70	74	71	287	14364.00	10260.00
	David CARTER (Eng)	73	72	68	74	287	14364.00	10260.00
33	Soren HANSEN (Den)	72	74	71	71	288	13104.00	9360.00
	José COCERES (Arg)	73	70	74	71	288	13104.00	9360.00
	Jamie SPENCE (Eng)	75	72	71	70	288	13104.00	9360.00
	Anthony WALL (Eng)	74	72	72	70	288	13104.00	9360.00
	Roger CHAPMAN (Eng)	70	74	70	74	288	13104.00	9360.00
38	Greg TURNER (NZ)	73	74	70	72	289	11592.00	8280.00
	Raphaël JACQUELIN (Fr)	73	70	74	72	289	11592.00	8280.00
	Padraig HARRINGTON (Ire)	73	73	70	73	289	11592.00	8280.00
	Roger WESSELS (SA)	77	70	69	73	289	11592.00	8280.00
42	David HOWELL (Eng)	72	70	74	74	290	9912.00	7080.00
	Patrik SJÖLAND (Swe)	69	73	74	74	290	9912.00	7080.00
	Jeremy ROBINSON (Eng)	70	73	73	74	290	9912.00	7080.00
	Alex CEJKA (Ger)	69	75	72	74	290	9912.00	7080.00
	Gary EVANS (Eng)	74	72	70	74	290	9912.00	7080.00
	Ian WOOSNAM (Wal)	73	71	71	75	290	9912.00	7080.00
48	Stephen FIELD (Eng)	76	71	70	74	291	8232.00	5880.00
	Derrick COOPER (Eng)	71	74	74	72	291	8232.00	5880.00
	Mark ROE (Eng)	73	72	76	70	291	8232.00	5880.00
	Silvio GRAPPASONNI (It)	74	69	72	76	291	8232.00	5880.00
52	Eduardo ROMERO (Arg)	72	74	73	73	292	7056.00	5040.00
	Heinz Peter THÜL (Ger)	74	73	73	72	292	7056.00	5040.00
	Mark O'MEARA (USA)	71	73	76	72	292	7056.00	5040.00
55	Christopher HANELL (Swe)	71	75	72	75	293	6048.00	4320.00
	Warren BENNETT (Eng)	72	74	74	73	293	6048.00	4320.00
	Per HAUGSRUD (Nor)	73	72	75	73	293	6048.00	4320.00
58	Van PHILLIPS (Eng)	72	73	74	75	294	5040.00	3600.00
	Andrew OLDCORN (Scot)	72	73	74	75	294	5040.00	3600.00
	Domingo HOSPITAL (Sp)	73	74	73	74	294	5040.00	3600.00
	Ricardo GONZALEZ (Arg)	75	72	74	73	294	5040.00	3600.00
	Thomas GÖGELE (Ger)	70	77	69	78	294	5040.00	3600.00
63	Dean ROBERTSON (Scot)	71	76	72	76	295	3906.00	2790.00
	Paul MCGINLEY (Ire)	70	74	76	75	295	3906.00	2790.00
	Jorge BERENDT (Arg)	71	75	76	73	295	3906.00	2790.00
	Mark MOULAND (Wal)	74	73	79	69	295	3906.00	2790.00
67	Angel CABRERA (Arg)	73	73	73	77	296	2512.50	1794.64
	Des SMYTH (Ire)	74	69	77	76	296	2512.50	1794.64
	Thomas LEVET (Fr)	73	73	77	73	296	2512.50	1794.64
	Massimo SCARPA (It)	71	76	77	72	296	2512.50	1794.64
71	Eamonn DARCY (Ire)	73	74	75	75	297	2503.50	1788.21
	Clinton WHITELAW (SA)	71	75	77	74	297	2503.50	1788.21
73	Nick FALDO (Eng)	71	75	73	79	298	2497.50	1783.93
	Michael JONZON (Swe)	71	74	77	76	298	2497.50	1783.93
75	Max ANGLERT (Swe)	69	76	78	76	299	2491.50	1779.64
	Steven RICHARDSON (Eng)	70	75	81	73	299	2491.50	1779.64
77	Olle KARLSSON (Swe)	70	77	75	78	300	2485.50	1775.36
	Fredrik LINDGREN (Swe)	70	74	80	76	300	2485.50	1775.36

NICK PRICE: swept through the pack

Welcome TPC fans!

Deutsche Bank - SAP Open
May 18 – 21, 2000

Golf Club Gut Kaden near Hamburg

Tiger Woods, winner 1999

For further information please contact the
Deutsche Bank - SAP Tournament office
Tel. + 49 (0) 4193 9 000 -0 · Fax -111
http://www.deutschebank-sap-open.de

Mission accomplished

Colin Montgomerie fulfils prediction

with "as good as I can play"

victory at magnificent Wentworth Club

On reflection, there seemed to be an air of inevitability about Colin Montgomerie's triumph at Wentworth Club. It was rather like reading the last page of a thriller and ignoring the preceding chapters with their intriguing twists and turns because their relevance is lost once the denouement is known.

After all, the towering Scottish professional simply reaffirmed a self-evident truth when he became only the second golfer in history after Nick Faldo to retain the Volvo PGA Championship – namely that he remains the dominant force in the European game or, as he puts it, the man his fellow professionals least like to see in their rear-view mirrors.

The plain fact is that nobody can

MARK JAMES: Ryder Cup captain's form sparks more speculation

really feel safe when Montgomerie is around and no leading margin is ever large enough to allow its possessor to feel totally secure from his grasp. In truth, the pattern of his triumph over the West Course underlined that point in that he started his title defence in the supporting acts yet still emerged to top the bill.

And yet before that winning moment arrived a full cast of characters figured in the drama and some of them had cause to hope with some justification that their hour had come and that the title could fall to them. Each had a moment of fleeting glory then stepped aside as Montgomerie,

ERNIE ELS: "If I shot 80 I'd still be smiling."

STEPHEN LEANEY: golf is a thirsty game

SANDY LYLE: four sub-par rounds

inspired by overpowering self-belief, charged through in the fast lane.

Earlier, he had outlined an astounding agenda by stating that it was his plan to win two of three successive tournaments in his schedule. Accordingly he snapped up the Benson and Hedges International Open then left the stage to Tiger Woods in Germany a week later and thus came to Wentworth with the added burden of having to justify and complete his earlier prediction of victory.

And yet for some time at least it seemed that others intended to spoil the plot. Indeed, Montgomerie himself cast a wary eye towards Ernie Els, who had twice thwarted his US Open chances of success, and offered the not-too-serious hope that as the South African's wife Liezl had just given birth to their first child – daughter Samantha Leigh – that week, he might be too distracted to display his customary competitive prowess.

Els admitted that his thoughts were elsewhere as he played, but such lack of focus caused no serious damage as he

COLIN MONTGOMERIE: "He just lapped the field."

STEPHEN LEANEY: not far to look for his place in the field

SERGIO GARCIA: command performance closing 66

opened with a 68 to find himself three strokes off the pace-setting target set by Bernhard Langer, who had won the title three times previously and was therefore a proven campaigner on Wentworth's rolling terrain.

Langer was clearly running into powerful form, as was Ulsterman Darren Clarke after a lacklustre start to the season during which he decided to consult Butch Harmon, who coaches Tiger Woods, for some help in restoring his game. That decision looked to have paid off when he opened with a 67 that was matched by European Ryder Cup captain Mark James, whose own run of success was already prompting speculative discussion that his playing talents rather than his

BRUT IMPÉRIAL
BRUT IMPÉRIAL
BRUT IMPÉRIAL
MOËT & CHANDON
CHAMPAGNE
Official
champagne
to the
PGA
European
Tour

SHOT OF THE WEEK

Colin Montgomerie called it the shot that changed the tournament for him and it came during the second round in the most dramatic circumstances. He had played his tee shot down the last fairway when a violent electrical storm broke and play was suspended for two hours. Colin had marked the position of his golf ball with a tee peg, but when he returned the marker had disappeared. Officials then told him he would have to drop the ball as near as possible to the original spot, but he was concerned that dropping a ball from shoulder height on to a wet fairway could cause a worse lie. But as he could not identify the original location there was no alternative. After more discussion with the referee he dropped the ball then reached for a five iron and drilled the ball 198 yards to within eight feet of the hole and sank the putt for an eagle three to lift himself back into contention and eventual victory.

powers of leadership might be required for the squad.

Meanwhile, the reigning US Masters champion José Maria Olazábal had settled comfortably into the early pace with a 68 after birdies at the last two holes, and Lee Westwood, recovering from problems to his right shoulder, kept within range with a 69. Sandy Lyle revived glorious memories of the past when he birdied the last three holes for a 70. Only Montgomerie, it seemed, found cause for dissatisfaction when he played the last four holes in one over par and toiled vainly over the par fives he would normally dismiss with ease (and in fact later did that weekend).

By the end of the second day Clarke had become the main attraction at ten under par with Els just a stroke behind him. It was prima facie evidence that Clarke had touched his mercurial best again and that the South African's enormous natural talent might just have guided him to success on automatic pilot, even though his mind might have been elsewhere.

He had played the outward nine holes in 31 strokes, and even though he failed to birdie those last two holes in his 67, his face still broke into a huge grin and he said: "These days are great for Liezl and myself. If I shot 80 I'd still be smiling."

James kept pace with his rivals and was three strokes off the lead along with Dean Robertson, winner of the Fiat and Fila Italian Open earlier in the season. The scoreboard also revealed the first signs of a mounting threat being posed by Montgomerie who finished in spectacular style – for several reasons – with a 70. He and playing companion Clarke faced their second shots to the final green when a violent electrical thunderstorm held up play for two hours.

BERNHARD LANGER: a drive to impress Ryder Cup team-mate Darren Clarke

Upon their return they discovered that the tee pegs they had used to mark the position of their tee shots had been removed and they were obliged to drop their golf balls as close as possible to the original spot. Clarke then struck his ball to the edge of the green and two putted for a birdie. It was a cool-headed response to a setback that in times past might have seriously unsettled him. Meanwhile, Montgomerie rifled his approach within nine feet of the flagstick and holed the putt for an eagle three, then said afterwards that he felt the shot had changed the tournament for him, and, as it turned out, for others too.

At the halfway stage Montgomerie was still five strokes behind the leader with some hefty contenders, including Els, Olazábal and Langer, among others, in between. Moreover, the quiet man of golf, Retief Goosen, had started to make his self-effacing presence felt as he moved within two strokes of the lead. Els and fellow South African Goosen have been friends and rivals since boyhood, and Els's judgement of Goosen is that he has an immense talent but has

developed late because of an inherent uneasiness with the fame that accompanies success.

Yet Goosen's style and standard of play have pushed him into prominence and he moved to the top of the Volvo Order of Merit table for a period prior to his appearance at Wentworth Club. If he had bothered to look in his rear-view mirror in the third round he would have seen the towering figure of Montgomerie looming closer and closer, and by the end of a spectacular day's play, the Surrey-based Scot had caught up with a 67 while Clarke faltered to a 77 and forfeited both lead and prospect.

Montgomerie's extraordinary barrage contained two eagles. The first came on the long 12th when he drilled a four iron to 12 feet for a single putt, and the second flourish was saved until the last hole when his four iron again left him close enough for a single putt. That effort left him tied for the lead at ten under par with Goosen.

And quite clearly he was getting

DARREN CLARKE: touched mercurial best

better as each day passed although he sounded a note of caution – which ironically seemed like a warning to others –

PAUL EALES: growing consistency reaps rich reward

THE COURSE

Constant rain throughout the winter caused extra work for course superintendent Chris Kennedy and his team to successfully bring the condition of the West Course to Championship level in time for the flagship event of the European Tour. Subsequent lengthy spells of sunshine transformed the whole course into a majestic riot of colour that rivalled Augusta National at its best. Wentworth looked magnificent and the clever contour mowing of the fairways gave professionals essential definition for their shots. Moreover, the changes introduced last year have proved to be significant, particularly on the 11th hole which was formerly the third easiest hole on the course. By pushing the tee back even further and introducing a right-hand fairway bunker it has now become the third toughest.

when he said: "They don't pay out after three rounds no matter how far ahead you are. They pay out after four."

But they might as well have written his name on the cheque there and then, because he erupted on the final day with a quality of golf he believes he has attained only once previously in his career – at the 1997 US Open at Congressional – and left all his rivals struggling to catch up, particularly Goosen, his playing companion and early rival.

Montgomerie was in ruthless mood and moved two strokes clear after his

RETIEF GOOSEN: the "Quiet Man" of golf

TOMMY HORTON: among many who made good use of the Mizuno workshop

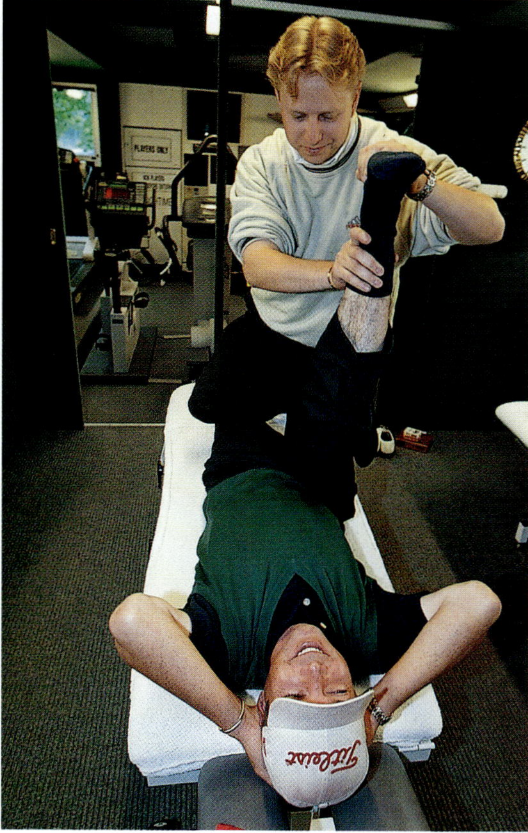

DEAN ROBERTSON: 3M physio

JOSÉ MARIA OLAZÁBAL: Tour dinner gave his Masters
jacket a rare outing

birdie at the second hole, then played the three holes from the tenth in a breath-taking four under par to finish with a best of the week 64 and admitted: "That is as good as I can play." Els, his old rival, finished with a 68 and reflected: "He just lapped the field and is now playing better than he has ever played."

Goosen, perhaps rather shell-shocked, slipped to fourth place along with Els and Stephen Leaney. Meanwhile, James had ambled into second place with a stirring 66, albeit five strokes behind the winner. His consistency throughout the tournament fuelled a debate over what if he found himself among the top ten automatic qualifiers for the Ryder Cup team. It was a dilemma he refused to consider until the bulk of the qualifying events had been completed and he could make a more realistic judgement, although he insisted that he would not add any extra tournaments to his personal schedule. "I've got other things to do. Like gardening," he said.

One heartening aspect of the last day scenario was the confident manner in which Paul Eales confirmed his growing consistency with a third place finish, one stroke behind James, after closing with a spirited 67. The Lancashire-based professional held his nerve down the final hole and struck a three iron to the green for an eagle three and a handsome 113,930 euro (£81,378) payout, which was more than he earned for the entire 1998 season.

Spanish prodigy Sergio Garcia transformed what had been a muted week into a command performance with a last round 66 which hoisted him into a share of 19th place, prompting more speculation about his Ryder Cup prospects. Mercifully, at Wentworth Club in May there was still much pivotal golf to be played before that question could be resolved.

And what of those others who started the Championship with such high hopes and commanded attention for a few fleeting moments? Clarke finished in tied 13th place after that damaging third round 77 interrupted his positive stride. Olazábal took tenth place. Oh yes, and Montgomerie stuck to the script. Two wins in three weeks. As predicted.

Michael McDonnell

Wentworth Club, Surrey, England, May 28–31, 1999 · Par 72 · Yards 7006

Pos	Name & Country	Rnd 1	Rnd 2	Rnd 3	Rnd 4	Total	Prize Money €	Prize Money £
1	Colin MONTGOMERIE (Scot)	69	70	67	64	270	303350.00	216678.57
2	Mark JAMES (Eng)	67	70	72	66	275	202300.00	144500.00
3	Paul EALES (Eng)	68	70	71	67	276	113930.00	81378.57
4	Stephen LEANEY (Aus)	73	67	69	68	277	77233.33	55166.66
	Ernie ELS (SA)	68	67	74	68	277	77233.33	55166.66
	Retief GOOSEN (SA)	67	69	70	71	277	77233.33	55166.66
7	Bernhard LANGER (Ger)	65	73	70	70	278	46900.00	33500.00
	David CARTER (Eng)	71	70	69	68	278	46900.00	33500.00
	Mathias GRÖNBERG (Swe)	69	73	67	69	278	46900.00	33500.00
10	Jarmo SANDELIN (Swe)	70	72	71	66	279	33716.67	24083.34
	Sven STRÜVER (Ger)	75	69	69	66	279	33716.67	24083.34
	José Maria OLAZÁBAL (Sp)	68	70	72	69	279	33716.67	24083.34
13	Darren CLARKE (N.Ire)	67	67	77	69	280	26262.33	18758.81
	David HOWELL (Eng)	72	72	71	65	280	26262.33	18758.81
	Robert KARLSSON (Swe)	70	68	71	71	280	26262.33	18758.81
	Warren BENNETT (Eng)	70	74	69	67	280	26262.33	18758.81
	Ian GARBUTT (Eng)	74	68	68	70	280	26262.33	18758.81
	Jean VAN DE VELDE (Fr)	67	75	70	68	280	26262.33	18758.81
19	Stephen ALLAN (Aus)	72	69	71	69	281	20774.00	14838.57
	Michael CAMPBELL (NZ)	68	70	72	71	281	20774.00	14838.57
	Eduardo ROMERO (Arg)	71	71	67	72	281	20774.00	14838.57
	Dean ROBERTSON (Scot)	68	69	73	71	281	20774.00	14838.57
	Jesper PARNEVIK (Swe)	70	69	72	70	281	20774.00	14838.57
	Sergio GARCIA (Sp)	72	73	70	66	281	20774.00	14838.57
	Paul BROADHURST (Eng)	73	69	72	67	281	20774.00	14838.57
26	Mark ROE (Eng)	70	70	73	69	282	18018.00	12870.00
	Ian WOOSNAM (Wal)	72	73	70	67	282	18018.00	12870.00
	Sandy LYLE (Scot)	70	70	71	71	282	18018.00	12870.00
29	Roger WESSELS (SA)	71	73	68	71	283	15045.33	10746.66
	Costantino ROCCA (It)	71	71	72	69	283	15045.33	10746.66
	Joakim HAEGGMAN (Swe)	71	72	69	71	283	15045.33	10746.66
	Thomas LEVET (Fr)	71	71	71	70	283	15045.33	10746.66
	Jeev Milkha SINGH (Ind)	72	69	71	71	283	15045.33	10746.66
	Des SMYTH (Ire)	69	72	72	70	283	15045.33	10746.66
	Peter LONARD (Aus)	69	70	70	74	283	15045.33	10746.66
	Gary ORR (Scot)	71	70	73	69	283	15045.33	10746.66
	Sam TORRANCE (Scot)	70	68	75	70	283	15045.33	10746.66
38	Mark MCNULTY (Zim)	71	70	67	76	284	12922.00	9230.00
	Rolf MUNTZ (Hol)	71	72	73	68	284	12922.00	9230.00
40	Phillip PRICE (Wal)	73	69	72	71	285	12012.00	8580.00
	Greg TURNER (NZ)	73	67	74	71	285	12012.00	8580.00
	Pedro LINHART (Sp)	67	76	72	70	285	12012.00	8580.00
43	Raymond RUSSELL (Scot)	71	72	74	69	286	10738.00	7670.00
	Andrew OLDCORN (Scot)	72	68	73	73	286	10738.00	7670.00
	John BICKERTON (Eng)	73	72	74	67	286	10738.00	7670.00
	Miguel Angel JIMÉNEZ (Sp)	73	72	75	66	286	10738.00	7670.00
47	Paul LAWRIE (Scot)	70	71	76	70	287	8736.00	6240.00
	Andrew COLTART (Scot)	72	73	73	69	287	8736.00	6240.00
	Michael LONG (NZ)	71	73	71	72	287	8736.00	6240.00
	Pierre FULKE (Swe)	73	68	73	73	287	8736.00	6240.00
	Craig HAINLINE (USA)	73	72	72	70	287	8736.00	6240.00
	Barry LANE (Eng)	70	74	71	72	287	8736.00	6240.00
	Santiago LUNA (Sp)	71	71	75	70	287	8736.00	6240.00
54	Francisco CEA (Sp)	72	73	72	71	288	7098.00	5070.00
	David GILFORD (Eng)	70	70	75	73	288	7098.00	5070.00
56	Lee WESTWOOD (Eng)	69	73	75	72	289	6188.00	4420.00
	Ignacio GARRIDO (Sp)	74	70	73	72	289	6188.00	4420.00
	Padraig HARRINGTON (Ire)	74	70	72	73	289	6188.00	4420.00
59	Nick FALDO (Eng)	74	71	74	71	290	5460.00	3900.00
	José RIVERO (Sp)	67	76	71	76	290	5460.00	3900.00
	Lian-Wei ZHANG (ROC)	74	71	73	72	290	5460.00	3900.00
62	Patrik SJÖLAND (Swe)	73	71	73	74	291	5096.00	3640.00
63	Derrick COOPER (Eng)	67	76	74	75	292	4732.00	3380.00
	Per NYMAN (Swe)	74	70	78	70	292	4732.00	3380.00
	Paul CURRY (Eng)	70	74	71	77	292	4732.00	3380.00
66	Philip WALTON (Ire)	73	72	74	75	294	2730.00	1950.00

OPERATIONAL EXCELLENCE
VOLVO
VOLVO

Las Vegas inspiration

Darren Clarke took a flight to Nevada

and found the answer to an ailing

golf swing for success at Hanbury Manor

The English Open returned to the Marriott Hanbury Manor for a third time, but under new sponsorship, The Compass Group of catering companies giving notice of what they hope will be a long term association with the European Tour.

Hanbury Manor is a daunting 7016 yards for most amateurs, but seems ideally suited to the strength and skills of the modern professional. Last year Greg Chalmers got within striking distance of becoming the first player to break 60 on the European Tour, just a short putt missed at the 17th and no closing birdie getting in the way.

This time, the course was playing long after heavy rain earlier in the week, but softer putting surfaces more than compensated for that, and a dry spring had left the rough sparse compared with previous years. Even so chill winds from a strange quarter should have made any score under 70 in the first round something special, but many of the morning

COLIN MONTGOMERIE: hugely successful campaign

players brushed par aside and by lunchtime there were two 64s on the board.

The first came from Geoff Ogilvy, another fine product from the Australian amateur game, who is finding his feet on the European Tour. Then there was John Bickerton, a European Challenge Tour graduate who this season had already tied for one tournament (losing the play-off for the Algarve Portuguese Open title to Van Phillips) and done sufficiently well in others to have put all worries for the year behind him.

The best story to come from that first morning though was Sam Torrance. Sidelined through injury for much of the early part of the year, he started by dropping three shots in his first four holes, but recovered to such good effect that he turned in a 67 including chipping in for an eagle at the last. A first swallow perhaps of his golfing summer.

Heavy rain after lunch had the second half of the field struggling to keep up. Colin Montgomerie, still counting his chips from a hugely successful campaign in May, made few mistakes in going round in 70. It was

a score matched by defending champion Lee Westwood, but he would follow that with a 75 and so miss out on the weekend.

For a time on day two, it looked like we might have the narrowest margin ever between the halfway leader and those just making the cut; six shots covered the top 70 players until late in the afternoon. That was until Darren Clarke chose to make his move. He'd opened with a more than adequate 68, but had made little progress in terms of par after going out in 35. Then,

while all around him were treading water, he suddenly found inspiration, and came home in 30, finishing with five consecutive birdies.

For the second week in a row he had the halfway lead, but fresh in his mind would be the 77 he had taken in the third round at Wentworth Club in the Volvo PGA Championship. Marriott Hanbury Manor is not the West Course, but memories like that must be exorcised if they are not to fester.

STEPHEN LEANEY: shared third place

We're the driving force behind the PGA European Tour.

National CarRental.
OFFICIAL CAR RENTAL COMPANY OF THE PGA EUROPEAN TOUR

With over 250,000 vehicles available from nearly 3,000 international locations, National Car Rental are ideally placed for the perfect drive.
As the Tour's official car rental company we'll be supporting five of the largest tournaments, including

The Compass Group English Open, Spanish and German Opens, as well as the Volvo PGA championship and The Victor Chandler British Masters.
So. if you want to be first on the green, call our international reservation line on +44 (0) 1273 223308 or visit our website at www.nationalcar-europe.com

National CarRental.

Green means go

SHOT OF THE WEEK

A clear winner as shot of the week was Darren Clarke's second to the par five 17th in the second round. Slightly stymied by a tree on the left, he set his three wood out over the lake and the trees to the right of the green, trusting the wind and a bit of draw to bring the ball back in. It pitched no more than ten feet from the hole.

ROBERT KARLSSON: 63 despite shank

Clarke, however, had good reason to feel confident. After taking a long break from the game during the winter, he had struggled to find his rhythm. It required hard work, lots of it, and Clarke was determined that he would cure the swing faults on the practice range, He had also turned for advice to Butch Harmon, who coaches Tiger Woods.

"I flew to Las Vegas to see Butch,"

NICK FALDO: timing counts for all

THE COURSE

Marriott Hanbury Manor is a course of two distinct halves. The newer front nine is set on a western facing slope, much exposed to the prevailing winds, and is certainly tougher. The back nine meandering through the parkland setting in front of the old manor has more charm and would undoubtedly be the choice of those going out for a few holes after tea.

explained Clarke. "I worked hard while I was there, and on my return we continued to talk on the telephone. He helped straighten out a lot of things.

"Derrick Cooper also had a look at me to make sure I kept doing what I worked on with Butch. It was a nice change-around. Things hadn't gone well in the early part of the year, and it was a tough time. I wasn't the best of company in the world, I imagine. But I have a solid foundation in that I have a lot of support from my wife Heather, Andrew Chandler, my manager, and Butch. Sometimes I play well, sometimes I don't."

This time, Clarke continued to play well. Saturday provided the best weather and instantly the field made hay, Sweden's Robert Karlsson showing what was possible with a 63, despite a full blooded shank at the short 16th. That score was already on the board when Clarke teed off, just to add to the pressure.

He took 36 to the turn to allow those behind to catch up, including the intimidating name of Montgomerie who posted a 65 just as Clarke was turning for home. But as the round progressed and it became clear the previous week's 'Sunset Strip' had been an isolated aberration, Clarke again finished with a flourish; each of the last five holes once more producing a birdie.

A five-shot lead is comfortable but not conclusive, and of the half dozen in closest pursuit, it was joint first round leader Bickerton who took up the challenge. Clarke seemed to have made his task even easier by holing a bunker shot at the first for an eagle, but later fluffed a couple of chips. Turning in 32, Bickerton at one point got within a single stroke, but he, too, required two chips from the back of the 13th, and that was all the room Clarke needed to go ahead and win by two shots with a closing 68 for a 20-under-par total of 268.

Bruce Critchley

JOHN BICKERTON: closed to within one shot

Marriott Hanbury Manor, Ware, England, June 3–6, 1999 • Par 72 • Yards 7016

Pos	Name & Country	Rnd 1	Rnd 2	Rnd 3	Rnd 4	Total	Prize Money €	Prize Money £
1	Darren CLARKE (N.Ire)	68	65	67	68	268	166660.00	119042.86
2	John BICKERTON (Eng)	64	73	68	65	270	111100.00	79357.14
3	David CARTER (Eng)	67	71	67	69	274	56300.00	40214.29
	Stephen LEANEY (Aus)	68	70	67	69	274	56300.00	40214.29
5	Andrew COLTART (Scot)	68	73	64	70	275	38700.00	27642.86
	Colin MONTGOMERIE (Scot)	70	70	65	70	275	38700.00	27642.86
7	Dean ROBERTSON (Scot)	69	70	70	67	276	22143.33	15816.66
	Fredrik LINDGREN (Swe)	71	71	67	67	276	22143.33	15816.66
	Gary ORR (Scot)	68	71	66	71	276	22143.33	15816.66
	Mark ROE (Eng)	71	72	68	65	276	22143.33	15816.66
	Olle KARLSSON (Swe)	67	72	70	67	276	22143.33	15816.66
	Peter SENIOR (Aus)	69	68	69	70	276	22143.33	15816.66
13	Emanuele CANONICA (It)	71	67	70	69	277	15690.00	11207.14
	Robert KARLSSON (Swe)	71	72	63	71	277	15690.00	11207.14
15	John SENDEN (Aus)	69	72	69	68	278	14400.00	10285.71
	Thomas GÖGELE (Ger)	67	69	70	72	278	14400.00	10285.71
17	Costantino ROCCA (It)	69	69	68	73	279	12316.67	8797.62
	Jeev Milkha SINGH (Ind)	68	73	67	71	279	12316.67	8797.62
	Lian-Wei ZHANG (PRC)	70	71	71	67	279	12316.67	8797.62
	Paul BROADHURST (Eng)	69	73	67	70	279	12316.67	8797.62
	Paul LAWRIE (Scot)	69	70	71	69	279	12316.67	8797.62
	Peter MITCHELL (Eng)	68	69	70	72	279	12316.67	8797.62
23	Geoff OGILVY (Aus)	64	71	72	73	280	10950.00	7821.43
	Paul CURRY (Eng)	68	71	72	69	280	10950.00	7821.43
25	Ian GARBUTT (Eng)	70	72	67	72	281	10200.00	7285.71
	Peter LONARD (Aus)	75	67	68	71	281	10200.00	7285.71
	Wayne WESTNER (SA)	70	73	69	69	281	10200.00	7285.71
28	Pedro LINHART (Sp)	72	70	70	70	282	9000.00	6428.57
	Retief GOOSEN (SA)	70	71	68	73	282	9000.00	6428.57
	Robert COLES (Eng)	70	70	73	69	282	9000.00	6428.57
	Sam TORRANCE (Scot)	67	73	71	71	282	9000.00	6428.57
	Stephen GALLACHER (Scot)	72	71	68	71	282	9000.00	6428.57
33	Andrew RAITT (Eng)	70	70	72	71	283	7700.00	5500.00
	Bob MAY (USA)	72	68	69	74	283	7700.00	5500.00
	Gary EMERSON (Eng)	72	71	66	74	283	7700.00	5500.00
	Jamie SPENCE (Eng)	69	73	69	72	283	7700.00	5500.00
	Mark MCNULTY (Zim)	67	77	71	68	283	7700.00	5500.00
	Mats HALLBERG (Swe)	71	72	72	68	283	7700.00	5500.00
39	Alberto BINAGHI (It)	70	68	69	77	284	5900.00	4214.29
	Anders HANSEN (Den)	73	71	69	71	284	5900.00	4214.29
	Daniel CHOPRA (Swe)	71	70	72	71	284	5900.00	4214.29
	Ignacio GARRIDO (Sp)	69	74	71	70	284	5900.00	4214.29
	Jim PAYNE (Eng)	74	67	71	72	284	5900.00	4214.29
	Mark JAMES (Eng)	71	72	69	72	284	5900.00	4214.29
	Mats LANNER (Swe)	70	72	71	71	284	5900.00	4214.29
	Michael CAMPBELL (NZ)	70	72	74	68	284	5900.00	4214.29
	Miles TUNNICLIFF (Eng)	71	71	68	74	284	5900.00	4214.29
	Roger WINCHESTER (Eng)	68	70	72	74	284	5900.00	4214.29
	Søren KJELDSEN (Den)	73	69	70	72	284	5900.00	4214.29
	Thomas LEVET (Fr)	71	71	71	71	284	5900.00	4214.29
51	Gary EVANS (Eng)	72	71	70	72	285	4400.00	3142.86
	Jean VAN DE VELDE (Fr)	70	73	71	71	285	4400.00	3142.86
	Nick FALDO (Eng)	70	74	73	68	285	4400.00	3142.86
54	Christian CÉVAER (Fr)	72	72	70	72	286	3600.00	2571.43
	Malcolm MACKENZIE (Eng)	72	72	70	72	286	3600.00	2571.43
	Marc FARRY (Fr)	72	72	71	71	286	3600.00	2571.43
	Mathias GRÖNBERG (Swe)	66	74	73	73	286	3600.00	2571.43
	Roger WESSELS (SA)	72	71	72	71	286	3600.00	2571.43
59	Anthony WALL (Eng)	73	70	74	70	287	3000.00	2142.86
	Paul EALES (Eng)	70	69	73	75	287	3000.00	2142.86
	Ross MCFARLANE (Eng)	73	69	73	72	287	3000.00	2142.86
62	Eamonn DARCY (Ire)	72	72	72	72	288	2750.00	1964.29
	Tom GILLIS (USA)	68	75	71	74	288	2750.00	1964.29
64	Joakim HAEGGMAN (Swe)	75	69	70	75	289	1918.20	1370.14
	Anders FORSBRAND (Swe)	69	72	74	74	289	1918.20	1370.14
	Christopher HANELL (Swe)	73	71	73	72	289	1918.20	1370.14
	Raphaël JACQUELIN (Fr)	70	72	73	74	289	1918.20	1370.14
	Stephen DODD (Wal)	70	70	73	76	289	1918.20	1370.14
69	Massimo FLORIOLI (It)	70	73	72	75	290	1488.00	1062.86
	Andrew BONHOMME (Aus)	70	73	70	77	290	1488.00	1062.86
	Steve WEBSTER (Eng)	69	72	73	76	290	1488.00	1062.86
72	Stuart CAGE (Eng)	74	70	75	74	293	1482.00	1058.57
73	Carlos RODILES (Sp)	75	69	72	81	297	1477.50	1055.36
	Francisco CEA (Sp)	71	71	81	74	297	1477.50	1055.36
75	Jeremy ROBINSON (Eng)	70	73	81	75	299	1473.00	1052.14

The world's finest golfers expect the world's finest caterers. Which is why Payne and Gunter is the preferred corporate hospitality and foodservice provider at world-class golfing events.

THE OPEN CHAMPIONSHIP
THE VOLVO PGA CHAMPIONSHIP
BENSON & HEDGES INTERNATIONAL OPEN
THE VICTOR CHANDLER BRITISH MASTERS
THE COMPASS GROUP ENGLISH OPEN
SMURFIT EUROPEAN OPEN
PAYNE AND GUNTER

Undisputed Masters

PAYNE AND GUNTER

Payne and Gunter, Mayfair House, Belvue Road, Northolt, Middlesex UB5 5QJ.
A member of Compass Group PLC – the world's largest foodservice organisation
catering to customers in over 50 countries. Tel: 0181 842 2224 Fax: 0181 845 2319

Golf's most exclusive club

Jarmo Sandelin joins the
international elite with
a prize money cannot buy

Drivers motoring from Tegel Airport in Berlin towards Leipzig cannot avoid being reminded that they are passing through the former East Germany. For mile after mile the roadside scenery consists of unremitting tenement blocks, which for all their expensive refurbishment remain bleak reminders of a past age.

The destination for the European Tour in early June was the Sporting Club Berlin, and a greater contrast between the apartments past which the players had driven and this sybaritic oasis could not possibly be imagined.

Things are not what they used to be in these parts; the people who live in and around the little village of Bad Saarow, home of Hotel Kempinski and the golf courses that surround it, today enjoy a better quality of life. The fact remains, though, that the television people, golfers, officials and press corps who made the trip still inhabit a different world to most of the local populace.

RETIEF GOOSEN: gracious in defeat

How much of that communicated itself to the playing personnel in the 65th German Open is subject to doubt. All they knew – and why should it have been otherwise? – was that they were about to play a tournament on a fine golf course in ideal conditions. The tournament started on the morning of Thursday, June 10, and by the early evening of Sunday, June 13, one man had produced the performance that would change his life, perhaps for ever. Jarmo Sandelin was that man, and on that golden Sunday afternoon, after a play-off against a doughty foe, he became a Ryder Cup player.

Sandelin, born in Finland but a Swedish national for all but a handful of his 32 years, thus became the fourth Swede behind Joakim Haeggman, Per-Ulrik Johansson and Jesper Parnevik, to claim Cup honours, but he did not do so without a fight. At the end of 72 hotly contested holes, Sandelin was locked inseparably with South African Retief Goosen on 274, 14 under par. Much had contributed to the deadlock as they completed matching 68s, but all that mattered now was that they would go out again and fight, head-to-head, one-against-one, with no quarter asked or given.

It did not take long to settle the issue. Sandelin struck a marvellous drive at the first play-off hole, the 18th, hit the green and was never going to take more than two putts. Goosen, meanwhile, came off his second stroke and was left with a horrible shot for his third. The ball came to rest a foot from the right edge of a bunker and he had no choice but to stand in the sand to play the shot.

His feet were a good three feet below the ball, which he would be striking at around waist level. In the circumstances, he did pretty well to get it within 15 feet of the hole, but pretty well was not pretty enough this time. Sandelin duly holed out for a par four and Goosen faced his putt to stay alive. He almost did it – the ball shaved the hole but stayed above ground. Game over; winner and loser equally gracious in victory and defeat.

Although Goosen's shot from Hades by the side of that bunker was important enough, the piece could have been settled without the need for extra time. Throughout a tense and steamy afternoon, Goosen and Sandelin, joint leaders at the start

Retief Goosen's missed putt for victory from three feet on the last hole of regulation play reprieved Sandelin, and he capitalised on his second chance with a wonderful drive on the first extra hole. He used his driver for a stroke that started left and cut back into position "A" on the fairway. He would have to do something tragic to mess things up from there, and didn't. But Goosen did; the Swede's tee shot had put just enough pressure on him to deny him the chance of re-grouping after the putt that had got away.

PIERRE FULKE: closing 67

THE COURSE

A fine course in superb condition. Throughout the week the players extolled the virtues of the putting surfaces; the principal focus of their praise was that, even at the end of the day, they remained true and unspiked. It has the character of an inland links – by common consent, one of the best layouts the European Tour would visit all year.

of the day, had established such a powerful position that by the time they reached the 17th tee they were as fireproof as asbestos, immune from the flames of ambition that had licked at their ankles from other sources during the day.

Ten minutes later Sandelin had bogeyed the hole to surrender the lead he had held since Friday night. Now all the quiet South African had to do to claim the title was hold his nerve on the last. He didn't. He had to hole a three-foot putt for victory, and, horror of horrors, he pulled it left. As errors go, it was an absolute gem. "I thought it was left-to-right, but it went straight," he said. It didn't, actually – from right behind the putt, the line was an inch outside the right lip. But no matter. The fact is that he missed it.

The nature of the beast meant that the final round was the most gripping of the four, but the tournament was packed with incident from the start. On day one Gary Evans, on a working holiday with his wife, Sam, and their daughter, Olivia, had an immaculate 62 that was to win him a Rolex watch for the lowest round of the week, while the second round was illuminated by a 64 from Sandelin that put him a stroke clear of the field.

Raymond Russell, the quiet Scot, rode into town with a 63 in his saddle-bag on Saturday, a round that propelled him from joint 59th into a tie for second place. Sandelin, meanwhile, had a 73. If he had a slice of luck in the entire tournament, it was that, even with such an ordinary score chalked up against his name, he retained the lead, even if he had to share it with Goosen, who had a 68.

And so to that last, tense 18 holes that ultimately denied Goosen his second victory of the season and gave Sandelin another honour to add to the Peugeot Open de España title he had won in April. He pocketed 166,660 euro (£119,042), but this time, the money was of secondary importance. He had joined the most exclusive club in world golf; and not even the richest man on the planet can buy that.

GARY EVANS: Rolex watch for a 62

Mel Webb   171

Sporting Club Berlin, Berlin, Germany, June 10–13, 1999 · Par 72 · Yards 7082

Pos	Name & Country	Rnd 1	Rnd 2	Rnd 3	Rnd 4	Total	Prize Money €	Prize Money £
1	Jarmo SANDELIN (Swe)	69	64	73	68	274	166660.00	119042.86
2	Retief GOOSEN (SA)	67	71	68	68	274	111100.00	79357.14
3	Pierre FULKE (Swe)	69	69	71	67	276	62600.00	44714.29
4	Roger WESSELS (SA)	67	67	75	68	277	46200.00	33000.00
	Thomas GÖGELE (Ger)	71	71	70	65	277	46200.00	33000.00
6	Padraig HARRINGTON (Ire)	69	70	69	70	278	30000.00	21428.57
	Alex CEJKA (Ger)	66	71	73	68	278	30000.00	21428.57
	Santiago LUNA (Sp)	71	70	69	68	278	30000.00	21428.57
9	David CARTER (Eng)	69	68	73	69	279	20226.67	14447.62
	Raymond RUSSELL (Scot)	74	70	63	72	279	20226.67	14447.62
	Gary EVANS (Eng)	62	75	70	72	279	20226.67	14447.62
12	Geoff OGILVY (Aus)	70	66	73	71	280	15815.00	11296.43
	Robert KARLSSON (Swe)	72	68	69	71	280	15815.00	11296.43
	Steve WEBSTER (Eng)	70	70	71	69	280	15815.00	11296.43
	Jorge BERENDT (Arg)	66	71	72	71	280	15815.00	11296.43
16	Jean VAN DE VELDE (Fr)	72	68	72	69	281	13500.00	9642.86
	Fabrice TARNAUD (Fr)	71	72	68	70	281	13500.00	9642.86
	Paolo QUIRICI (Swi)	72	72	67	70	281	13500.00	9642.86
19	Soren HANSEN (Den)	70	71	73	68	282	11720.00	8371.43
	Ian HUTCHINGS (SA)	71	69	72	70	282	11720.00	8371.43
	Peter MITCHELL (Eng)	69	73	74	66	282	11720.00	8371.43
	Ricardo GONZALEZ (Arg)	70	73	71	68	282	11720.00	8371.43
	Peter O'MALLEY (Aus)	69	70	73	70	282	11720.00	8371.43
24	Raphaël JACQUELIN (Fr)	71	72	68	72	283	9750.00	6964.29
	Christopher HANELL (Swe)	70	72	67	74	283	9750.00	6964.29
	Per NYMAN (Swe)	70	73	69	71	283	9750.00	6964.29
	Søren KJELDSEN (Den)	67	72	75	69	283	9750.00	6964.29
	Paul BROADHURST (Eng)	71	70	71	71	283	9750.00	6964.29
	Jean-Francois REMESY (Fr)	68	71	72	72	283	9750.00	6964.29
	Costantino ROCCA (It)	69	72	70	72	283	9750.00	6964.29
	Mark ROE (Eng)	71	69	74	69	283	9750.00	6964.29
32	Bernhard LANGER (Ger)	72	69	72	71	284	8100.00	5785.71
	Mark MCNULTY (Zim)	70	72	72	70	284	8100.00	5785.71
	Gary ORR (Scot)	70	71	70	73	284	8100.00	5785.71
	Andrew OLDCORN (Scot)	73	67	75	69	284	8100.00	5785.71
36	Michael CAMPBELL (NZ)	69	72	73	71	285	6600.00	4714.29
	Fredrik JACOBSON (Swe)	72	70	74	69	285	6600.00	4714.29
	Paul MCGINLEY (Ire)	70	69	75	71	285	6600.00	4714.29
	Sven STRÜVER (Ger)	72	71	74	68	285	6600.00	4714.29
	John BICKERTON (Eng)	72	71	70	72	285	6600.00	4714.29
	Joakim HAEGGMAN (Swe)	68	75	70	72	285	6600.00	4714.29
	Ian GARBUTT (Eng)	68	71	73	73	285	6600.00	4714.29
	Roger WINCHESTER (Eng)	72	72	72	69	285	6600.00	4714.29
	Alberto BINAGHI (It)	69	72	74	70	285	6600.00	4714.29
	Malcolm MACKENZIE (Eng)	71	71	72	71	285	6600.00	4714.29
	Robert Jan DERKSEN (Hol)	67	69	72	77	285	6600.00	4714.29
47	John SENDEN (Aus)	70	70	75	71	286	5100.00	3642.86
	Greg TURNER (NZ)	66	74	72	74	286	5100.00	3642.86
	Peter LONARD (Aus)	72	69	73	72	286	5100.00	3642.86
	Andrew RAITT (Eng)	69	74	73	70	286	5100.00	3642.86
51	Carl WATTS (Eng)	69	72	72	74	287	4600.00	3285.71
52	Erol SIMSEK (Ger)	68	73	72	75	288	3900.00	2785.71
	Peter BAKER (Eng)	71	72	73	72	288	3900.00	2785.71
	Johan RYSTRÖM (Swe)	71	70	72	75	288	3900.00	2785.71
	Andrew MCLARDY (SA)	72	72	74	70	288	3900.00	2785.71
	Anthony WALL (Eng)	71	73	72	72	288	3900.00	2785.71
	John MELLOR (Eng)	69	70	77	72	288	3900.00	2785.71
58	Greg OWEN (Eng)	74	69	72	74	289	3200.00	2285.71
	Marcel SIEM (AM) (Ger)	73	71	72	73	289		
	Michael THANNHAUSER (AM) (Ger)	73	69	74	73	289		
59	Russell CLAYDON (Eng)	73	71	73	73	290	3100.00	2214.29
60	Tom GILLIS (USA)	72	68	77	74	291	2950.00	2107.14
	Daren LEE (Eng)	71	69	76	75	291	2950.00	2107.14
62	Silvio GRAPPASONNI (It)	73	71	74	74	292	2800.00	2000.00
63	Miles TUNNICLIFF (Eng)	76	67	74	76	293	2325.00	1660.71
	Max ANGLERT (Swe)	73	71	75	74	293	2325.00	1660.71
	Carlos RODILES (Sp)	72	69	80	72	293	2325.00	1660.71
	Paul EALES (Eng)	72	72	73	76	293	2325.00	1660.71
67	Barry LANE (Eng)	70	74	74	76	294	1495.50	1068.21
	Jim PAYNE (Eng)	72	72	76	74	294	1495.50	1068.21
69	Craig RONALD (Scot)	71	73	76	76	296	1491.00	1065.00

ALEX CEJKA: head up for a good shot

PHOTOGRAPHER JULES ALEXANDER

BOSS
HUGO BOSS GOLF

HUGO BOSS UK LTD,
TEL. 0171 534 2700

Experience settles marathon

Miguel Angel Martin conquered injury and a remarkable European Tour newcomer to complete his comeback

When David Park decided to turn professional after the 1997 Walker Cup match, the world of golf was guardedly hesitant to recognise the potential he possessed despite his achievement in winning the Brabazon Trophy and La Manga Masters in his final amateur year.

Then the clouds of obscurity began to gather ominously after he took himself off to the 1997 European Tour Qualifying School at San Roque and fell at the first hurdle. The youngster from Hereford was unable to get beyond the 72 holes stage and there was to be no early "ticket" to Europe's theatre of dreams for finishing 114th.

But 20 months later, despite another Qualifying School failure (tied 116th) in the meantime, Park's name became known and respected by all after a remarkable first appearance on the European Tour in the Moroccan Open at Golf Royal D'Agadir.

He did not win - that honour went to the talented, determined and experienced Spaniard Miguel Angel Martin, completing a great comeback after an injury needing two operations - but it took until the sixth

extra hole of their sudden-death duel before the Wimbledon-born Welshman succumbed after never being headed over the scheduled 72 holes.

How Park's career progressed from aspiring amateur to the brink of creating history as the first to win on his European Tour debut is an object lesson to all young players. It is a testament to good sense, allied to the great knowledge accumulated by his coach David Llewellyn during his own career as a tournament

golfer. "Lulu" had partnered Ian Woosnam to World Cup victory for Wales in Hawaii in 1987, and the following season in Biarritz joined the select group of golfers who have shot 60 on the European Tour.

Llewellyn knew that Park, whom he had helped to reach Walker Cup status, had little chance of making a successful transition to the professional tournament ranks without first "learning his trade". For the majority who don't it is a bridge that is far too wide. The ideal vehicle was provided by the European Challenge Tour and, helped by a cash grant from the "Elite Cymru" sports body of which Sky TV commentator Philip Parkin is a member-selector, Park set out to prove himself on the best of all proving grounds.

In his first season on the European Challenge Tour he finished a creditable 29th, winning his eleventh event, the Rolex Trophy in Geneva after a play-off with Per Nyman. Visits to the Ivory Coast, Kenya, Turkey, Russia, Finland, Italy, Austria and Portugal introduced him to the nomadic life of a tournament golfer, with its attendant travel, hotel and language challenges.

More importantly the campaign enabled Park to discover himself. "The European Challenge Tour is a great training ground for life on the European Tour, but the most valuable thing I have learned is self-reliance. Most important is getting to know your own swing. You have to be able to sort things out yourself if something is going wrong," said Park.

In 1999 Park, who has regular Monday sessions with coach Llewellyn at his base near Chester, has shown how much he has learnt at home and away. Before arriving in Morocco he was 58 under par for his eight appearances on the European Challenge Tour after winning the second event in Spain, and adding four other top ten finishes to top the money list.

Park was 12 under par on the exacting Golf Royal D'Agadir course after opening with rounds of 67-69-68, then concluding with a regulation 72 for a 276 total which was matched only by Martin. Third man Klas Eriksson of Sweden was three strokes further back, with another Swede Eric Carlberg and Argentinian Jorge Berendt sharing fourth spot on 280.

There had not been such a remarkable debut in Europe since the arrival in 1977 of Greg Norman who, when after missing the cut at the PGA Championship, won on his second British outing in the Martini International tournament at Blairgowrie.

That Park's performance was not crowned to the fullest extent of victory was because of Martin's stubborn refusal to give up what seemed a lost cause. He hit his tee shot into the lake at the 12th on the final afternoon and handed an understandably cautious Park a three-shot lead.

Park was still three shots clear with two holes remaining, but ahead lay the tortuous par five 17th, where he had been in heavy rough from the tee on each of the two previous days, and the 457-yards dogleg 18th, where trouble lurks on both sides of the fairway, and the elevated, heavily-contoured green is an elusive target.

Martin reckoned he needed at least one three to have a chance of winning; as it transpired two finishing fours got him into a play-off as Park followed an untidy bogey six after driving into rough and bunkering his fourth shot, with another mistake at the last. Again he paid the penalty for a drive that missed the fairway.

DAVID PARK: agony at the sixth extra hole

THE COURSE

Golf Royal D'Agadir was designed by Robert Trent Jones inside the turreted walls of King Hassan II's seaside palace. It is one of the most demanding tests of a player's shot-making skills, especially when the "chergi" desert wind rises over the exposed seaside holes. Elsewhere the course meanders through dense scrub and clumps of eucalyptus trees. Narrow fairways and small, elevated, sloping greens demand accuracy from the tee, precise iron play and an assured putting touch. It is also notable for an unusual configuration. There are five long holes and five par threes, with water a feature at most of them.

It was an agonising repeat of his finish 24 hours earlier when three dropped shots in the last three holes cost him a commanding advantage over his last day challengers.

Further heartbreak followed when the putter that had been his faithful ally turned tepid in the most protracted play-off since Seve Ballesteros beat Jesper Parnevik over six holes in the 1992 Open de Baleares at Santa Ponsa. Park missed birdie chances from ten feet on the second sudden-death return to the 17th and from seven feet on more or less the same left to right downhill line on his fifth. Martin who twice had to scramble desperately and also hole from 15 feet on trip number three to stay alive, made his experience count at the sixth extra hole.

With his opponent bunkered in two and unable to get down in two more, the Spaniard coolly two-putted from 25 feet for a par four to secure his third European Tour victory, and cement his comeback from the career-threatening injury to his left wrist that had resulted in his missing the 1997 Ryder Cup contest at Valderrama.

After two operations, the 1998 season had been a virtual write-off for the 37-year-old from Madrid. "It was tough to come back from that and there were many times that I did not feel good at being out of the game for 18 months," he said. "Now my ambition is just to continue playing well. If I do that, maybe another Ryder Cup place will come."

For Park the disappointment of his near-miss was acute. But he had played with such character and aplomb that it was abundantly clear that an exciting new British star had arrived on the European golf stage. Only one question remained. It was no longer a question of if or when he would become a Tour champion, but simply, how soon?

Mike Britten

KLAS ERIKSSON: third with strong finish

GOLF ROYAL D'AGADIR, AGADIR, MOROCCO, JUNE 17–20, 1999 • PAR 72 • YARDS 6657

Pos	Name & Country	Rnd 1	Rnd 2	Rnd 3	Rnd 4	Total	Prize Money €	Prize Money £
1	Miguel Angel MARTIN (Sp)	67	71	70	68	276	81660.00	58328.57
2	David PARK (Wal)	67	69	68	72	276	54430.00	38878.57
3	Klas ERIKSSON (Swe)	75	67	69	68	279	30670.00	21907.14
4	Jorge BERENDT (Arg)	68	71	72	69	280	22635.00	16167.86
	Eric CARLBERG (Swe)	67	72	66	75	280	22635.00	16167.86
6	Nick O'HERN (Aus)	70	70	70	71	281	17150.00	12250.00
7	Andrew RAITT (Eng)	73	68	72	70	283	12632.67	9023.34
	Daren LEE (Eng)	68	74	69	72	283	12632.67	9023.34
	Carlos LARRAIN (Ven)	68	70	70	75	283	12632.67	9023.34
10	Stephen SCAHILL (NZ)	71	71	70	72	284	9800.00	7000.00
11	Scott WATSON (Eng)	71	74	72	68	285	8722.00	6230.00
	Jesus Maria ARRUTI (Sp)	73	71	71	70	285	8722.00	6230.00
13	David LYNN (Eng)	73	72	71	70	286	7882.00	5630.00
14	Marcello SANTI (It)	71	74	73	69	287	6640.00	4742.86
	Scott DOWNTON (Eng)	74	71	71	71	287	6640.00	4742.86
	Carl SUNESON (Sp)	72	69	74	72	287	6640.00	4742.86
	Geoff OGILVY (Aus)	72	73	70	72	287	6640.00	4742.86
	Johan SELBERG (Swe)	71	72	70	74	287	6640.00	4742.86
	Alex CEJKA (Ger)	74	68	69	76	287	6640.00	4742.86
	Simon WAKEFIELD (Eng)	71	72	64	80	287	6640.00	4742.86
21	Brian NELSON (USA)	77	68	72	71	288	5586.00	3990.00
	Van PHILLIPS (Eng)	72	74	71	71	288	5586.00	3990.00
	Fabrice TARNAUD (Fr)	77	67	71	73	288	5586.00	3990.00
24	Clinton WHITELAW (SA)	72	73	72	72	289	5071.50	3622.50
	Henrik NYSTROM (Swe)	74	71	73	71	289	5071.50	3622.50
	Mikael LUNDBERG (Swe)	73	70	76	70	289	5071.50	3622.50
	David HOWELL (Eng)	74	71	69	75	289	5071.50	3622.50
28	Anders HANSEN (Den)	74	71	73	72	290	4284.00	3060.00
	Alexandre BALICKI (Fr)	73	73	72	72	290	4284.00	3060.00
	Simon D. HURLEY (Eng)	68	74	76	72	290	4284.00	3060.00
	Charles CHALLEN (Eng)	71	72	73	74	290	4284.00	3060.00
	Ignacio GARRIDO (Sp)	74	70	72	74	290	4284.00	3060.00
	Lucas PARSONS (Aus)	73	67	75	75	290	4284.00	3060.00
	Costantino ROCCA (It)	73	72	69	76	290	4284.00	3060.00
35	Alvaro SALTO (Sp)	78	68	71	74	291	3430.00	2450.00
	Heinz Peter THÜL (Ger)	69	74	74	74	291	3430.00	2450.00
	John WADE (Aus)	70	73	74	74	291	3430.00	2450.00
	Oa ELIASSON (Swe)	74	71	74	72	291	3430.00	2450.00
	Matthew BLACKEY (Eng)	73	72	74	72	291	3430.00	2450.00
	Hennie OTTO (SA)	70	71	75	75	291	3430.00	2450.00
	Gordon SHERRY (Scot)	73	69	73	76	291	3430.00	2450.00
	Philip WALTON (Ire)	72	70	73	76	291	3430.00	2450.00
	Robert COLES (Eng)	73	66	73	79	291	3430.00	2450.00
44	Erol SIMSEK (Ger)	76	67	74	75	292	2744.00	1960.00
	Benoit TEILLERIA (Fr)	70	71	77	74	292	2744.00	1960.00
	Martin ERLANDSSON (Swe)	73	72	76	71	292	2744.00	1960.00
	Knud STOREGAARD (Den)	73	73	75	71	292	2744.00	1960.00
	Ian HUTCHINGS (SA)	73	69	73	77	292	2744.00	1960.00
49	Ashley ROESTOFF (SA)	73	72	73	75	293	2254.00	1610.00
	Wayne RILEY (Aus)	72	69	78	74	293	2254.00	1610.00
	Pedro LINHART (Sp)	74	71	78	70	293	2254.00	1610.00
	Ross DRUMMOND (Scot)	73	73	70	77	293	2254.00	1610.00
	Morten BACKHAUSEN (Den)	74	68	72	79	293	2254.00	1610.00
54	Andrew MCLARDY (SA)	70	74	75	75	294	1911.00	1365.00
	Jean Pierre CIXOUS (Fr)	67	73	80	74	294	1911.00	1365.00
56	Daniel WESTERMARK (Swe)	71	71	76	77	295	1666.00	1190.00
	Rafael BENITEZ (Sp)	71	74	75	75	295	1666.00	1190.00
	Carlos RODILES (Sp)	71	73	71	80	295	1666.00	1190.00
59	Steve ALKER (NZ)	72	72	73	79	296	1494.50	1067.50
	Philip GOLDING (Eng)	74	71	75	76	296	1494.50	1067.50
61	Tony JOHNSTONE (Zim)	74	70	80	73	297	1396.50	997.50
	Juan NUTT (Ven)	77	66	71	83	297	1396.50	997.50
63	Elliot BOULT (NZ)	73	70	78	77	298	1323.00	945.00
64	Michele REALE (It)	75	71	77	76	299	1249.50	892.50
	John HAWKSWORTH (Eng)	73	70	82	74	299	1249.50	892.50
66	Mohamed MAKROUNE (Mor)	71	72	79	83	305	735.00	525.00

JORGE BERENDT: poised for tied fourth

MOROCCAN OPEN
Royal Golf Links Agadir

ONMT

AN OUTSTANDING WEEK OF GOLF

Sahara Cup

PRO AMS of Moroccan Open

Moroccan Open

FOR INFORMATION CALL OR WRITE TO

Royal Moroccan Golf Federation

Royal Golf Dar Es Salam Route des Zaërs - Rabat -
Tél. :(212/7) 75.56.36 / 75.59.60 - Fax : (212/7) 75.10.26. - Télex : 36.774 (FRMGOLF)

Listening to inner demons

Meticulous preparation guided
Payne Stewart to the title
he felt he was owed at Pinehurst

*I*t was peaceful and uncrowded as Payne Stewart and Chuck Cook, Stewart's swing coach, walked Pinehurst No. 2 course on the Saturday before the US Open Championship. Stewart, who had missed the halfway cut in Memphis and flown to North Carolina, had only a few clubs and balls with him as he tried to familiarise himself with every aspect of the famous course, from its rough, which Stewart noted was not quite so penal as US Open rough often was, to the well-sited bunkers and the greens that resembled upturned saucers with their attendant run-offs. The two men made this walk again on Sunday, checking each hole not only from tee to green but also from green to tee. As they walked they talked, about how to meet its challenges, stay focussed and calm because so many of the other competitors would not be able to do that.

On Sunday afternoon a week later, this thorough preparation was proved to have been worth it as Stewart became the 17th man to win two US Opens in the same decade. Just as Ben Hogan's meticulous preparation at Carnoustie in 1953 was instrumental in his success in that year's Open Championship, so the hours Stewart had spent the previous weekend yielded him the ultimate prize. On a course that was so difficult Chris Perry waved a white flag of surrender on the 72nd fairway and then crawled the last few yards to the green on his hands and

PAYNE STEWART: this putt for the Open

PHIL MICKELSON: special strengths, chipping and putting, let him down

knees, Stewart was the only man under par after rounds of 68, 69, 72 and 70 and won by one stroke from Phil Mickelson.

What drives one man to rise above another at one particular moment? In Stewart's case it was his inner demons. Having been second in 1993 and 1998, both times to Lee Janzen, the 1991 US Open champion felt he was owed a second championship of his country. He knew that though he was 137th in driving accuracy and 123rd in greens hit in regulation, his short game was a match for anyone's. Perhaps most important of all, he knew that though he suffered from Attention Deficit Disorder, which made it hard for him to remain focused on things, he had matured into a calmer,

quieter and more thoughtful person, one who was more at peace with himself and, as such, was a prime candidate to win this event. It did no harm to his chances that since winning at Hazeltine in 1991, Stewart had undergone a transformation in character, turning himself into one of the more popular Tour members, a believer in God, wearer of a WWJD – What Would Jesus Do – bracelet on a wrist who begins each day by reading a passage from the bible.

This was the Open that was supposed to favour Europeans. Indeed, José Maria Olazábal, the reigning Masters champion, was certainly the first European to be the clear favourite to win this event. On the first morning there was a hint of low

cloud around the tops of the trees that lined every hole and a light rain was falling. Umbrellas were up. The scene was reminiscent of Wentworth or Sunningdale or Swinley Forest on a damp autumn day.

In fact, the 22-strong squad of Europeans covered themselves in glory as they fought with a course that seemed to be so similar to those at home. Darren Clarke, tenth equal, finished the highest European and Colin Montgomerie's rounds of 72, 72, 74, 72 earned him a share of 15th place with Justin Leonard. Lee Westwood missed the cut, which seemed in keeping with his downbeat mood and his view that the course did not resemble any course in Europe.

Most bizarre of all was the way

182

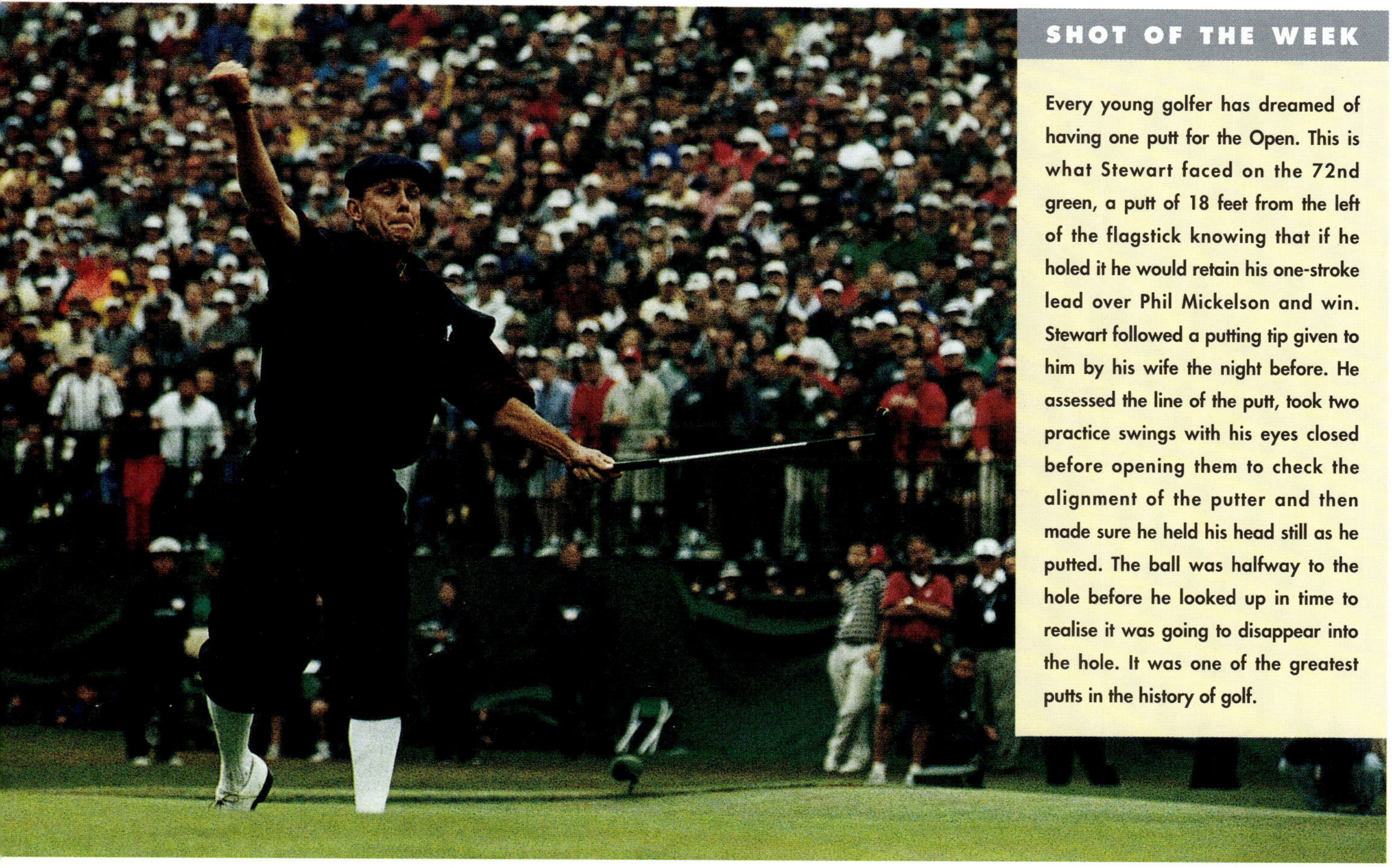

Every young golfer has dreamed of having one putt for the Open. This is what Stewart faced on the 72nd green, a putt of 18 feet from the left of the flagstick knowing that if he holed it he would retain his one-stroke lead over Phil Mickelson and win. Stewart followed a putting tip given to him by his wife the night before. He assessed the line of the putt, took two practice swings with his eyes closed before opening them to check the alignment of the putter and then made sure he held his head still as he putted. The ball was halfway to the hole before he looked up in time to realise it was going to disappear into the hole. It was one of the greatest putts in the history of golf.

Olazábal's chances of winning the second, and his second, major championship of the year ended on Friday morning when he withdrew because he had broken a bone in his right hand the previous night by punching a wall in his hotel in frustration. "I was upset with myself," Olazábal, whose first round had been 75, said. "I was disappointed at the way I played and I did something I should not have done and now I am paying the price."

This injury was only marginally more

DARREN CLARKE: best of the European challengers

THE COURSE

The 7,175 yards par 70 No.2 course at Pinehurst was designed by Donald Ross, the Scot who was born in Dornoch in 1872. Ross began as a clubmaker at the local golf club in Dornoch before journeying south to St Andrews where he served as an apprentice under Old Tom Morris. Ross also served an apprenticeship at Carnoustie before returning to Dornoch and in 1899 emigrating to the US. He arrived in Pinehurst in December 1900 and completed work on the No. 2 course, which he always regarded as his best, in 1907. Though heavily treed, the course is not narrow. Its fairways enjoy the sandy turf you would expect from a course built in an area known as the sandhills of North Carolina. Its greens are large, usually raised with considerable subtleties on the putting surface and tend to fall away at the edges.

bizarre than the one that had befallen David Duval the week before the event when the world number one had burned his right thumb and fore-finger while making a cup of coffee and was unable to practise. Duval started well enough and was level with Stewart and Mickelson after 36 holes, but never quite figured out what went wrong in his third round, a 75.

In practise player after player spoke of the importance of chipping and putting. They acknowledged that it was a US Open course on which the rough and was not overly penal and they would be able to use their drivers, but they said again and again that the event would be determined on and around the greens. "This was the first US Open course I've played that tests every area of a player's game," Mickelson said. It was to test the 29-year-old to the limit before his special strengths of

VIJAY SINGH: matched Tiger Woods for tied third

TIGER WOODS: high on a charge

COLIN MONTGOMERIE: tied 15th

DAVID DUVAL: hot coffee a painful handicap

chipping and putting let him down over the last three holes. Mickelson's mind may have been with Amy, his wife, who was expecting their first born child at the end of June. Mickelson had a pager inside his golf bag and had vowed to abandon the event no matter where he was on the course and return home to his wife if she went into labour.

John Daly might as well have gone home after 54 holes. He ran up an 11 on the par four, eighth hole in Sunday's last round, including twice failing to get an uphill putt to remain on the putting surface, and incurring a two-stroke penalty for hitting a moving ball. There followed the traditional blast at the USGA for the

way the course was set up, an outburst that was followed by a hand-written letter of apology from Daly to the USGA.

Whoever said that major championships come down to the last nine holes was wrong. This one came down to the last three holes and perhaps even to the three strokes hit in the space of 30 seconds when Stewart and Mickelson were putting on the 16th green and Tiger Woods was putting on the 17th green. First Stewart holed from 23 feet to save his par. Then Woods missed from three feet having been in a bunker. Next Mickelson missed his putt of seven feet, which meant that Stewart, who had fallen out of a share of the lead with Mickelson on the previous

hole, had regained a share of the lead at level par while Woods had fallen back to one over par, one stroke behind.

Stewart cemented his place with an arrow-straight six iron to three feet on the 17th, which enabled him to birdie the hole, and take a one-stroke lead. Then, using a nine iron, he got out of the rough into which he had driven on the right of the fairway and pitched with his lob wedge to 18 feet of the flag on the 18th green. All that remained, he knew, was to hole the putt and avoid a play-off the next day. He did so brilliantly to bring to an end the best US Open of recent memory with the best finish of recent memory.

John Hopkins

Pinehurst No. 2, North Carolina, USA, June 17–20, 1999 · Par 70 · Yards 7175

Pos	Name & Country	Rnd 1	Rnd 2	Rnd 3	Rnd 4	Total	Prize Money €	Prize Money £
1	Payne STEWART (USA)	68	69	72	70	279	543647.10	388319.35
2	Phil MICKELSON (USA)	67	70	73	70	280	321839.08	229885.06
3	Vijay SINGH (Fiji)	69	70	73	69	281	171176.20	122268.72
	Tiger WOODS (USA)	68	71	72	70	281	171176.20	122268.72
5	Steve STRICKER (USA)	70	73	69	73	285	113648.34	81177.38
6	Tim HERRON (USA)	69	72	70	75	286	101714.20	72653.00
7	David DUVAL (USA)	67	70	75	75	287	83730.64	59807.60
	Jeff MAGGERT (USA)	71	69	74	73	287	83730.64	59807.60
	Hal SUTTON (USA)	69	70	76	72	287	83730.64	59807.60
10	Darren CLARKE (N.Ire)	73	70	74	71	288	68597.39	48998.14
	Bill MAYFAIR (USA)	67	72	74	75	288	68597.39	48998.14
12	Paul AZINGER (USA)	72	72	75	70	289	58580.80	41843.43
	Paul GOYDOS (USA)	67	74	74	74	289	58580.80	41843.43
	Davis LOVE III (USA)	70	73	74	72	289	58580.80	41843.43
15	Justin LEONARD (USA)	69	75	73	73	290	50637.03	36169.31
	Colin MONTGOMERIE (Scot)	72	72	74	72	290	50637.03	36169.31
17	Jim FURYK (USA)	69	73	77	72	291	40670.17	29050.12
	Jay HAAS (USA)	74	72	73	72	291	40670.17	29050.12
	Dudley HART (USA)	73	73	76	69	291	40670.17	29050.12
	John HUSTON (USA)	71	69	75	76	291	40670.17	29050.12
	Jesper PARNEVIK (Swe)	71	71	76	73	291	40670.17	29050.12
	Scott VERPLANK (USA)	72	73	72	74	291	40670.17	29050.12
23	Miguel Angel JIMÉNEZ (Sp)	73	70	72	77	292	29144.18	20817.27
	Nick PRICE (Zim)	71	74	74	73	292	29144.18	20817.27
	Tom SCHERRER (USA)	72	72	74	74	292	29144.18	20817.27
	Brian WATTS (USA)	69	73	77	73	292	29144.18	20817.27
	D A WEIBRING (USA)	69	74	74	75	292	29144.18	20817.27
28	David BERGANIO Jnr (USA)	68	77	76	72	293	22777.07	16269.34
	Tom LEHMAN (USA)	73	74	73	73	293	22777.07	16269.34
30	Bob ESTES (USA)	70	71	77	76	294	20706.00	14790.00
	Geoffrey SISK (USA)	71	72	76	75	294	20706.00	14790.00
32	Stewart CINK (USA)	72	74	78	71	295	19526.50	13947.50
	Sven STRÜVER (Ger)	70	76	75	74	295	19526.50	13947.50
34	Brad FABEL (USA)	69	75	78	74	296	16599.72	11856.94
	Carlos Danie FRANCO (Par)	69	77	73	77	296	16599.72	11856.94
	Gabriel HJERTSTEDT (Swe)	75	72	79	70	296	16599.72	11856.94
	Rocco MEDIATE (USA)	69	72	76	79	296	16599.72	11856.94
	Craig PARRY (Aus)	69	73	79	75	296	16599.72	11856.94
	Steve PATE (USA)	70	75	75	76	296	16599.72	11856.94
	Corey PAVIN (USA)	74	71	78	73	296	16599.72	11856.94
	Esteban TOLEDO (Mex)	70	72	76	78	296	16599.72	11856.94
42	Stephen ALLAN (Aus)	71	74	77	75	297	13106.24	9361.60
	Gary HALLBERG (USA)	74	72	75	76	297	13106.24	9361.60
	Len MATTIACE (USA)	72	75	75	75	297	13106.24	9361.60
	Chris PERRY (USA)	72	74	75	76	297	13106.24	9361.60
46	Robert ALLENBY (Aus)	74	72	76	76	298	10490.56	7493.26
	Brandel CHAMBLEE (USA)	73	74	74	77	298	10490.56	7493.26
	Lee JANZEN (USA)	74	73	76	75	298	10490.56	7493.26
	David LEBECK (USA)	74	70	78	76	298	10490.56	7493.26
51	Steve ELKINGTON (Aus)	71	72	79	77	299	8963.65	6402.61
	Chris TIDLAND (USA)	71	75	75	78	299	8963.65	6402.61
53	Greg KRAFT (USA)	70	73	82	75	300	8316.93	5940.66
	Spike MCROY (USA)	70	74	76	80	300	8316.93	5940.66
	Phillip PRICE (Wal)	71	73	75	81	300	8316.93	5940.66
	Jason TYSKA (USA)	72	74	75	79	300	8316.93	5940.66
57	Jerry KELLY (USA)	73	74	79	75	301	7689.34	5492.39
	Tom WATSON (USA)	75	70	77	79	301	7689.34	5492.39
	Kaname YOKOO (Jpn)	68	74	78	81	301	7689.34	5492.39
60	John COOK (USA)	74	73	77	78	302	7358.37	5255.98
	Tom KITE (USA)	74	72	80	76	302	7358.37	5255.98
62	Christopher SMITH (USA)	69	77	77	80	303	7113.08	5080.77
	Bob TWAY (USA)	69	77	79	78	303	7113.08	5080.77
64	Larry MIZE (USA)	69	75	84	76	304	6929.11	4949.36
	Henry KUEHNE (Am) (USA)	72	75	81	78	306		
66	Bob BURNS (USA)	71	76	84	77	308	6745.14	4817.96
	Ted TRYBA (USA)	72	75	82	79	308	6745.14	4817.96
68	John DALY (USA)	68	77	81	83	309	6561.17	4686.55

So dreams do come true

David Park just missed a winning

European Tour debut but he

waited only a week to make amends

David Park matched the feat of Greg Norman and equalled a 22-year-old record when he won the Compaq European Grand Prix at De Vere Slaley Hall on only his second European Tour appearance.

More than 20,000 enthusiastic fans enjoyed glorious weather while watching Park prove that golfing dreams do come true. Just one week after losing to Miguel Angel Martin in a six-hole play-off for the Moroccan Open, Park showed he had the nerve to win in another tense battle with proven champion David Carter and fast-finishing Slaley specialist Retief Goosen.

This time, the 25-year-old Welshman holed a putt of two feet on the 18th for his first European Tour title, a cheque for 151,660 euro (£108,328), a two-year Tour exemption, and a place in the Open Championship at Carnoustie. It equalled the achievement of the Australian legend Norman, who won the 1977 Martini

DAVID CARTER: looked favourite at the turn

International on his second appearance on the European Tour.

Park, a self-possessed young man, was very much unaware of what his success had brought him, concentrating with almost Ben Hogan-like intensity on each shot and letting the rest take care of itself. When celebrating his 25th birthday on the Friday of the tournament, he was fully prepared to return to the European Challenge Tour and play in the Rolex Open, but his win, by one shot from Carter and Goosen with a 14 under par score of 274, underlined the importance of the European Tour's policy of opportu-nity and incentive. Now the door was open to compete in the Open Championship and take on the superstars of world golf week after week.

It was, as The Times reported, a cele-bration of the fact that romance is not dead, even in the sometimes cynical world of modern sport.

Park's winning putt on the 18th, which ranked as the most difficult hole on a rain-hit final day, came after he and Carter had been locked together, trading shot for shot over the final two rounds. The pair were 14 under par playing the last, and a play-off was looming until Carter missed the fairway and was unable to reach the green in two. Park hit the green with a superb approach and Carter just failed to pitch and single putt, leaving Park to hole from two feet for a terrific win.

Carter, who partnered Nick Faldo to England's 1998 World Cup victory, had looked favourite when he went to turn in level par with Park two over. But three crucial blows brought the Welshman into contention and tied for the lead. After he hooked his drive at the tenth hole across a brook and behind a tree, he played a marvellous approach under the branches, carried a bunker to a raised green and made par.

Then he birdied the next to move within one shot and holed a great putt at the 14th to match Carter at 14 under par. And when Carter found the rough at the 18th, Park played a superb approach to hit the green to take command. "It was a tough putt," said Park of his winning stroke. "But it was uphill and it was a bit left to right. There were lots of things going through my head, but I gave myself a slap around the chops and said 'come on, hole it' and it went in the left side of the hole. It was a great feeling."

SHOT OF THE WEEK

David Park's approach to the 18th on the last day to set up a winning par was a real challenger for Shot of the Week. But even more impressive was his nine iron from the fairway bunker on the 395 yards 16th in the third round. Park had an awkward stance with his feet half in and out of the hazard, and his cleanly struck recov-ery carried the ball 140 yards to a foot from the pin for a birdie.

THE COURSE

Architect Dave Thomas's creation commands increasing respect as a challenging examination for world-class golfers. All of his own vast experience as a tournament winner and Ryder Cup star has been used to make the 7,088 yards course call for a carefully measured blend of power and finesse. In a stunning Tyne Valley setting in the 1,000-acre Slaley Hall estate with spectacular views, it demands the kind of golf that attracts and excites galleries. The exceptional talents of Europe's number one, Colin Montgomerie, excelled at Slaley Hall when he won two years ago, and now the course has inspired the dramatic arrival of a new champion, David Park.

Declared Carter: " I could not believe it when my putt on the 18th missed – I thought it was dying into the hole, but congratulations to David Park, we had a good day together." South African Goosen, winner at Slaley Hall in 1996 and second the next year, continued his love affair with the Northumberland layout, shooting a closing 66 to share the runner-up role. "Slaley seems to suit my game," he said. "I love the course and the hotel."

Joe McNally, Managing Director of Compaq UK, was a happy man with the support and enthusiasm of big crowds. He said: "It's the third year we have sponsored this event. The venue is superb and under the stewardship of De Vere we have a very professional tournament, and having been born in Gateshead, nothing pleases me more than attracting a major tournament to this part of the world."

Alan Hedley

PETER MITCHELL: second round 65 equalled course record

DE VERE SLALEY HALL, NORTHUMBERLAND, ENGLAND, JUNE 24–27, 1999 · PAR 72 · YARDS 7088

Pos	Name & Country	Rnd 1	Rnd 2	Rnd 3	Rnd 4	Total	Prize Money €	£
1	David PARK (Wal)	67	65	70	72	274	151660.00	108328.57
2	David CARTER (Eng)	65	69	68	73	275	79030.00	56450.00
	Retief GOOSEN (SA)	70	68	71	66	275	79030.00	56450.00
4	Peter O'MALLEY (Aus)	66	71	71	70	278	45500.00	32500.00
5	Lee WESTWOOD (Eng)	72	70	67	70	279	38540.00	27528.57
6	Ricardo GONZALEZ (Arg)	70	70	71	71	282	29575.00	21125.00
	Dean ROBERTSON (Scot)	72	70	72	68	282	29575.00	21125.00
8	Stephen LEANEY (Aus)	71	72	69	71	283	20423.33	14588.09
	Warren BENNETT (Eng)	73	70	73	67	283	20423.33	14588.09
	José COCERES (Arg)	69	68	73	73	283	20423.33	14588.09
11	Sven STRÜVER (Ger)	69	67	74	74	284	14864.80	10617.71
	Padraig HARRINGTON (Ire)	71	71	71	71	284	14864.80	10617.71
	Jamie SPENCE (Eng)	68	71	71	74	284	14864.80	10617.71
	Darren CLARKE (N.Ire)	71	69	76	68	284	14864.80	10617.71
	Emanuele CANONICA (It)	72	69	69	74	284	14864.80	10617.71
16	Johan RYSTRÖM (Swe)	69	72	71	73	285	11810.40	8436.00
	Massimo SCARPA (It)	72	67	74	72	285	11810.40	8436.00
	Stephen SCAHILL (NZ)	73	69	73	70	285	11810.40	8436.00
	Peter MITCHELL (Eng)	72	65	75	73	285	11810.40	8436.00
	Andrew COLTART (Scot)	73	69	71	72	285	11810.40	8436.00
21	Geoff OGILVY (Aus)	71	72	73	70	286	10374.00	7410.00
	Robert LEE (Eng)	70	70	77	69	286	10374.00	7410.00
	Stephen GALLACHER (Scot)	72	71	72	71	286	10374.00	7410.00
24	John MCHENRY (Ire)	72	71	72	72	287	9009.00	6435.00
	Paul AFFLECK (Wal)	72	69	73	73	287	9009.00	6435.00
	Ian GARBUTT (Eng)	70	68	73	76	287	9009.00	6435.00
	Russell CLAYDON (Eng)	71	69	74	73	287	9009.00	6435.00
	Ross MCFARLANE (Eng)	70	71	73	73	287	9009.00	6435.00
	Thomas GÖGELE (Ger)	70	74	73	70	287	9009.00	6435.00
	Alex CEJKA (Ger)	71	71	76	69	287	9009.00	6435.00
31	Gary EMERSON (Eng)	68	75	75	70	288	7200.38	5143.13
	Greg TURNER (NZ)	72	70	73	73	288	7200.38	5143.13
	David HOWELL (Eng)	71	69	75	73	288	7200.38	5143.13
	Thomas LEVET (Fr)	71	73	71	73	288	7200.38	5143.13
	Jeev Milkha SINGH (Ind)	68	69	72	79	288	7200.38	5143.13
	Miles TUNNICLIFF (Eng)	69	68	73	78	288	7200.38	5143.13
	Massimo FLORIOLI (It)	74	67	74	73	288	7200.38	5143.13
	Diego BORREGO (Sp)	70	70	71	77	288	7200.38	5143.13
39	Daren LEE (Eng)	68	70	76	75	289	5369.00	3835.00
	Robert Jan DERKSEN (Hol)	69	73	76	71	289	5369.00	3835.00
	Michael CAMPBELL (NZ)	69	70	76	74	289	5369.00	3835.00
	Jonathan LOMAS (Eng)	69	73	76	71	289	5369.00	3835.00
	Richard BOXALL (Eng)	75	69	74	71	289	5369.00	3835.00
	Ian HUTCHINGS (SA)	71	73	75	70	289	5369.00	3835.00
	Seve BALLESTEROS (Sp)	73	69	74	73	289	5369.00	3835.00
	Fabrice TARNAUD (Fr)	71	71	75	72	289	5369.00	3835.00
	Brian DAVIS (Eng)	70	73	71	75	289	5369.00	3835.00
	Stephen BENNETT (Eng)	68	70	75	76	289	5369.00	3835.00
	Paul MCGINLEY (Ire)	67	73	74	75	289	5369.00	3835.00
	David GILFORD (Eng)	74	65	71	79	289	5369.00	3835.00
51	David LYNN (Eng)	67	72	78	73	290	4095.00	2925.00
	Van PHILLIPS (Eng)	70	73	73	74	290	4095.00	2925.00
53	Barry LANE (Eng)	70	74	72	75	291	3219.13	2299.38
	Anders FORSBRAND (Swe)	71	73	74	73	291	3219.13	2299.38
	Roger WESSELS (SA)	71	73	74	73	291	3219.13	2299.38
	Gary ORR (Scot)	71	70	74	76	291	3219.13	2299.38
	Jarrod MOSELEY (Aus)	70	73	75	73	291	3219.13	2299.38
	Eric CARLBERG (Swe)	73	70	75	73	291	3219.13	2299.38
	Carlos LARRAIN (Ven)	72	72	74	73	291	3219.13	2299.38
	John SENDEN (Aus)	70	69	76	76	291	3219.13	2299.38
61	Andrew RAITT (Eng)	74	70	73	76	293	2502.50	1787.50
	Carlos RODILES (Sp)	73	66	78	76	293	2502.50	1787.50
	Richard GREEN (Aus)	72	72	73	76	293	2502.50	1787.50
	Henrik BJORNSTAD (Nor)	74	69	76	74	293	2502.50	1787.50
65	Anders HANSEN (Den)	69	73	79	73	294	1667.33	1190.95
	Ignacio GARRIDO (Sp)	68	73	75	78	294	1667.33	1190.95
	Paul EALES (Eng)	75	69	78	72	294	1667.33	1190.95
68	Philip WALTON (Ire)	72	71	77	75	295	1356.00	968.57
	Peter BAKER (Eng)	72	70	77	76	295	1356.00	968.57
	Andrew BEAL (Eng)	73	68	74	80	295	1356.00	968.57
71	Stuart CAGE (Eng)	73	71	76	76	296	1348.50	963.21
	Stephen DODD (Wal)	74	70	73	79	296	1348.50	963.21
	Kenneth FERRIE (AM) (Eng)	73	70	78	76	297		
73	Nick O'HERN (Aus)	72	71	80	75	298	1344.00	960.00
74	Jorge BERENDT (Arg)	72	72	82	73	299	1339.50	956.79
	Justin ROSE (Eng)	75	69	82	73	299	1339.50	956.79

RETIEF GOOSEN: Slaley Hall specialist

El Nino blows all aside

Still a lad among men, his professional

career only six tournaments old, now

Sergio Garcia joins the Tour champions

The exciting career of Sergio Garcia is destined to be measured by many milestones before he takes his eventual leave of the game in the far off distant future. But none will be more significant than his first professional victory and the manner in which he achieved it in the Murphy's Irish Open.

Put in perspective, he was still a schoolboy even though he had turned professional 74 days before the championship. He was 19 years old and by definition, therefore, a mere lad amongst men when they assembled at the awesome Druids Glen course in County Wicklow for the championship.

But he was to prove himself beyond doubt before the week was out as he outplayed more seasoned rivals to win what was only his sixth professional event. Moreover, his performance on the final day entered the realms of pure match-play as he took on Argentinian Angel Cabrera and emerged triumphant from their duel and in so doing added fuel to the debate about his eligibilty for Ryder Cup team service.

At the start of the week public attention had focused firmly on former Open champion John Daly who had planned the make the Irish event part of his build-up for the Open Championship and looked to be regaining his vintage form when he opened with a 69. Sadly, the touch was not to last and an 81 in the third round convinced him that perhaps

he was not yet ready for the rigours of Carnoustie.

Even so, there had been moments of sheer brilliance from the American star who was well aware that the fans had come to see him perform the spectacular – whether sublime or ridiculous – and did not disappoint them.

Not once did Wild Thing back away from a difficult stroke yet philosophically accepted whatever outcome came his way. It was vintage stuff even if it did not quite come off this time.

Garcia – nicknamed El Nino in childhood because of his brisk style – had also opened with a 69 and was part of a general throng of campaigners settling down to what promised to be a low scoring contest that looked likely to be won – or lost – by the narrowest of margins. The leaderboard showed Colin Montgomerie and Lee Westwood neatly placed in the pack as they too became the focus of the thousands of exuberant Irish fans who turned up to witness the contest in the majestic region known as the Garden of Ireland.

Other characters however were to stroll across the stage before the dramatic

MIGUEL ANGEL MARTIN: final round 62

Sergio Garcia knew he had to kill off Angel Cabrera's challenge in decisive manner – he even referred to it afterwards as "a great match" between them – and chose the long 11th to widen a gap that was never to be closed. He lashed a three wood from the fairway towards the green, then trotted after the ball, urging it to reach the putting surface. It obliged, and Garcia took two putts for the first of three successive birdies that kept him beyond serious threat. It was the precise stroke when nothing less would do.

ANGEL CABRERA: duel in the Garden of Ireland

denouement and all of them had reason to hope that perhaps their moment had come. American professional Craig Hainline set a sparkling pace with a first day 65 and Welshman Phillip Price and Denmark's Søren Hansen subsequently broke free to share the halfway lead on ten under par 132.

Price has been acknowledged among his peers to be a solid performer ever since winning the Portuguese Open in 1994, but while his talent earned him a regular week-to-week income from

tournaments there had been no subsequent victories. For that reason he decided to kick-start his career in 1998 and employed a psychologist and coach to such beneficial effect that he finished 15th on the Volvo Order of Merit.

However, there still had been no wins when the 32-year-old professional came to Ireland, but at least he was more frequently in contention these days and reasoned that sooner or later another chance would come his way.

Not this time though, because both

THE COURSE

Druids Glen rewards the eternal virtues of accuracy and power and is also prepared to near-perfection and fairness which is the reason it remains such a favourite with European Tour professionals. The wide variation in character and direction of holes also makes it an exhaustive test of judgement with no serious "breather" holes on the homeward stretch. Once the extremely demanding 13th is negotiated, other perils lie in wait before the card can be signed.

he and Hansen were overtaken by the genial Cabrera edging past on the third day with a 66 to hold a two-stroke advantage going into the final round.

As it happened, an enduring local hero had moved within reach of the lead as 47-year-old Ryder Cup veteran Eamonn Darcy ambled across the scene to the delight of Irish fans who had not witnessed a fellow-countryman taking the

national title since John O'Leary became champion in 1982. The seasoned campaigner from just down the road at Delgany had seen active service on Tour since 1971 and moved within three strokes of the halfway lead to prove that the old touch had not diminished.

He still lurked going into the final round although he could be forgiven for not keeping pace when Garcia moved to overdrive. Even so, Darcy finished joint fourth to remind his rivals that he is still very much on the active list.

When Garcia found himself paired with Cabrera in the final round there was an instant man-to-man aspect about their encounter, particularly to the young Spaniard who had already won the British Amateur Championship in that form of play. He moved into swift action with a birdie at the first hole from 30 feet and after nine holes of intensive play had taken the lead.

Garcia looked to have put the title beyond reach when he birdied three successive holes from the long 11th where he reached the green with his second stroke and took two putts.

He then holed from 45 feet on the short 12th and from 30 feet at the next. But Cabrera was not quite finished and hit back with successive birdies at the 14th and 15th to narrow the gap. Then Garcia moved two strokes clear with a birdie four on the 16th that looked more like a salvage operation when he missed the green into a difficult lie but chipped down delicately and holed the putt.

At that moment the contest was essentially over and he had only to avoid disaster over the closing holes to become champion. He did even better and birdied the last – his eighth birdie of the day – to finish with a 64 and 16 under par 268 total.

He said afterwards: "I have been waiting all my life for this time." With respect, that is still not very long even for a prodigy. What sets him apart is that like players of rare quality, he works to his own standards just as Severiano Ballesteros and José Maria Olazábal did before him. And like them, there is a sense of greater destiny about the young man. Truly, the best is yet to come.

EAMONN DARCY: delighted Irish fans

Michael McDonnell

197

Druids Glen GC, Dublin, Ireland, July 1–4, 1999 • Par 71 • Yards 7012

Pos	Name & Country	Rnd 1	Rnd 2	Rnd 3	Rnd 4	Total	Prize Money €	Prize Money £
1	Sergio GARCIA (Sp)	69	68	67	64	268	233320.00	166657.14
2	Angel CABRERA (Arg)	70	66	66	69	271	155540.00	111100.00
3	Jarrod MOSELEY (Aus)	66	69	69	69	273	87640.00	62600.00
4	Miguel Angel MARTIN (Sp)	71	71	72	62	276	59453.33	42466.66
	Thomas BJÖRN (Den)	70	66	71	69	276	59453.33	42466.66
	Eamonn DARCY (Ire)	68	67	71	70	276	59453.33	42466.66
7	Malcolm MACKENZIE (Eng)	72	70	67	68	277	34055.00	24325.00
	Lee WESTWOOD (Eng)	70	68	71	68	277	34055.00	24325.00
	Colin MONTGOMERIE (Scot)	68	67	71	71	277	34055.00	24325.00
	Sven STRÜVER (Ger)	69	70	70	68	277	34055.00	24325.00
11	Gary ORR (Scot)	68	71	72	67	278	24890.00	17778.57
	Phillip PRICE (Wal)	67	65	75	71	278	24890.00	17778.57
13	Craig HAINLINE (USA)	65	72	72	70	279	21970.00	15692.86
	Emanuele CANONICA (It)	68	72	72	67	279	21970.00	15692.86
15	Russell CLAYDON (Eng)	69	69	71	71	280	18573.33	13266.66
	Stephen LEANEY (Aus)	70	71	67	72	280	18573.33	13266.66
	Ricardo GONZALEZ (Arg)	71	69	68	72	280	18573.33	13266.66
	John MELLOR (Eng)	68	71	73	68	280	18573.33	13266.66
	Alex CEJKA (Ger)	67	68	72	73	280	18573.33	13266.66
	David HOWELL (Eng)	69	73	67	71	280	18573.33	13266.66
21	Paul LAWRIE (Scot)	72	69	70	70	281	15750.00	11250.00
	Miguel Angel JIMÉNEZ (Sp)	68	72	75	66	281	15750.00	11250.00
	David CARTER (Eng)	70	70	70	71	281	15750.00	11250.00
	Peter O'MALLEY (Aus)	70	66	72	73	281	15750.00	11250.00
25	Roger WESSELS (SA)	67	73	71	71	282	14070.00	10050.00
	Des SMYTH (Ire)	73	69	67	73	282	14070.00	10050.00
	Andrew MCLARDY (SA)	69	67	72	74	282	14070.00	10050.00
	Soren HANSEN (Den)	69	63	76	74	282	14070.00	10050.00
29	Paul AFFLECK (Wal)	69	73	69	72	283	12390.00	8850.00
	Michael CAMPBELL (NZ)	68	69	68	78	283	12390.00	8850.00
	Jeev Milkha SINGH (Ind)	66	69	75	73	283	12390.00	8850.00
	Jim PAYNE (Eng)	68	73	70	72	283	12390.00	8850.00
33	Bernhard LANGER (Ger)	71	67	76	70	284	11200.00	8000.00
	Ignacio GARRIDO (Sp)	70	71	71	72	284	11200.00	8000.00
	Søren KJELDSEN (Den)	70	70	75	69	284	11200.00	8000.00
36	Steve WEBSTER (Eng)	72	68	70	75	285	10080.00	7200.00
	Ian GARBUTT (Eng)	72	68	69	76	285	10080.00	7200.00
	Paolo QUIRICI (Swi)	69	72	69	75	285	10080.00	7200.00
	Michael JONZON (Swe)	66	75	69	75	285	10080.00	7200.00
	Massimo SCARPA (It)	67	72	77	69	285	10080.00	7200.00
41	Silvio GRAPPASONNI (It)	69	71	75	71	286	8400.00	6000.00
	Jean Francois REMESY (Fr)	69	72	71	74	286	8400.00	6000.00
	David GILFORD (Eng)	69	71	76	70	286	8400.00	6000.00
	Costantino ROCCA (It)	72	70	74	70	286	8400.00	6000.00
	Paul BROADHURST (Eng)	70	71	74	71	286	8400.00	6000.00
	Greg TURNER (NZ)	69	68	72	77	286	8400.00	6000.00
	Paul EALES (Eng)	71	68	75	72	286	8400.00	6000.00
48	Fabrice TARNAUD (Fr)	72	70	71	74	287	6860.00	4900.00
	Wayne RILEY (Aus)	71	69	74	73	287	6860.00	4900.00
	Anders HANSEN (Den)	67	73	75	72	287	6860.00	4900.00
	Peter BAKER (Eng)	70	68	78	71	287	6860.00	4900.00
52	Derrick COOPER (Eng)	66	74	73	75	288	5600.00	4000.00
	Jonathan LOMAS (Eng)	72	70	73	73	288	5600.00	4000.00
	Joakim HAEGGMAN (Swe)	69	73	76	70	288	5600.00	4000.00
	Barry LANE (Eng)	74	67	74	73	288	5600.00	4000.00
	Brian DAVIS (Eng)	70	70	75	73	288	5600.00	4000.00
57	Peter LONARD (Aus)	71	67	75	76	289	4760.00	3400.00
58	Stephen GALLACHER (Scot)	72	70	78	71	291	4340.00	3100.00
	David PARK (Wal)	70	72	71	78	291	4340.00	3100.00
	Marc FARRY (Fr)	70	71	74	76	291	4340.00	3100.00
61	Ross MCFARLANE (Eng)	70	69	79	74	292	3850.00	2750.00
	Thomas LEVET (Fr)	71	71	71	79	292	3850.00	2750.00
	Alberto BINAGHI (It)	68	73	77	74	292	3850.00	2750.00
	Patrik SJÖLAND (Swe)	69	70	79	74	292	3850.00	2750.00
65	Anthony WALL (Eng)	72	68	78	75	293	3500.00	2500.00
66	Mathias GRÖNBERG (Swe)	72	69	77	77	295	2100.00	1500.00
67	John DALY (USA)	69	72	81	74	296	2097.00	1497.86
68	Richard COUGHLAN (Ire)	71	71	76	79	297	2094.00	1495.71

JARROD MOSELEY: *tied third rewarded consistency*

End of a long wait

Colin Montgomerie answers the need

for a Scot to win in Scotland

with a charge of nine birdies in 12 holes

The previews of The Standard Life Loch Lomond in the local newspapers followed familiar lines. Who was the last Scot to win a top-flight professional tournament on Scottish soil? It was, in fact, Ken Brown in the Glasgow Open at Haggs Castle in 1984. But even that statistic did not quite satisfy those who delight in delving deeper into the tournament history of the nation which claims to have invented the game.

Previous to The Standard Life Loch Lomond, the last Scot born in Scotland to win north of the border was Eric Brown in the 1960 Match-Play Championship at Turnberry, and if that still did not suffice, one had to go back to Tommy Armour in 1931 at Carnoustie to discover the last Scots-born player to win the Open Championship in his homeland. The odds, therefore, were stacked as high as Ben Lomond against the Tartan Army of Colin Montgomerie, Sam Torrance, Andrew Coltart,

Paul Lawrie and Dean Robertson when they arrived at Rossdhu House, the seat of the Clan Colquhoun.

Not only was history against them, so was 19-year-old Spaniard Sergio Garcia, who, the previous week, had emerged from Druids Glen with the Murphy's Irish Open title added to his burgeoning cv. He had rounded off on the Sunday with a 64, and on the Wednesday he resumed his slaying of the Celts with a 62 at Loch Lomond. Not only that, he asserted that he had played well enough to have shot a 59.

Montgomerie had to settle for a 69, dropping shots at each of the last two holes, confessing afterwards that he had not played well. At the top of the leaderboard, the precocious Garcia was being pursued by Sweden's Jesper Parnevik, who shot a 64, with the seasoned Roger Winchester stepping out from the chorus line with a 65 to join two other Swedes, Patrik Sjöland and Mats Lanner. One behind them, and menacing, following encouraging performances at Slaley Hall and Druids Glen, was the title holder Lee Westwood.

In ideal scoring conditions on the second day, Montgomerie lit up the tournament and his own visage with a 65. Had his putter been warmer he would have equalled Garcia's first round 62. Even so, it was a typically invigorating performance by Europe's number one, providing food to all his rivals on the leaderboard as he finished two shots behind Garcia and three behind Parnevik at the halfway stage.

Parnevik went to 11 under par with a 67 which he achieved at the same time as wrestling with a bizarre arithmetical problem. The extrovert Swede wanted to

SERGIO GARCIA: 62 but thought he deserved 59

Roger Winchester's seven iron for an eagle two at the 425 yards par four first hole in the second round. The shot, into the wind, measured 171 yards. It guided him to a score of 69 to add to his opening 65, and, eventually, a confidence-building top ten finish for the 1998 European Challenge Tour graduate.

know the difference in distance between a rope on the ground encircling the earth and another one three feet off the ground. For someone endeavouring to win the 233,320 euro (£166,657) first prize and

LEE WESTWOOD: looking dangerous once more

THE COURSE

In its usual immaculate condition and with the greens, as ever, among the best encountered during the season, the Loch Lomond course, designed by Tom Weiskopf, deserved its general high praise. Among the most scenic in the world, it achieves the fine balance of rewarding those with the boldness and ability to attack, but always implanting in the mind of the player that a loose shot can, and often will, be severely punished, Certainly, Loch Lomond is a course that demands constant and maximum concentration.

JESPER PARNEVIK: arithmetical problem solved

precious Ryder Cup points, it seemed an unnecessary distraction. But that's Jesper. If you are prepared to consume volcanic dust, anything is possible, and he was close to providing the correct answer which is, according to the best sources, 18.84 feet.

Garcia having returned to normality with a 70, the leaderboard was more congested, but nothing like what it was at the end of 54 holes. Westwood broke 70 for the third day, a 67 taking him into the lead at 12 under par. This was more like the Westwood of 1998. He had been frustrated by his form, and a shoulder injury, but now, the week before the Open Championship at Carnoustie, he was looking dangerous again.

However, his lead was the minimum. There were 11 players within four strokes of him, among them Garcia, the Challenge Tour discovery David Park, and, inevitably,

Montgomerie, who was round in 70 despite missing five putts of 15 feet and under.

"You can't afford to miss chances like that, but I'll sort it out tonight and give it my best shot tomorrow," Montgomerie said.

Midway through the final round, five players were locked together on 12 under par: Westwood, Garcia, Montgomerie, Lanner and Michael Jonzon. But, like middleweights in the ring with a super heavyweight, one by one they were all floored by the determined Scotsman. He began with a bogey, but in 12 holes from the fifth he had nine birdies, and by the time he strode off the 18th green with a 64 and the 15,000 gallery in tumult, he was three shots clear at 16 under par.

"This is my 20th win in Europe, and it's the one that means most to me," said an emotional Montgomerie. Yes, Scotland's long wait for a home winner was over.

Jock MacVicar   203

LOCH LOMOND, GLASGOW, SCOTLAND, JULY 7–10, 1999 • PAR 71 • YARDS 7050

Pos	Name & Country	Rnd 1	Rnd 2	Rnd 3	Rnd 4	Total	Prize Money €	Prize Money £
1	Colin MONTGOMERIE (Scot)	69	65	70	64	268	233320.00	166657.14
2	Michael JONZON (Swe)	69	66	70	66	271	104393.33	74566.66
	Sergio GARCIA (Sp)	62	70	71	68	271	104393.33	74566.66
	Mats LANNER (Swe)	65	71	66	69	271	104393.33	74566.66
5	Lee WESTWOOD (Eng)	66	68	67	71	272	54180.00	38700.00
	Jesper PARNEVIK (Swe)	64	67	71	70	272	54180.00	38700.00
7	Bob MAY (USA)	71	68	68	67	274	36073.33	25766.66
	Eduardo ROMERO (Arg)	69	67	70	68	274	36073.33	25766.66
	Michael CAMPBELL (NZ)	66	68	70	70	274	36073.33	25766.66
10	Roger WINCHESTER (Eng)	65	69	70	71	275	25075.00	17910.71
	David PARK (Wal)	69	65	68	73	275	25075.00	17910.71
	Patrik SJÖLAND (Swe)	65	73	69	68	275	25075.00	17910.71
	Retief GOOSEN (SA)	71	65	68	71	275	25075.00	17910.71
14	Robert ALLENBY (Aus)	72	67	69	68	276	21420.00	15300.00
15	Ian GARBUTT (Eng)	68	68	69	72	277	18928.00	13520.00
	Phillip PRICE (Wal)	68	71	69	69	277	18928.00	13520.00
	Angel CABRERA (Arg)	69	70	69	69	277	18928.00	13520.00
	Russell CLAYDON (Eng)	71	68	68	70	277	18928.00	13520.00
	Max ANGLERT (Swe)	71	71	67	68	277	18928.00	13520.00
20	Jean VAN DE VELDE (Fr)	69	68	69	72	278	16380.00	11700.00
	Thomas BJÖRN (Den)	70	66	66	76	278	16380.00	11700.00
	Fredrik LINDGREN (Swe)	71	69	68	70	278	16380.00	11700.00
23	Jamie SPENCE (Eng)	72	70	71	66	279	14490.00	10350.00
	Mark ROE (Eng)	69	71	69	70	279	14490.00	10350.00
	David CARTER (Eng)	72	66	70	71	279	14490.00	10350.00
	Darren CLARKE (N.Ire)	69	70	74	66	279	14490.00	10350.00
	Thomas LEVET (Fr)	69	70	70	70	279	14490.00	10350.00
	David HOWELL (Eng)	67	70	70	72	279	14490.00	10350.00
29	Greg OWEN (Eng)	71	71	71	67	280	12040.00	8600.00
	Miguel Angel JIMÉNEZ (Sp)	72	69	67	72	280	12040.00	8600.00
	Bradley HUGHES (Aus)	69	74	68	69	280	12040.00	8600.00
	Andrew COLTART (Scot)	68	70	69	73	280	12040.00	8600.00
	Nick FALDO (Eng)	68	70	68	74	280	12040.00	8600.00
	David GILFORD (Eng)	72	66	69	73	280	12040.00	8600.00
35	Craig HAINLINE (USA)	67	76	70	68	281	10780.00	7700.00
	Clinton WHITELAW (SA)	69	73	67	72	281	10780.00	7700.00
37	Jean-Francois REMESY (Fr)	70	68	72	72	282	9660.00	6900.00
	Billy MAYFAIR (USA)	70	69	71	72	282	9660.00	6900.00
	Stephen ALLAN (Aus)	71	69	69	73	282	9660.00	6900.00
	Stephen LEANEY (Aus)	73	66	72	71	282	9660.00	6900.00
	John SENDEN (Aus)	71	67	69	75	282	9660.00	6900.00
	Des SMYTH (Ire)	74	64	72	72	282	9660.00	6900.00
43	Miguel Angel MARTIN (Sp)	71	69	72	71	283	8400.00	6000.00
	Marc FARRY (Fr)	72	69	74	68	283	8400.00	6000.00
	Jarmo SANDELIN (Swe)	72	70	70	71	283	8400.00	6000.00
46	Mark JAMES (Eng)	70	70	71	73	284	6860.00	4900.00
	Peter SENIOR (Aus)	69	73	74	68	284	6860.00	4900.00
	Francisco CEA (Sp)	70	73	73	68	284	6860.00	4900.00
	Peter O'MALLEY (Aus)	71	66	74	73	284	6860.00	4900.00
	Anthony WALL (Eng)	75	68	73	68	284	6860.00	4900.00
	Steve WEBSTER (Eng)	71	69	71	73	284	6860.00	4900.00
	Glen DAY (USA)	71	72	71	70	284	6860.00	4900.00
	Gary ORR (Scot)	70	72	70	72	284	6860.00	4900.00
54	Sam TORRANCE (Scot)	68	74	72	71	285	5320.00	3800.00
	Craig SPENCE (Aus)	74	68	69	74	285	5320.00	3800.00
	Malcolm MACKENZIE (Eng)	69	73	70	73	285	5320.00	3800.00
57	Raymond RUSSELL (Scot)	72	69	73	72	286	4620.00	3300.00
	Per-Ulrik JOHANSSON (Swe)	70	67	77	72	286	4620.00	3300.00
59	Ignacio GARRIDO (Sp)	73	69	72	73	287	4130.00	2950.00
	Domingo HOSPITAL (Sp)	71	71	72	73	287	4130.00	2950.00
	Paul LAWRIE (Scot)	67	73	73	74	287	4130.00	2950.00
	Ricardo GONZALEZ (Arg)	70	70	72	75	287	4130.00	2950.00
63	Thomas GÖGELE (Ger)	70	69	74	75	288	3640.00	2600.00
	Alex CEJKA (Ger)	74	69	72	73	288	3640.00	2600.00
	Paolo QUIRICI (Swi)	74	68	72	74	288	3640.00	2600.00
66	Greg TURNER (NZ)	68	75	74	72	289	2100.00	1500.00
67	Tom GILLIS (USA)	70	73	72	75	290	2097.00	1497.86
	Matt KUCHAR (AM) (USA)	74	69	71	76	290		
68	Brian DAVIS (Eng)	69	72	71	79	291	2092.50	1494.64
	Andrew OLDCORN (Scot)	68	74	74	75	291	2092.50	1494.64
70	Barry LANE (Eng)	74	68	72	79	293	2088.00	1491.43
71	Daniel CHOPRA (Swe)	72	71	78	73	294	2085.00	1489.29
72	Richard BOXALL (Eng)	71	72	75	77	295	2082.00	1487.14

DAVID PARK: stepping out for a score of 65

VOLVO
PGA CHAMPIONSHIP
1988. IAN WOOSNAM
1989. NICK FALDO
1990. MIKE HARWOOD
1991. SEVE BALLESTEROS
1992. TONY JOHNSTONE
1993. BERNHARD LANGER
1994. JOSE MARIA OLAZABAL
1995. BERNHARD LANGER
1996. COSTANTINO ROCCA
1997. IAN WOOSNAM
1998. COLIN MONTGOMERIE
BY APPOINTMENT
TO H.M. THE QUEEN
JEWELLERS, GOLDSMITHS
& SILVERSMITHS
ASPREY & GARRARD LTD
LONDON
BY APPOINTMENT
TO H.M. QUEEN ELIZABETH
THE QUEEN MOTHER
JEWELLERS & SILVERSMITHS
ASPREY & GARRARD LTD
LONDON
BY APPOINTMENT
TO H.R.H. THE PRINCE OF WALES
JEWELLERS, GOLDSMITHS
& SILVERSMITHS
ASPREY & GARRARD LTD
LONDON

Carnoustie's inspiring hero

A face in the crowd, ten shots behind, then

Scotsman Paul Lawrie completes

an incredible journey as The Open winner

"There is a tide in the affairs of men,
Which, taken at the flood, leads on to fortune."

This couplet by William Shakespeare captures precisely the incredible drama of a Scottish afternoon in July when the personal destinies of a few brave men became entwined in the chase for glory until one of them reached out and grabbed it.

By coincidence, what happened at Carnoustie also underlined the wisdom of an old golf professional who once observed: "You don't win the Open. The Open wins you." The implication was that sometimes the great event lays in wait for a new and unsuspecting champion, then plucks him from the ranks.

So it was that Scottish professional Paul Lawrie turned up at the beginning of the 128th Open Golf Championship week to join a gathering throng of hopefuls whose simple and collective task was to prove themselves good enough for a place in the Championship. By the end of that week the Aberdeen golfer was holding the famous silver claret jug aloft as the last Open champion of the 20th century. It was an amazing journey that is destined to become part of golf's legend.

It is also the inspiring story of how a hitherto little known, but determined, campaigner leapt from 159th place in the

JESPER PARNEVIK: another top ten finish

ANGEL CABRERA: shared fourth place

PATRIK SJÖLAND: leaning to chip

Official World Golf Ranking to catch all the established stars by surprise with a measure of talent, persistence and – of course – good fortune that turned what had seemed the daydream of every aspiring golfer into breathtaking reality.

And yet his success story was linked inextricably to the fate of the Frenchman, Jean Van de Velde, who stood on the tee of the 72nd hole with what seemed an unassailable three-stroke lead and the title within his grasp only to see it all slip away, even though he lifted himself for one defiant flourish and joined the play-off with Lawrie and 1997 champion Justin Leonard where his chances were to be dashed again.

Even so, he bore that cruel experience with a sense of amused perspective not given to many of us as he shrugged off the loss of a place in history and the handsome fortune that went with it. It was, he reflected, still only a game and his misfortune was really of little consequence in the wider context of real tragedies that beset the world.

Such an uplifting attitude earned him huge admiration for the manner in which he had accepted what many considered to be self-inflicted defeat by his refusal in those closing moments to make full use of his stroke advantage and play safely down the final hole. In any case he had proved to himself that he could produce an

unbeaten 72-hole score in the Open Championship – albeit six over par 290 – and he reasoned that if he could do it once he could certainly do it again and be better prepared next time.

That winning score was in itself

commentary on the degree of difficulty both climate and course presented to the great players of the world, many of whom were seeing Carnoustie for the first time because 24 years had elapsed since the venue was last on the Open rota. Its

COLIN MONTGOMERIE: rough treatment

SERGIO GARCIA: The Open becomes a learning experience

TIGER WOODS: teeth-gritting strength

NICK FALDO: three times winner of The Open

reputation had preceded it in terms of the challenge offered as well as the calibre of previous winners – Tommy Armour, Henry Cotton, Ben Hogan, Gary Player and Tom Watson – it rewarded.

Consequently, even though the visiting stars were prepared for an exhaustive examination, they were clearly taken aback at the level of test that confronted them through narrow contoured fairways, sometimes only fifteen yards wide in the landing areas, as well as seemingly acres of savage rough that impinged too closely for their comfort on many fairways. If they had come to Carnoustie expecting routine tee-to-green stuff of the kind they experienced week-to-week, they were due for serious disappointment.

Carnoustie in these conditions required ingenuity, imagination and a repertoire of strokes that could not be acquired in just a few days. It also demanded a mind-set that accepted the inevitable disasters, ignored all conventional notions about par golf but concentrated instead on just producing the lowest score. However, none of these self-evident truths deterred the stars airing their disgruntled views in no uncertain terms when they arrived.

Meanwhile, at Downfield, in the audition for the supporting acts, Lawrie was working hard to earn his place on the big stage. Although he had won the Qatar Masters earlier in the season there was no obvious sign that he was about to move into such towering form. Indeed, his father Jim, who had taught him to play and acted as his caddie in the early days, was actually on holiday with the rest of the family in Spain during Open week.

JEAN VAN DE VELDE: happiness at the Open …

… is making birdies to take the lead …

… but serious grief is being in the Barry Burn at the 72nd hole and losing a three-shot advantage

Paul Lawrie held a slender one-stroke advantage as he stood over his second shot 221 yards from the final green in the play-off and was well aware of the menace of the Barry Burn which had previously taken its toll on both Justin Leonard and Jean Van de Velde. The slightest hint of self-doubt would almost certainly make him a victim too and throw the title back to his rivals. Under intense pressure he selected a four iron, gazed at the target then made a measured swing at the ball which rose majestically, bounced close to the greenside bunker but then rolled obediently to within four feet of the hole for a birdie. It was the stroke of a champion.

Lawrie qualified safely at Downfield yet still escaped public attention because another qualifier, 16-year-old English amateur Zane Scotland, took the headlines as the second youngest golfer ever to win a place in the Championship. Indeed, it was characteristic of Lawrie's progress that week that he remained out of the spotlight until his last-day charge when he made up a ten-stroke deficit on overnight leader Van de Velde, who had also come into the Championship the hard way by winning the qualifying tournament at Monifieth with a brace of 67s.

In the meantime, some of the main contenders who had dared to hope their crowning moment might be imminent had to revise their thoughts after punishing encounters with wind and rough on the first day. David Duval was dismayed to discover his style of play failed to fit the Carnoustie pattern.

Tiger Woods decided on negative strategy and left his driver in the bag, relying instead on long irons from the tee but in so doing giving away his obvious power advantage over his rivals.

In essence, the great players had failed to discover the correct way to play Carnoustie and their scorecards proved it. Defending champion Mark O'Meara signed for an 83 and went on to miss the halfway cut. Severiano Ballesteros had 80. Tom Watson took 82. Sergio Garcia scored 89, and Duval settled for 79 and observed wryly that he had just produced one of the worst scores of his career but was still in contention.

The first indication that the 128th Open Championship might not follow a customary pattern came when Australian professional Rodney Pampling marched over the links in 71 strokes to remind the stars that the fearless approach can bring its own rewards. It can also bring its own

JUSTIN LEONARD: a shot dropped and The Open is lost

ANDREW COLTART (top): it went thataway …

JOSÉ MARIA OLAZÁBAL (middle): it's in there somewhere …

GREG NORMAN (bottom): head up and press on

disasters too because on the second day he found such trouble that he missed the halfway cut.

His fate confirmed the more conventional view that the real title contenders – Colin Montgomerie, Ernie Els, Woods, Greg Norman and Jesper Parnevik, twice a runner-up at the Open – were simply waiting for their moment to strike and turn the Championship into the predicted showdown amongst themselves. Perhaps for that reason nobody paid too much attention to 30-year-old Lawrie who at the halfway stage was still just a face in the crowd.

Even Van de Velde himself, who had snatched the halfway lead with a 68 and 143 total, was being discussed in terms of how long his nerve might endure during the third round once the superstars put him under collective pressure. But the 33-year-old Frenchman refused to give way and after 54 holes had increased his lead to a five-stroke margin while none of the top-of-the-bill performers – except Leonard – made serious advance.

Woods had muzzled his firepower and spent the day without scoring a birdie. Montgomerie lost his edge with three bogeys in the last four holes. Norman was barely within range. In truth, time was running out for them so that the possibility of the Open being won by the first Frenchman since Arnaud Massy took the title in 1907 at Hoylake began to take serious shape.

Moreover, the Frenchman was playing with such colossal flair that nothing seemed to bother him and even the occasional crisis was negotiated with consummate ease. At this stage there were thirteen players as well as a margin of ten strokes between the leader and Lawrie who toiled to a third day 76 showing no signs of what was to come.

A book could be written – and probably will – about the events of that last day at Carnoustie with all its twists and turns of fate that left contenders and spectators utterly bemused as the title slipped one way and then the other. Earlier, the diminutive Australian Craig Parry menaced but then left the scene with a

THE COURSE

The toughest of all the Open venues because its 7,361 yardage follows all quarters of the compass with no more than two successive holes ever following the same direction. Consequently, all manner of shots are required when the wind blows and the closing three holes present the most awesome challenge over which the menacing Barry Burn and rough must be avoided at all costs. Extensive refinements to the course had been made including nine new Championship tees and additional bunkering.

couple of double bogeys and nobody else in that distinguished field seemed able to give chase.

What nobody knew – not even the central characters – was that an incredible drama was about to unfold. It began quietly enough with a best-of-the-day 67 from Lawrie which left him six over par with Leonard and three strokes worse than Van de Velde as the Frenchman came to the final tee.

That cushion of three strokes should have meant Carnoustie's last hole, menaced by the Barry Burn which winds across it, held no terror for him.

Indeed, it could have been negotiated safely with three successive seven iron shots to reach the heart of the green with the subsequent comfort of three putts to become Open champion.

But the Frenchman clearly wanted to win in style and reached for his driver to launch the ball and his destiny into a

nightmare sequence of errors – each more punishing than the previous one – and seemingly unable to stop the decline. The ball was pushed massively off line but miraculously found a decent lie. Van de Velde shrugged off any notion of caution and went for the green with a shot that clattered against the righthand grandstand and bounced back into deep rough.

The crisis was taking gruesome proportion because he hacked his third into the Barry Burn, thought about playing the ball – even removing his shoes and socks and standing in the water – but took a penalty drop instead. His fifth attempt landed in a bunker. His sixth finished six feet away and he sank a brave putt to earn a place in the play-off.

If nothing else he had given the lie to that old expression that nobody remembers who came second. The fact is that nobody will ever forget who came second at Carnoustie in 1999. Or how he did it either.

Nor will those who were present ever forget the fearless manner in which Lawrie stepped forward to claim the Open Championship as his own with a magnificent finish in the four-hole play-off, even though there had been clear signs of nervousness between Leonard, Van de Velde and himself at the start of their encounter. All that changed however when Lawrie took control with a four iron to ten feet in the gathering gloom for a birdie on the 17th and followed up with another on the last hole.

The game had found a true champion and Scotland a new golfing hero. It had been a long wait but well worth it and the words of Robert Burns seemed to define the nation's joy: "Now's the day, and now's the hour." And Paul Lawrie had shared it with them all.

Michael McDonnell

CARNOUSTIE, ANGUS, SCOTLAND, JULY 15–18, 1999 · PAR 71 · YARDS 7361

Pos	Name & Country	Rnd 1	Rnd 2	Rnd 3	Rnd 4	Total	Prize Money €	£
1	Paul LAWRIE (Scot)	73	74	76	67	290	490000.00	350000.00
2	Justin LEONARD (USA)	73	74	71	72	290	259000.00	185000.00
	Jean VAN DE VELDE (Fr)	75	68	70	77	290	259000.00	185000.00
4	Craig PARRY (Aus)	76	75	67	73	291	140000.00	100000.00
	Angel CABRERA (Arg)	75	69	77	70	291	140000.00	100000.00
6	Greg NORMAN (Aus)	76	70	75	72	293	98000.00	70000.00
7	David FROST (SA)	80	69	71	74	294	70000.00	50000.00
	Davis LOVE III (USA)	74	74	77	69	294	70000.00	50000.00
	Tiger WOODS (USA)	74	72	74	74	294	70000.00	50000.00
10	Jesper PARNEVIK (Swe)	74	71	78	72	295	48720.00	34800.00
	Scott DUNLAP (USA)	72	77	76	70	295	48720.00	34800.00
	Retief GOOSEN (SA)	76	75	73	71	295	48720.00	34800.00
	Hal SUTTON (USA)	73	78	72	72	295	48720.00	34800.00
	Jim FURYK (USA)	78	71	76	70	295	48720.00	34800.00
15	Tsuyoshi YONEYAMA (Jpn)	77	74	73	72	296	36400.00	26000.00
	Colin MONTGOMERIE (Scot)	74	76	72	74	296	36400.00	26000.00
	Scott VERPLANK (USA)	80	74	73	69	296	36400.00	26000.00
18	Bernhard LANGER (Ger)	72	77	73	75	297	28700.00	20500.00
	Andrew COLTART (Scot)	74	74	72	77	297	28700.00	20500.00
	Frank NOBILO (NZ)	76	76	70	75	297	28700.00	20500.00
	Patrik SJÖLAND (Swe)	74	72	77	74	297	28700.00	20500.00
	Lee WESTWOOD (Eng)	76	75	74	72	297	28700.00	20500.00
	Costantino ROCCA (It)	81	69	74	73	297	28700.00	20500.00
24	Peter O'MALLEY (Aus)	76	75	74	73	298	21420.00	15300.00
	Ernie ELS (SA)	74	76	76	72	298	21420.00	15300.00
	Brian WATTS (USA)	74	73	77	74	298	21420.00	15300.00
	Ian WOOSNAM (Wal)	76	74	74	74	298	21420.00	15300.00
	Miguel Angel MARTIN (Sp)	74	76	72	76	298	21420.00	15300.00
29	Padraig HARRINGTON (Ire)	77	74	74	74	299	18900.00	13500.00
30	Jeff MAGGERT (USA)	75	77	75	73	300	16180.00	11557.14
	Darren CLARKE (N.Ire)	76	75	76	73	300	16180.00	11557.14
	Payne STEWART (USA)	79	73	74	74	300	16180.00	11557.14
	Pierre FULKE (Swe)	75	75	77	73	300	16180.00	11557.14
	Thomas BJÖRN (Den)	79	73	75	73	300	16180.00	11557.14
	Tim HERRON (USA)	81	70	74	75	300	16180.00	11557.14
	Len MATTIACE (USA)	73	74	75	78	300	16180.00	11557.14
37	Mark MCNULTY (Zim)	73	77	76	75	301	13300.00	9500.00
	Dudley HART (USA)	73	79	75	74	301	13300.00	9500.00
	Peter BAKER (Eng)	77	74	78	72	301	13300.00	9500.00
	Nick PRICE (Zim)	77	74	73	77	301	13300.00	9500.00
	Michael WEIR (Can)	83	71	72	75	301	13300.00	9500.00
	Paul AFFLECK (Wal)	79	75	74	73	301	13300.00	9500.00
43	Duffy WALDORF (USA)	80	72	76	74	302	12180.00	8700.00
	Mark JAMES (Eng)	76	74	74	78	302	12180.00	8700.00
45	Steve PATE (USA)	73	76	80	74	303	11357.50	8112.50
	Naomichi OZAKI (Jpn)	74	78	75	76	303	11357.50	8112.50
	Jeff SLUMAN (USA)	80	74	77	72	303	11357.50	8112.50
	David HOWELL (Eng)	76	78	79	70	303	11357.50	8112.50
49	Neil PRICE (Eng)	79	74	76	75	304	10103.33	7216.66
	Thomas LEVET (Fr)	78	76	76	74	304	10103.33	7216.66
	Katsuyoshi TOMORI (Jpn)	74	75	79	76	304	10103.33	7216.66
	Kyoung-Ju CHOI (Kor)	76	72	81	75	304	10103.33	7216.66
	Bradley HUGHES (Aus)	76	71	78	79	304	10103.33	7216.66
	Dean ROBERTSON (Scot)	76	75	78	75	304	10103.33	7216.66
	Bob ESTES (USA)	75	76	77	76	304	10103.33	7216.66
	Stephen ALLAN (Aus)	79	73	83	69	304	10103.33	7216.66
	Peter LONARD (Aus)	76	78	74	76	304	10103.33	7216.66
58	Dennis PAULSON (USA)	74	78	79	74	305	9187.50	6562.50
	Jeremy ROBINSON (Eng)	77	76	77	75	305	9187.50	6562.50
	Santiago LUNA (Sp)	78	74	80	73	305	9187.50	6562.50
	Phillip PRICE (Wal)	77	76	77	75	305	9187.50	6562.50
62	Johan RYSTRÖM (Swe)	78	75	76	77	306	8890.00	6350.00
	David DUVAL (USA)	79	75	76	76	306	8890.00	6350.00
	Mark BROOKS (USA)	82	70	76	78	306	8890.00	6350.00
65	Jarmo SANDELIN (Swe)	75	78	77	77	307	8750.00	6250.00
66	Sven STRÜVER (Ger)	77	73	79	79	308	8680.00	6200.00
67	Lee THOMPSON (Eng)	75	78	76	80	309	8610.00	6150.00
68	Brian DAVIS (Eng)	80	71	82	77	310	8505.00	6075.00
	John HUSTON (USA)	80	71	77	82	310	8505.00	6075.00
70	Lee JANZEN (USA)	80	74	79	78	311	8400.00	6000.00
71	Katayama SHINGO (Jpn)	76	75	78	83	312	8330.00	5950.00
72	Martyn THOMPSON (Eng)	76	78	78	81	313	8225.00	5875.00
	Derrick COOPER (Eng)	75	77	76	85	313	8225.00	5875.00

Play-off:

Paul LAWRIE: 5 4 3 3

Justin LEONARD: 5 4 4 5

Jean VAN DE VELDE: 6 4 3 5

Barclays Premier is pleased to be associated with the PGA European Tour.

Barclays Premier Central Office, PO Box 122, 2 The Oaks, Westwood Business Park, Coventry CV4 8YZ. Telephone: (01203) 534642.

Dutch treat from Westwood

Five behind, then Englishman's
record-equalling 63 denies
three wins in a row for Scots

*I*t was rather like the
morning after the night
before when the players
arrived at Hilversumsche for
the 75th TNT Dutch Open.
Those contestants who had
played in the 128th Open
Championship the week
before were still recovering
from their sufferings at
Carnoustie and were look-
ing for some degree of
respite.

Hilversumsche, with its
tree-lined holes, can, rather
like the West Course at
Wentworth Club, prove
punishing when the fairways
are firm, hard and bouncy.

"This is a very different
course from the one I won
on last year," said stylish
Stephen Leaney. So he and
his colleagues were relieved
when heavy rain slowed
everything down.

In contrast to Carnoustie,
the Hilversumsche course
played comparatively friendly.
Scoring, as it is usually these
days on the European Tour,
was excellent. There were
birdies aplenty, and you lost
ground with a par-matching
71. Carnoustie had also been
a par 71 but it was 725 yards

SHOT OF THE WEEK

No player hit such a towering second shot as close to the stick at the 493 yards par five last hole as Darren Clarke did in his second round 65. But it is a putt on the home hole green which gets the vote as the shot of many great shots during the week. Putts seldom win the top accolade but the one from 20 feet Gary Orr holed under the severest pressure for a birdie four at the last on the final day was a beauty. He may not have won but that delicious putt was worth 42,000 euro (£30,000) and earned him well-deserved runner-up spot.

longer, the rough was thicker and fairways narrower. At Carnoustie there were nine scores under 70 on the week. At Hilversumsche there were 129.

The field in Holland was a strong one. Former Open and double US PGA champion Nick Price was in town playing his last event before flying off in his private jet with the family for a South African safari and a visit to Zimbabwe. He had finished joint third the previous year and had had high hopes of winning the title on this visit. Sadly, except for the third day, his putter was warm, not hot. He finished tied eighth.

There were Ryder Cup points at stake for the Europeans with the battle for a place in the automatic top ten intensifying, but what happened at Hilversumsche had only a marginal effect on the placings. True, Andrew Coltart and Bernhard Langer moved into the top ten ahead of Mark James, who missed the cut, but neither was seriously in contention to win at Hilversumsche. Langer finished tied 15th, Coltart tied 20th, and Alex Cejka, who made the cut, hardly improved his chances of travelling to Brookline when finishing 37th.

After a rainy first day six players shared the lead, and at one point on day two there were ten log-jammed at the top of the board. With two rounds to go there were just eight shots separating the leading players and the group that just made the cut setting up a weekend of nail-biting drama. It was a good week for the fans.

On that first day Argentinean Eduardo Romero, winner of 83 events in South America, and Angel Cabrera, tied fourth at Carnoustie, one shot off the play-off, both fired 67. Spain's Ignacio Garrido, Japan's Katsuyoshi Tomori, Italy's Emanuele Canonica and, much to the delight of the locals, Rolf Muntz, Holland's leading player, were on the same mark. For Muntz it was a welcome return to form after having missed 14 halfway cuts in 18 starts.

Romero stayed in the lead after two rounds and was joined by Oak Hill Ryder Cup hero Philip Walton, another golfer whose form had given him much cause for grief during the year. Holing putts had been his problem, or rather not holing them. Yet in a second round 66 he used a recently acquired putter only 24 times. He had been given the putter by the son-in-law of his gardener whom he had met at a petrol station. The fairytale of the second day was short-lived as Walton tumbled to 75, 75 over the weekend and ended tied 60th.

Three British players shared third spot at halfway. Jonathan Lomas, John Bickerton and Gary Orr, close friend of Open champion Paul Lawrie. It was Orr's faultless third round 65 which gave him

EDUARDO ROMERO: shared halfway lead

ROLF MUNTZ: gave Dutch fans a treat

the lead on the 54-hole mark two ahead of the diligent Muntz and three in front of Lomas, Darren Clarke, who had been second the year before, and Roger Chapman, the still-to-win Englishman whose six second place finishes include two in Holland.

It was not to be for Chapman or Lomas. Orr had the chance to become the third Scottish golfer to win a European title in as many weeks, a feat last achieved in 1984 through Sandy Lyle, Sam Torrance and Gordon Brand Junior. Orr, however, finished runner-up.

The winner was a golfer whose presence on the leaderboard or just off it can never be ignored and he won it in style. Not Stephen Leaney, the defending champion who finished seven back, not Heineken Classic winner Jarrod Moseley, who closed with a 66, nor Romero who made up for a disappointing Saturday 72 by firing a second best of the day last-round 64.

In fact, the golfer who came sweeping through to victory from five strokes back with a record-equalling last day 63 for 15 under-par 269 was Lee Westwood, whose

NICK PRICE: putter cold

PHILIP WALTON: warm work

Hilversumsche, staging the TNT Dutch Open for the 20th time, is one of Holland's best known courses, cut through the trees in an area east of Amsterdam now designated a national recreation area. Former Dutch champion W. Burrows and Harry Colt were the architects. It is inland and tree-lined but, curiously, the undulating fairways give the course a seaside feel. There is plenty of scope for the old-fashioned chip-and-run. The quality of the much-admired design has produced a series of fine champions over the years. In Lee Westwood this tradition was maintained in 1999.

only victory to date in 1999 had been the Macao Open on the Asian Tour. The previous year at Hilversumsche Westwood had finished joint third after opening with a 63. This time his spectacular finish gave him the victory he needed to encourage him in his bid to topple Colin Montgomerie from the Volvo Order of Merit No. 1 spot at season's end.

Westwood, who had dispensed with a prototype set of clubs for his old ones despatched by TNT to him in Holland just in time for him to use them in the second round at Hilversumsche, had insisted on Saturday night he was playing well enough through the green but putting like a chump. Make that champ on Sunday.

Orr doggedly stayed in the hunt until three-putting the 71st hole. He failed in his bid to make a last hole eagle to force a play-off, but he did make a birdie to grab second place on his own. Muntz was less fortunate. Needing a birdie to finish fifth on his own he took a bogey six. For him disappointment, but for champion Westwood, troubled by injury in the earlier part of the season, delight. Maybe the fans did not get their home-bred winner but the 75th TNT Dutch Open had not disappointed.

Renton Laidlaw

JARROD MOSELEY: tied third after 66

HILVERSUMSCHE G.C., HILVERSUM, AMSTERDAM, HOLLAND, JULY 22–25, 1999 • PAR 71 • YARDS 6636

Pos	Name & Country	Rnd 1	Rnd 2	Rnd 3	Rnd 4	Total	Prize Money €	£
1	Lee WESTWOOD (Eng)	72	68	66	63	269	186660.00	133328.57
2	Gary ORR (Scot)	69	67	65	69	270	124430.00	88878.57
3	Eduardo ROMERO (Arg)	67	68	72	64	271	63050.00	45035.71
	Jarrod MOSELEY (Aus)	68	70	67	66	271	63050.00	45035.71
5	Maarten LAFEBER (Hol)	73	68	64	69	274	40076.67	28626.19
	Darren CLARKE (N.Ire)	72	65	67	70	274	40076.67	28626.19
	Craig SPENCE (Aus)	73	67	66	68	274	40076.67	28626.19
8	John HUSTON (USA)	69	72	65	69	275	21488.57	15348.98
	Angel CABRERA (Arg)	67	71	67	70	275	21488.57	15348.98
	Rolf MUNTZ (Hol)	67	70	66	72	275	21488.57	15348.98
	Ian GARBUTT (Eng)	70	72	68	65	275	21488.57	15348.98
	Nick PRICE (Zim)	73	66	67	69	275	21488.57	15348.98
	Andrew OLDCORN (Scot)	76	66	67	66	275	21488.57	15348.98
	Jonathan LOMAS (Eng)	70	66	68	71	275	21488.57	15348.98
15	Paul MCGINLEY (Ire)	68	69	71	68	276	15142.40	10816.00
	Eamonn DARCY (Ire)	71	67	69	69	276	15142.40	10816.00
	Bernhard LANGER (Ger)	70	69	68	69	276	15142.40	10816.00
	Stephen LEANEY (Aus)	71	69	65	71	276	15142.40	10816.00
	Dean ROBERTSON (Scot)	73	68	70	65	276	15142.40	10816.00
20	Andrew COLTART (Scot)	72	67	68	70	277	12768.00	9120.00
	Ricardo GONZALEZ (Arg)	69	69	68	71	277	12768.00	9120.00
	David GILFORD (Eng)	68	70	70	69	277	12768.00	9120.00
	Anders HANSEN (Den)	75	68	64	70	277	12768.00	9120.00
	Katsuyoshi TOMORI (Jpn)	67	72	70	68	277	12768.00	9120.00
25	Roger WINCHESTER (Eng)	74	68	65	71	278	11088.00	7920.00
	Jim PAYNE (Eng)	71	71	67	69	278	11088.00	7920.00
	Roger CHAPMAN (Eng)	69	70	65	74	278	11088.00	7920.00
	Mark MCNULTY (Zim)	71	68	67	72	278	11088.00	7920.00
	Jeremy ROBINSON (Eng)	74	68	66	70	278	11088.00	7920.00
30	Paolo QUIRICI (Swi)	73	66	66	74	279	9232.00	6594.29
	Paul EALES (Eng)	68	70	71	70	279	9232.00	6594.29
	Massimo SCARPA (It)	74	69	66	70	279	9232.00	6594.29
	Peter LONARD (Aus)	74	65	70	70	279	9232.00	6594.29
	Geoff OGILVY (Aus)	71	67	70	71	279	9232.00	6594.29
	John BICKERTON (Eng)	69	67	72	71	279	9232.00	6594.29
	Jean-Francois REMESY (Fr)	71	72	68	68	279	9232.00	6594.29
37	Ignacio GARRIDO (Sp)	67	71	74	68	280	7840.00	5600.00
	Robert Jan DERKSEN (Hol)	71	68	72	69	280	7840.00	5600.00
	Christopher HANELL (Swe)	72	69	69	70	280	7840.00	5600.00
	Mats LANNER (Swe)	72	68	71	69	280	7840.00	5600.00
	Alex CEJKA (Ger)	71	72	70	67	280	7840.00	5600.00
42	Michael LONG (NZ)	69	70	70	72	281	6496.00	4640.00
	Henrik NYSTROM (Swe)	73	70	72	66	281	6496.00	4640.00
	Stephen FIELD (Eng)	69	71	71	70	281	6496.00	4640.00
	Henrik BJORNSTAD (Nor)	73	68	67	73	281	6496.00	4640.00
	Jeev Milkha SINGH (Ind)	72	70	70	69	281	6496.00	4640.00
	Massimo FLORIOLI (It)	69	68	73	71	281	6496.00	4640.00
	Pedro LINHART (Sp)	72	68	71	70	281	6496.00	4640.00
49	Santiago LUNA (Sp)	72	68	69	73	282	5152.00	3680.00
	Diego BORREGO (Sp)	71	72	72	67	282	5152.00	3680.00
	Andrew MCLARDY (SA)	70	72	66	74	282	5152.00	3680.00
	José RIVERO (Sp)	74	69	70	69	282	5152.00	3680.00
	Stephen GALLACHER (Scot)	70	72	69	71	282	5152.00	3680.00
54	Ian HUTCHINGS (SA)	70	72	75	66	283	4256.00	3040.00
	John MELLOR (Eng)	71	71	70	71	283	4256.00	3040.00
	Michael JONZON (Swe)	70	72	71	70	283	4256.00	3040.00
57	Francisco CEA (Sp)	69	72	75	68	284	3621.33	2586.66
	Stephen MCALLISTER (Scot)	73	70	75	66	284	3621.33	2586.66
	Jorge BERENDT (Arg)	71	70	73	70	284	3621.33	2586.66
60	Steen TINNING (Den)	70	70	73	72	285	3192.00	2280.00
	Fredrik JACOBSON (Swe)	75	67	71	72	285	3192.00	2280.00
	Tom GILLIS (USA)	73	69	74	69	285	3192.00	2280.00
	Philip WALTON (Ire)	69	66	75	75	285	3192.00	2280.00
64	Pierre FULKE (Swe)	70	72	70	74	286	2856.00	2040.00
	Joakim HAEGGMAN (Swe)	71	72	72	71	286	2856.00	2040.00
66	Daren LEE (Eng)	75	68	70	74	287	1680.00	1200.00
67	Stephen DODD (Wal)	69	73	71	76	289	1677.00	1197.86
68	Stephen BENNETT (Eng)	72	71	74	74	291	1671.00	1193.57
	Greg OWEN (Eng)	69	71	73	78	291	1671.00	1193.57
	Emanuele CANONICA (It)	67	72	72	80	291	1671.00	1193.57
	Maarten VAN DEN BERG (AM) (Hol)	73	70	76	73	292		
71	Olle KARLSSON (Swe)	71	72	75	74	292	1665.00	1189.29

Friendship feeds rivalry

Lee Westwood snatches title
after Darren Clarke scores
60 and goes six shots clear

The wind didn't even whisper in the willows. The birds suspended singing. The river hardly flowed and the salmon certainly didn't dare leap. Even the Irish spectators, starved of a home victory for 17 years, stood still in respectful silence. It was Saturday and the second round of the Smurfit European Open at the spectacular K Club. One of Ireland's own stood on the threshold of history. The magic number was 59. No one had ever broken 60 in a European Tour tournament. David Duval had done so in America earlier in the year, but 59 remained an impregnable barrier in Europe.

Darren Clarke was on his penultimate hole of the second round just eight feet from his 13th birdie. There was no reason to suppose he would miss. He had holed everything within that range and beyond throughout the round, but this time the ball shaved the cup and stayed above ground. There was one more hole left to play, one more chance at the jackpot. Again the big Irishman hit the green in regulation, again the crowd went into mute mode, waiting wishfully for that extra special something. But again he missed.

It seemed ludicrous to be disappointed. The man had just shot 60, twelve under par, to tie a European record. Sure, he had recorded 60 before in Monte Carlo but that was nine under and the K Club's Arnold Palmer design was a much tougher

DARREN CLARKE: It's going to take me a long time to get over it

A close run thing between Lee Westwood's three wood to the 18th hole on the last day to seal his victory and Darren Clarke's hole-in-one in his third round of 66. Westwood's was a draw of 239 yards which "wasn't a piece of cake but I started it exactly where I wanted to and drew it into the centre of the green." The par three fifth is in a pretty setting with a man-made waterfall as a spectacular backdrop. Clarke hit a "nice, high six iron 205 yards and it just trickled into the hole from the front of the green for my first hole-in-one as a professional. It was a fantastic feeling."

test, a course decreed worthy of hosting the Ryder Cup in 2005. But there was that unmasked feeling of an opportunity lost, even in Clarke's mind.

Yet, it was a magnificently compiled score, a flawless exhibition, four shots better than the previous record. Good enough for playing companion Ian Woosnam to say with conviction: "The way he played it should have been better." When Clarke added 66 on Sunday he went six shots ahead of one of the strongest fields to assemble on the European Tour's 1999 schedule. Australia's Peter O'Malley was second and Lee Westwood third, a shot further back.

But there was still a tournament to be won and the biggest prize ever offered by the European Tour, 316,660 euro (£226,185). One round, or even two, does

not win a tournament and, as Clarke was to learn the hard way, even three rounds with a lead of six shots fell short of the full requirement. The weekend days of Saturday and Sunday were certainly his but this was a Monday finish and the last day belonged, indisputably, to his friend, the irrepressible Westwood.

Ask Clarke which would he take 59 or the title? "That was a big one for me. I had a six-shot lead. I shot 60, had a hole-in-one and all that stuff, but I still didn't win the championship. It's going to take me a long time to get over it." Westwood knew the feeling: "The way Darren was playing I thought I could hear the Fat Lady starting to tune her voice but anything's possible. People think you're not under lot of pressure when you're six shots in front but you look back to when

"If golf was an accurate metaphor for business, the bunkers would be bigger and the holes would be smaller."

Business isn't one of the easiest forms of human endeavour.
But it is the one we're best qualified to give you advice on.
See if we can help; get in touch soon.

IF YOU'RE IN BUSINESS, WE'RE IN BUSINESS

Visit any AIB branch   **www.aib.ie**

PETER O'MALLEY: glimmer of hope

Nick Faldo beat Greg Norman in the 1996 Masters and situations like that and you see it can be done. I've had it done to me by Colin Montgomerie in the Murphy's Irish Open. I was due one in Ireland."

So, an Englishman came waltzing past an Irishman, scoring 65 to 75. The previous week it was Scotsman Gary Orr who felt the lethal whiplash of Westwood's tail as he came from five behind to win the TNT Dutch Open by a shot. Few will deny that it is often easier to win from behind than in front. The pressure is not the same, and even Westwood faltered when he had the lead. He found water at the treacherous 16th and took double bogey six to give Clarke and O'Malley a glimmer of hope, but neither could capitalise. In the end Westwood finished in style with a brilliant 239 yards three wood into the heart of the spectacular par five 18th for a closing two-putt birdie.

Apart from Westwood's win, there were other significant aspects of the championship. It marked the first appearance since the extraordinary events at Carnoustie of Paul Lawrie, the Scot who won the Open Championship, and Jean Van de Velde, the Frenchman who so nearly succeeded. How would fame affect them? Not a lot it seemed as Lawrie opened with 67 and closed with 70 to share 15th place at eight under and Van

PER-ULRIK JOHANSSON: Tour golf is a stage – with spotlights

THE COURSE

The K Club is ideally placed in the heartland of County Kildare just about 40 minutes from Dublin Airport. Designed by Arnold Palmer, it is endowed with magnificent and varied species of trees. Many more semi-mature varieties are to be planted before the Ryder Cup is played there in 2005. It has a par of 72 with a championship length of 7,179 yards. Darren Clarke set a new course record of 60 during the Smurfit European Open. The Ryder Cup teams in 2005 will stay in the magnificent, five star on-site Hotel.

PAUL LAWRIE (above) and JEAN VAN DE VELDE (right): coping well with new fame

de Velde achieved his stated targets to make the cut and consolidate his Ryder Cup position.

Even so the Smurfit European Open title belonged to Lee Westwood, and for Darren Clarke there were thoughts of what might have been.

Colm Smith

The K Club, Dublin, Ireland, July 30–August 2, 1999 • Par 72 • Yards 7179

Pos	Name & Country	Rnd 1	Rnd 2	Rnd 3	Rnd 4	Total	Prize Money €	Prize Money £
1	Lee WESTWOOD (Eng)	69	67	70	65	271	316660.00	226185.71
2	Darren CLARKE (N.Ire)	73	60	66	75	274	165020.00	117871.43
	Peter O'MALLEY (Aus)	68	69	68	69	274	165020.00	117871.43
4	Costantino ROCCA (It)	69	73	70	65	277	87760.00	62685.71
	Robert KARLSSON (Swe)	70	72	69	66	277	87760.00	62685.71
6	John SENDEN (Aus)	67	73	69	69	278	53350.00	38107.14
	Angel CABRERA (Arg)	69	69	70	70	278	53350.00	38107.14
	José COCERES (Arg)	67	70	70	71	278	53350.00	38107.14
	Gary EMERSON (Eng)	70	69	70	69	278	53350.00	38107.14
10	Richard GREEN (Aus)	71	69	69	70	279	33044.00	23602.86
	Peter LONARD (Aus)	72	67	72	68	279	33044.00	23602.86
	Andrew COLTART (Scot)	71	67	71	70	279	33044.00	23602.86
	Per-Ulrik JOHANSSON (Swe)	73	66	72	68	279	33044.00	23602.86
	Russell CLAYDON (Eng)	72	69	68	70	279	33044.00	23602.86
15	Paul LAWRIE (Scot)	67	71	72	70	280	26776.67	19126.19
	Colin MONTGOMERIE (Scot)	67	71	69	73	280	26776.67	19126.19
	Katsuyoshi TOMORI (Jpn)	66	69	73	72	280	26776.67	19126.19
18	Jarrod MOSELEY (Aus)	70	71	71	69	281	22641.67	16172.62
	Jamie SPENCE (Eng)	71	67	74	69	281	22641.67	16172.62
	Padraig HARRINGTON (Ire)	69	73	71	68	281	22641.67	16172.62
	Mark MCNULTY (Zim)	72	69	70	70	281	22641.67	16172.62
	Michael CAMPBELL (NZ)	66	74	72	69	281	22641.67	16172.62
	Brian DAVIS (Eng)	69	73	68	71	281	22641.67	16172.62
24	Silvio GRAPPASONNI (It)	68	72	70	72	282	18810.00	13435.71
	Steen TINNING (Den)	69	73	69	71	282	18810.00	13435.71
	Retief GOOSEN (SA)	70	68	73	71	282	18810.00	13435.71
	Stephen ALLAN (Aus)	68	75	68	71	282	18810.00	13435.71
	Craig SPENCE (Aus)	68	73	70	71	282	18810.00	13435.71
	Nick O'HERN (Aus)	70	72	70	70	282	18810.00	13435.71
	Paul EALES (Eng)	72	68	70	72	282	18810.00	13435.71
31	Greg TURNER (NZ)	71	71	71	70	283	15817.50	11298.21
	Nick FALDO (Eng)	70	73	70	70	283	15817.50	11298.21
	Andrew SHERBORNE (Eng)	73	69	73	68	283	15817.50	11298.21
	Francisco CEA (Sp)	71	68	70	74	283	15817.50	11298.21
35	Craig HAINLINE (USA)	69	70	69	76	284	13110.00	9364.29
	Stephen GALLACHER (Scot)	68	72	73	71	284	13110.00	9364.29
	Domingo HOSPITAL (Sp)	71	70	75	68	284	13110.00	9364.29
	Paul BROADHURST (Eng)	73	70	72	69	284	13110.00	9364.29
	Jean VAN DE VELDE (Fr)	70	71	70	73	284	13110.00	9364.29
	Gary ORR (Scot)	69	71	73	71	284	13110.00	9364.29
	Ian WOOSNAM (Wal)	67	72	72	73	284	13110.00	9364.29
	Eduardo ROMERO (Arg)	71	72	72	69	284	13110.00	9364.29
	Peter BAKER (Eng)	70	71	74	69	284	13110.00	9364.29
	Ricardo GONZALEZ (Arg)	68	75	72	69	284	13110.00	9364.29
45	Roger CHAPMAN (Eng)	68	73	74	70	285	10450.00	7464.29
	Jorge BERENDT (Arg)	68	73	68	76	285	10450.00	7464.29
	Barry LANE (Eng)	70	71	73	71	285	10450.00	7464.29
	Des SMYTH (Ire)	72	70	72	71	285	10450.00	7464.29
49	Alex CEJKA (Ger)	69	73	70	74	286	8550.00	6107.14
	Søren KJELDSEN (Den)	71	71	70	74	286	8550.00	6107.14
	Malcolm MACKENZIE (Eng)	67	72	76	71	286	8550.00	6107.14
	Soren HANSEN (Den)	73	70	73	70	286	8550.00	6107.14
	Sergio GARCIA (Sp)	71	69	73	73	286	8550.00	6107.14
	Anthony WALL (Eng)	73	70	71	72	286	8550.00	6107.14
55	Stephen LEANEY (Aus)	70	71	74	72	287	6127.50	4376.79
	Pedro LINHART (Sp)	75	68	76	68	287	6127.50	4376.79
	Diego BORREGO (Sp)	73	70	73	71	287	6127.50	4376.79
	Damian MCGRANE (Ire)	72	70	72	73	287	6127.50	4376.79
	David GILFORD (Eng)	68	68	79	72	287	6127.50	4376.79
	Daniel CHOPRA (Swe)	72	71	73	71	287	6127.50	4376.79
	Andrew RAITT (Eng)	72	71	69	75	287	6127.50	4376.79
	Paolo QUIRICI (Swi)	73	66	71	77	287	6127.50	4376.79
63	Ignacio GARRIDO (Sp)	70	72	71	75	288	4417.50	3155.36
	Roger WESSELS (SA)	73	70	73	72	288	4417.50	3155.36
	Raymond RUSSELL (Scot)	70	71	74	73	288	4417.50	3155.36
	Bob MAY (USA)	69	72	72	75	288	4417.50	3155.36
67	Clinton WHITELAW (SA)	69	69	77	74	289	2844.00	2031.43
	Dean ROBERTSON (Scot)	69	73	75	72	289	2844.00	2031.43
	Peter MITCHELL (Eng)	67	70	72	80	289	2844.00	2031.43
70	David CARTER (Eng)	74	69	75	74	292	2836.50	2026.07
	Miguel Angel JIMÉNEZ (Sp)	67	75	81	69	292	2836.50	2026.07
72	Philip WALTON (Ire)	72	71	76	78	297	2832.00	2022.86

NICK FALDO: three rounds of 70 win attention

future

Developing
packaging solutions
for future
generations

The development of global export markets has created sophisticated demands for packaging which will protect, present and promote a diverse range of products. Jefferson Smurfit Group has over sixty years' experience in meeting these demands innovatively and cost-effectively.

Together with its associates, Jefferson Smurfit Group is the world's largest paper-based packaging organisation and largest recycler of paper, with operations throughout Europe, Scandinavia and North and South America.

Smurfit has total control of the packaging manufacturing process, starting with sourcing and sorting waste paper for its own mills and producing virgin pulp from its own sustainable forests, through to the manufacture of paper and board and the production of a wide range of packaging for diverse markets.

From corrugated board to sturdy cases and complex cartons, Smurfit is skilled in answering the world's packaging needs, and with specialist Research and Design centres in Europe and the USA supporting its operations and customers globally, Smurfit is uniquely placed to develop paper and packaging solutions which meet today's needs and those of generations to come.

Jefferson Smurfit Group plc, World Headquarters, Beech Hill, Clonskeagh, Dublin 4, Ireland,
Phone: 00 353 1 2027000 Web Site: www.smurfit.ie

Another win, another record

Four European Tour titles in one year

sweep Colin Montgomerie

to a new milestone in his career

Colin Montgomerie, European No. 1 for the past six years, arrived at Barsebäck in Malmo for the Volvo Scandinavian Masters, the only European Tour event played in Sweden, on a mission. He had taken the decision quite deliberately not to head off for early practice at Medinah, Chicago, venue of the upcoming US PGA Championship.

He had also decided not to enter the Buick Open, the US Tour event opposite the Volvo Scandinavian Masters. Better, he thought, to compete in Europe in the week leading up to the last major of the year, and the Swedish tournament fitted the bill perfectly for him. After all, he did have a history of playing well in the European country where golf has boomed so dramatically in the past 20 years. Back in 1991 he won the event at Drottningholm in Stockholm, and had come second at Barsebäck in 1995 after a great battle with Jesper Parnevik. He had made nearly 350,000 euro (£250,000) in prize-money in the eight-year history of the event that succeeded Sven Tumba's Scandinavian Enterprise Open. In short, he liked the people, and the courses, and he had

another strong reason for being in Barsebäck. After successive wins, Lee Westwood, whose own aim was to end Montgomerie's extended reign as top money-earner, was snapping at the Scot's heels at the head of the Volvo Order of Merit.

In 1994, 1996 and again in 1998, Montgomerie had picked up three titles, and with first prize cheques already banked from the Benson and Hedges International Open, the Volvo PGA Championship and The Standard Life Loch Lomond, he now reckoned he could

win a fourth European Tour title in one year for the first time, and put some distance between Westwood and himself again.

Montgomerie knew, however, that he would face stiff opposition from Swedish favourite Parnevik who was keen to successfully defend the title in order to boost his chances of making the European Ryder Cup team automatically instead of having to rely on a wild card selection from captain Mark James. That invitation seemed hopeful after he had putted superbly to win his second US PGA Tour title – the Greater Greensboro Chrysler Classic – but he knew it would help if James did not need to use a captain's pick to take him to The Country Club, Brookline.

It was the perfect scenario for four days of superb golf over the course which overlooks the Oresund, across which it is possible to see Copenhagen on a clear day. Fans from Denmark and Northern Germany traditionally head by hydrofoil and helicopter to Barsebäck at the weekend for the tournament, joining the locals and the many golfing visitors who flock to an area where there are 50 courses within an hour's drive of Malmo's city centre. By the year 2000 a bridge and tunnel will link

SHOT OF THE WEEK

Although Australian Rodger Davis had his own "first" – a three wood second shot hit into the hole for an albatross two – the second of the season – at the 547 yards par five 16th, the shot of the tournament was produced by Swede Patrik Sjöland. In the first round, he stepped on to the tee at the 170 yards eighth, pulled out a six iron and promptly holed-in-one. He went on to miss the halfway cut, which came at level par, but had the consolation of winning a £25,000 car from sponsors Volvo for his feat. It was his second hole-in-one of the season – he aced the 17th in the Qatar Masters – and it was the Tour's 25th ace of 1999.

PATRIK SJÖLAND: won Volvo car

Denmark and Sweden, making the journey for the fans even easier.

Although he had dashed from Dublin, and the Smurfit European Open, Montgomerie competed cheerily in the Eurocard Challenge, in which he partnered Touring Car champion Rickard Rydell in the pre-tournament pro-am. If he was tired he did not show it and was more than happy with his game as he teed up on the first afternoon.

Montgomerie, the only golfer with a sub 70 average score for the season, got off to a good start with a five under par, competently compiled 67. It tied him for second place with fellow Scot Dean Robertson, but both were two shots behind a former Ryder Cup player, Paul Broadhurst, who surprised himself with his course record-equalling pace-setting score.

Tony Johnstone had set the record of 65 in 1992, the year Nick Faldo won the title. Vijay Singh had equalled it in 1995, but Broadhurst, having dispensed with the help of long-time coach Bill Ferguson to concentrate more on the mental side of the game with psychologist John Alsopp, was hardly having one of his best seasons. Ninetieth in the Volvo Order of Merit he had made only nine cuts in 21 starts. He was concerned about his game and his opening 65 gave him a much-needed boost of confidence.

While Broadhurst shot a second round 72, Montgomerie added another 67 for ten under par to move smoothly into the lead even if he did not grab all the headlines. Rookie Geoff Ogilvy, the 22-year-old Australian, improved 12 shots on his opening round 74 with a staggering 62, shattering the old record by three. It was his best ever career round and moved him

JESPER PARNEVIK: Swedish favourite putting on the style

THE COURSE

Many of the original holes at Barsebäck, one of Sweden's best known golf complexes, were altered substantially several years ago by British architect Donald Steel. The last six used for the Volvo Scandinavian Masters were all designed by Steel with the 438-yard 17th named as Sweden's best golf hole in 1998. What makes the course unusual is that four holes – the short eighth, the ninth, tenth and 11th – are all played along the shores of the Oresund and have a distinctly Scottish links-look about them. At 7,318 yards the Barsebäck course is an excellent test which made long-hitting Geoff Ogilvy's eight birdies and an eagle record 62 justifiably one of the rounds of the year.

ROBERT KARLSSON: well placed and hoping

into contention as Robertson slipped back. Parnevik was tied with Broadhurst, three back, after rounds of 69 and 68.

The Ryder Cup hopes of Ian Woosnam and Patrik Sjöland were dented when they missed the halfway cut, the Swede despite an ace at the eighth on the first day. But Andrew Coltart and Robert Karlsson, ninth and tenth in the points table, were well placed at halfway to increase their chances of a Cup debut, and both David Carter and Per-Ulrik Johansson were in form, too. The prospect of a weekend battle between Parnevik and Montgomerie was especially intriguing.

While Montgomerie completed a near flawless third round 65, Parnevik, losing his putting touch on the back nine, lost ground with a 69. So Montgomerie's last day partner was Broadhurst, six behind after 54 holes. Parnevik was seven behind in the second last group with Carter, who had abandoned his "broomstick" for a regular length putter.

The weather, which had been so wonderful for the first three days, finally broke. On Sunday it was windy and rainy, and the course played at its most difficult which helped Montgomerie. It was not a day for anyone to make a last day charge. Montgomerie knew if he shot 70 then Broadhurst would need 63 to beat him;

Parnevik or Carter would need to equal Ogilvy's new course record – virtually impossible in the conditions.

As a contest it was clear early on the last day that Montgomerie had ended it on Saturday. There would be a battle for second prize between Parnevik, Ogilvy, Francisco Cea, the impressive young Spaniard, and Las Vegas-based American Bob May, having his most consistent season – a battle Parnevik would win. Montgomerie simply strolled to his 21st European Tour victory, shooting one better than his planned 70 to win by nine – his biggest winning margin since taking the Portuguese Open in 1989 by 11 shots.

His four-round total of 268 was two better than the previous best winning score at Barsebäck, and his 20 under par performance better than his 15 under par win at the Benson and Hedges International Open, his 18 under par defence of his Volvo PGA Championship title at Wentworth and his 16 under par win at The Standard Life Loch Lomond. He had achieved his goal. He had won four titles for the first time and had moved 407,400 euro (£293,000) ahead of rival Westwood in the Volvo Order of Merit.

Renton Laidlaw

Barsebäck G & C.C., Malmo, Sweden, August 5–8, 1999 • Par 72 • Yards 7318

Pos	Name & Country	Rnd 1	Rnd 2	Rnd 3	Rnd 4	Total	Prize Money €	£
1	Colin MONTGOMERIE (Scot)	67	67	65	69	268	233320.00	166657.14
2	Jesper PARNEVIK (Swe)	69	68	69	71	277	155540.00	111100.00
3	Bob MAY (USA)	71	71	67	69	278	78820.00	56300.00
	Geoff OGILVY (Aus)	74	62	71	71	278	78820.00	56300.00
5	Francisco CEA (Sp)	68	72	67	72	279	46340.00	33100.00
	Andrew MCLARDY (SA)	70	71	66	72	279	46340.00	33100.00
	Robert KARLSSON (Swe)	71	69	71	68	279	46340.00	33100.00
	Katsuyoshi TOMORI (Jpn)	72	69	69	69	279	46340.00	33100.00
9	Russell CLAYDON (Eng)	72	70	67	71	280	26304.00	18788.57
	Brian DAVIS (Eng)	73	70	70	67	280	26304.00	18788.57
	Jarrod MOSELEY (Aus)	68	70	73	69	280	26304.00	18788.57
	Paul BROADHURST (Eng)	65	72	68	75	280	26304.00	18788.57
	Greg TURNER (NZ)	70	68	70	72	280	26304.00	18788.57
14	Michael CAMPBELL (NZ)	70	67	72	72	281	20160.00	14400.00
	Gary ORR (Scot)	69	72	71	69	281	20160.00	14400.00
	Steen TINNING (Den)	71	66	72	72	281	20160.00	14400.00
	David CARTER (Eng)	70	68	68	75	281	20160.00	14400.00
18	Richard BOXALL (Eng)	72	70	70	70	282	17406.67	12433.34
	Per NYMAN (Swe)	70	70	67	75	282	17406.67	12433.34
	Mathias GRÖNBERG (Swe)	76	68	68	70	282	17406.67	12433.34
21	Peter O'MALLEY (Aus)	73	71	69	70	283	14700.00	10500.00
	David PARK (Wal)	74	70	68	71	283	14700.00	10500.00
	Padraig HARRINGTON (Ire)	73	69	69	72	283	14700.00	10500.00
	Dean ROBERTSON (Scot)	67	70	73	73	283	14700.00	10500.00
	Gary EMERSON (Eng)	72	72	67	72	283	14700.00	10500.00
	Wayne WESTNER (SA)	69	72	71	71	283	14700.00	10500.00
	Jamie SPENCE (Eng)	73	69	70	71	283	14700.00	10500.00
	Paolo QUIRICI (Swi)	70	68	75	70	283	14700.00	10500.00
	Gary EVANS (Eng)	69	69	72	73	283	14700.00	10500.00
30	Jonathan LOMAS (Eng)	72	72	67	73	284	11540.00	8242.86
	Henrik STENSON (Swe)	69	71	72	72	284	11540.00	8242.86
	Adam MEDNICK (Swe)	72	70	73	69	284	11540.00	8242.86
	Jarmo SANDELIN (Swe)	74	70	68	72	284	11540.00	8242.86
	Tony JOHNSTONE (Zim)	74	70	68	72	284	11540.00	8242.86
	Stephen ALLAN (Aus)	73	67	68	76	284	11540.00	8242.86
	Søren KJELDSEN (Den)	70	71	72	71	284	11540.00	8242.86
37	Michael LONG (NZ)	69	71	74	71	285	9380.00	6700.00
	Ignacio GARRIDO (Sp)	70	73	71	71	285	9380.00	6700.00
	Johan RYSTRÖM (Swe)	71	73	72	69	285	9380.00	6700.00
	Jean VAN DE VELDE (Fr)	70	70	72	73	285	9380.00	6700.00
	Per-Ulrik JOHANSSON (Swe)	71	68	68	78	285	9380.00	6700.00
	Ian GARBUTT (Eng)	70	70	72	73	285	9380.00	6700.00
	Rodger DAVIS (Aus)	71	72	71	71	285	9380.00	6700.00
	Fredrik JACOBSON (Swe)	71	69	75	70	285	9380.00	6700.00
45	Henrik NYSTROM (Swe)	72	72	68	74	286	7280.00	5200.00
	Raphaël JACQUELIN (Fr)	69	74	71	72	286	7280.00	5200.00
	Malcolm MACKENZIE (Eng)	72	71	74	69	286	7280.00	5200.00
	Andrew COLTART (Scot)	69	70	75	72	286	7280.00	5200.00
	Rolf MUNTZ (Hol)	74	69	69	74	286	7280.00	5200.00
	Miguel Angel MARTIN (Sp)	72	70	70	74	286	7280.00	5200.00
	Paul MCGINLEY (Ire)	72	71	68	75	286	7280.00	5200.00
52	Paul EALES (Eng)	73	71	71	72	287	5320.00	3800.00
	John MELLOR (Eng)	68	72	70	77	287	5320.00	3800.00
	Richard GREEN (Aus)	71	70	70	76	287	5320.00	3800.00
	José RIVERO (Sp)	69	69	72	77	287	5320.00	3800.00
	Thomas BJÖRN (Den)	77	66	72	72	287	5320.00	3800.00
	Emanuele CANONICA (It)	77	64	69	77	287	5320.00	3800.00
	Greg OWEN (Eng)	73	69	73	72	287	5320.00	3800.00
59	Barry LANE (Eng)	71	69	74	74	288	3990.00	2850.00
	Sven STRÜVER (Ger)	71	69	73	75	288	3990.00	2850.00
	Retief GOOSEN (SA)	73	71	71	73	288	3990.00	2850.00
	Costantino ROCCA (It)	68	73	74	73	288	3990.00	2850.00
	Alex CEJKA (Ger)	72	69	71	76	288	3990.00	2850.00
	Craig STADLER (USA)	72	71	71	74	288	3990.00	2850.00
65	Ian HUTCHINGS (SA)	71	73	70	75	289	2293.57	1638.26
	Miles TUNNICLIFF (Eng)	75	68	74	72	289	2293.57	1638.26
	Phillip PRICE (Wal)	72	69	72	76	289	2293.57	1638.26
	Richard S JOHNSON (Swe)	70	73	72	74	289	2293.57	1638.26
	Christopher HANELL (Swe)	72	70	71	76	289	2293.57	1638.26
	Stephen FIELD (Eng)	76	68	68	77	289	2293.57	1638.26
	Jorge BERENDT (Arg)	73	69	73	74	289	2293.57	1638.26
72	Anders HANSEN (Den)	72	69	73	76	290	2076.00	1482.86
	Stephen GALLACHER (Scot)	72	72	73	73	290	2076.00	1482.86
	Mats LANNER (Swe)	74	70	72	74	290	2076.00	1482.86
	Andrew SHERBORNE (Eng)	72	70	73	75	290	2076.00	1482.86
	Silvio GRAPPASONNI (It)	70	73	71	76	290	2076.00	1482.86
77	Mikael LUNDBERG (Swe)	70	73	75	74	292	2064.00	1474.29
	Anders FORSBRAND (Swe)	72	70	72	78	292	2064.00	1474.29
	Ross MCFARLANE (Eng)	71	73	77	71	292	2064.00	1474.29
80	Paul AFFLECK (Wal)	68	76	73	76	293	2058.00	1470.00
81	Peter HANSSON (Swe)	70	74	75	77	296	2055.00	1467.86
82	Niclas FASTH (Swe)	75	69	75	82	301	2052.00	1465.71

GEOFF OGILVY: shattered course record

Skinny, *adj.-*
thin, weedy,
haggard,
emaciated,
slicey, cutty.

Fat Shaft, *n.*
- deadly
accuracy,
remarkable
distance!

This is the true meaning of Fat Shaft.

The Fat Shaft tip diameter is bigger where you need it, near the club head. This dramatically reduces club head twist - the result - **deadly accuracy**.

However, that is not the full story.

With less twist, energy from the club transfers to the ball more efficiently at impact - the result - **remarkable distance**.

Fat Shaft Technology is now available on our Oversized Titanium Wood and our range of forged and cast Irons.

But don't just take our word for it – experience the meaning of Fat Shaft yourself at one of our Fat Shaft Demo Days.

Visit us online at: www.wilsonsports.com

Golf Pride® UST

Fat Shaft®
DEADLY ACCURACY   REMARKABLE DISTANCE™

Italian job perfected

Costantino Rocca made the most

of a late call to Galway Bay

by winning first twin Tours title

The tournament was unique, the venue ideal. The West of Ireland Golf Classic at Galway Bay Golf and Country Club represented a new dimension in the European Tour's ever-expanding programme and the Irish Tourist Board's commitment to the game. What better place to launch the first "double badge" event with an equal number of golfers from the European and Challenge Tours eligible to compete for the same rewards, than in the spectacular surroundings and convivial atmosphere of one of Ireland's newest golf resorts.

The prize money of 357,046 euro (£255,033) counted for both the Volvo Order of Merit and for Ryder Cup points and also carried a one-year European Tour exemption for the winner. In other words there was something for everyone who made it through the weekend.

Costantino Rocca got what he came for. The popular Italian made no secret of his desire to play for Europe against America in the Ryder Cup at The Country Club, Brookline. He had twice tasted victory in 1995 and 1997 but had dropped so far down the rankings that something beyond the ordinary was required in the two remaining weeks before final selection. The hoped for 11th hour call to the US PGA Championship never arrived so he promptly applied for a late invitation to Galway and said on arrival: "I'm here because I want to be in the Ryder Cup team. I need to win."

Padraig Harrington was also seeking Ryder Cup recognition but he did not seem to view victory in Galway as vital to his cause as Rocca did to his. That is not to say he was in any way less committed, for Harrington is well known as one of the toughest competitors in the game. He was to prove the point several times through the four days as he exploited his considerable ability at the short game to chase Rocca home.

Winning is no easy task and Galway Bay's par of 72 no easy target. But they got lucky with the wind. In fact, the

COSTANTINO ROCCA: *"I got the job done"*

THE COURSE

Galway Bay was designed in 1993 by Christy O'Connor Junior. Although built along the shores of the famous Bay, it is not of links texture but one of the finest parkland type courses in the country. Cleverly bunkered, it also has a series of lakes to add to the natural difficulties of its championship length of 7,148 yards.

players must have wondered was it just a quirk of nature that the trees on the course were all bending in one direction – to the east away from the wild, prevailing winds that can blow from the bay. There was wind and some rain but, even at its strongest over the four days, those who live along the western seaboard would say it was no more than a fresh breeze. Still, there was enough of a draught to present a stiff test.

Even with Europe's top ranking players on other business in Chicago, the strength in depth of talent through both Tours was demonstrated by figures of a two over par cut and a 12 under par winning aggregate. Still, it was always a good bet that the regular Tour players would be the main contenders when it came to the wire on the final day. So it came to pass with Rocca, Ireland's Harrington and Des

SHOT OF THE WEEK

The sixth, a par five of 526 yards, with a green flanked on the right by out-of-bounds and a lake on the left, calls for a decision on whether to lay up or take on the narrow entrance with the second shot. Rocca, after a massive drive, hit a superb three wood to 15 feet for an eagle to set up a round of 68 and a share of the lead going into the final round.

Smyth, and England's Gary Evans and Paul Broadhurst vying for the principal places, but through the first three rounds there was always a Challenge Tour presence at or near the top of the leaderboard.

For instance, Elliott Boult, a 33-year-old New Zealander, shot 66 on the first day to lead the unrelated Hansens from Sweden, Anders and Søren, and fellow Challenge Tour player Nils Rörbaek from Denmark by one shot. Yet another Swede, Eric Carlberg, took over at the top on Friday at nine under (68,67) with Gary Evans a shot behind and Rörbaek still in contention at seven under with Scotland's Stephen Gallacher and Ireland's Paul McGinley.

But the men of experience were gathering for attack, and as they entered the final round Rocca and Harrington were tied for the lead at ten under par; Evans was nine under and Smyth at eight under. Smyth had played well enough from tee to green over the four days but failed on the greens and a trip to the water at the eighth virtually destroyed his chances. Evans was always within striking distance on the last day but became a little erratic. Thus, it was left to the Italian-Irish alliance to make the final decision. They kept opening the door for one another until Harrington closed it on himself on the 16th tee. They were level at 11 under par but the Irishman carved his tee shot over the boundary wall and onto the shore.

PADRAIG HARRINGTON:
tough competitor

Rocca then locked up at the last when he holed for birdie from 35 feet, leaving Harrington with a putt of six feet to secure second place on his own. By this time the crowd had grown to more than 4,000, the biggest golf gallery ever seen west of the Shannon river and, although their preference was to cheer home the first Irish winner of a European Tour event on home soil since John O'Leary in 1982, Rocca responded to a rousing reception with hands aloft and a happy smile to declare: "I got the job done. That was what I wanted to do this week."

Colm Smith

GALWAY BAY G & CC, IRELAND, AUGUST 12–15, 1999 • PAR 72 • YARDS 7148

Pos	Name & Country	Rnd 1	Rnd 2	Rnd 3	Rnd 4	Total	Prize Money €	£
1	Costantino ROCCA (It)	70	68	68	70	276	58330.00	41664.29
2	Padraig HARRINGTON (Ire)	69	69	68	72	278	38380.00	27414.29
3	Paul BROADHURST (Eng)	73	66	72	68	279	18080.00	12914.29
	Gary EVANS (Eng)	70	66	71	72	279	18080.00	12914.29
	Des SMYTH (Ire)	71	68	69	71	279	18080.00	12914.29
6	Anders HANSEN (Den)	67	74	71	68	280	10500.00	7500.00
	Paul MCGINLEY (Ire)	68	69	74	69	280	10500.00	7500.00
	Michael LONG (NZ)	69	72	73	66	280	10500.00	7500.00
9	Eric CARLBERG (Swe)	68	67	74	72	281	7410.00	5292.86
	Mats HALLBERG (Swe)	70	71	71	69	281	7410.00	5292.86
11	Gary EMERSON (Eng)	68	71	72	71	282	6440.00	4600.00
12	Soren HANSEN (Den)	67	72	72	72	283	5666.67	4047.62
	Knud STOREGAARD (Den)	68	71	74	70	283	5666.67	4047.62
	Elliot BOULT (NZ)	66	75	71	71	283	5666.67	4047.62
15	Maarten LAFEBER (Hol)	71	68	73	72	284	4931.67	3522.62
	Andrew RAITT (Eng)	68	75	66	75	284	4931.67	3522.62
	Benoit TEILLERIA (Fr)	70	72	72	70	284	4931.67	3522.62
18	Peter LAWRIE (Ire)	70	76	72	67	285	4287.50	3062.50
	Andrew OLDCORN (Scot)	68	76	71	70	285	4287.50	3062.50
	Bradley DREDGE (Wal)	69	71	76	69	285	4287.50	3062.50
	Andrew BUTTERFIELD (Eng)	71	70	72	72	285	4287.50	3062.50
22	Ian HUTCHINGS (SA)	69	74	71	72	286	3727.50	2662.50
	Christian CÉVAER (Fr)	72	72	71	71	286	3727.50	2662.50
	Raimo SJÖBERG (Swe)	74	68	74	70	286	3727.50	2662.50
	Carl SUNESON (Sp)	71	73	68	74	286	3727.50	2662.50
	Leif WESTERBERG (Swe)	74	72	70	70	286	3727.50	2662.50
	Fredrik HENGE (Swe)	70	70	71	75	286	3727.50	2662.50
28	Scott HENDERSON (Scot)	69	73	74	71	287	3055.71	2182.65
	Matthew BLACKEY (Eng)	70	73	71	73	287	3055.71	2182.65
	Dominique NOUAILHAC (Fr)	70	72	76	69	287	3055.71	2182.65
	Marcus WHEELHOUSE (NZ)	74	72	70	71	287	3055.71	2182.65
	Andrew CLAPP (Eng)	74	71	71	71	287	3055.71	2182.65
	Philip GOLDING (Eng)	70	72	75	70	287	3055.71	2182.65
	Nils RORBAEK (Den)	67	70	78	72	287	3055.71	2182.65
35	Stephen GALLACHER (Scot)	68	69	77	74	288	2520.00	1800.00
	Gary MURPHY (Ire)	72	72	73	71	288	2520.00	1800.00
	Jon ROBSON (Eng)	70	73	72	73	288	2520.00	1800.00
	Johan SKOLD (Swe)	71	72	75	70	288	2520.00	1800.00
	Daniel WESTERMARK (Swe)	70	73	73	72	288	2520.00	1800.00
	Carlos LARRAIN (Ven)	72	73	75	68	288	2520.00	1800.00
	Adam MEDNICK (Swe)	72	74	71	71	288	2520.00	1800.00
42	Nick O'HERN (Aus)	71	73	74	71	289	1995.00	1425.00
	Martin ERLANDSSON (Swe)	70	75	73	71	289	1995.00	1425.00
	Gary CLARK (Eng)	70	71	75	73	289	1995.00	1425.00
	Justin ROSE (Eng)	71	73	70	75	289	1995.00	1425.00
	Simon D. HURLEY (Eng)	69	71	77	72	289	1995.00	1425.00
	Stephen DODD (Wal)	68	74	76	71	289	1995.00	1425.00
	Henrik NYSTROM (Swe)	74	71	74	70	289	1995.00	1425.00
	Klas ERIKSSON (Swe)	72	74	70	73	289	1995.00	1425.00
50	Lee S JAMES (Eng)	69	75	72	74	290	1505.00	1075.00
	Gordon SHERRY (Scot)	72	71	73	74	290	1505.00	1075.00
	Stephen SCAHILL (NZ)	71	75	74	70	290	1505.00	1075.00
	Eamonn DARCY (Ire)	71	75	72	72	290	1505.00	1075.00
	Anssi KANKKONEN (Fin)	71	73	73	73	290	1505.00	1075.00
	Mark BOOTH (Eng)	73	71	76	70	290	1505.00	1075.00
56	David LYNN (Eng)	74	72	71	74	291	1190.00	850.00
	Jesus Maria ARRUTI (Sp)	68	76	76	71	291	1190.00	850.00
	Greig HUTCHEON (Scot)	72	74	72	73	291	1190.00	850.00
59	Brian NELSON (USA)	69	76	74	73	292	1015.00	725.00
	Juan NUTT (Ven)	70	76	76	70	292	1015.00	725.00
	Mike MILLER (Scot)	72	74	73	73	292	1015.00	725.00
	Philip WALTON (Ire)	75	70	75	72	292	1015.00	725.00
	Wayne WESTNER (SA)	70	74	77	71	292	1015.00	725.00
64	Daniel CHOPRA (Swe)	70	73	72	78	293	781.67	558.34
	Rudi SAILER (Aut)	71	74	78	70	293	781.67	558.34
	Magnus PERSSON (Swe)	68	74	78	73	293	781.67	558.34
67	José Manuel CARRILES (Sp)	75	70	76	73	294	552.50	394.64
	Lucas PARSONS (Aus)	72	71	76	75	294	552.50	394.64
	Euan LITTLE (Scot)	71	74	75	74	294	552.50	394.64
	José Antonio SOTA (Sp)	72	74	74	74	294	552.50	394.64
71	Robert LEE (Eng)	70	74	76	75	295	545.00	389.29
72	Marc PENDARIES (Fr)	69	76	78	73	296	540.50	386.07
	Gianluca BARUFFALDI (It)	72	73	74	77	296	540.50	386.07
74	Steven RICHARDSON (Eng)	70	76	77	74	297	534.50	381.79
	Alvaro SALTO (Sp)	68	76	80	73	297	534.50	381.79
76	Damian MOONEY (N.Ire)	73	71	77	77	298	528.50	377.50
	Paul DWYER (Eng)	77	69	76	76	298	528.50	377.50
78	Gustavo ROJAS (Arg)	72	74	80	74	300	524.00	374.29

ERIC CARLBERG: commanded halfway lead

Tiger hunt grips world

A second major championship for Tiger Woods

but only after holding off a fantastic

challenge to the last green by Sergio Garcia

The history books will record that Tiger Woods won his second major title at the 81st United States PGA Championship at the Medinah Country Club, Chicago, Illinois. The memory will always recall the way Sergio Garcia, the 19-year-old Spanish 'Wonderkid' or 'El Nino', leapt into the hearts of everyone waiting to embrace the game's newest star.

This was a very different victory for Woods, himself only 23, than his record-breaking, runaway triumph at the 1997 Masters Tournament. Having seen a five-stroke lead with seven holes to play dwindle alarmingly quickly to just one, the American displayed a tenacious determination to complete the victory.

The crucial moment for the world number one came when he missed the green at the par three 17th and chipped to eight feet. It was the sort of clutch putt many would have dribbled wide of the hole, but Woods, bravely, found the centre of the cup. "My caddie said it was inside left and I thought, 'perfect'," Woods said. "I knew it didn't break as much as it looked."

Woods deserved to win against what the statisticians called the strongest field

ever for a major championship. Yet by the time he had, the gallery and a worldwide television audience was won over by the precocious Garcia.

The magical moment everyone will remember came on the 16th hole. The young Spaniard's drive ended by the roots of a tree to the right of the fairway. It appeared the tree blocked out any attempt to find a green 189 yards away, and Jerry Higginbotham, Garcia's experienced caddie, advised chipping out sideways.

So did the Spanish commentators Severiano Ballesteros was listening to at home. Seve, who when 19 himself had captured the public's imagination by finishing as runner-up to Johnny Miller in the 1976 Open Championship at Royal Birkdale, screamed at his television that they were all wrong.

He knew Sergio would go for the green, and he did with a huge, slicing lash with a six iron to pull off a stroke of brilliance. "I just opened the clubface and made a full swing," Garcia said. "I closed my eyes on the downswing and went backwards in case the ball came back off the tree, and when I opened my eyes the ball was going to the green. I was pretty excited and wanted to see where it finished."

Joyfully unrestrained, Garcia started running down the fairway and then jumped in the air to see the ball land on the green. Then he bent over and patted his heart. Never once did that smile of his leave his face. This was only Garcia's second major in the United States and his second as a professional. In his first major in America, Garcia won the low amateur honours at the 1999 Masters. In his first major as a professional he missed the cut at The Open Championship, finishing dead last at Carnoustie at 30 over par. But by the end of the first round at Medinah, Garcia, the second youngest player ever to appear in the US PGA Championship, was first. He led with a 66 that equalled the course record Skip Kendall was to lower to 65 the following day.

Garcia likes "to shoot the lights out"; after his 62 at Loch Lomond, the power in the clubhouse failed. On the Thursday night of the US PGA, thousands in down-

SERGIO GARCIA: "I don't think anybody has seen a shot like it," praised Ben Crenshaw

Only one contender: Sergio Garcia's amazing escape from the roots of a tree at the 16th hole with a six iron onto a green 189 yards away. "I don't think anybody has ever seen a shot like it," said Ben Crenshaw, the US Ryder Cup captain who still seemed awestruck a day later. "That shot captured America's imagination. It was one of the most beautiful things I've ever seen on a golf course. I spoke to his caddie last night, Jerry Higginbotham, and he said: 'You know, I'm dumbfounded. I'm speechless.' He was just trying to save a stroke when he's driven into a place like that. This kid goes for the shot knowing that if he goes into the ground hard, he could break the clubhead. That's the reason he did not look at the ball.

"The verve, creativity and imagination with that shot, I mean, is something you just don't see. The enthusiasm with which he ran after the ball – and the tremendous athleticism – encapsulates everything we thought about the game when we were 19. I mean, your mouth's open about it. Really, how tremendous that was. Taking his hat off and putting it over his heart, that's wonderful. How can you not love this kid? He is unbelievable."

Ben Crenshaw

Top: The "shot that captured America's imagination" is on its way, and so is young Garcia, sprinting down the fairway

Right: The impatience and athleticism of youth, a running jump to see the ball land safely on the green

Above: The strains of an incredible, injury-defying gamble leave a pounding heart to be steadied

COLIN MONTGOMERIE: tied for sixth

and Miguel Angel Jiménez, tied tenth, made it the first occasion when four Europeans had finished in the top ten at the US PGA. Garcia started the final round two behind the joint leaders, Woods and Canadian Mike Weir. The Spaniard hooked his tee-shot into the water at the short second but holed from 12 feet for only his third bogey of the week. He birdied the fifth and the tenth, but by going out in 33 Woods had opened up a lead of four strokes which he extended with a birdie at the 11th hole.

Nick Price, the experienced Zimbabwean, seemed to be the most likely challenger until Garcia holed a downhill putt of 20 feet for a birdie at the short 13th. He looked back at Woods on the tee and raised a challenging, but friendly, fist. "I wanted him to know that he still had to play well to win," Garcia said. Woods then put his tee shot over the back, played ping pong across the green and eventually holed from four feet for a double bogey five. Garcia heard the roar go up and knew he had a chance.

town Chicago were blacked out. "I think I've proved myself today," Garcia said. "I think the Open Championship is done so I don't want to hear any more questions about the Open. But I'm going to tell you this: the difference is that I played very well.

"Everything went the right way, I made some good putts, had a couple of good breaks. At the Open, I started with a triple bogey and everything went the wrong way."

All 7,401 yards of the Medinah course, the second longest in major championship history, proved fertile ground for European hopes, with 15 players making the cut, including the Open Champion Paul Lawrie and Carnoustie runner-up Jean Van de Velde in their first majors in America. The man leading the challenge at halfway was Lee Westwood, continuing his fine form from Europe, but he suffered in the wake of playing with Woods in the third round and had to be treated for dehydration on Saturday night.

Then the challenge was taken up by Garcia, who along with Colin Montgomerie, tied sixth, Jesper Parnevik

JESPER PARNEVIK: made it four Europeans in top ten

THE COURSE

At 7,401 yards, Medinah's No 3 Course, originally designed as a "sporty little course for women" but which turned into the fearsome 'Monster of the Midwest', was the second longest course in major championship history. The longest, the 7,436-yard Columbine Country Club in Colorado, was at altitude and so played shorter. Medinah did not quite play up to its full length as a number of holes dogleg one way or the other, but with 4,101 trees on the estate, mostly oaks, it was inevitable that someone would get behind one of them, as Garcia did at the 16th in the final round.

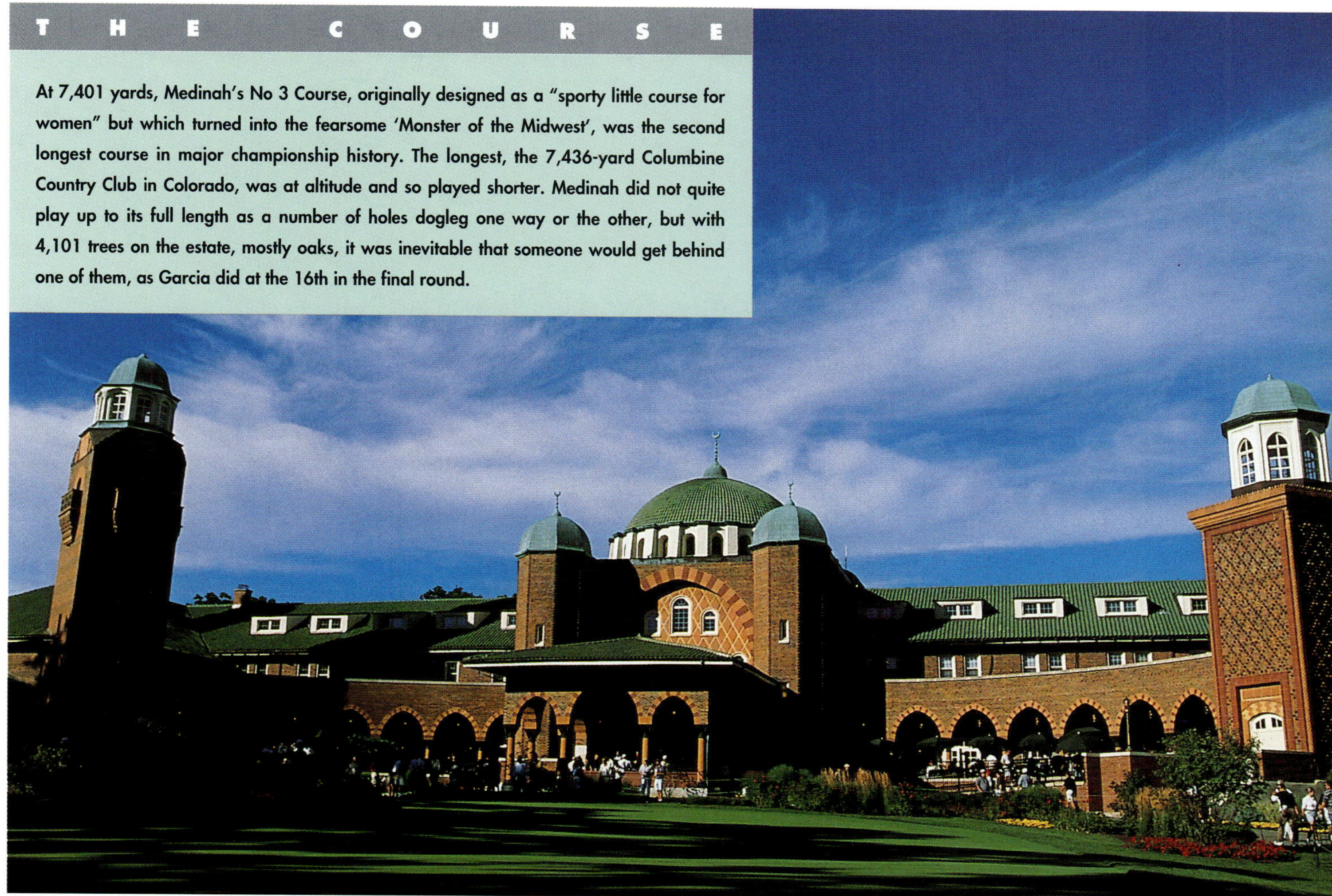

The margin was down to one but Garcia slipped two behind with a bogey at the 15th despite a fine recovery from the trees on the right with his second shot. The even more miraculous recovery at the next meant he finished with three pars, and though Woods dropped a shot at the 16th, he hung on. But it was "Sergio, Sergio" that the gallery was chanting at the 18th.

"It was amazing," said Garcia, who clinched a place in the European Ryder Cup team. "It's the best week of my life. I've never had so much fun playing golf. The crowds were amazing. I almost couldn't hear. They must have thought I was an American. I am a little unhappy that I didn't win," he added, "but inside of me I feel I won. At 19 years old, and three months since I turned professional, you can't ask for more. This is a little more than my expectations and I really love it. When I turned pro I was hoping to win my first tournament and get on the Ryder Cup team. If you had said I was going to be first in the Murphy's Irish Open, tied second at The Standard Life Loch Lomond, runner-up at the US PGA, and miss the cut at the Open Championship by hundreds, I'd have taken it."

"It's a relief," Woods admitted, "to finally get a second major championship title. Sergio played wonderfully and although I had a five-stroke lead, I knew that with a couple of mistakes that could go in a couple of holes, which is what happened. It was completely different from Augusta when I led by nine. I would have killed myself if I had lost that one.

"It was fun playing under all that pressure. The crowd got behind Sergio and rightfully so. He and I play a very similar game. We are both aggressive, hit the ball a long way and both like to be creative. He turns a bad shot into a positive. He wears his emotions on his sleeve. The media was all over me for that but hopefully they'll leave him alone because he is a wonderful kid."

The last major of the millennium seemed to have shown the way for the start of the next century: Woods vs Garcia. But Woods did not want to make it an exclusive rivalry. "There are a lot of good players in their 20s who are going to be around for another 20 years. Sergio is still a teenager and then you have David Duval, Justin Leonard, Phil Mickelson and a number of wonderful players from around the world like Ernie Els, Lee Westwood and Darren Clarke. There is no rivalry between just two of those but there are a handful of players who will lead golf into the next millennium."

As for himself, Woods now found himself halfway to winning all four major championships, something only achieved by four players in the history of the game. "Whether this win puts me on track with Jack Nicklaus, I don't know. He won the Grand Slam by the time he was 26 and hopefully I can do the same."

Andy Farrell

Medinah Country Club, Chicago, Illinois, USA, August 12–15, 1999 · Par 72 · Yards 7401

Pos	Name & Country	Rnd 1	Rnd 2	Rnd 3	Rnd 4	Total	Prize Money €	£
1	Tiger WOODS (USA)	70	67	68	72	277	545522.02	389658.58
2	Sergio GARCIA (Sp)	66	73	68	71	278	327313.21	233795.15
3	Stewart CINK (USA)	69	70	68	73	280	175779.32	125556.66
	Jay HAAS (USA)	68	67	75	70	280	175779.32	125556.66
5	Nick PRICE (Zim)	70	71	69	71	281	111702.13	79787.23
6	Bob ESTES (USA)	71	70	72	69	282	96981.69	69272.64
	Colin MONTGOMERIE (Scot)	72	70	70	70	282	96981.69	69272.64
8	Jim FURYK (USA)	71	70	69	74	284	83560.12	59685.80
	Steve PATE (USA)	72	70	73	69	284	83560.12	59685.80
10	David DUVAL (USA)	70	71	72	72	285	62489.69	44635.49
	Miguel Angel JIMÉNEZ (Sp)	70	70	75	70	285	62489.69	44635.49
	Jesper PARNEVIK (Swe)	72	70	73	70	285	62489.69	44635.49
	Corey PAVIN (USA)	69	74	71	71	285	62489.69	44635.49
	Chris PERRY (USA)	70	73	71	71	285	62489.69	44635.49
	Mike WEIR (Can)	68	68	69	80	285	62489.69	44635.49
16	Mark BROOKS (USA)	70	73	70	74	287	42083.13	30059.38
	Gabriel HJERTSTEDT (Swe)	72	70	73	72	287	42083.13	30059.38
	Brandt JOBE (USA)	69	74	69	75	287	42083.13	30059.38
	Greg TURNER (NZ)	73	69	70	75	287	42083.13	30059.38
	Lee WESTWOOD (Eng)	70	68	74	75	287	42083.13	30059.38
21	David FROST (SA)	75	68	74	71	288	28748.14	20534.39
	Scott HOCH (USA)	71	71	75	71	288	28748.14	20534.39
	Skip KENDALL (USA)	74	65	71	78	288	28748.14	20534.39
	J.L. LEWIS (USA)	73	70	74	71	288	28748.14	20534.39
	Kevin WENTWORTH (USA)	72	70	72	74	288	28748.14	20534.39
26	Fred COUPLES (USA)	73	69	75	72	289	20781.79	14844.14
	Carlos Daniel FRANCO (Par)	72	71	71	75	289	20781.79	14844.14
	Jerry KELLY (USA)	69	74	71	75	289	20781.79	14844.14
	Hal SUTTON (USA)	72	73	73	71	289	20781.79	14844.14
	Jean VAN DE VELDE (Fr)	74	70	75	70	289	20781.79	14844.14
31	Paul GOYDOS (USA)	73	70	71	76	290	17318.16	12370.11
	Mark JAMES (Eng)	70	74	79	67	290	17318.16	12370.11
	Ted TRYBA (USA)	70	72	76	72	290	17318.16	12370.11
34	Steve FLESCH (USA)	73	71	72	75	291	13359.72	9542.66
	Paul LAWRIE (Scot)	73	72	72	74	291	13359.72	9542.66
	Tom LEHMAN (USA)	70	74	76	71	291	13359.72	9542.66
	Billy MAYFAIR (USA)	75	69	75	72	291	13359.72	9542.66
	Kenny PERRY (USA)	74	69	72	76	291	13359.72	9542.66
	Scott VERPLANK (USA)	73	72	73	73	291	13359.72	9542.66
	Lanny WADKINS (USA)	72	69	74	76	291	13359.72	9542.66
41	Paul AZINGER (USA)	77	69	71	75	292	9741.46	6958.19
	Angel CABRERA (Arg)	73	73	74	72	292	9741.46	6958.19
	Chris DIMARCO (USA)	74	71	74	73	292	9741.46	6958.19
	Nick FALDO (Eng)	71	71	75	75	292	9741.46	6958.19
	Hale IRWIN (USA)	70	69	78	75	292	9741.46	6958.19
	Robert KARLSSON (Swe)	70	76	73	73	292	9741.46	6958.19
	Duffy WALDORF (USA)	74	71	70	77	292	9741.46	6958.19
	Brian WATTS (USA)	69	71	72	80	292	9741.46	6958.19
49	Olin BROWNE (USA)	73	72	74	74	293	7083.13	5059.38
	Davis LOVE III (USA)	71	72	75	75	293	7083.13	5059.38
	Rocco MEDIATE (USA)	71	72	78	72	293	7083.13	5059.38
	Vijay SINGH (Fiji)	74	70	77	72	293	7083.13	5059.38
	Kirk TRIPLETT (USA)	73	70	70	80	293	7083.13	5059.38
54	JP HAYES (USA)	68	76	76	74	294	6407.72	4576.94
	Andrew MAGEE (USA)	72	72	77	73	294	6407.72	4576.94
	Jeff SLUMAN (USA)	72	73	73	76	294	6407.72	4576.94
57	Phil MICKELSON (USA)	72	72	74	77	295	6212.89	4437.78
	Mark O'MEARA (USA)	72	74	73	76	295	6212.89	4437.78
	Payne STEWART (USA)	75	71	75	74	295	6212.89	4437.78
	Bob TWAY (USA)	73	71	80	71	295	6212.89	4437.78
61	Mark CALCAVECCHIA (USA)	71	75	76	74	296	6039.71	4314.08
	Brad FAXON (USA)	72	73	77	74	296	6039.71	4314.08
	Greg KRAFT (USA)	74	70	75	77	296	6039.71	4314.08
	Bernhard LANGER (Ger)	71	75	74	76	296	6039.71	4314.08
65	Alex CEJKA (Ger)	71	73	75	78	297	5888.17	4205.84
	Andrew COLTART (Scot)	72	74	80	71	297	5888.17	4205.84
	Mike REID (USA)	72	74	76	75	297	5888.17	4205.84
68	Scott DUNLAP (USA)	74	72	71	81	298	5779.94	4128.53
	Bruce ZABRISKI (USA)	70	75	77	76	298	5779.94	4128.53
70	Rich BEEM (USA)	72	73	78	76	299	5671.70	4051.21
	Thomas BJÖRN (Den)	73	73	78	75	299	5671.70	4051.21
	Naomichi OZAKI (Jpn)	73	73	78	75	299	5671.70	4051.21
73	Fred FUNK (USA)	75	69	76	80	300	5585.11	3989.36
74	Joey SINDELAR (USA)	73	70	75		218	5541.81	3958.44

SERGIO GARCIA and TIGER WOODS: "It was fun"

You may never go there, but it's nice to know your phone will work if you do.

BT Cellnet. The world's largest roaming mobile network.
No one else is as well connected.

£1 million barrier is broken

Winner Colin Montgomerie sets prize money

record while runner-up Padraig Harrington

clinches Ryder Cup place in final-putt drama

Every two years an extra dimension is added to the BMW International Open at the Golfclub München Nord-Eichenried just outside Munich. Every two years, the week is deadline time for Ryder Cup points as well as a confrontation for serious prize money, enough this time to see Colin Montgomerie become the first to pass £1million (1,400,000 euro) winnings in a single season. Every two years, the tournament provides riveting entertainment on two fronts.

How riveting depends on your point of view, of course. Take Padraig Harrington. In 1997 the Irishman, three times a Walker Cup player, shot 19 under par for four circuits of Nord-Eichenried, finished joint ninth in the tournament, yet left heartbroken. Had the young Dubliner taken two shots fewer he would have been part of Severiano Ballesteros's winning squad at Valderrama – and the memory still hurts.

"To be so close to qualifying and not make it is easily the biggest disappointment of my professional career," said Harrington on the eve of the 1999 event. "This time I hope to do better."

Easier said than done. Harrington arrived in Germany fresh from a second place finish in the West of Ireland Golf Classic, but was only one of a host of players in with a chance of claiming one of the last remaining places in the European side. With 1,983 points available to the winner, most of those in the top 30 of the qualifying standings could qualify. More realistically, however, only the top 20 were genuine contenders.

Just to complicate things even more, European skipper Mark James had a chance to make it as a player. Not that he was telling anyone of his plans should he make it. "I've made a decision on whether I'll play if I win an automatic place," he said, after an opening round of 70 left him trailing eight shots behind first-day leader David Park's astonishing 62. "But it's a secret." Cue wicked grin.

PADRAIG HARRINGTON: wiping out a bad memory

JOHN BICKERTON: another top ten finish

ROBERT KARLSSON: man in the hottest seat

Elsewhere, the man in the hottest seat, tenth-placed Swede Robert Karlsson matched James's score, while Harrington was in a group of three on 66. European number one Colin Montgomerie, already the winner of four European Tour events in 1999, took 69 and professed to need a "big improvement" if he was to increase that number to five.

One day later, two things happened. First, Montgomerie made his intimidating presence felt on the rest of the field with a mouth-watering round of 64 to take the lead over a faltering Park. And second, Harrington confirmed that he was on the leaderboard to stay. His 67 put him alongside the Scot. If things stayed the same for 36 more holes, Harrington would make his Ryder Cup debut.

SHOT OF THE WEEK

It was only a putt of ten feet. Only. But Padraig Harrington thought he had to hole it on the 72nd green if he was to make the European Ryder Cup team for the first time. Taking the left-to-right borrow perfectly, it went in dead centre. It was only afterwards the Irishman realised that two putts would have seen him safely into captain Mark James's team. Still, his was a fine example of pressure putting at its best.

"I hope the next two days are a wash-out," he said with a smile. "But I can't expect that. I have got to do battle with Monty. If you can beat him you aren't doing too badly."

True enough. But no one, least of all Harrington, thought that would be easy. The Irishman shot another 66 in the third round yet still found himself trailing Montgomerie by a shot. The pair were, by now, well clear of the chasing pack, which included the likes of James and late-charging John Bickerton in joint seventh spot. Both, along with Karlsson and Scot Andrew Coltart, needed low closing

ANDREW COLTART: on a late charge to impress

The Golfclub München Nord-Eichenried asks many questions of the professional's short-iron play. Only precisely struck approaches to the deceptive, but much praised, greens set up easy birdie chances. Water hazards add to the challenge of this parkland test which has been toughened in a dedicated programme of improvements over recent years.

JARROD MOSELEY: closing 66 worth third place

rounds as well as some help from Harrington. Given the positions of his closest challengers, the Irishman now knew that staying in second place would almost certainly see him on the Concorde to Boston a month later.

Early in the fourth round Harrington was providing that help, too. Four over par after four holes, the former Peugeot Open de España champion had virtually handed the title to Montgomerie, and,

perhaps even more importantly from his point of view, given his pursuers encouragement.

Harrington's ready smile belies his competitiveness, however. He never did catch Montgomerie, who scored a closing 70 for 20 under par 268 to win by three shots in the end, and raise his prize money total to a precise 1,422,247 euro (£1,087,319) for the season. But Harrington fought his way back to level

par for the day and kept his runner-up spot. The brave putt of ten feet he holed on the last green raised the biggest cheer of the day.

"This won't sink in until tomorrow morning," said Harrington. "I'm on a high and certainly won't sleep at all, even less than I did last night. But right now it's a lovely feeling."

Better than 1997 certainly.

John Huggan

Golfclub München Nord-Eichenried, Munich, Germany, August 19–22, 1999 · Par 72 · Yards 6914

Pos	Name & Country	Rnd 1	Rnd 2	Rnd 3	Rnd 4	Total	Prize Money €	Prize Money £
1	Colin MONTGOMERIE (Scot)	69	64	65	70	268	198320.00	141657.14
2	Padraig HARRINGTON (Ire)	66	67	66	72	271	132210.00	94435.71
3	Jarrod MOSELEY (Aus)	67	68	71	66	272	74500.00	53214.29
4	John BICKERTON (Eng)	67	69	69	69	274	59500.00	42500.00
5	Mark JAMES (Eng)	70	69	66	70	275	39375.00	28125.00
	Gary ORR (Scot)	70	68	69	68	275	39375.00	28125.00
	David HOWELL (Eng)	67	70	72	66	275	39375.00	28125.00
	Andrew COLTART (Scot)	70	68	71	66	275	39375.00	28125.00
9	Mathias GRÖNBERG (Swe)	72	68	67	69	276	22375.60	15982.57
	Robert KARLSSON (Swe)	70	71	70	65	276	22375.60	15982.57
	Jean-Francois REMESY (Fr)	69	69	66	72	276	22375.60	15982.57
	Paul BROADHURST (Eng)	69	73	66	68	276	22375.60	15982.57
	Peter BAKER (Eng)	67	71	71	67	276	22375.60	15982.57
14	Dean ROBERTSON (Scot)	70	71	71	65	277	18200.00	13000.00
15	Domingo HOSPITAL (Sp)	66	71	67	74	278	15782.67	11273.34
	Bernhard LANGER (Ger)	69	68	72	69	278	15782.67	11273.34
	Ian WOOSNAM (Wal)	70	66	68	74	278	15782.67	11273.34
	Phillip PRICE (Wal)	67	69	68	74	278	15782.67	11273.34
	Stephen FIELD (Eng)	67	73	69	69	278	15782.67	11273.34
	Andrew MCLARDY (SA)	70	72	68	68	278	15782.67	11273.34
21	Dennis EDLUND (Swe)	66	71	72	70	279	13030.50	9307.50
	Andrew BEAL (Eng)	71	69	69	70	279	13030.50	9307.50
	Nick FALDO (Eng)	67	73	72	67	279	13030.50	9307.50
	Tony JOHNSTONE (Zim)	68	69	73	69	279	13030.50	9307.50
	Santiago LUNA (Sp)	71	69	71	68	279	13030.50	9307.50
	Søren KJELDSEN (Den)	73	69	68	69	279	13030.50	9307.50
27	Mark MOULAND (Wal)	69	70	68	73	280	10727.00	7662.14
	Wayne RILEY (Aus)	72	63	73	72	280	10727.00	7662.14
	Miles TUNNICLIFF (Eng)	67	73	71	69	280	10727.00	7662.14
	Greg OWEN (Eng)	72	71	67	70	280	10727.00	7662.14
	Sven STRÜVER (Ger)	73	69	69	69	280	10727.00	7662.14
	Francisco CEA (Sp)	70	68	70	72	280	10727.00	7662.14
	Paul LAWRIE (Scot)	69	73	70	68	280	10727.00	7662.14
34	Rodger DAVIS (Aus)	73	70	64	74	281	8806.00	6290.00
	Michael LONG (NZ)	73	69	70	69	281	8806.00	6290.00
	Peter O'MALLEY (Aus)	73	70	70	68	281	8806.00	6290.00
	Thomas BJÖRN (Den)	70	70	70	71	281	8806.00	6290.00
	David CARTER (Eng)	74	67	71	69	281	8806.00	6290.00
	Barry LANE (Eng)	74	68	71	68	281	8806.00	6290.00
	Henrik BJORNSTAD (Nor)	73	70	69	69	281	8806.00	6290.00
41	Andrew RAITT (Eng)	70	70	71	71	282	7378.00	5270.00
	David GILFORD (Eng)	73	69	71	69	282	7378.00	5270.00
	Jamie SPENCE (Eng)	72	65	72	73	282	7378.00	5270.00
	Thomas GÖGELE (Ger)	70	69	71	72	282	7378.00	5270.00
	Van PHILLIPS (Eng)	70	73	69	70	282	7378.00	5270.00
46	John MELLOR (Eng)	71	69	70	73	283	6307.00	4505.00
	Peter FOWLER (Aus)	71	70	67	75	283	6307.00	4505.00
	Mark MCNULTY (Zim)	69	68	74	72	283	6307.00	4505.00
	Roger WESSELS (SA)	73	70	68	72	283	6307.00	4505.00
50	Emanuele CANONICA (It)	70	69	74	71	284	5236.00	3740.00
	Ignacio GARRIDO (Sp)	73	65	76	70	284	5236.00	3740.00
	Jonathan LOMAS (Eng)	70	69	72	73	284	5236.00	3740.00
	Paolo QUIRICI (Swi)	70	68	73	73	284	5236.00	3740.00
	Carlos RODILES (Sp)	72	71	72	69	284	5236.00	3740.00
55	Trevor IMMELMAN (SA)	70	72	74	69	285	3910.00	2792.86
	Peter MITCHELL (Eng)	69	70	70	76	285	3910.00	2792.86
	Retief GOOSEN (SA)	70	69	74	72	285	3910.00	2792.86
	Silvio GRAPPASONNI (It)	70	71	73	71	285	3910.00	2792.86
	Per-Ulrik JOHANSSON (Swe)	71	72	71	71	285	3910.00	2792.86
	Jeremy ROBINSON (Eng)	72	69	70	74	285	3910.00	2792.86
	Nick O'HERN (Aus)	67	74	70	74	285	3910.00	2792.86
62	Jean VAN DE VELDE (Fr)	68	73	73	72	286	3272.50	2337.50
	Warren BENNETT (Eng)	73	67	73	73	286	3272.50	2337.50
64	David PARK (Wal)	62	72	73	80	287	2283.00	1630.71
	Derrick COOPER (Eng)	71	70	71	75	287	2283.00	1630.71
	Per HAUGSRUD (Nor)	68	74	73	72	287	2283.00	1630.71
	Fabrice TARNAUD (Fr)	74	69	73	71	287	2283.00	1630.71
	Soren HANSEN (Den)	72	69	72	74	287	2283.00	1630.71
69	Paul MCGINLEY (Ire)	69	72	74	73	288	1771.50	1265.36
	Andrew SHERBORNE (Eng)	72	71	71	74	288	1771.50	1265.36
	Katsuyoshi TOMORI (Jpn)	70	72	73	73	288	1771.50	1265.36
	Scott HENDERSON (Scot)	70	71	75	72	288	1771.50	1265.36
73	Russell CLAYDON (Eng)	74	68	73	74	289	1764.00	1260.00
74	Marc FARRY (Fr)	69	73	78	71	291	1759.50	1256.79
	Philip WALTON (Ire)	73	70	71	77	291	1759.50	1256.79
76	Alberto BINAGHI (It)	72	71	70	82	295	1755.00	1253.57
77	Stephen DODD (Wal)	69	74	75	80	298	1752.00	1251.43

COLIN MONTGOMERIE: playing to billboard orders

Ripping it for fun

Doing what he enjoys most, Tiger Woods

takes on the world's best, shoots 62

and adds another title to his collection

All week at Akron, television had been showing the now famous advertisement of Tiger Woods juggling with a ball and club – right hand, left hand, through his legs – before dispatching a volley into the distance.

And for months afterwards life imitated advert as professionals around the world honed their powers of prestidigitation by way of a welcome diversion to the hard slog of the practice range. Gary Evans proved himself better than most but Mark Roe remained 'King of the Trick Shot'.

That same week in Ohio, a media party at a driving range appropriately called 'Hackers' saw journalists attempt various daft shots with rubbish bins, coke cans, and a tomato sauce bottle. It seemed that everyone wanted to ape Tiger. Copying tricks is one thing, however. Matching him on a golf course is a quite different, much more elusive proposition, as the events at Firestone Country Club – and, increasingly, courses around the world – demonstrated.

This was the summer in which Tiger Woods drew away from the rest of golf's leading players and his victory in the World Golf Championships – NEC Invitational served only to emphasise his pre-eminence in the game. A second major championship had been secured with a thrilling US PGA Championship success a fortnight earlier at Medinah and now he was showing another elite field precisely who was boss.

The 24 European and American Ryder Cup players had been invited, as had been those international and US players who had participated in the Presidents Cup. Forty one of the best players in the world competing over one of the most liked and admired courses on the planet. It was a case for salivation.

Colin Montgomerie, Lee Westwood, Sergio Garcia, Masters champion José Maria Olazábal and Open champion Paul Lawrie headed the European Challenge, while Woods was joined by the likes of David Duval, Phil Mickelson, Davis Love III and US Open champion Payne Stewart in flying the Stars and Stripes.

The presence of Nick Price and Ernie Els ensured that this would be no

exclusively transatlantic tussle even if both boasted strong British connections. Price's mother still lives in England while Els, having bought a house at Wentworth in Surrey, is both a member and neighbour of the European Tour.

The Orient – and we are not talking about Leyton – was most prominently represented by Shigeki Maruyama whose final round of 68 was to clinch sixth place and enough yen to worry the beads on an abacus.

The action in this second World Golf Championships event was as thrilling as everyone had anticipated, but only after first-day

TOM LEHMAN: 75 finish was costly

PHIL MICKELSON: closing 65 gave him runner-up mantle

It would almost have been possible to select any of Tiger Woods's 62 blows in his brilliant third round as the shot of the week. But Saturday is moving day, not closing day and for any single shot to be placed above others there has to be several elements.

Technique, of course, is important, as is significance to the eventual outcome. There also has to be an element of withstanding pressure since most professionals can play most shots. It is those who can do so when absolutely necessary who become champions.

That applies more to putting than any other aspect of the game. Woods had seen a five-stroke lead cut to one and was in danger of bogeying the 71st. At the time he did not know that Phil Mickelson was taking five at the par four last. The 15 footer to save par was vital. His concentration, nerve and technique held as he slammed the ball into the cup.

He had holed an even more crucial one at the 71st at Medinah with Sergio Garcia breathing down his neck. "It seems like I always have to make putts on 17," Woods said. "I did it in my amateur days as well. I am not complaining about it."

That putt at Akron gave him a two-stroke lead and allowed him to bogey the last for victory. It was the shot of the week.

FRED COUPLES: shot 63 on Day Three

TIGER WOODS: golf of the Gods

thunderstorms had disappeared. A handful of players finished their opening rounds on Thursday and Paul Lawrie, for example, managed just a single shot.

The 36 holes he was required to play on Friday took its toll over the weekend, though not before he grabbed the halfway lead. His first round 67 was his lowest in the States and a second round 68 took him to the top of the leaderboard. The combination of heat and humidity and downright fatigue did for the Aberdonian. Tiredness did for Lee Westwood in what turned out to be a generally draining week for the European contingent.

SERGIO GARCIA: chased winner to the finishing line

CARLOS FRANCO: challenger from Paraguay

ERNIE ELS: European Tour Member and Wentworth H.Q. neighbour

T H E   C O U R S E

Firestone Country Club was designed by Englishman Bertie Way in 1929, but it was only after the comparatively easy South Course was toughened up by famous architect Robert Trent Jones in the 1950s that it became acclaimed as one of the finest in the world.

A 6,585-yard par 72 became a 7,180-yard par 70 with the addition of 50 bunkers, two new ponds and the rebuilding and reshaping of all 18 greens. The redesign was specifically for the 1960 US PGA Championship, which returned to Akron in 1966 and 1975. A US Open is thought to be long overdue.

Professionals love Firestone because 'what you see is what you get', as the maxim goes. There is nothing fancy, nothing tricked up, just a long course in which fine play is rewarded and poor play suitably punished. Although there is an element of up and back or up and down in the layout, each hole offers something different and bears the closest scrutiny.

The 16th is the so-called signature hole, a 625-yard par five which even Tiger Woods would hesitate about trying to reach in two. Mortals require a four iron second shot just to lay up. Many a tee shot is bunkered right, merely adding to the length and difficulty.

The course record of 61 is held by José Maria Olazábal, playing his first competitive round there in 1990. He even missed from six feet for birdie on the 17th and signed his card thinking he was 11 under par. He had thought the par was 72. Seventy years earlier, it had been.

Sergio Garcia was an exception. The amazing Spanish teenager chased Woods to the finishing line, just as he had done at the US PGA Championship, his challenge only ending at the 70th hole with a watery quadruple bogey nine. "I wanted to hit it close and maybe I got a little too aggressive and put it in the water," he said of his approach to the green. "I didn't hit a good lob wedge after that and put it in the water again. But, you know, sometimes these things happen." Such equanimity belied his tender years.

Which left Woods, pressed, too, by Mickelson, who finished runner-up, one shot behind, to take the euro 865,961 (£618,543) first prize with a ten under par total of 270. His prodigious length had been key on a long course made longer by days of heavy rain with fairways wide

COLIN MONTGOMERIE: draining week for Europeans

JIM FURYK: nicely poised to share tenth place

enough to permit the use of a driver. "I only rip it for fun these days," he claimed. He was having fun alright.

His 62 on the Saturday will live in the memory for all those who witnessed it. This was golf of the Gods. Lee Westwood, an early finisher, had watched on a television in his hotel bedroom. He was transfixed. "I don't think you could ever see a better nine holes of golf," Westwood later said of Woods's inward half. "Every shot was just perfect."

So, the questioner asked in the wake of victory, do you feel invincible? Woods smiled. "No," he replied, before pausing and smiling again. "Sorry," he added, recognising from where the journalist was coming and ensuring she did not go any further.

Maybe not invincible, but surely, tricks apart, inimitable.

Alan Fraser

PAUL LAWRIE: halfway leader

JOSÉ MARIA OLAZÁBAL: Masters champion

FIRESTONE COUNTRY CLUB, AKRON, OHIO, USA, AUGUST 26–29, 1999 • PAR 70 • YARDS 7139

Pos	Name & Country	Rnd 1	Rnd 2	Rnd 3	Rnd 4	Total	Prize Money €	£
1	Tiger WOODS (USA)	66	71	62	71	270	865961.53	618543.95
2	Phil MICKELSON (USA)	69	67	70	65	271	441640.38	315457.41
3	Craig PARRY (Aus)	71	66	69	69	275	283602.40	202573.14
	Nick PRICE (Zim)	67	69	68	71	275	283602.40	202573.14
5	Ernie ELS (SA)	71	69	67	69	276	202635.00	144739.29
6	Shigeki MARUYAMA (Jpn)	72	67	70	68	277	155007.11	110719.36
7	Jeff MAGGERT (USA)	71	67	69	71	278	133358.08	95255.77
	Sergio GARCIA (Sp)	67	70	69	72	278	133358.08	95255.77
	Carlos Daniel FRANCO (Para)	68	67	70	73	278	133358.08	95255.77
10	Jim FURYK (USA)	67	72	69	71	279	111709.04	79792.17
	Davis LOVE III (USA)	68	69	70	72	279	111709.04	79792.17
12	Mark CALCAVECCHIA (USA)	68	69	73	70	280	94389.81	67421.29
	Padraig HARRINGTON (Ire)	72	67	70	71	280	94389.81	67421.29
	Steve PATE (USA)	69	71	68	72	280	94389.81	67421.29
15	Vijay SINGH (Fij)	71	67	72	71	281	76204.61	54431.86
	Hal SUTTON (USA)	69	67	72	73	281	76204.61	54431.86
	Payne STEWART (USA)	70	67	69	75	281	76204.61	54431.86
	Tom LEHMAN (USA)	67	72	67	75	281	76204.61	54431.86
	Fred COUPLES (USA)	71	70	63	77	281	76204.61	54431.86
20	Justin LEONARD (USA)	73	68	69	72	282	63215.19	45153.71
21	Paul LAWRIE (Scot)	67	68	74	74	283	57153.46	40823.90
	Greg TURNER (NZ)	70	71	68	74	283	57153.46	40823.90
23	Stuart APPLEBY (Aus)	72	70	72	70	284	50225.77	35875.55
	Scott HOCH (USA)	68	73	71	72	284	50225.77	35875.55
25	Mark O'MEARA (USA)	73	70	71	71	285	43298.08	30927.20
	Greg NORMAN (Aus)	70	75	66	74	285	43298.08	30927.20
27	Miguel Angel JIMÉNEZ (Sp)	72	70	70	74	286	35792.79	25566.28
	David DUVAL (USA)	67	72	71	76	286	35792.79	25566.28
	Jesper PARNEVIK (Swe)	75	69	66	76	286	35792.79	25566.28
30	Jarmo SANDELIN (Swe)	71	71	73	72	287	32040.58	22886.13
	Lee JANZEN (USA)	71	70	72	74	287	32040.58	22886.13
	Colin MONTGOMERIE (Scot)	69	75	67	76	287	32040.58	22886.13
33	Lee WESTWOOD (Eng)	74	72	70	72	288	29442.69	21030.49
	Andrew COLTART (Scot)	71	71	69	77	288	29442.69	21030.49
	John HUSTON (USA)	69	71	70	78	288	29442.69	21030.49
36	Darren CLARKE (N.Ire)	73	72	69	75	289	27277.79	19484.14
	Jean VAN DE VELDE (Fr)	75	71	68	75	289	27277.79	19484.14
38	Frank NOBILO (NZ)	73	69	75	73	290	25978.85	18556.32
39	Steve ELKINGTON (Aus)	70	74	71	76	291	25112.88	17937.77
40	José Maria OLAZÁBAL (Sp)	70	80	69	73	292	24246.92	17319.23
41	Naomichi OZAKI (Jpn)	75	74	75	72	296	23380.96	16700.69

SERGIO GARCIA and TIGER WOODS: oh no, not you again

Success on a higher plane

Challenge Tour experience rewards
Warren Bennett with first win on
the European Tour at Gleneagles

As the Monarch's Course ambles towards the glen of eagles, the Scottish PGA Championship could hardly have wished for a more beautiful setting or exacting test. If Jack Nicklaus's spectacular layout at Gleneagles ensured that bogeys were usually in richer supply than eagles, England's Warren Bennett did his level best to tame the beast.

The 28-year-old from Watford edged out Holland's Rolf Muntz in a sudden-death play-off after both golfers completed four rounds on the six under par total of 282. The graduate of the European Challenge Tour admitted he drew on his track record of success in 1998, when he won five times, to hole a winning birdie putt of some four feet at the first extra hole.

"In 1998 I contended so many times as well as winning that I think it helps you to focus on what's required when you get another chance," said Bennett. "It's pretty much automatic. You know you can't afford to make any mistakes or you'll lose."

Bennett's closing round of 69 was a sterling effort, though the golfer thought he should have been more aggressive playing the 72nd hole.

"I learned my lesson from that in the play-off," he added. "I knew a birdie would be needed to win and I had to attack the pin more. When the putt went in, it was the highlight of my career."

As he took away a cheque for 58,330 euro (£41,664), as well as his first victory on the European Tour, Bennett could look back on a week in which he'd needed to demonstrate patience as well as resolve in demanding conditions.

Muntz, like Bennett, who was top amateur at Turnberry in the 1994 Open, came into the tournament with fond recollections of past visits to Scotland, having won the Amateur Championship at Muirfield in 1990. The spectacular scenery of the Ochil Hills certainly seemed to bring back good memories about this part of the world for the Dutchman. After missing 17 cuts in a dispiriting season, Muntz took command of the first round in Perthshire with a splendid opening score of 66 which established the Monarch's Course record.

Sam Torrance's hopes of winning a sixth Scottish PGA title were sabotaged before the tournament even started when he was the victim of a sting on the practice ground. He inadvertently grasped a wasp with his left hand, the doctor was called for and vinegar applied, Sam joked after five holes that he reeked so strongly of vinegar he felt like a bag of chips. The sting did nothing for his feel, either, and Torrance took 75.

To his credit, Torrance bounced back with a 68 in the second round, inspired in part by the feats of his 11-year-old son,

SHOT OF THE WEEK

Although David Howell made a claim when he aced the tenth hole with a five iron, the key shot for Warren Bennett was a thumping fairway wood onto the 16th green. A daunting par five, this 543-yard hole, protected at the front by a loch, gave Bennett problems all week. "But I really got into my tee shot and then I put a great three wood on the green," he recalled. "The shot set up an easy two-putt birdie." His four was enough to secure a play-off with Rolf Muntz.

Daniel, who pulled off the first hole-in-one of his young life on the little par three course which skirts the lawns in front of the five star Gleneagles Hotel.

Muntz, though, was still the man to catch at the top of the leaderboard, thanks to a tidy 71 which gave him the half-way lead on the seven under par mark of 137. Bennett, who added a 69 to his opening 70, was just two shots adrift.

The third round is traditionally regarded as moving day in professional golf and Bennett must have felt as if he'd moved right out of contention when he ran up 74 in the most testing conditions of the week. Muntz took 73 and slipped out of first place, leaving Sweden's Klas Eriksson, another golfer with a track record of success on the European Challenge Tour, to take over at the top courtesy of a chip-in from 50 feet for an eagle at the 12th which took him onto the 209 mark after 54 holes.

A 74 for 283 in the final round meant the Swede eventually had to settle for a share of third spot and a cheque for 19,705 euro (£14,075) with Roger Winchester. The main title ended up in a showdown between Bennett and Muntz, while the honour of top Scot, and the accolade of SPGA Champion of Scotland, went to Aberdeen's Greig Hutcheon, who was eighth.

A reserve who only got into the tournament at the 11th hour, Hutcheon, aged 26, made the most of his

WARREN BENNETT: grateful champion

KLAS ERIKSSON: Challenge Tour success

The debut of the Monarch's as a championship venue could hardly have been more auspicious. Designed by Jack Nicklaus, the Monarch's is Scotland's longest inland course. In a blustery week punctuated by frequent showers, the course played to its full length and provided a demanding test. In the end, only seven players broke the par of 288. Sam Torrance wasn't one of them but the Scot heaped praise on the layout, which he described as a more fearsome challenge than the renowned King's Course. "But it's just as beautiful," he added.

ROGER WINCHESTER: tied third

opportunity after he revealed how he'd played with Paul Lawrie as a lad at Banchory and had been inspired by his fellow Aberdonian's success in winning the Open Championship at Carnoustie.

With a prize fund of 350,000 euro (£250,000), the revived Scottish PGA Championship was an experience akin to pouring old wine into a new bottle. Although the original event had been around since 1907, the tournament fell on hard times. But the move to Gleneagles and the start of a new chapter in the championship's history was rewarded with a grateful champion.

Mike Aitken

ROLF MUNTZ: fond memories of Scotland

MONARCH'S COURSE, GLENEAGLES HOTEL, SCOTLAND, AUGUST 27–30, 1999 • PAR 72 • YARDS 7053

Pos	Name & Country	Rnd 1	Rnd 2	Rnd 3	Rnd 4	Total	Prize Money €	Prize Money £
1	Warren BENNETT (Eng)	70	69	74	69	282	58330.00	41664.29
2	Rolf MUNTZ (Hol)	66	71	73	72	282	38880.00	27771.43
3	Klas ERIKSSON (Swe)	68	70	71	74	283	19705.00	14075.00
	Roger WINCHESTER (Eng)	71	68	72	72	283	19705.00	14075.00
5	Per NYMAN (Swe)	72	69	72	73	286	14830.00	10592.86
6	Ian HUTCHINGS (SA)	70	74	70	73	287	11375.00	8125.00
	Andrew MCLARDY (SA)	73	71	69	74	287	11375.00	8125.00
8	Greig HUTCHEON (Scot)	69	73	73	73	288	8750.00	6250.00
9	Roger CHAPMAN (Eng)	71	72	74	72	289	7410.00	5292.86
	Fredrik JACOBSON (Swe)	70	71	77	71	289	7410.00	5292.86
11	Stuart CAGE (Eng)	70	75	75	70	290	5860.00	4185.71
	Raymond RUSSELL (Scot)	70	75	71	74	290	5860.00	4185.71
	Grant HAMERTON (Eng)	71	73	73	73	290	5860.00	4185.71
	Gary EVANS (Eng)	68	75	73	74	290	5860.00	4185.71
15	Stephen DODD (Wal)	72	75	70	74	291	4563.57	3259.69
	Brian NELSON (USA)	72	72	74	73	291	4563.57	3259.69
	Russell WEIR (Scot)	68	75	76	72	291	4563.57	3259.69
	Daren LEE (Eng)	71	72	75	73	291	4563.57	3259.69
	Daniel CHOPRA (Swe)	71	75	72	73	291	4563.57	3259.69
	Justin ROSE (Eng)	68	71	82	70	291	4563.57	3259.69
	Henrik BJORNSTAD (Nor)	72	69	82	68	291	4563.57	3259.69
22	Paul NILBRINK (Swe)	67	73	77	75	292	3780.00	2700.00
	Andrew CLAPP (Eng)	68	72	76	76	292	3780.00	2700.00
	Ross DRUMMOND (Scot)	72	73	72	75	292	3780.00	2700.00
	Katsuyoshi TOMORI (Jpn)	71	75	71	75	292	3780.00	2700.00
	Juan NUTT (Ven)	74	69	73	76	292	3780.00	2700.00
27	Elliot BOULT (NZ)	74	71	78	70	293	3360.00	2400.00
	Wayne RILEY (Aus)	73	74	75	71	293	3360.00	2400.00
	David HOWELL (Eng)	72	75	75	71	293	3360.00	2400.00
30	Murray URQUHART (Scot)	72	73	74	75	294	2885.00	2060.71
	Andrew BONHOMME (Aus)	70	73	78	73	294	2885.00	2060.71
	Massimo FLORIOLI (It)	76	71	75	72	294	2885.00	2060.71
	Jeev Milkha SINGH (Ind)	72	72	76	74	294	2885.00	2060.71
	Peter FOWLER (Aus)	72	73	77	72	294	2885.00	2060.71
	David J RUSSELL (Eng)	72	69	76	77	294	2885.00	2060.71
	Kalle BRINK (Swe)	71	72	74	77	294	2885.00	2060.71
37	Peter SMITH (Scot)	71	71	77	76	295	2520.00	1800.00
	Sam TORRANCE (Scot)	75	68	75	77	295	2520.00	1800.00
	Andrew BARNETT (Wal)	78	68	71	78	295	2520.00	1800.00
40	Greg OWEN (Eng)	69	74	80	73	296	2310.00	1650.00
	Lee VANNET (Scot)	72	75	72	77	296	2310.00	1650.00
	Nigel PRESTON (Eng)	72	74	76	74	296	2310.00	1650.00
43	Richard BOXALL (Eng)	75	69	75	78	297	1960.00	1400.00
	Johan RYSTRÖM (Swe)	70	73	80	74	297	1960.00	1400.00
	Colin GILLIES (Scot)	75	71	77	74	297	1960.00	1400.00
	Mathias GRÖNBERG (Swe)	78	69	74	76	297	1960.00	1400.00
	Brian MARCHBANK (Scot)	69	75	77	76	297	1960.00	1400.00
	Neil RODERICK (Wal)	73	72	75	77	297	1960.00	1400.00
	John GREAVES (Scot)	75	68	74	80	297	1960.00	1400.00
50	Gordon SHERRY (Scot)	70	75	77	76	298	1610.00	1150.00
	Scott HENDERSON (Scot)	71	70	76	81	298	1610.00	1150.00
	Marcello SANTI (It)	77	69	76	76	298	1610.00	1150.00
53	Jean Pierre CIXOUS (Fr)	70	75	75	79	299	1295.00	925.00
	Stephen FIELD (Eng)	73	74	79	73	299	1295.00	925.00
	Robert COLES (Eng)	73	73	76	77	299	1295.00	925.00
	Henrik NYSTROM (Swe)	72	74	77	76	299	1295.00	925.00
	John CHILLAS (Scot)	76	71	77	75	299	1295.00	925.00
	Kevin STABLES (Scot)	75	72	76	76	299	1295.00	925.00
59	Jorgen AKER (Swe)	71	75	74	80	300	1050.00	750.00
	Mark KING (Scot)	74	73	80	73	300	1050.00	750.00
	Steven THOMPSON (Eng)	69	72	81	78	300	1050.00	750.00
62	Alan REID (Scot)	71	76	76	78	301	980.00	700.00
63	Andrew OLDCORN (Scot)	68	75	83	77	303	910.00	650.00
	Grant DODD (Aus)	73	74	76	80	303	910.00	650.00
	Fabrice TARNAUD (Fr)	74	72	79	78	303	910.00	650.00
66	Colin BROOKS (Scot)	75	68	83	78	304	560.00	400.00

DAVID HOWELL: hole-in-one at new Tour venue

Avalanche of success

High in the Swiss Alps, Lee Westwood

turns a "fun week" into his

third European Tour victory in a row

Lee Westwood's third successive European Tour victory of 1999 on home soil at the Canon European Masters was a triumph of mind over matter. He flew to Switzerland after three frustrating tournaments in America anticipating "a fun week" with his family in the alpine resort of Crans-sur-Sierre, with its snowy peaks, panoramic vistas and luxury shops and hotels, and an avalanche of birdies and eagles being required to carry off the title.

After all, Sven Strüver's winning total in 1998 was 263, and Colin Montgomerie, the man Westwood was desperate to topple from the European number one spot, ended with a record 260 tally two years before after a blistering 61, 63 finale.

What Westwood found, however, was a much more formidable test awaiting him following Severiano Ballesteros's completion of his two-year contract to turn the Crans course into a true championship challenge. Some of the changes, he openly confessed, were not to his liking, but, typically, he buckled down to turn in a professional performance to rank among his best.

"Normally you are thinking 18 to 24 under par to win, but I reckon eight to ten under will do the trick this week," Westwood declared, after opening up with a brace of 69s to share the halfway lead as the cut fell at five over par compared with two under 12 months before. That Westwood's winning score was eventually a 14 under par 270 bore

testimony to the way he came to terms with the new layout – and the way Denmark's Thomas Björn chased him all the way.

"I got used to the greens as the week went on, they looked faster than they

were," he added. "I didn't feel under pressure, I was enjoying battling with Thomas so much.

"I'd hit a great shot in close, then he'd do the same. I'd knock in a big birdie putt and he'd follow me or vice versa. It was

THOMAS BJÖRN: chased winner all the way

pure match-play and great fun. It's one of the best days I've ever had on a golf course – really special.

"Thomas said to me: 'The next time you spend three weeks in America please take a week off when you get back!' Even though the margin was two shots the result was in doubt to the last putts. When he bogeyed the 17th it gave me a bit of breathing space. But on 18, I was six feet away putting for par and he was 12 feet away putting for birdie – he missed and I holed."

Westwood had closed 67, 65. Björn,

Australian Wayne Riley sent his six iron tee shot soaring over the road straight into the cup for a hole-in-one at the 188-yard third hole in round three to win a gold ingot worth around euro 7,000 (£5,000) presented by Credit Suisse Private Banking. Remarkably, he was the last man to have an ace in this event, at the 13th in 1995 to win an Ebel watch.

after following an opening 72 with a Friday 66, made 68, 66. Many had predicted Westwood's Ryder Cup teammate and great friend Darren Clarke (they were the top ranked contenders in the field in second and sixth place in the Volvo Order of Merit) would chase him hardest for the 210,000 euro (£150,000) jackpot, but it was Björn, in 40th spot on the money list, who took up the challenge.

He had missed out on a Ryder Cup return after starring alongside fellow rookies Westwood and Clarke at Valderrama in 1997, when he partnered Ian Woosnam to a fourball triumph and then came battling from four down to the then Open champion Justin Leonard to force a vital half in the singles.

Victories in the Heineken Classic and Peugeot Open de España in 1998 kept the Björn bandwagon rolling, but the wheels came off when injury hit later in the year and he admitted: "My form suffered when I missed tournaments and

ALEX CEJKA: third with closing 66

THE COURSE

The Crans course on which shots travel ten per cent further at 5,000 feet is used as nursery ski slopes in winter and has been extensively strengthened by Severiano Ballesteros. He has remodelled the greens and in 1999 reshaped the 17th into a demanding dogleg and sited a pond front right of the 18th green.

SAM TORRANCE: fit again after frustrating summer

couldn't practise and I think I tried too hard when I came back. I told myself it wasn't the end of the world if I didn't make the Ryder Cup, and it hurt badly. But I've proved in Switzerland that I'm back in the right direction.

"It's tough when you haven't been in this situation for a while. Lee's attitude on the golf course is fantastic. He's very calm and completely in control of his game. He's getting to a stage where he's won so many tournaments he doesn't feel the pressure the same as the rest of us. He and Montgomerie are probably in a league of their own. We all want to be where they are and the most impressive thing is that they can stay at the top of the Official World Ranking playing mostly in Europe. There are a few of us who should be in that league, like Darren and myself, but we are lagging a little behind. We've just got to keep plugging away."

Westwood was delighted to have kept the pressure on Montgomerie in the race to top the Volvo Order of Merit. He said: "Every time I win it makes it more interesting. Every time I play well it's an incentive to him and vice versa. After I won in Holland and Ireland he won in Sweden and Germany. Every time he sets new targets, like winning by nine in Sweden, it gives you that bit of a kick up the backside to concentrate harder. It shows you what sort of standard you have to be at to win the Volvo Order of Merit – and he's going for his seventh year on the trot!"

Alex Cejka, another man on many shortlists who failed to make the Ryder Cup, closed with a 66 to finish third, four behind Björn, and Sam Torrance underlined his return to full fitness after a frustrating summer with weekend rounds of 65, 67 to tie Marc Farry for fourth, two shots further back.

But the man with the biggest smile at the finish was Westwood. "Shooting 65 under the kind of pressure Thomas put on me after starting favourite with the bookmakers back home was very satisfying," he said, adding: "especially as my dad had a few bob on me!"

Gordon Richardson   269

Crans-sur-Sierre, Switzerland, September 2–5, 1999 • Par 71 • Yards 6848

Pos	Name & Country	Rnd 1	Rnd 2	Rnd 3	Rnd 4	Total	Prize Money €	£
1	Lee WESTWOOD (Eng)	69	69	67	65	270	210000.00	150000.00
2	Thomas BJÖRN (Den)	72	66	68	66	272	140000.00	100000.00
3	Alex CEJKA (Ger)	70	70	70	66	276	78860.00	56328.57
4	Marc FARRY (Fr)	70	70	68	70	278	58200.00	41571.43
	Sam TORRANCE (Scot)	75	71	65	67	278	58200.00	41571.43
6	Sven STRÜVER (Ger)	70	70	69	71	280	37800.00	27000.00
	Miguel Angel JIMÉNEZ (Sp)	70	73	72	65	280	37800.00	27000.00
	Ignacio GARRIDO (Sp)	70	76	66	68	280	37800.00	27000.00
9	Nick O'HERN (Aus)	71	71	71	68	281	24527.50	17519.64
	Eduardo ROMERO (Arg)	70	73	68	70	281	24527.50	17519.64
	Stephen FIELD (Eng)	68	74	68	71	281	24527.50	17519.64
	Patrik SJÖLAND (Swe)	72	71	71	67	281	24527.50	17519.64
13	Bob MAY (USA)	69	73	69	71	282	19775.00	14125.00
	Domingo HOSPITAL (Sp)	72	72	69	69	282	19775.00	14125.00
15	Peter O'MALLEY (Aus)	73	72	69	69	283	17388.00	12420.00
	Michael CAMPBELL (NZ)	72	66	71	74	283	17388.00	12420.00
	Dean ROBERTSON (Scot)	72	72	71	68	283	17388.00	12420.00
	Diego BORREGO (Sp)	73	70	70	70	283	17388.00	12420.00
19	Roger WESSELS (SA)	70	72	69	73	284	15624.00	11160.00
20	Eamonn DARCY (Ire)	74	73	71	67	285	14364.00	10260.00
	Geoff OGILVY (Aus)	71	73	69	72	285	14364.00	10260.00
	Miles TUNNICLIFF (Eng)	72	70	66	77	285	14364.00	10260.00
	John BICKERTON (Eng)	70	74	72	69	285	14364.00	10260.00
	Ross DRUMMOND (Scot)	73	72	68	72	285	14364.00	10260.00
25	Ricardo GONZALEZ (Arg)	71	75	72	68	286	12852.00	9180.00
	Tom GILLIS (USA)	66	80	69	71	286	12852.00	9180.00
	Ian GARBUTT (Eng)	77	69	70	70	286	12852.00	9180.00
28	Mats HALLBERG (Swe)	73	74	72	68	287	10584.00	7560.00
	Mark MOULAND (Wal)	74	71	70	72	287	10584.00	7560.00
	Peter FOWLER (Aus)	73	74	71	69	287	10584.00	7560.00
	Steen TINNING (Den)	73	72	69	73	287	10584.00	7560.00
	Angel CABRERA (Arg)	68	75	72	72	287	10584.00	7560.00
	Massimo SCARPA (It)	72	75	71	69	287	10584.00	7560.00
	Per-Ulrik JOHANSSON (Swe)	76	70	70	71	287	10584.00	7560.00
	Darren CLARKE (N.Ire)	70	70	72	75	287	10584.00	7560.00
	Francisco CEA (Sp)	68	72	75	72	287	10584.00	7560.00
	Barry LANE (Eng)	72	74	70	71	287	10584.00	7560.00
38	Roger CHAPMAN (Eng)	71	74	71	72	288	8694.00	6210.00
	Nick FALDO (Eng)	71	73	73	71	288	8694.00	6210.00
	Jarrod MOSELEY (Aus)	74	71	72	71	288	8694.00	6210.00
	Richard BOXALL (Eng)	71	75	71	71	288	8694.00	6210.00
42	Peter SENIOR (Aus)	71	71	77	70	289	7686.00	5490.00
	Andrew SHERBORNE (Eng)	70	72	75	72	289	7686.00	5490.00
	Phillip PRICE (Wal)	72	73	71	73	289	7686.00	5490.00
	Christopher HANELL (Swe)	75	72	70	72	289	7686.00	5490.00
46	Daren LEE (Eng)	71	74	73	72	290	6678.00	4770.00
	Jean-Francois REMESY (Fr)	69	78	71	72	290	6678.00	4770.00
	Andrew BEAL (Eng)	72	75	73	70	290	6678.00	4770.00
	Gary ORR (Scot)	72	72	70	76	290	6678.00	4770.00
50	Ian HUTCHINGS (SA)	71	76	74	70	291	5418.00	3870.00
	Mathias GRÖNBERG (Swe)	69	78	75	69	291	5418.00	3870.00
	David PARK (Wal)	73	73	73	72	291	5418.00	3870.00
	Anthony WALL (Eng)	70	76	72	73	291	5418.00	3870.00
	David CARTER (Eng)	73	71	72	75	291	5418.00	3870.00
	Pierre FULKE (Swe)	69	74	70	78	291	5418.00	3870.00
56	Craig HAINLINE (USA)	74	73	70	75	292	4284.00	3060.00
	Malcolm MACKENZIE (Eng)	70	76	73	73	292	4284.00	3060.00
	Massimo FLORIOLI (It)	73	74	75	70	292	4284.00	3060.00
59	Thomas GÖGELE (Ger)	73	74	68	78	293	3843.00	2745.00
	Gilberto MORALES (Ven)	75	72	75	71	293	3843.00	2745.00
61	Olle KARLSSON (Swe)	76	69	74	75	294	3528.00	2520.00
	Warren BENNETT (Eng)	70	74	74	76	294	3528.00	2520.00
	Kim FELTON (Aus)	71	76	73	74	294	3528.00	2520.00
64	Stuart CAGE (Eng)	73	70	76	76	295	3213.00	2295.00
	Wayne RILEY (Aus)	75	71	76	73	295	3213.00	2295.00
66	David HOWELL (Eng)	72	75	75	74	296	1890.00	1350.00
67	Steve REY (Swi)	73	74	71	79	297	1887.00	1347.86
68	Per NYMAN (Swe)	74	73	78	73	298	1882.50	1344.64
	Mats LANNER (Swe)	72	75	75	76	298	1882.50	1344.64
70	Van PHILLIPS (Eng)	73	70	82	75	300	1878.00	1341.43

Canon is proud to be an Official Sponsor of the PGA European Tour.
http://sport.canon-europa.com

No racing certainties on Tour

Bob May saves new bookmaker sponsor

£70,000 with short-head win

over favourite Colin Montgomerie

As a bookmaker famed for fearlessly taking on the world's highest rollers, Victor Chandler has made his fortune out of 50-1 outsiders beating the favourites at Royal Ascot.

So it was fitting that when the genial Victor decided to sponsor the British Masters at Woburn, to the tune of £5 million over five years in his first golf venture, the first winner, the little-considered American Bob May, a serial runner-up who had played bridesmaid 22 times, should short-head the supposed "good thing", Colin Montgomerie, in front of a record 15,000-plus crowd who thought they had come to salute the sixth victory of another memorable year for Europe's main man.

When the sponsor said his thank-yous to the course staff at the prize giving, the paramedics came in for special mention. "I would have needed assistance from them if Monty had won," he joked. A Montgomerie victory would indeed

WINNING DOUBLE: new sponsor Victor Chandler and first-time champion Bob May

have cost his firm £70,000. May, in contrast, went totally unbacked when the magnificent state-of-the-art Chandler betting palace opened for business, and he repaid a fair proportion of his winner's cheque by coming to their rescue.

In one of the most surprising turn-arounds of the year, Montgomerie, start-ing the final day 17 under par and three shots clear after 54 almost perfect holes marred by just one bogey, lost the plot. In little more than an hour he had increased his bogey tally to five with a series of unusual errors, eventually triple-putting three times in a closing 71 to May's 67.

An unbackable 1-8 chance when play began, with May at 7-1 and the rest any price you liked, the Scot was expected to enjoy a Sunday afternoon stroll in the park. How wrong we all were. After seven holes, Montgomerie had dropped four shots. May picked up two, and the favourite's three-shot lead was now a three-shot deficit. But would the 30-year-old Californian, never a winner in almost 200 tournaments on the Nike, US, Asian and European Tours since turning professional following the 1991 Walker Cup, manage to hold his nerve?

That was the 200,000-dollar question, but, under the calming influence of new caddie Max Cunning, only a jabby putt of six feet at the 18th that shot a good two feet past the hole – "it seemed like ten" – gave Montgomerie just the tiniest play-off hope, and betrayed May's past record of missed opportunities.

Nicknamed "Top-Ten Bob" – Woburn was his tenth such finish of the year – May had one credential exactly right for this tournament: he lives in the gambling capital of the world, Las Vegas. Though no wild punter, he still backs Montgomerie to win all the Majors in the Vegas sportsbooks and is waiting to collect. "It's just a matter of time," insists May. "Monty is one the of the best players in the world, if not the best player. I never

COLIN MONTGOMERIE: unbackable at 1-8 odds before play started

dreamed when I set out that I would beat him. But Colin did not play the way he knows how to play."

May had already backed a winner with the second shot of his second round, a three iron that travelled 298 yards for an albatross two at the 502-yard tenth. If that rare bird had come at the 18th, May would have claimed Chandler's special prize, ownership of a racehorse for next year, but the sponsors came up with a consolation, and May will see his own

SHOT OF THE WEEK

When Bob May holed his three iron second shot for an albatross two at the 502-yard tenth hole on Friday, everybody thought "bad luck" because Victor Chandler had put up a prize worth euro 35,000 (£25,000) for an albatross at a different hole, the 514-yard 18th – ownership of a racehorse for a year. By the end of the week, that shot was worth a good deal more – euro 131,660 (£94,043) more, to be precise - because it made the difference between victory and, at best, a play-off for the likeable Californian.

CHRISTOPHER HANELL: reason to keep smiling

THE COURSE

It had been five long years since wonderful Woburn had hosted the British Masters and the players were unanimous in praising the way it had matured. The slick greens sorted the men out from the boys and the encroaching trees trapped their usual crop of victims. The crowds also voted with their feet for the easy-to-get-to course, close to the M1. More than 41,000 basked in the four sunny days, 90 per cent up on Woburn in 1994.

LEE WESTWOOD: 72 was punishing

colours carried by a horse Chandler will have leased to him for a day. More importantly, as it turned out, that three under par bonus gave May the cushion he needed to pass the post safely on Sunday with a 19 under par 269 that proved beyond even Montgomerie.

With wife and son in Vegas, the loneliness of the long distance golfer was revealed when May admitted that, had he not received an invitation from Sunningdale golfer Anthony Wall to spend Sunday night with his family, he would have had to celebrate his maiden victory alone in a hotel room. Next year, thanks to this breakthrough, it will be different. If his bid to regain his US Tour card fails, he will bring his family over to a more permanent home in England.

Christopher Hanell, an ever-smiling Swede, had plenty to smile about with his biggest cheque for third, while English prospect Greg Owen grabbed a share of fourth with Lee Westwood (whose own chance had disappeared with a 72 on day three) by holing his pitch for an eagle three at the last to clinch his card for 2000.

The ground-breaking flair which Chandler had demonstrated by removing his off-course business to Gibraltar earlier in the summer to help clients avoid the nine per cent British betting tax was seamlessly transferred to a golfing environment at Woburn and it was hard to believe that Richard Thomas, Chandler's Business Development Director, and his team had not done it all before.

Spectators who bought £4 programmes received £4-worth of free bets in return, one of many nice touches from Chandler's on-course debut, the most important, as far as serious punters were concerned, being the absence of tax or "administration" charges on bets. The first bookmaker to sponsor on Tour since Coral backed the Welsh Classic in 1980-1982, Chandler have now taken over from William Hill as the European Tour's Official Bookmaker for the duration of their sponsorship.

Jeremy Chapman

275

Woburn, Buckinghamshire, England, September 9–12, 1999 • Par 72 • Yards 6973

Pos	Name & Country	Rnd 1	Rnd 2	Rnd 3	Rnd 4	Total	Prize Money €	£
1	Bob MAY (USA)	69	67	66	67	269	166666.00	119047.14
2	Colin MONTGOMERIE (Scot)	67	64	68	71	270	111100.00	79357.14
3	Christopher HANELL (Swe)	70	69	66	67	272	62600.00	44714.29
4	Lee WESTWOOD (Eng)	68	66	72	68	274	46200.00	33000.00
	Greg OWEN (Eng)	68	70	70	66	274	46200.00	33000.00
6	Steve WEBSTER (Eng)	67	70	70	68	275	35000.00	25000.00
7	Sam TORRANCE (Scot)	72	67	69	68	276	27500.00	19642.86
	Paul BROADHURST (Eng)	68	71	72	65	276	27500.00	19642.86
9	Stephen LEANEY (Aus)	67	70	70	70	277	22300.00	15928.57
10	Michael CAMPBELL (NZ)	70	71	67	70	278	16155.00	11539.29
	Raymond RUSSELL (Scot)	71	65	70	72	278	16155.00	11539.29
	Tony JOHNSTONE (Zim)	71	69	68	70	278	16155.00	11539.29
	John BICKERTON (Eng)	68	68	71	71	278	16155.00	11539.29
	Steen TINNING (Den)	69	72	70	67	278	16155.00	11539.29
	Paul MCGINLEY (Ire)	71	71	70	66	278	16155.00	11539.29
	Retief GOOSEN (SA)	69	71	68	70	278	16155.00	11539.29
	Darren CLARKE (N.Ire)	71	66	74	67	278	16155.00	11539.29
18	Mathias GRÖNBERG (Swe)	72	67	67	73	279	11600.00	8285.71
	Ian WOOSNAM (Wal)	68	69	69	73	279	11600.00	8285.71
	Mark MCNULTY (Zim)	73	69	68	69	279	11600.00	8285.71
	Eduardo ROMERO (Arg)	70	68	66	75	279	11600.00	8285.71
	Daren LEE (Eng)	70	71	71	67	279	11600.00	8285.71
	Per NYMAN (Swe)	72	67	73	67	279	11600.00	8285.71
	Peter MITCHELL (Eng)	68	74	70	67	279	11600.00	8285.71
	Robert Jan DERKSEN (Hol)	74	68	68	69	279	11600.00	8285.71
26	Marc FARRY (Fr)	72	68	70	70	280	9450.00	6750.00
	Jamie SPENCE (Eng)	70	69	71	70	280	9450.00	6750.00
	Santiago LUNA (Sp)	73	68	74	65	280	9450.00	6750.00
	Patrik SJÖLAND (Swe)	70	73	70	67	280	9450.00	6750.00
	Sven STRÜVER (Ger)	73	69	72	66	280	9450.00	6750.00
	Jeev Milkha SINGH (Ind)	68	72	71	69	280	9450.00	6750.00
32	Paolo QUIRICI (Swi)	69	69	72	71	281	7900.00	5642.86
	Jonathan LOMAS (Eng)	73	70	70	68	281	7900.00	5642.86
	David CARTER (Eng)	71	71	70	69	281	7900.00	5642.86
	Thomas BJÖRN (Den)	70	70	72	69	281	7900.00	5642.86
	Derrick COOPER (Eng)	68	75	68	70	281	7900.00	5642.86
	Des SMYTH (Ire)	70	71	69	71	281	7900.00	5642.86
38	Anthony WALL (Eng)	71	69	72	70	282	6400.00	4571.43
	Pierre FULKE (Swe)	70	72	71	69	282	6400.00	4571.43
	Miguel Angel MARTIN (Sp)	74	65	73	70	282	6400.00	4571.43
	Jarmo SANDELIN (Swe)	70	73	66	73	282	6400.00	4571.43
	Angel CABRERA (Arg)	71	68	70	73	282	6400.00	4571.43
	Andrew MCLARDY (SA)	70	72	71	69	282	6400.00	4571.43
	Richard BOXALL (Eng)	70	69	72	71	282	6400.00	4571.43
	Gary ORR (Scot)	70	69	73	70	282	6400.00	4571.43
	Søren KJELDSEN (Den)	67	72	72	71	282	6400.00	4571.43
47	Greg TURNER (NZ)	73	70	70	70	283	5000.00	3571.43
	Stephen ALLAN (Aus)	65	72	75	71	283	5000.00	3571.43
	Jesus Maria ARRUTI (Sp)	69	70	70	74	283	5000.00	3571.43
	Emanuele CANONICA (It)	71	70	75	67	283	5000.00	3571.43
	Richard GREEN (Aus)	73	70	68	72	283	5000.00	3571.43
52	David GILFORD (Eng)	71	70	72	71	284	4200.00	3000.00
	Raphaël JACQUELIN (Fr)	70	71	73	70	284	4200.00	3000.00
	Nick O'HERN (Aus)	69	73	68	74	284	4200.00	3000.00
55	Stephen GALLACHER (Scot)	72	68	73	72	285	3420.00	2442.86
	José COCERES (Arg)	70	69	72	74	285	3420.00	2442.86
	Silvio GRAPPASONNI (It)	67	68	75	75	285	3420.00	2442.86
	Peter BAKER (Eng)	70	73	71	71	285	3420.00	2442.86
	John MELLOR (Eng)	70	73	72	70	285	3420.00	2442.86
60	Eamonn DARCY (Ire)	69	73	72	73	287	2800.00	2000.00
	Anders HANSEN (Den)	71	72	70	74	287	2800.00	2000.00
	Andrew RAITT (Eng)	70	73	73	71	287	2800.00	2000.00
	Richard COUGHLAN (Ire)	72	71	71	73	287	2800.00	2000.00
	Søren HANSEN (Den)	68	70	73	76	287	2800.00	2000.00
65	Mark MOULAND (Wal)	72	70	77	69	288	2009.00	1435.00
	Massimo SCARPA (It)	70	70	74	74	288	2009.00	1435.00
67	Carlos RODILES (Sp)	72	69	74	74	289	1515.00	1082.14
68	Olle KARLSSON (Swe)	68	75	77	70	290	1512.00	1080.00
69	Bernhard LANGER (Ger)	68	75	74	74	291	1507.50	1076.79
	Marcello SANTI (It)	71	71	80	69	291	1507.50	1076.79
71	Andrew OLDCORN (Scot)	69	74	76	73	292	1501.50	1072.50
	John MCHENRY (Ire)	72	71	73	76	292	1501.50	1072.50
73	Peter SENIOR (Aus)	71	70	79	74	294	1497.00	1069.29

Bob May's victory was perfectly timed – so was his bonus prize, an Omega watch from executive Brian Jowle

Seven years of toil rewarded

When a last green, fast, downhill putt of 25 feet

finally offered Pierre Fulke his chance

to become a new Tour champion - he didn't miss

*I*f golf clubs could talk, it would be educational and amusing to sit a bunch of putters down in some locker-room or other and invite them to chat about their cousins that nestle and clank alongside them in those big, mobile homes their masters call golf bags.

The shorter in stature among them would probably feel some small affinity with the wedges, if only because they, too, are little fellows, while even the taller branch of the family, the broomhandles, would appreciate the subtleties of which they are capable.

The first reservations might be expressed for irons nine to four, but even they would be likely to escape complete condemnation on the grounds that they were honest enough fellows doing a routine job as best they could. Hardly inspired, unambitious, but salt-of-the-earth types who neither seek nor are granted much glory in life.

So far, so good. Stainless steel-shafted perestroika preserved thus far. But how about the big boys? The long irons, the fairway woods and, crucially, the drivers? Only now, one fancies, would the real bile kick in. You can just hear, can't you? "Well, the long irons are just so ignorant. All they're good for is giving the ball a dirty great clout, but they shouldn't be blamed, because, by and large, they're pretty stupid.

"But the woods are really beyond the pale. They're no more than thugs, totally brain-dead, not one grey cell between the lot of them. If we're the sensitive ones in here, the woods are the bully boys. Can't stand the sight of them. They might give the ball a headache, but it's about time they remembered that it's us who win golf tournaments, not them. If we were as bad at our jobs as they are at theirs - all crash, bang, wallop and never mind the fairway - we'd be out of work in ten minutes."

They would be right, too. Woods, be they giga-headed, warp factor five titanium, or anything else, serve a purpose, of that there is no doubt. But if the player who wields them is to do something as significant as win a golf tournament, he must, above all else, have a putter that is doing its job. Ask Colin Montgomerie - one week in the middle of September his little green machine suddenly went as mental as the widest, wildest driver in creation, and it cost him a great deal of spending fodder.

For all four days of the Trophée

Lancôme in the autumnal, sylvan splendour of Saint-Nom-la-Bretèche, Montgomerie used his heavy artillery with the precision of a surgeon's knife. He hit fairways with them, he put his ball on greens with monotonous regularity with those dull sorts, the mid-irons, he gave himself birdie chances with Messrs Sand, Pitching and Lob. But when he needed a bit of help from that mercurial little chap with the small head and the short shaft, he found, to his cost, that it was indulging itself in a fit of the sulks.

In the four days of the tournament,

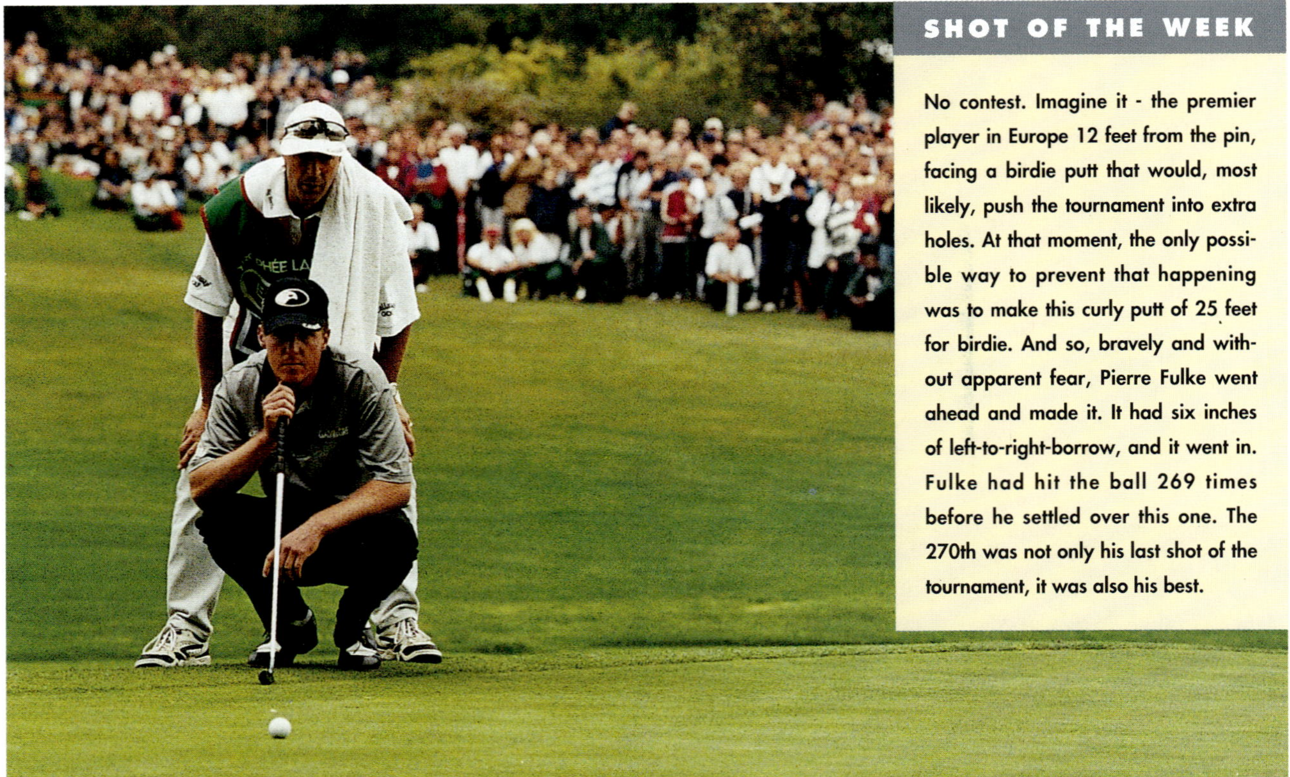

No contest. Imagine it - the premier player in Europe 12 feet from the pin, facing a birdie putt that would, most likely, push the tournament into extra holes. At that moment, the only possible way to prevent that happening was to make this curly putt of 25 feet for birdie. And so, bravely and without apparent fear, Pierre Fulke went ahead and made it. It had six inches of left-to-right-borrow, and it went in. Fulke had hit the ball 269 times before he settled over this one. The 270th was not only his last shot of the tournament, it was also his best.

Montgomerie struck the ball 272 times, of which 120 were putts. In his last round alone, he took 35 strokes on the greens – and putting like that wouldn't win a monthly medal at the local muni, never mind an important European Tour event. It all added up to a hair-shirt sort of a week for Europe's No 1, narrow failure suffered rather than the triumphant success the rest of his golf deserved immediately ahead of the Ryder Cup at Brookline.

The man himself was in mental turmoil after he had been beaten by two shots by the courage and dogged persistence of Sweden's Pierre Fulke, who won one of the European Tour's most coveted titles with a total of 270, 14 under par. "It was sad," said Montgomerie, profound *tristesse* enveloping him like the tattered cloak of a beggar, in the immediate aftermath of Fulke's triumph and his failure. "I should have had this wrapped up after five holes. That's the best I have ever hit the ball in a round of golf, but 35 putts doesn't win you anything."

True, but the most amazing thing about all Montgomerie's travails was that as he reached the green on Saint-Nom's treacherous 18th hole he still had the chance to win the tournament. Ignacio Garrido was already in on 13 under par, hardly knowing whether to look or not. Fulke was also on 13 under, Montgomerie on minus 12. Par for the stocky Swede and birdie for Montgomerie would put it into a three-way play-off and, for all Montgomerie's failings on the putting surfaces, few would have bet against him then.

Montgomerie put his tee shot on the 209-yard hole

IGNACIO GARRIDO: to look or not to look?

The combined test that Saint-Nom-la-Bretèche comes up with as a distillation from the best of its two courses proved once again that for all its apparent benevolence, it is utterly unforgiving on anything the slightest bit loose. Demanding of total concentration, it is one of the best parkland courses that mainland Europe has to offer. It emerged from the week with its considerable reputation unsullied.

to within 12 feet, just on the right fringe, flirting with but safely away from the pond that lures so many to a watery disaster. Fulke, on the other hand, was facing a slippery, downhill, breaking putt of 25 feet on a lightning-fast green. In spite of all that had gone before, the actuarial odds must have favoured Montgomerie at that instant.

He stalked, restless, he glowered in that massively magisterial way of his, he could not wait to play his master-stroke. It never came to that. Instead, the touch of genius came from Fulke. His line was, perhaps, two and a half cup-widths to the left of the hole. His destiny was in his hands and, outwardly calm but inwardly shaking

like an aspen leaf in the breezes of a New England fall, he stepped up to his ball, settled, then sent it on its way.

Montgomerie did not look at first, but eventually his eyes were attracted to Fulke's ball like iron filings to a magnet. From six feet out, Fulke knew, Montgomerie knew, the gallery knew, that it was going nowhere but in the hole. And that, of course, is where it ended its journey. Fulke punched the air in his understated, Swedish way. He had done it. The breakthrough that had been so long in the coming through seven long years of toil on the European Tour had finally happened.

There was scarcely a glimmer of reaction from Montgomerie. He had fallen short; by his own superlative standards he had failed, because for such people as he, not winning represents failure.

But there was still a job to be done, still the first birdie for ten holes to be sought. It almost goes without saying that he missed. The moment had been there, waiting to be seized, and somebody had grabbed it before he had the chance. For a man who lives so much of his life in the sun, a little rain had suddenly fallen. And all because a small, dissident servant had, just for a few days, decided to stage its own quiet little rebellion.

COLIN MONTGOMERIE: life in the sun gave way to rain

Mel Webb   281

SAINT-NOM-LA-BRETÈCHE, PARIS, FRANCE, SEPTEMBER 16–19, 1999 • PAR 71 • YARDS 6903

Pos	Name & Country	Rnd 1	Rnd 2	Rnd 3	Rnd 4	Total	Prize Money €	£
1	Pierre FULKE (Swe)	69	69	65	67	270	186660.00	133328.57
2	Ignacio GARRIDO (Sp)	67	70	68	66	271	124430.00	88878.57
3	Santiago LUNA (Sp)	70	66	70	66	272	57843.33	41316.66
	Colin MONTGOMERIE (Scot)	66	70	68	68	272	57843.33	41316.66
	Greg OWEN (Eng)	73	66	67	66	272	57843.33	41316.66
6	Jarmo SANDELIN (Swe)	70	66	69	69	274	36400.00	26000.00
	Gary EVANS (Eng)	71	64	73	66	274	36400.00	26000.00
8	Steve WEBSTER (Eng)	69	71	68	67	275	26490.00	18921.43
	Marc FARRY (Fr)	75	68	66	66	275	26490.00	18921.43
10	Peter SENIOR (Aus)	66	72	70	68	276	19488.00	13920.00
	Miguel Angel JIMÉNEZ (Sp)	68	64	70	74	276	19488.00	13920.00
	Angel CABRERA (Arg)	71	69	67	69	276	19488.00	13920.00
	Mark MCNULTY (Zim)	71	69	68	68	276	19488.00	13920.00
	Alex CEJKA (Ger)	64	73	73	66	276	19488.00	13920.00
15	Tom GILLIS (USA)	69	74	66	68	277	15792.00	11280.00
	Retief GOOSEN (SA)	78	65	69	65	277	15792.00	11280.00
	José COCERES (Arg)	66	71	71	69	277	15792.00	11280.00
18	Ricardo GONZALEZ (Arg)	67	72	71	68	278	13346.67	9533.34
	Michael CAMPBELL (NZ)	68	68	70	72	278	13346.67	9533.34
	Paul LAWRIE (Scot)	72	68	70	68	278	13346.67	9533.34
	Costantino ROCCA (It)	68	72	67	71	278	13346.67	9533.34
	Dennis EDLUND (Swe)	68	71	72	67	278	13346.67	9533.34
	Jeev Milkha SINGH (Ind)	72	67	70	69	278	13346.67	9533.34
24	John MELLOR (Eng)	69	71	71	68	279	11088.00	7920.00
	Bob MAY (USA)	73	68	68	70	279	11088.00	7920.00
	Thomas BJÖRN (Den)	72	70	67	70	279	11088.00	7920.00
	Paul MCGINLEY (Ire)	72	69	68	70	279	11088.00	7920.00
	Russell CLAYDON (Eng)	67	73	70	69	279	11088.00	7920.00
	Domingo HOSPITAL (Sp)	72	71	68	68	279	11088.00	7920.00
	Roger WESSELS (SA)	72	70	73	64	279	11088.00	7920.00
31	Emanuele CANONICA (It)	71	69	70	70	280	8748.44	6248.89
	Rolf MUNTZ (Hol)	68	71	72	69	280	8748.44	6248.89
	Søren KJELDSEN (Den)	73	69	68	70	280	8748.44	6248.89
	Jean VAN DE VELDE (Fr)	68	70	71	71	280	8748.44	6248.89
	Stephen FIELD (Eng)	71	67	73	69	280	8748.44	6248.89
	Mark JAMES (Eng)	70	70	72	68	280	8748.44	6248.89
	Stephen LEANEY (Aus)	68	70	73	69	280	8748.44	6248.89
	Steen TINNING (Den)	67	72	73	68	280	8748.44	6248.89
	Brian DAVIS (Eng)	68	72	71	69	280	8748.44	6248.89
40	Paolo QUIRICI (Swi)	69	72	70	70	281	7392.00	5280.00
	Miles TUNNICLIFF (Eng)	67	73	69	72	281	7392.00	5280.00
	Peter O'MALLEY (Aus)	71	71	68	71	281	7392.00	5280.00
43	Barry LANE (Eng)	72	71	72	67	282	6384.00	4560.00
	Fredrik JACOBSON (Swe)	72	69	70	71	282	6384.00	4560.00
	José Maria OLAZABAL (Sp)	68	70	71	73	282	6384.00	4560.00
	Ian WOOSNAM (Wal)	70	70	75	67	282	6384.00	4560.00
	Anthony WALL (Eng)	72	71	72	67	282	6384.00	4560.00
	Klas ERIKSSON (Swe)	69	73	68	72	282	6384.00	4560.00
49	Fredrik LINDGREN (Swe)	71	72	71	69	283	5488.00	3920.00
	Mats LANNER (Swe)	73	68	73	69	283	5488.00	3920.00
51	Jean-Francois REMESY (Fr)	69	69	74	72	284	4592.00	3280.00
	Paul BROADHURST (Eng)	72	71	71	70	284	4592.00	3280.00
	Silvio GRAPPASONNI (It)	74	68	71	71	284	4592.00	3280.00
	Peter MITCHELL (Eng)	71	71	74	68	284	4592.00	3280.00
	José RIVERO (Sp)	67	72	76	69	284	4592.00	3280.00
	Stuart LITTLE (Eng)	72	70	70	72	284	4592.00	3280.00
57	Miguel Angel MARTIN (Sp)	72	69	71	73	285	3376.00	2411.43
	Andrew OLDCORN (Scot)	71	69	74	71	285	3376.00	2411.43
	Sven STRÜVER (Ger)	75	68	72	70	285	3376.00	2411.43
	Sam TORRANCE (Scot)	68	71	72	74	285	3376.00	2411.43
	Christopher HANELL (Swe)	71	69	75	70	285	3376.00	2411.43
	Didier DE VOOGHT (Bel)	70	70	75	70	285	3376.00	2411.43
	Des SMYTH (Ire)	69	70	73	73	285	3376.00	2411.43
64	David GILFORD (Eng)	72	71	71	72	286	2267.25	1619.46
	Andrew BEAL (Eng)	72	71	73	70	286	2267.25	1619.46
	Mathias GRÖNBERG (Swe)	72	68	78	68	286	2267.25	1619.46
	Tony JOHNSTONE (Zim)	70	73	73	70	286	2267.25	1619.46
68	Massimo FLORIOLI (It)	68	71	73	75	287	1674.00	1195.71
69	Ross MCFARLANE (Eng)	70	73	76	69	288	1668.00	1191.43
	Francisco CEA (Sp)	71	72	74	71	288	1668.00	1191.43
	Ernie ELS (SA)	72	69	76	71	288	1668.00	1191.43
72	John SENDEN (Aus)	73	70	75	71	289	1660.50	1186.07
	Raphaël JACQUELIN (Fr)	72	71	71	75	289	1660.50	1186.07
74	Jarrod MOSELEY (Aus)	75	68	72	75	290	1653.00	1180.71
	Mark DAVIS (Eng)	71	72	76	71	290	1653.00	1180.71
	Thomas LEVET (Fr)	71	69	76	74	290	1653.00	1180.71
77	Per-Ulrik JOHANSSON (Swe)	70	72	76	73	291	1645.50	1175.36
	Stephen GALLACHER (Scot)	69	73	75	74	291	1645.50	1175.36
79	Andrew SHERBORNE (Eng)	74	69	73	76	292	1641.00	1172.14
80	Massimo SCARPA (It)	70	72	71	80	293	1638.00	1170.00
81	Phillip PRICE (Wal)	73	70	77	74	294	1635.00	1167.86

It's the little things in life that need care and attention.

That's why we put a lot of care and attention into designing and making innovative products that will help make your day a little easier and better, a little healthier and safer.

Every day, 3M products touch people's lives in many ways . . . from home care to health care, from transportation and construction to business, education and recreation . . .

Some, like Scotch® Magic™ Tape and Post-it® Notes, are brands found in households and offices all over the world. Others become essential components of customer products such as computers, cars and drug delivery systems. Still others, like the reflective materials used in traffic signs and number plates, are standards in their industry.

If you would like more information on over 50,000 3M products that could improve your day, just call us on 08705 360036. Better still, visit our web site at **http://www.3M.com/uk**

Thriving on pressure

Sergio Garcia remedies the stresses

and disappointments of Brookline

by capturing his second Tour title

The Linde German Masters in Cologne was a case of the morning after the night before, and the survival of the fittest.

Lee Westwood, Darren Clarke, Paul Lawrie and Jesper Parnevik all opted to take a breather after their pressure-cooker exertions in the Ryder Cup the week before, while Europe's remaining eight team members teed up on cue at Gut Lärchenhof. But physical fatigue and mental exhaustion took their toll at one time or another on most of them.

Colin Montgomerie, the 'Lion of Boston', looked none the worse for wear after a 70-67 start, but then faded with two 72s, fluffing two chips and a putt of two feet for a hugely uncharacteristic triple-bogey seven in round three to admit: "The concentration just went – I gave 110 per cent in America and it finally caught up with me."

Miguel Angel Jiménez, hero of the foursomes and fourballs on his Ryder Cup debut, opened with a 66 but took 73 next day, settling eventually for joint 12th place, three spots behind Montgomerie. And José Maria Olazábal, who launched the week with a 67, succumbed to a painful neck and more driving problems, tailing off with disappointing scores of 75 and 74 to end tied 26th – a stroke behind Frenchman Jean Van de Velde, who followed a third round 76 with a defiant 68, and level with Andrew Coltart, who managed a closing 69 after a lacklustre opening

74. Jarmo Sandelin suffered the severest Ryder Cup hangover by finishing last of the 69 qualifiers, 25 strokes behind after a pair of 78s.

But both 19-year-old Spaniard Sergio Garcia and youthful Irishman Padraig Harrington impressively survived all the trials and tribulations of their Ryder Cup baptisms, not to mention a strength-and-stamina sapping week of high winds and violent rain squalls in Germany. They battled it out toe to toe, Brookline-style, with Welsh wizard Ian Woosnam in a cliff-hanging sudden-death play-off for the title.

To nobody's surprise it was teenager Garcia who continued the fairytale start to his professional career by grabbing the glory in typically swashbuckling fashion. Woosnam, who amassed 20 birdies over the four days, could have won in normal time after dramatically rediscovering his scoring touch with a Saturday 66 containing only 24 putts.

Yet the man with 43 world-wide victories and European Tour winnings of more than 8.4 million euro (£6 million) under his belt, agonisingly missed a putt of five feet for a par four at the 72nd hole. It cost him 139,725 euro (£99,804), the difference between the winners purse of 291,700 euro (£208,357) and his cheque for joint second place.

Woosnam, who had struggled all week with a new, softer-shafted driver, still looked in command after a closing 69 left him 11 under par on 277 with Garcia, who ended as he began the week with a 68, and Harrington, who piled up eight birdies but then bogeyed the last for a 67.

When Harrington drove into the lake at the first extra hole to pick up a penalty stroke, and Garcia drove within a couple of feet of the water before hitting under the grandstand, Woosnam was faced with a putt of six feet for a par four that looked like being good enough for victory.

Sadly, he failed to make it to stay alive after Harrington, the conqueror of Mark

PADRAIG HARRINGTON: chipped in during play-off

"It's been a great start to life as a pro. My goals were to gain my card in Europe and the USA, to prove to Mark James I was worth a Ryder Cup place and to win a tournament, and I've achieved them all. I feel comfortable playing in the States but Europe is my Continent and I will play on both Tours wherever the top players are playing."

O'Meara in Boston, audaciously chipped in off a bank from 40 feet and Garcia, who so dazzlingly partnered Parnevik in the Ryder Cup, followed him in for his four from 25 feet.

Next time around, Harrington drove in a bunker and again missed the green and Garcia pounced to plunge home the dagger, this time with a cool-as-you-like putt from 18 feet for a title-winning birdie three.

It was his second European Tour triumph in nine outings since turning professional after the Masters Tournament – he won the Murphy's Irish Open at Druids Glen in July – and he insisted the Ryder Cup had helped: "I was really tired the first couple of days in Germany, even though I shot good scores, and very disappointed at the Brookline result after we went so close to winning. But the Ryder Cup gave me some great things. It put me under pressure and I had to handle it, which helped in Cologne. It was very good to be there again so soon and I stayed really focused to hole those two big putts.

IAN WOOSNAM: putt of five feet denied victory

THE COURSE

The Jack Nicklaus-designed layout 20 miles from Cologne has water coming into play on a dozen holes. It was stretched to a testing 7,289 yards after Colin Montgomerie's 22 under par winning performance in 1998, when Rodger Davis set the course record of 63. But officials reduced the ninth from 469 yards to 388 and the 18th from 456 yards to 383 on the final day of the 1999 event because of strong winds and heavy rain.

COLIN MONTGOMERIE: "The concentration just went"

There were disappointments for Ernie Els, a non-qualifier after twice hitting into the lake at the last; Fred Couples, who marked his 40th birthday on Sunday with a second successive 73 to finish 22nd after opening with a 68; and for Vijay Singh, last year's runner-up, who had to settle for joint 12th place.

Two former Ryder Cup Europeans with something to celebrate were Peter Baker, without a win for six years, and José Rivero. They both fired ten under par 278s to end just one shot behind Garcia, Harrington and Woosnam. Rivero's 80,815 euro (£57,725) prize secured his Tour card after he had started the week in 132nd place in the Volvo Order of Merit.

But it was another Spaniard less than half his age who left Germany wearing the biggest smile.

Gordon Richardson

GUT LÄRCHENHOF, COLOGNE, GERMANY, SEPTEMBER 30–OCTOBER 3, 1999 · PAR 72 · YARDS 7289

Pos	Name & Country	Rnd 1	Rnd 2	Rnd 3	Rnd 4	Total	Prize Money €	£
1	Sergio GARCIA (Sp)	68	69	72	68	277	291700.00	208357.14
2	Padraig HARRINGTON (Ire)	70	70	70	67	277	151975.00	108553.57
	Ian WOOSNAM (Wal)	68	74	66	69	277	151975.00	108553.57
4	José RIVERO (Sp)	68	66	75	69	278	80815.00	57725.00
	Peter BAKER (Eng)	70	68	69	71	278	80815.00	57725.00
6	Alex CEJKA (Ger)	66	73	69	71	279	61250.00	43750.00
7	Carlos Daniel FRANCO (Par)	69	75	68	68	280	48125.00	34375.00
	Retief GOOSEN (SA)	67	69	74	70	280	48125.00	34375.00
9	Bernhard LANGER (Ger)	70	71	71	69	281	35420.00	25300.00
	Peter MITCHELL (Eng)	72	70	70	69	281	35420.00	25300.00
	Colin MONTGOMERIE (Scot)	70	67	72	72	281	35420.00	25300.00
12	David GILFORD (Eng)	69	76	72	65	282	27676.50	19768.93
	Joakim HAEGGMAN (Swe)	71	70	72	69	282	27676.50	19768.93
	Miguel Angel JIMÉNEZ (Sp)	66	73	72	71	282	27676.50	19768.93
	Vijay SINGH (Fij)	68	70	70	74	282	27676.50	19768.93
16	Thomas BJÖRN (Den)	72	69	70	72	283	24654.00	17610.00
17	Paul MCGINLEY (Ire)	72	74	70	68	284	21875.00	15625.00
	Richard GREEN (Aus)	72	73	71	68	284	21875.00	15625.00
	Steen TINNING (Den)	69	72	74	69	284	21875.00	15625.00
	Marc FARRY (Fr)	68	73	74	69	284	21875.00	15625.00
	Greg TURNER (NZ)	67	74	71	72	284	21875.00	15625.00
22	Fred COUPLES (USA)	68	71	73	73	285	19950.00	14250.00
23	Jean VAN DE VELDE (Fr)	71	71	76	68	286	18900.00	13500.00
	Paul BROADHURST (Eng)	70	71	73	72	286	18900.00	13500.00
	Mark MOULAND (Wal)	69	69	75	73	286	18900.00	13500.00
	Kariem BARAKA (AM) (Ger)	71	71	77	67	286		
26	Andrew COLTART (Scot)	74	72	72	69	287	17062.50	12187.50
	Thomas LEVET (Fr)	67	76	72	72	287	17062.50	12187.50
	Miguel Angel MARTIN (Sp)	72	72	71	72	287	17062.50	12187.50
	José Maria OLAZÁBAL (Sp)	67	71	75	74	287	17062.50	12187.50
30	Pierre FULKE (Swe)	72	69	77	70	288	15006.25	10718.75
	Michael CAMPBELL (NZ)	70	75	75	68	288	15006.25	10718.75
	Gary EVANS (Eng)	73	73	71	71	288	15006.25	10718.75
	Mark MCNULTY (Zim)	72	73	70	73	288	15006.25	10718.75
34	Russell CLAYDON (Eng)	74	71	75	69	289	13650.00	9750.00
	Anthony WALL (Eng)	71	72	78	68	289	13650.00	9750.00
	Daniel CHOPRA (Swe)	71	76	70	72	289	13650.00	9750.00
37	Tony JOHNSTONE (Zim)	74	67	75	74	290	12775.00	9125.00
	Craig HAINLINE (USA)	72	71	73	74	290	12775.00	9125.00
39	Miles TUNNICLIFF (Eng)	72	75	71	73	291	11900.00	8500.00
	Ignacio GARRIDO (Sp)	70	73	75	73	291	11900.00	8500.00
	Thomas GÖGELE (Ger)	74	72	75	70	291	11900.00	8500.00
42	Phillip PRICE (Wal)	72	74	73	73	292	10325.00	7375.00
	Gary ORR (Scot)	75	71	73	73	292	10325.00	7375.00
	Fredrik JACOBSON (Swe)	73	73	73	73	292	10325.00	7375.00
	Jean-Francois REMESY (Fr)	75	70	75	72	292	10325.00	7375.00
	David HOWELL (Eng)	74	72	74	72	292	10325.00	7375.00
	Mats LANNER (Swe)	73	70	77	72	292	10325.00	7375.00
48	Andrew BEAL (Eng)	71	76	74	72	293	8750.00	6250.00
	Raphaël JACQUELIN (Fr)	72	73	77	71	293	8750.00	6250.00
	Scott HENDERSON (Scot)	75	70	72	76	293	8750.00	6250.00
51	Stuart CAGE (Eng)	72	69	77	76	294	7175.00	5125.00
	Greg OWEN (Eng)	70	70	79	75	294	7175.00	5125.00
	Costantino ROCCA (It)	72	75	74	73	294	7175.00	5125.00
	Malcolm MACKENZIE (Eng)	72	71	78	73	294	7175.00	5125.00
	Raymond RUSSELL (Scot)	74	71	77	72	294	7175.00	5125.00
	Steve WEBSTER (Eng)	72	72	73	77	294	7175.00	5125.00
57	Rolf MUNTZ (Hol)	75	70	75	75	295	5556.25	3968.75
	Paolo QUIRICI (Swi)	70	77	73	75	295	5556.25	3968.75
	Paul EALES (Eng)	76	70	76	73	295	5556.25	3968.75
	Van PHILLIPS (Eng)	76	71	76	72	295	5556.25	3968.75
61	Gerry NORQUIST (USA)	76	70	76	75	297	4987.50	3562.50
	Derrick COOPER (Eng)	71	75	79	72	297	4987.50	3562.50
63	Jarrod MOSELEY (Aus)	71	73	78	76	298	4550.00	3250.00
	Patrick PLATZ (Ger)	74	70	81	73	298	4550.00	3250.00
	Ross MCFARLANE (Eng)	74	73	79	72	298	4550.00	3250.00
66	Steven RICHARDSON (Eng)	76	71	77	75	299	2625.00	1875.00
67	Philip WALTON (Ire)	73	73	77	78	301	2620.50	1871.79
	Stephen LEANEY (Aus)	74	72	78	77	301	2620.50	1871.79
69	Jarmo SANDELIN (Swe)	74	72	78	78	302	2616.00	1868.57

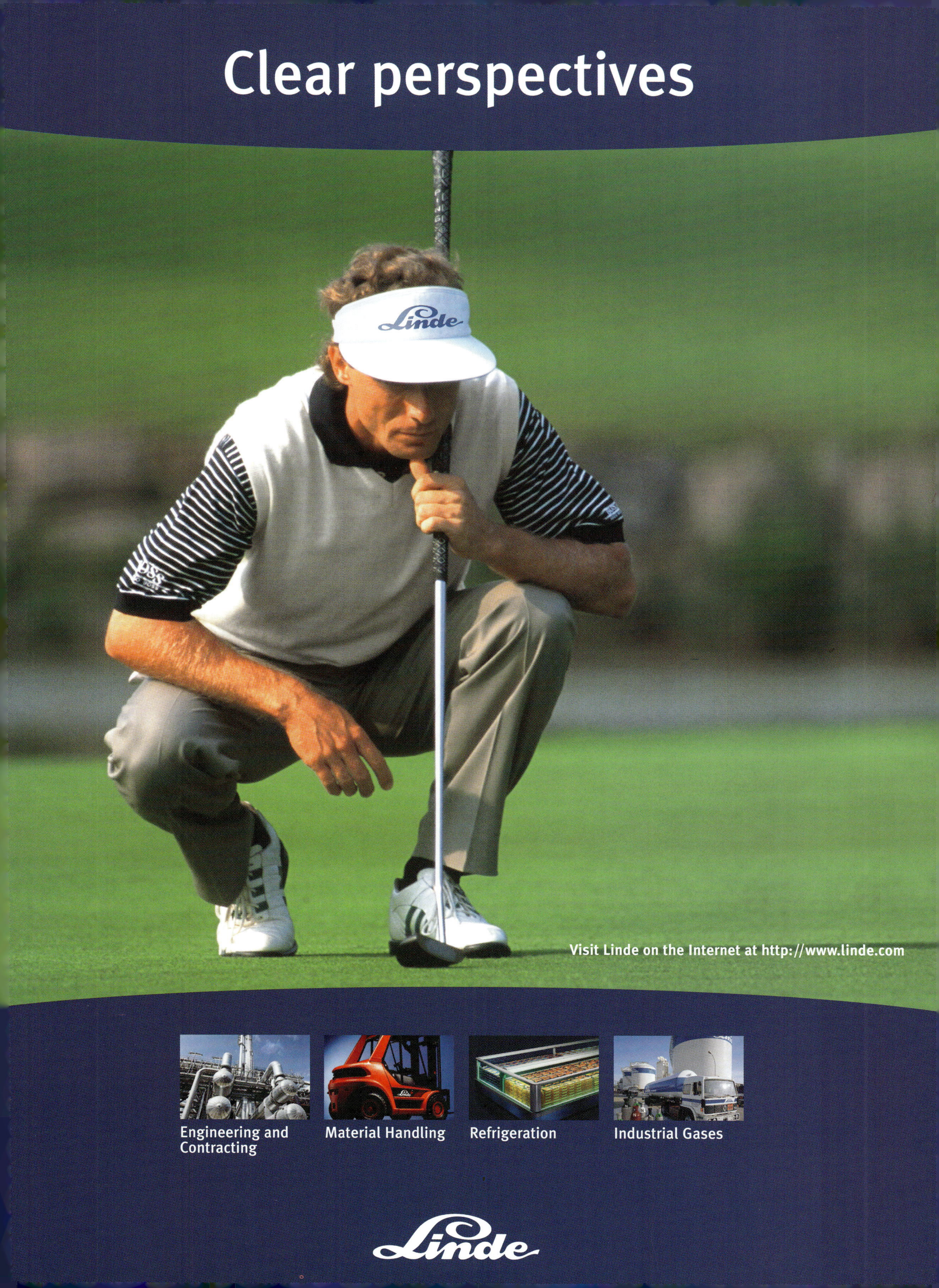
Clear perspectives
Linde
Visit Linde on the Internet at http://www.linde.com
Engineering and Contracting
Material Handling
Refrigeration
Industrial Gases
Linde

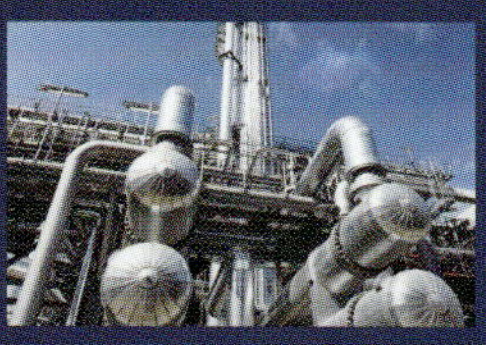

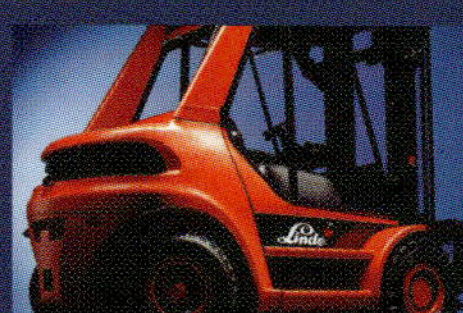

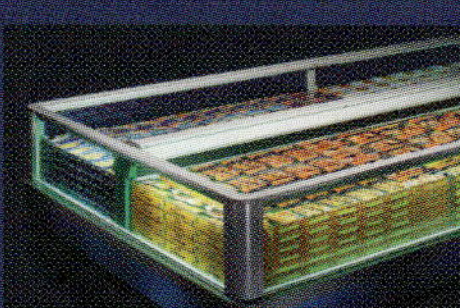

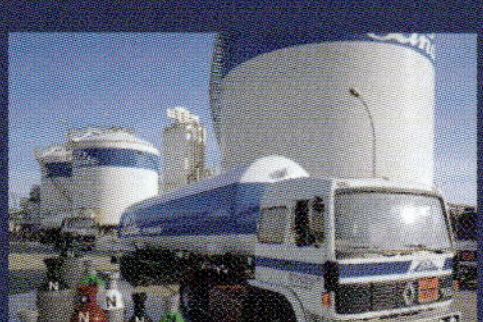

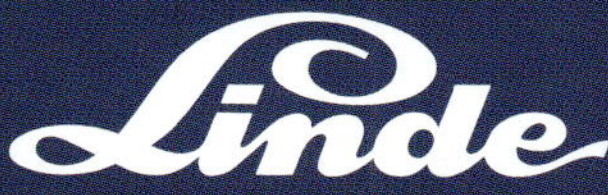

Viva España

Great golf, superb sportsmanship
and a memorable victory
for three all-conquering amigos

This was the 15th Alfred Dunhill Cup at St. Andrews – and surely the best. Which, come to think of it, really shouldn't come as too much of a surprise. All the elements were in place for a great tournament.

A strong "40-something" American side of Tom Lehman, Mark O'Meara and Payne Stewart, all three fresh from the United States's Ryder Cup victory two weeks earlier, were installed as number one seeds; Spain, in the shapes of Masters champion José Maria Olazábal, Miguel Angel Jiménez and Sergio Garcia, were always going to be strong challengers; and two-time defending champions South Africa were returning in search of an unprecedented hat-trick of wins.

Mix well, toss in the Home Countries and the likes of Australia and New Zealand and you have a recipe for success – and some super golf.

Which is just what we got. You want eagles? We had plenty, including two in succession by Carlos Franco. After making a sizeable putt for a three at the long fifth in his match with Isao Aoki of Japan, the Paraguayan holed his pitch at the 416-yard sixth for a two. Three holes later he was out in 30, six under par – and he missed from six feet at the ninth.

Indeed, nowhere was immune to these great players. Craig Parry, of

SERGIO GARCIA: we've won the Cup

Australia, and Scotland's Open champion Paul Lawrie both pitched in for eagle twos at the most famous closing hole in all of golf. And both, like Franco, did the deed against the Japanese. Eliminated by the Australians only on individual matches won, it just wasn't their week.

Nor was it Colin Montgomerie's. The Scot, an ever-present in the home side since 1991, arrived in St. Andrews on Wednesday morning, played five holes in the pro-am, then retired to the comfort of his hotel room complaining of toothache. Only the day before Europe's number one had undergone root canal surgery. Ouch. The next morning Montgomerie was still suffering and reluctantly gave up his place to Sam Torrance, himself no stranger to Alfred Dunhill Cup play.

Still, it didn't take long for the personality of the week to emerge. Garcia had never been to St. Andrews before, but he knew he was going to like it. Anywhere his compatriot Severiano Ballesteros had won an Open Championship was sure to suit the 19-year-old rising star of European golf equally well.

And so it proved. Par at the Old Course may be 72 on the card, but for Garcia, Spain's captain for the week, it was more like, oh, 67. Three days in succession the teenager toured the home of golf in five under par. Three times he emerged

victorious. Three times he led his side to victory.

That last win, over Ireland, was the hardest and, it must be said, the most unlikely. After 11 holes of his match with Darren Clarke, Garcia, although four under par, was three shots behind the inspired Ulsterman. Worse for Spain, Paul McGinley was in the midst of seeing off Olazábal 68-70 and Padraig Harrington was two shots ahead of Jiménez with only three holes to play.

It was a grim situation, but, as it turned out, no problem for the Spaniards. Against Clarke, who would stumble sadly to a double bogey at the notorious 17th Road Hole, Garcia played the last six holes of the match in three under par, good enough for an unlikely one-shot win. Then, in the last match, Jiménez made three birdies in the last five holes against his Ryder Cup foursomes partner, then won the first extra hole with another

three. No wonder Olazábal, standing by the side of the green, was delighted.

The next morning, reprieved, the Spaniards took on their conquerors in last year's final, the formidable South African trio of Ernie Els, David Frost and Retief Goosen. In the other semi-final, Sweden would face Australia. Both were close. Both finished 2-1. And it was Spain and Australia who emerged to fight out the final.

It, too, turned out to be a superbly played match. In the top game Parry and Garcia had a magnificent tussle. Both were round in 69, great golf in the increasingly blustery conditions, and only the Spaniard's three putts at the first extra hole decided it.

For all his disappointment, the

MIGUEL ANGEL JIMÉNEZ: three birdies from 14th

DARREN CLARKE: victim of the 17th

Describing the Old Course at St. Andrews is like assessing the Mona Lisa's smile. The Home of Golf is the original on which every course is modelled. For all that, with its massive double greens and absence of rough, it remains a unique test of golf – especially when the wind blows.

youngster – a cumulative 18 under par for his five rounds - had nothing to worry about. His experienced countrymen both had shots in hand. Olazábal saw off Stephen Leaney by six and Jiménez was two too good for Peter O'Malley. Spain had its first ever Alfred Dunhill Cup victory.

Afterwards, an emotional Olazábal dedicated the win to his manager, Sergio Gomez. Sadly, Gomez's brother had died earlier in the week. "This is for Sergio and his family," said the Masters champion.

Yes, and for the three amigos. For them and the appreciative galleries, it was a truly memorable week's golf richly blessed with exemplary international sportsmanship. Ole!

John Huggan

CARLOS FRANCO: two successive eagles

JOSÉ MARIA OLAZÁBAL: emotional win

Old Course, St. Andrews, 7th - 10th October, 1999 • Par 72 • Yards 7094

Final

SPAIN	2	1	AUSTRALIA
Sergio Garcia	69	69	Craig Parry*
José Maria Olazábal	72	78	Stephen Leaney
Miguel Angel Jiménez	73	75	Peter O'Malley

* won at 1st extra hole

Semi-Final

AUSTRALIA	2	1	SWEDEN
Craig Parry	72	75	Gabriel Hjertstedt
Peter O'Malley	78	76	Patrik Sjöland
Stephen Leaney*	80	80	Jarmo Sandelin

* won at 1st extra hole

Semi-Final

SPAIN	2	1	SOUTH AFRICA
Sergio Garcia	72	70	Ernie Els
Miguel Angel Jiménez	73	77	David Frost
José Maria Olazábal	75	76	Retief Goosen

Group One

DAY 1

USA beat NEW ZEALAND 2-1
Mark O'Meara (73) beat Greg Turner (74)
Payne Stewart (76) lost to Michael Long (72)
Tom Lehman (71) beat Michael Campbell (74)

SWEDEN beat ITALY 3-0
Gabriel Hjertstedt (71) beat Costantino Rocca (75)
Jarmo Sandelin (72) beat Massimo Scarpa (79)
Patrik Sjöland (68) beat Emanuele Canonica (74)

DAY 2

USA lost to ITALY 3-0
Mark O'Meara (72) lost to Costantino Rocca (70)
Tom Lehman (74) lost to Emanuele Canonica (72)
Payne Stewart (72) lost to Massimo Scarpa (71)

SWEDEN lost to NEW ZEALAND 1-2
Gabriel Hjertstedt (72) lost to Michael Campbell (71)
Patrik Sjöland (74) lost to Michael Long (73)
Jarmo Sandelin (69) beat Greg Turner (70)

DAY 3

NEW ZEALAND beat ITALY 2-1
Greg Turner (70) beat Emanuele Canonica (72)
Michael Long (72) lost to Massimo Scarpa (71)
Michael Campbell (70) beat Costantino Rocca (74)

USA lost to SWEDEN 1-2
Mark O'Meara (69) beat Patrik Sjöland (73)
Payne Stewart (74) lost to Gabriel Hjertstedt (69)
Tom Lehman (74) lost to Jarmo Sandelin (71)

Group Two

DAY 1

AUSTRALIA beat JAPAN 2-1
Craig Parry (69) beat Tsuyoshi Yoneyama (70)
Peter O'Malley (74) lost to Isao Aoki (72)
Stephen Leaney (69) beat Katsuyoshi Tomori (70)

SCOTLAND beat PARAGUAY 2-1
Sam Torrance (75) beat Raul Fretes (77)
Gary Orr (73) lost to Carlos Franco (65)
Paul Lawrie (71) beat Angel Franco (73)

DAY 2

AUSTRALIA lost to PARAGUAY 1-2
Peter O'Malley (73) beat Raul Fretes (76)
Stephen Leaney (74) lost to Angel Franco (73)
Craig Parry (70) lost to Carlos Franco (70)*
* won at 2nd extra hole

SCOTLAND lost to JAPAN 1-2
Sam Torrance (76) lost to Isao Aoki (71)
Paul Lawrie (71) lost to Katsuyoshi Tomori (71)*
Gary Orr (69) beat Tsuyoshi Yoneyama (71)
* won at 1st extra hole

DAY 3

PARAGUAY lost to JAPAN 1-2
Angel Franco (72) lost to Katsuyoshi Tomori (68)
Raul Fretes (69) lost to Tsuyoshi Yoneyama (68)
Carlos Franco (65) beat Isao Aoki (77)

SCOTLAND lost to AUSTRALIA 1-2
Paul Lawrie (71) beat Peter O'Malley (73)
Sam Torrance (71) lost to Craig Parry (70)
Gary Orr (70) lost to Stephen Leaney (67)

Group Three

DAY 1

SOUTH AFRICA beat CHINA 2-1
Ernie Els (72) beat Zhang Lian-Wei (74)
David Frost (69) beat Cheng Jun (72)
Retief Goosen (73) lost to Wu Xiang-Bing (72)

ENGLAND beat INDIA :2-1
Lee Westwood (73) lost to Jeev Milkha Singh (70)
Mark James (72) beat Jyoti Randhawa (73)
David Howell (71) beat Vijay Kumar (72)

DAY 2

SOUTH AFRICA beat INDIA 3-0
Ernie Els (69) beat Jeev Milkha Singh (72)
Retief Goosen (67) beat Vijay Kumar (75)
David Frost (68) beat Jyoti Randhawa (74)

ENGLAND beat CHINA 2-1
Lee Westwood (69) beat Zhang Lian-Wei (72)
David Howell (75) lost to Cheng Jun (70)
Mark James (72) beat Wu Xiang-Bing (74)

DAY 3

SOUTH AFRICA beat ENGLAND 3-0
Ernie Els (67) beat David Howell (69)
David Frost (71) beat Mark James (72)
Retief Goosen (66) beat Lee Westwood (70)

CHINA lost to INDIA 0-3
Zhang Lian-Wei (74) lost to Jyoti Randhawa (73)
Cheng Jun (74) lost to Jeev Milkha Singh (72)
Wu Xiang-Bing (77) lost to Vijay Kumar (73)

Group Four

DAY 1

IRELAND beat ZIMBABWE 3-0
Paul McGinley (70) beat Tony Johnstone (75)
Darren Clarke (69) beat Mark McNulty (74)
Padraig Harrington (71) beat Nick Price (72)

SPAIN beat FRANCE 2-1
Miguel Angel Jiménez (73) lost to Marc Farry (68)
Sergio Garcia (67) beat Jean Francois Remesy (70)
José Maria Olazábal* (74) beat Jean Van De Velde (74)
* won at 1st extra hole

DAY 2

SPAIN beat ZIMBABWE 2-1
Sergio Garcia (67) beat Nick Price (70)
José Maria Olazábal (67) beat Tony Johnstone (73)
Miguel Angel Jiménez (73) lost to Mark McNulty (68)

IRELAND beat FRANCE 2-1
Darren Clarke (67) beat Marc Farry (75)
Paul McGinley (74) lost to Jean Van De Velde (70)
Padraig Harrington (73) beat Jean Francois Remesy (74)

DAY 3

FRANCE lost to ZIMBABWE 0-2
Marc Farry (73) lost to Mark McNulty (69)
Jean Francois Remesy (68) — Tony Johnstone (68)~
Jean Van De Velde (68) lost to Nick Price (68)*
~ did not conclude play-off
* won at 3rd extra hole

SPAIN beat IRELAND 2-1
Sergio Garcia (67) beat Darren Clarke (68)
José Maria Olazábal (70) lost to Paul McGinley (68)
Miguel Angel Jiménez* (69) beat Padraig Harrington (69)
* won at 1st extra hole

Prize Money

Country	Team €	Team £	Player €	Player £	Total €	Total £
Winners						
SPAIN (2)	420,000	300,000	140,000	100,000	420,000	300,000
Runners-Up						
AUSTRALIA (5)	210,000	150,000	70,000	50,000	210,000	150,000
Losing Semi-Finalists						
SOUTH AFRICA (3)	133,000	95,000	44,332	31,666	266,000	190,000
SWEDEN (8)	133,000	95,000	44,332	31,666	266,000	190,000

* Number in parentheses indicates seeds

Country	Team €	Team £	Player €	Player £	Total €	Total £
Group One						
SWEDEN(8)						
NEW ZEALAND	63,000	45,000	21,000	15,000		
ITALY	35,700	25,500	11,900	8,500		
USA(1)	27,300	19,500	9,100	6,500	126,000	90,000
Group Two						
AUSTRALIA(5)						
JAPAN	63,000	45,000	21,000	15,000		
SCOTLAND(4)	35,700	25,500	11,900	8,500		
PARAGUAY	27,300	19,500	9,100	6,500	126,000	90,000

Country	Team €	Team £	Player €	Player £	Total €	Total £
Group Three						
SOUTH AFRICA(3)						
ENGLAND(6)	63,000	45,000	21,000	15,000		
INDIA	35,700	25,500	11,900	8,500		
CHINA	27,300	19,500	9,100	6,500	126,000	90,000
Group Four						
SPAIN(2)						
IRELAND(7)	63,000	45,000	21,000	15,000		
ZIMBABWE	35,700	25,500	11,900	8,500		
FRANCE	27,300	19,500	9,100	6,500	126,000	90,000

ALFRED DUNHILL

Facet Sport

For further information call 0171 290 8720

Aching for another win

Colin Montgomerie painfully delays

an urgent need to visit a dentist

until he claims his sixth title of the season

A sublime English autumn week-end; the Wentworth Club's West Course in pristine condition; and some record-breaking scoring to match. Yes, it was Cisco World Match Play Championship time again for the many thousands of fascinated fans, who, for the 36th year in succession, flocked to the famous Surrey course on their annual October pilgrimage.

And the bonus for them this time was to witness Colin Montgomerie who, as a schoolboy in his native Scotland, used to watch the event avidly on television, finally achieve one of his lifetime golfing ambitions by defeating defending champion Mark O'Meara 3 and 2 in an absorbing final to become the 20th golfer to have won this coveted title.

This was Montgomerie's sixth win of his 1999 campaign, and it took his earnings for just two weeks' work at Wentworth, following victory at the Volvo PGA Championship in May, to 540,400 euro

(£386,000). Clutching the impressive silver trophy, a beaming Montgomerie declared: "There is a word on this championship that means a lot to me. It is the first one, the word *world*, and anytime you are a world champion in anything it means an awful lot and to get my name on this incredible role of honour means everything to me. Isao Aoki and I are the only ones in the past 20 years without a major to our names."

The day after his victory, Montgomerie faced a daunting trip to the dentist to finally remove the infected tooth which had forced him out of the Alfred Dunhill Cup the previous week and which had required antibiotics and painkillers to see him through the match

SHOT OF THE WEEK

Mark O'Meara has made a habit of winning his matches from off the green. He did it to Tiger Woods at the 36th in the 1998 final and again to Craig Parry at the 39th in this year's second round.

These were surpassed at the 36th in the semi-final against Nick Price when, from a tricky position in a grassy hollow beside the green, he lofted an inch-perfect wedge shot over the bunker to land three feet from the hole and roll straight in. "If you are going to get lucky there is no better place or time to do it," said a modest O'Meara.

play marathon.

But the title, the 238,000 euro (£170,000) winner's cheque, and sweet revenge for his semi-final defeat by O'Meara in 1998, must have provided their own anaesthetics. In fact, Montgomerie and O'Meara proved the perfect illustration of the old adage: "Beware the injured golfer".

O'Meara came desperately close to having to pull out of the event after trapping nerves in his neck and left shoulder, and only some intensive treatment by European Tour physiotherapist Jonathan Shrewsbury, who the 42-year-old American hailed as a "miracle worker", saw him through.

"Considering the way I felt on Thursday it is amazing that I got so far,"

SERGIO GARCIA: better-ball 25 for front nine

NOTAH BEGAY III: charming discovery

MARK O'MEARA: the Houdini of Wentworth Club

admitted O'Meara. "This whole year has been a battle, with my swing and my confidence. But it hasn't been for lack of giving everything, and I have got to take a lot of pride from that."

O'Meara, who had fought back from four down at lunch to beat Tiger Woods at the last hole of the 1998 final, proved the Houdini of Wentworth again in his semi-final against Nick Price, recovering from four down at the 17th to again win at the 36th, this time courtesy of an astonishing 40-yard chip-in from off the green. Montgomerie had a much easier time of it in his semi-final, cruising past his Ryder Cup teammate Padraig Harrington 7 and 6. Five up after 18, Montgomerie, using a favourite old putter he had pulled out of the attic just before the Ryder Cup, single putted four out of five greens between the 22nd and 26th. "He is almost unstoppable in that mood," admitted Harrington.

The standard of play throughout the Championship, for which the field was a record 165 under par (Montgomerie alone was 29 under), provided the spectators with great theatre.

Spanish prodigy Sergio Garcia and the unassuming South African Retief Goosen posted a breathtaking better-ball of ten under par 25 for the front nine of the afternoon round. Goosen eventually won 2 and 1.

PADRAIG HARRINGTON: tribute to "unstoppable" opponent

THE COURSE

There was unstinting and universal praise for course superintendent Chris Kennedy, head greenkeeper Graham Matheson and their team for producing the West Course in what Colin Montgomerie described as "the most magnificent condition I have ever seen it."

"It was a great team effort," declared Kennedy. "Three weeks before the event we were very worried. We experienced $10^{1}/_{2}$ inches of rain in September, when $2^{1}/_{2}$ is the average, but the sunshine came just in time to save us."

NICK PRICE: 13 under par success

The Australian Craig Parry outgunned Open champion Paul Lawrie 4 and 3, while Harrington achieved a decisive 7 and 6 demolition of Paraguayan star Carlos Franco, a multiple US Tour winner this year. And there was the 4 and 3 victory by charming, native-American discovery Notah Begay III over Masters Tournament winner José Maria Olazábal, clearly a victim of influenza.

The quarter-finals brought no change to the glorious weather nor the sensational scoring. This time Price led the way by being a remarkable 13 under par in beating Goosen 6 and 5. This match finished long before the other three, with Montgomerie finally shaking off Begay 2 and 1, while Harrington had to wait until the 38th to dismiss three times winner and pre-event favourite Ernie Els.

O'Meara had to battle on even further before chipping in from beside the green to beat Parry at the 39th.

The American's fighting qualities were again in evidence in the final, but Montgomerie's will to win was even stronger and O'Meara confidently predicted by way of a tribute: "He will go on to win a major and I won't be surprised if it is in the next 12 months."

John Whitbread

Wentworth Club, Surrey, England, October 14-17, 1999 • Par 72 • Yards 7006

First Round

		Prize money	
		€	£
Craig Parry (USA) (8) beat Paul Lawrie (Scot)	4 & 3	42,000	30,000
Retief Goosen (SA) beat Sergio Garcia (Sp) (5)	2 & 1	42,000	30,000
Padraig Harrington (Ire) beat Carlos Franco (Par) (6)	7 & 6	42,000	30,000
Notah Begay III (USA) beat José Maria Olazábal (Sp) (7)	4 & 3	42,000	30,000

Second Round

		Prize money	
		€	£
Mark O'Meara (USA) (1) beat Craig Parry	at 39th	56,000	40,000
Nick Price (Zim) (4) beat Retief Goosen	6 & 5	56,000	40,000
Padraig Harrington beat Ernie Els (SA) (3)	at 38th	56,000	40,000
Colin Montgomerie (Scot) (2) beat Notay Begay III	2 & 1	56,000	40,000

Semi-Finals

Mark O'Meara beat Nick Price	1 hole	70,000	50,000
Colin Montgomerie beat Padraig Harrington	7 & 6	70,000	50,000

Final

		Prize money	
		€	£
Colin Montgomerie beat	3 & 2	238,000	170,000
Mark O'Meara		126,000	90,000

Figures in parentheses indicate seedings

Final bonds true sportsmen

Born again Björn

PGA Golf de Catalunya revives

winning ways of Thomas Björn

after being sidelined by injury

Thomas Björn has been a trailblazer from the moment he struck the first ball of his professional career. So, few people were surprised when he became the first European golfer to win the first Sarazen World Open staged in Europe on the new, impressive PGA Golf de Catalunya course designed by PGA European Tour Chairman Neil Coles and Vice-Chairman Angel Gallardo.

The tall, imposing Dane has been relishing challenges since he played for his country at every level, including the Eisenhower Trophy, before turning professional in 1993.

In 1995 he won four titles on the way to topping the European Challenge Tour with a record haul of prize money. The following summer, in his first season on the European Tour, he burst to prominence by capturing one of its most prestigious titles from a world-class field in the Loch Lomond World Invitational at the exceptional Scottish course.

Then, he used that victory as a springboard to become the first Dane to play for Europe in the Ryder Cup, performing with the utmost distinction under the inspirational captaincy of Severiano Ballesteros at Valderrama in 1997. He produced one of the highlights of that momentous week by recovering from the loss of the first four holes to halve his singles match with the then Open champion Justin Leonard, whom he had beaten in company with Ian Woosnam in the fourballs.

In 1998 he scored two more wins to confirm his place among Europe's best and earn the right to compete for the game's biggest titles. So it was a major

disappointment when a neck muscle injury, incurred in the spring of the 1999 season, disrupted his schedule and kept him out of tournament golf for nearly

PAOLO QUIRICI: threatened until course evacuation

KATSUYOSHI TOMORI: tied runner-up from Japan

three months. Björn tried to make a comeback for the defence of his Peugeot Open de España title in Barcelona, but it was not until the Murphy's Irish Open in July that he was able to resume play without pain and, despite a sterling effort over the next eight weeks, he was unable to retain a Ryder Cup place for the 1999 match against the United States at Brookline.

Ironically, and as so often happens, he found top form the week after the European team was finalised, finishing runner-up in the Canon European Masters to Lee Westwood. Björn could have been forgiven for resting on his laurels, but he was determined to end the decade on a high note and start the new millennium as a serious contender for major honours.

With that incentive uppermost in his mind when he returned to Spain, Björn was delighted to find the European Tour's prestigious and newest venue was custom-built for his powerful, long game. The architects had set out to reward straight, long hitting, and Björn showed how much he appreciated this particular examination by completing an oft weather-disrupted 72 holes with three rounds under

S H O T   O F   T H E   W E E K

Katsuyoshi Tomori demonstrated his prowess with the pitching clubs by sinking a nine iron shot of 130 yards for an eagle two at the second (his 11th) hole of his third round 66. However, the Japanese was beaten to the honour of the week's outstanding stroke by his playing partner Domingo Hospital when they began at the 434-yard tenth. The Spaniard found himself 187 yards from the flag for his second stroke, but holed out a perfectly executed three iron shot for an eagle two. It inspired him to an outward 31 which also contained four birdies and another eagle at the par five 15th.

70 for a 15 under par total of 273, two shots ahead of Swiss Paolo Quirici and Japanese Katsuyoshi Tomori. Spaniard Francisco Cea was fourth, a stroke further back.

With ten different nations represented in the leading 13 players, American legend Gene Sarazen, who died earlier in the year, would surely have approved of the fierce, but friendly, international rivalry in the tournament that bears his name. That was evident from the start, although the torrential rain which washed out the pro-am had hampered the preparation of many of the contenders.

Cea from Malaga, who had beaten Sergio Garcia in the final of the Spanish Championship in his final year as an amateur, set the pace with a superb 65, one better than Björn, and the two Englishmen, Robert Coles and Roger Winchester. By halfway, despite delays from morning fog and afternoon thunderstorms, Italian Emanuele Canonica, Frenchman Thomas Levet and Dane Steen Tinning had joined Björn and Coles at the top of the leaderboard. After 54 holes, the veteran Catalan, Domingo Hospital, who in his days as a commercial pilot used to fly advertising planes over the nearby Costa Brava beaches, was among eight players chasing joint leaders Björn and Tomori, who was in sight of a first career victory.

Hospital had produced a remarkable first half to his third round, going out in 31 from the tenth with not a single par on his card. Three times he holed from off the green and had only nine putts, prompting architect Gallardo to surmise: "Perhaps he thinks he is playing a pitch and putt course!" A 67 lifted Hospital to ten under, but the popular 41-year-old was unable to sustain a challenge after losing a ball with his first tee shot of the final round, which rapidly became the preserve of Björn, Tomori, and the fast-finishing Quirici.

With the title and 93,320 euro (£66,657) at stake, Björn quickly seized the initiative with three birdies in the first four holes of the final round. But Tomori, often outdriven by as much as 40 yards, was in deadly form on the greens, and when Björn missed a very short putt to bogey the ninth, he was able to remain on level terms as both turned in 33.

Up ahead, Quirici had gone one better, and when the Swiss also birdied the 12th and 14th and got on the 15th with two woods to threaten another, Björn and Tomori looked like being presented with a clubhouse target they would have difficulty in matching. But the threat of lightning from a circling storm forced evacuation of the course for 45 minutes, and on the resumption Quirici three-

STEPHEN GALLACHER: top ten finish for the young Scot

THE COURSE

From the drawing board to fruition took 13 years, but PGA Golf de Catalunya is an impressive new addition to PGA European Tour Courses' portfolio of custom-built tournament venues. Designed by the PGA European Tour's chairman and vice-chairman, Neil Coles and Angel Gallardo, the 7,204 yards, par 72 course was conceived in 1986, completed in April 1999, and officially opened in the following June.

Their raw material was undulating heathland, well stocked with pine and cork trees, some up to 250 years old. Elevated tees, plunging fairways, and raised greens provide a panoramic, but eminently fair test. The feature hole is the 399-yard 13th, where an accurate drive from a high tee leaves a wedge shot over water to a green sited on a spit of land jutting into the large lake, which is also a backdrop to the third and 11th greens.

putted, while Tomori lost his accuracy from the tee. Despite missing good birdie chances at the 15th and 16th, Björn, who had made his sixth birdie at the 13th, holed from 15 feet to par the 17th and give himself the luxury of a two-stroke lead on the final tee.

After completing the formalities he said: "Sometimes when you have a break or a poor spell you start doubting yourself a little bit, doubting if you can come back and win. But I played probably my best golf from tee to green since the 1997 Ryder Cup. It was very strong. As I want to be there among the best, this win is a big step in the right direction. Everything is back in order."

Mike Britten

DOMINGO HOSPITAL: no pars in 31 out

PGA Golf de Catalunya, Barcelona, Spain, October 14–17, 1999 • Par 72 • Yards 7204

Pos	Name & Country	Rnd 1	Rnd 2	Rnd 3	Rnd 4	Total	€	£
1	Thomas BJÖRN (Den)	66	69	70	68	273	93320.00	66657.14
2	Paolo QUIRICI (Swi)	70	68	69	68	275	48630.00	34735.71
	Katsuyoshi TOMORI (Jpn)	72	67	66	70	275	48630.00	34735.71
4	Francisco CEA (Sp)	65	73	69	69	276	28000.00	20000.00
5	Stephen DODD (Wal)	72	71	67	68	278	20033.33	14309.52
	Emanuele CANONICA (It)	68	66	75	69	278	20033.33	14309.52
	Peter MITCHELL (Eng)	67	70	70	71	278	20033.33	14309.52
8	José COCERES (Arg)	72	71	68	68	279	13260.00	9471.43
	Domingo HOSPITAL (Sp)	69	70	67	73	279	13260.00	9471.43
10	Steen TINNING (Den)	69	67	74	70	280	10038.00	7170.00
	Stephen GALLACHER (Scot)	68	69	73	70	280	10038.00	7170.00
	Carlos RODILES (Sp)	67	71	71	71	280	10038.00	7170.00
	Thomas LEVET (Fr)	68	68	72	72	280	10038.00	7170.00
14	Gary ORR (Scot)	74	71	69	67	281	8232.00	5880.00
	Justin HOBDAY (SA)	73	69	70	69	281	8232.00	5880.00
	Fredrik JACOBSON (Swe)	71	72	67	71	281	8232.00	5880.00
17	José RIVERO (Sp)	74	70	71	67	282	7560.00	5400.00
18	Gary EVANS (Eng)	74	69	73	67	283	6584.00	4702.86
	Ignacio GARRIDO (Sp)	71	73	70	69	283	6584.00	4702.86
	Peter BAKER (Eng)	75	67	71	70	283	6584.00	4702.86
	Daren LEE (Eng)	68	72	72	71	283	6584.00	4702.86
	Miguel Angel MARTIN (Sp)	69	71	72	71	283	6584.00	4702.86
	Diego BORREGO (Sp)	73	69	68	73	283	6584.00	4702.86
	Miles TUNNICLIFF (Eng)	68	69	72	74	283	6584.00	4702.86
25	Fernando ROCA (Sp)	73	68	73	70	284	5460.00	3900.00
	Andrew OLDCORN (Scot)	71	70	73	70	284	5460.00	3900.00
	Roger WINCHESTER (Eng)	66	76	71	71	284	5460.00	3900.00
	Massimo SCARPA (It)	68	72	72	72	284	5460.00	3900.00
	Silvio GRAPPASONNI (It)	75	68	68	73	284	5460.00	3900.00
	David PARK (Wal)	71	68	71	74	284	5460.00	3900.00
31	Desvonde BOTES (SA)	74	69	72	70	285	4662.00	3330.00
	Fredrik LINDGREN (Swe)	76	69	70	70	285	4662.00	3330.00
	Anders HANSEN (Den)	77	67	73	68	285	4662.00	3330.00
	Anthony WALL (Eng)	69	69	73	74	285	4662.00	3330.00
35	Malcolm MACKENZIE (Eng)	69	75	70	72	286	4088.00	2920.00
	Jesus Maria ARRUTI (Sp)	70	75	69	72	286	4088.00	2920.00
	Alberto BINAGHI (It)	74	69	72	71	286	4088.00	2920.00
	Andrew SHERBORNE (Eng)	71	73	71	71	286	4088.00	2920.00
	Robert COLES (Eng)	66	70	79	71	286	4088.00	2920.00
	Johan RYSTRÖM (Swe)	69	74	73	70	286	4088.00	2920.00
41	John BICKERTON (Eng)	75	69	71	72	287	3360.00	2400.00
	Soren HANSEN (Den)	71	73	73	70	287	3360.00	2400.00
	Thomas GÖGELE (Ger)	69	74	71	73	287	3360.00	2400.00
	Henrik BJORNSTAD (Nor)	69	71	73	74	287	3360.00	2400.00
	Van PHILLIPS (Eng)	68	74	71	74	287	3360.00	2400.00
	Ross DRUMMOND (Scot)	70	71	70	76	287	3360.00	2400.00
	Søren KJELDSEN (Den)	70	72	69	76	287	3360.00	2400.00
48	Mark PILKINGTON (Wal)	72	71	72	73	288	2632.00	1880.00
	Costantino ROCCA (It)	72	73	70	73	288	2632.00	1880.00
	Ross MCFARLANE (Eng)	70	72	74	72	288	2632.00	1880.00
	Dean ROBERTSON (Scot)	72	72	74	70	288	2632.00	1880.00
	Raymond RUSSELL (Scot)	70	75	73	70	288	2632.00	1880.00
	Per NYMAN (Swe)	74	70	76	68	288	2632.00	1880.00
54	Christian CÉVAER (Fr)	67	75	74	73	289	2184.00	1560.00
	John MELLOR (Eng)	70	72	68	79	289	2184.00	1560.00
56	Andrew RAITT (Eng)	68	73	75	74	290	2016.00	1440.00
57	Andrew MCLARDY (SA)	71	70	73	78	292	1778.00	1270.00
	Juan QUIROS (Sp)	71	72	75	74	292	1778.00	1270.00
	Mark DAVIS (Eng)	73	72	74	73	292	1778.00	1270.00
	Carlos LARRAIN (Ven)	71	74	77	70	292	1778.00	1270.00
61	Jonathan LOMAS (Eng)	70	73	77	73	293	1596.00	1140.00
	Jamie SPENCE (Eng)	73	71	77	72	293	1596.00	1140.00
63	Daniel CHOPRA (Swe)	73	70	77	74	294	1484.00	1060.00
	Ian WOOSNAM (Wal)	71	72	77	74	294	1484.00	1060.00
65	Massimo FLORIOLI (It)	70	73	79	73	295	1400.00	1000.00
66	Scott HENDERSON (Scot)	73	71	78	76	298	840.00	600.00
67	Wayne RILEY (Aus)	72	73	81	74	300	837.00	597.86

Towering above adversity

Storm clouds added to the frustration

of Robert Karlsson, then came

the silver lining of a timely victory

Frustration at failing to qualify for Europe's Ryder Cup team by just one place; frustration at allowing five golden chances of victory slip away when you know you are having your best season in eight years; frustration at the weather, which left you not knowing most of the time if you would be on the course or in a players's lounge armchair. Those things were sent to try Robert Karlsson. The 6ft 5ins Swede, though, towered over all frustration and adversity.

His first success for over two years came just at the right time: Karlsson's return to Europe proved a triumphant journey after a brief spell in America following the crushing disappointment of missing Brookline when Ireland's Padraig

JAMIE SPENCE: fine finish to share runner-up role

Harrington swooped ahead of him in the final qualifying event. Typically, almost the first official words of the week from the modest 30-year-old giant had been: "At the time I thought 'good luck Padraig', because it was a great perfor-mance to make the team. But obviously I was very, very disappointed."

Asked if winning the Belgacom Open, and winning in such style, could make up for his Ryder Cup disappointment, Karlsson was in no doubt: "Definitely. And what is more, perhaps if I had played in the Ryder Cup, I may not have been fresh enough to win this tournament. Not winning this year would have proved even more disappointing than not getting my Ryder Cup place. It's been my best season

RETIEF GOOSEN: played his heart out

by far and if I had not been able to turn all my top ten finishes, and my five top fives, into a win, I would have never forgiven myself. Now, after winning the Belgacom Open, I don't feel I have to prove anything to anyone else."

Freshness was the key, felt Karlsson, freshness from sacrificing his Alfred

PER-ULRIK JOHANSSON: commanded half-way lead

Dunhill Cup team place to get over the staleness which had threatened to deteriorate his season. He recharged his batteries by playing fun golf in Philadelphia, then taking a couple of weeks off with his friends and family in Sweden. The ploy worked to perfection. Karlsson just got better and better as his batteries became fully charged.

And Karlsson needed to be at his best. Only his best would have been good enough to overcome a determined Retief Goosen, also having a supreme season. The South African, still harbouring hopes of deposing Colin Montgomerie as European number one, took a two-shot lead with a glorious, opening six under par 65. However, Goosen suffered after the deluge the next day, which caused over three hours' delay, and another Swede emerged as favourite.

Per-Ulrik Johansson at last found some form to clinch a one-stroke lead on seven under par when the second round was completed. Then, in the interrupted third round, Karlsson began his challenge, at one stage sharing the lead. But Goosen had it all to himself when they restarted in the morning, taking a lead of two shots into the final round, with Karlsson three off the pace.

Before any of the leading players could get to terms, though, a Boy's Own story was being written by 24-year-old Stephen Gallacher. Uncle Bernard would have been proud of the way his nephew, whose original aim had been to earn enough to keep his European Tour card, twice surged into the lead, playing the course the other way round as one of the back-markers. In the end, the Boy's Own story fell a chapter short as Gallacher had to settle for a share of sixth place. But the card he ensured made the perfect wedding present for his marriage the following Saturday.

Meanwhile, Karlsson's magnificent run of birdies around the turn and a fine finish, only matched by another long serviceman, Englishman Jamie Spence, earned him the 125,000 euro (£89,285) first prize and his third European Tour victory. A 66 for 12 under par was one better than Spence and Goosen, who played his heart out all week.

Karlsson's frustration was over.

Norman Dabell

ROYAL ZOUTE, BELGIUM, OCTOBER 21–24, 1999 · PAR 71 · YARDS 6907

Pos	Name & Country	Rnd 1	Rnd 2	Rnd 3	Rnd 4	Total	Prize Money €	Prize Money £
1	Robert KARLSSON (Swe)	69	68	69	66	272	125000.00	89285.71
2	Jamie SPENCE (Eng)	70	68	68	67	273	65130.00	46521.43
	Retief GOOSEN (SA)	65	71	67	70	273	65130.00	46521.43
4	Greg TURNER (NZ)	70	68	69	68	275	34635.00	24739.29
	Per-Ulrik JOHANSSON (Swe)	69	66	70	70	275	34635.00	24739.29
6	Mats LANNER (Swe)	72	68	70	66	276	21060.00	15042.86
	Thomas BJÖRN (Den)	73	68	69	66	276	21060.00	15042.86
	Paul BROADHURST (Eng)	73	69	68	66	276	21060.00	15042.86
	Stephen GALLACHER (Scot)	72	70	66	68	276	21060.00	15042.86
10	Des SMYTH (Ire)	70	70	68	69	277	15000.00	10714.29
11	Steen TINNING (Den)	70	69	69	70	278	13350.00	9535.71
	Ian WOOSNAM (Wal)	70	70	68	70	278	13350.00	9535.71
13	Anthony WALL (Eng)	72	71	66	70	279	12070.00	8621.43
14	José RIVERO (Sp)	67	71	72	70	280	9991.88	7137.06
	Jean-Francois REMESY (Fr)	72	68	68	72	280	9991.88	7137.06
	Paul LAWRIE (Scot)	73	69	68	70	280	9991.88	7137.06
	Lee WESTWOOD (Eng)	73	66	67	74	280	9991.88	7137.06
	Søren KJELDSEN (Den)	69	71	69	71	280	9991.88	7137.06
	John BICKERTON (Eng)	69	71	69	71	280	9991.88	7137.06
	Bernhard LANGER (Ger)	72	70	71	67	280	9991.88	7137.06
	Jean VAN DE VELDE (Fr)	72	69	69	70	280	9991.88	7137.06
22	Roger WINCHESTER (Eng)	75	66	71	69	281	7762.50	5544.64
	Greg OWEN (Eng)	74	67	74	66	281	7762.50	5544.64
	Thomas LEVET (Fr)	71	72	69	69	281	7762.50	5544.64
	Seve BALLESTEROS (Sp)	69	74	69	69	281	7762.50	5544.64
	Peter BAKER (Eng)	72	72	66	71	281	7762.50	5544.64
	Nicolas VANHOOTEGEM (Bel)	69	74	67	71	281	7762.50	5544.64
	Miguel Angel MARTIN (Sp)	72	70	66	73	281	7762.50	5544.64
	Mark MOULAND (Wal)	70	68	69	74	281	7762.50	5544.64
30	Brian DAVIS (Eng)	74	70	68	70	282	6262.50	4473.21
	José COCERES (Arg)	71	71	70	70	282	6262.50	4473.21
	Tony JOHNSTONE (Zim)	67	69	74	72	282	6262.50	4473.21
	Dean ROBERTSON (Scot)	67	70	73	72	282	6262.50	4473.21
	Paul MCGINLEY (Ire)	71	70	68	73	282	6262.50	4473.21
	Raphaël JACQUELIN (Fr)	72	69	67	74	282	6262.50	4473.21
36	Alex CEJKA (Ger)	68	73	71	72	284	5400.00	3857.14
	Andrew OLDCORN (Scot)	73	69	71	71	284	5400.00	3857.14
	Paul EALES (Eng)	73	69	71	71	284	5400.00	3857.14
	Mark JAMES (Eng)	68	71	72	73	284	5400.00	3857.14
	Phillip PRICE (Wal)	69	70	72	73	284	5400.00	3857.14
41	Dennis EDLUND (Swe)	71	70	71	73	285	4650.00	3321.43
	Van PHILLIPS (Eng)	70	72	72	71	285	4650.00	3321.43
	Marc FARRY (Fr)	76	69	69	71	285	4650.00	3321.43
	Philip WALTON (Ire)	73	67	74	71	285	4650.00	3321.43
	Joakim HAEGGMAN (Swe)	68	71	77	69	285	4650.00	3321.43
46	Darren CLARKE (N.Ire)	73	67	72	74	286	3900.00	2785.71
	Russell CLAYDON (Eng)	71	71	71	73	286	3900.00	2785.71
	Steve WEBSTER (Eng)	71	74	70	71	286	3900.00	2785.71
	Andrew BEAL (Eng)	73	72	71	70	286	3900.00	2785.71
	Peter MITCHELL (Eng)	75	70	72	69	286	3900.00	2785.71
51	Francisco CEA (Sp)	69	73	72	73	287	3225.00	2303.57
	Silvio GRAPPASONNI (It)	75	69	71	72	287	3225.00	2303.57
	Malcolm MACKENZIE (Eng)	72	72	71	72	287	3225.00	2303.57
	Tom GILLIS (USA)	71	72	69	75	287	3225.00	2303.57
55	Gary EVANS (Eng)	73	70	70	75	288	2850.00	2035.71
56	Arnaud LANGENAEKEN (Bel)	74	70	71	74	289	2493.75	1781.25
	Barry LANE (Eng)	72	68	75	74	289	2493.75	1781.25
	Michael CAMPBELL (NZ)	72	70	75	72	289	2493.75	1781.25
	Derrick COOPER (Eng)	74	70	73	72	289	2493.75	1781.25
60	Jonathan LOMAS (Eng)	69	72	75	74	290	2212.50	1580.36
	Olle KARLSSON (Swe)	72	70	75	73	290	2212.50	1580.36
62	Sven STRÜVER (Ger)	76	69	71	75	291	2062.50	1473.21
	Trevor IMMELMAN (SA)	72	73	76	70	291	2062.50	1473.21
64	Thomas GÖGELE (Ger)	70	73	72	77	292	1518.00	1084.29
	David GILFORD (Eng)	76	69	71	76	292	1518.00	1084.29
	Rolf MUNTZ (Hol)	73	71	73	75	292	1518.00	1084.29
	Miles TUNNICLIFF (Eng)	75	69	73	75	292	1518.00	1084.29
68	David HOWELL (Eng)	68	74	75	76	293	1119.00	799.29
69	Ove SELLBERG (Swe)	71	74	73	78	296	1116.00	797.14

ROBERT KARLSSON: triumphant escape from frustration

The Tour pays its respects

Winner Miguel Angel Jiménez and every other

player at Montecastillo were joined as a family

in grief by the death of Payne Stewart

*E*very week on the European Tour the 18th green is a place of jubilation, celebration and elation. And dejection and disappointment, too. Putts are holed, putts are missed. Dreams are fulfilled, hopes are dashed. In short, most human emotions are seen.

But at Montecastillo, on the evening of Friday, October 29, every single player competing in the Volvo Masters stood and shared the same feelings. Immense sadness and grief. In a scene which nobody hopes to see repeated, golf showed just how big a family it is and how much it hurts when there is a death in the family.

Four days earlier, Payne Stewart, the reigning United States Open Champion and only a few weeks before a member of the American side at both the Ryder Cup in Boston and Alfred Dunhill Cup at St Andrews, had taken off with five others on a private jet from Florida to Texas for America's Tour Championship.

They never arrived. For reasons which investigators quickly tried to discover, all those on board had been deprived of oxygen and died, leaving the jet, seemingly set on auto-pilot, to fly for 1,800 miles before running out of fuel and crashing more than four hours later in South Dakota.

The tragedy shocked the world, not just the world of golf, because Stewart was one of sport's most easily recognised and colourful characters, and at Pinehurst in

BERNHARD LANGER: "We have all been blessed by knowing and spending time with Payne."

June had capped an already glittering career by becoming a major champion again at the age of 42. And had done it in dramatic fashion by sinking a putt of 18 feet on the final green.

Everyone's heart went out to his wife, Tracey, and children, Chelsea (13) and Aaron (10), and tributes poured in. Inevitably, the tournaments which followed began as sombre occasions.

It was after the second round in Jerez that the entire Volvo Masters field gathered by the 18th green and paid their respects to the dead with a minute's silence, and these words by Bernhard

BERNHARD LANGER: in three-way tie for second place

Langer: "We are gathered here in remembrance of the six casualties of last Monday's airplane crash, one of them being our colleague and dear friend Payne Stewart.

"Payne was one of the most liked and respected players who has ever played the game. He treated everyone as very special, whether caddie, player, official, friend or

PAUL LAWRIE: two ways to enjoy a good drive

SHOT OF THE WEEK

There were a remarkable 43 eagles – a veritable convocation of them – during the week of the Volvo Masters, but as well as having a Spanish winner there was also a Spanish albatross. Francisco Cea, like Miguel Angel Jiménez from nearby Malaga, marked his debut in the event by holing a 220-yard three-wood for a two at the uphill 517-yard ninth. It was only the fifth albatross of the European Tour season and while Cea did not see it disappear into the hole, European Tour Productions TV cameras did. It was a perfect shot.

COLIN MONTGOMERIE: headed Volvo Bonus Pool

stranger. He took time and showed interest in all of us.

"We have all been blessed by knowing and spending time with Payne. Our hearts go out to Payne's wife Tracey and their children for the great loss of their loving father and husband. Payne, we know you have gone to a better place, to be with your Father in Heaven, but you will be greatly missed by all of us."

The show went on, as Stewart surely would have wanted, and to the delight of the home fans the Volvo Masters hailed its first Spanish winner in its 12-year history, nine at Valderrama and now three at Montecastillo.

Miguel Angel Jiménez was the man, coming from four strokes behind at the

PADRAIG HARRINGTON: 11 birdies spiced second round 65

MICHAEL CAMPBELL: New Zealander threatened through three rounds

start of the last day to triumph by two, his closing 65 including four birdies in the last seven holes and giving him a 19 under par total of 269, a tournament record. "I feel very proud being the first Spaniard to win the Volvo Masters," said the 35-year-old from Malaga, who in March captured the Turespaña Masters-Open Andalucia in his home town.

SERGIO GARCIA: but most of his year was bright

"This has been the best year of my career. It's been fantastic." He did, of course, make his Ryder Cup debut in Boston, and was so highly-rated by captain Mark James that he was used in all five sessions, then, in October, partnered José Maria Olazábal and Sergio Garcia to Alfred Dunhill Cup glory.

The Montecastillo course had over

SEVERIANO BALLESTEROS: talent, pride and experience at work

RETIEF GOOSEN: runner-up five times in season

eight inches of rain on it in the week prior to the tournament – five times the usual amount for the whole of October – but while the fairways showed the effect, the greens were rated by Retief Goosen as among the best of the season. The South African demonstrated his liking for them with a superb opening 62, good enough for a three-stroke lead over Welshman Phillip Price, but not for a new course record as preferred lies were in operation.

Goosen birdied the first three holes, quickly added two more and when he holed from 25 feet for eagle on the 517-yard ninth he was out in 29. Having led

from start-to-finish in both the Slaley Hall Northumberland Challenge in 1996 - his first European Tour victory – and the following year's Peugeot Open de France, the 30-year-old had no fears about finding himself out in front so early.

He improved from ten under par to 14 under on day two, although his lead was cut to one when Ireland's Padraig Harrington packed no fewer than 11 birdies into a 65. Then Goosen moved to 16 under with a Saturday 70, New Zealander Michael Campbell taking over in second place, two behind with a 67.

But Goosen could not then repel

Jiménez, whose decisive final round birdie burst was when he holed from 14 feet at the short 14th, 12 feet at the difficult 464-yard 15th and then from seven feet on the long 16th. The South African three-putted for bogey there and in the end had to birdie the last just to finish joint runner-up - for the fifth time in the season – with Harrington and Langer. It was also Harrington's fifth second place.

As well as the 232,400 euro (£166,000) first prize Jiménez was rewarded with a further 84,000 euro (£60,000) for coming second in the Volvo Bonus Pool, the mini-league table formed from the three

MIGUEL ANGEL JIMÉNEZ: the crowning of his career-best year

Volvo-sponsored events during 1999. Colin Montgomerie was the clear winner of that following his Volvo PGA Championship and Volvo Scandinavian Masters victories, and that was worth 140,000 euro (£100,000) to the Scot.

Unlike the previous six Volvo Masters, however, Montgomerie did not leave with the Volvo Order of Merit title as well. Finishing 16th put him 575,317 euro (£410,941) ahead of Sergio Garcia, but the Spanish teenager, Lee Westwood and Goosen all moved on to the WGC - American Express Championship at Valderrama, still with a chance of ending Montgomerie's long reign as Europe's number one.

Mark Garrod

Pos	Name & Country	Rnd 1	Rnd 2	Rnd 3	Rnd 4	Total	Prize Money €	£
1	Miguel Angel JIMÉNEZ (Sp)	68	67	69	65	269	232400.00	166000.00
2	Bernhard LANGER (Ger)	66	70	69	66	271	104346.67	74533.34
	Padraig HARRINGTON (Ire)	66	65	73	67	271	104346.67	74533.34
	Retief GOOSEN (SA)	62	68	70	71	271	104346.67	74533.34
5	Darren CLARKE (N.Ire)	67	70	70	66	273	54530.00	38950.00
	Sergio GARCIA (Sp)	69	68	67	69	273	54530.00	38950.00
7	Thomas BJÖRN (Den)	66	71	71	66	274	35933.33	25666.66
	Miguel Angel MARTIN (Sp)	69	68	67	70	274	35933.33	25666.66
	Michael CAMPBELL (NZ)	70	65	67	72	274	35933.33	25666.66
10	Peter O'MALLEY (Aus)	73	69	69	64	275	23286.67	16633.34
	Ian WOOSNAM (Wal)	71	68	69	67	275	23286.67	16633.34
	Jean VAN DE VELDE (Fr)	71	69	68	67	275	23286.67	16633.34
	Jarmo SANDELIN (Swe)	68	73	67	67	275	23286.67	16633.34
	Paul LAWRIE (Scot)	69	68	69	69	275	23286.67	16633.34
	José COCERES (Arg)	71	64	68	72	275	23286.67	16633.34
16	Peter MITCHELL (Eng)	70	71	67	68	276	19180.00	13700.00
	Ian GARBUTT (Eng)	68	69	70	69	276	19180.00	13700.00
	Colin MONTGOMERIE (Scot)	70	65	71	70	276	19180.00	13700.00
	Anthony WALL (Eng)	70	65	71	70	276	19180.00	13700.00
20	Paul BROADHURST (Eng)	73	68	69	67	277	17500.00	12500.00
	Per-Ulrik JOHANSSON (Swe)	69	70	67	71	277	17500.00	12500.00
22	Bob MAY (USA)	70	71	69	68	278	15855.00	11325.00
	Lian-Wei ZHANG (PRC)	67	72	70	69	278	15855.00	11325.00
	Robert KARLSSON (Swe)	73	67	69	69	278	15855.00	11325.00
	Mark MCNULTY (Zim)	69	68	71	70	278	15855.00	11325.00
26	Andrew COLTART (Scot)	69	69	70	71	279	14070.00	10050.00
	Greg TURNER (NZ)	75	67	66	71	279	14070.00	10050.00
	Jamie SPENCE (Eng)	66	75	66	72	279	14070.00	10050.00
	Patrik SJÖLAND (Swe)	69	69	68	73	279	14070.00	10050.00
30	Ignacio GARRIDO (Sp)	71	74	69	66	280	12810.00	9150.00
	Lee WESTWOOD (Eng)	72	68	70	70	280	12810.00	9150.00
32	Costantino ROCCA (It)	67	69	74	71	281	11550.00	8250.00
	Søren KJELDSEN (Den)	71	70	71	69	281	11550.00	8250.00
	Paul MCGINLEY (Ire)	72	71	70	68	281	11550.00	8250.00
	Stephen LEANEY (Aus)	79	67	69	66	281	11550.00	8250.00
36	David CARTER (Eng)	72	67	73	70	282	9450.00	6750.00
	David HOWELL (Eng)	72	68	73	69	282	9450.00	6750.00
	David PARK (Wal)	70	70	70	72	282	9450.00	6750.00
	Alex CEJKA (Ger)	75	69	66	72	282	9450.00	6750.00
	Kyi Hla HAN (Myr)	71	65	73	73	282	9450.00	6750.00
	Russell CLAYDON (Eng)	66	70	71	75	282	9450.00	6750.00
42	Dean ROBERTSON (Scot)	69	73	69	72	283	7560.00	5400.00
	Seve BALLESTEROS (Sp)	68	75	69	71	283	7560.00	5400.00
	Angel CABRERA (Arg)	71	71	71	70	283	7560.00	5400.00
	Paul EALES (Eng)	71	70	72	70	283	7560.00	5400.00
	Jarrod MOSELEY (Aus)	71	73	70	69	283	7560.00	5400.00
47	John BICKERTON (Eng)	73	71	69	71	284	6580.00	4700.00
	Gary EVANS (Eng)	71	73	70	70	284	6580.00	4700.00
49	Phillip PRICE (Wal)	65	74	72	74	285	5845.00	4175.00
	Eduardo ROMERO (Arg)	68	74	71	72	285	5845.00	4175.00
	Jean-Francois REMESY (Fr)	67	72	75	71	285	5845.00	4175.00
	Tony JOHNSTONE (Zim)	70	76	69	70	285	5845.00	4175.00
53	Steve WEBSTER (Eng)	66	72	76	72	286	5460.00	3900.00
54	Nico VAN RENSBURG (SA)	67	75	69	76	287	5040.00	3600.00
	Van PHILLIPS (Eng)	75	67	71	74	287	5040.00	3600.00
	Santiago LUNA (Sp)	74	69	71	73	287	5040.00	3600.00
	Gary ORR (Scot)	75	70	70	72	287	5040.00	3600.00
	Pierre FULKE (Swe)	71	72	78	66	287	5040.00	3600.00
59	Francisco CEA (Sp)	71	68	71	78	288	4550.00	3250.00
	Mark JAMES (Eng)	73	73	68	74	288	4550.00	3250.00
61	Peter BAKER (Eng)	69	73	70	77	289	4270.00	3050.00
	Marc FARRY (Fr)	69	72	77	71	289	4270.00	3050.00
63	Sven STRÜVER (Ger)	72	72	72	74	290	4060.00	2900.00
64	Ricardo GONZALEZ (Arg)	72	68	77	75	292	3850.00	2750.00
	Christopher HANELL (Swe)	69	78	72	73	292	3850.00	2750.00
66	José Maria OLAZÁBAL (Sp)	72	70	71	WD	213	3640.00	2600.00

Happiness is a popular Spaniard winning in Spain

Forsman & Bodenfors
VOLVO
for life
CGY 128
The Volvo S80 is probably the world's safest car. Side impact curtains, WHIPS (completely new protection against whiplash injuries) and everything else learnt about safety over the past 72 years, are standard features. A bi-turbo engine with 272 hp also protects you from boredom on long journeys. Unfortunately there is still no protection against insensitive birds, but we're working on it.
VOLVO S80. PROTECTS YOU AGAINST EVERYTHING. ALMOST.

Dynamic Duo strike again

Tiger Woods won another World Championship at Valderrama while Colin Montgomerie clinched his seventh European Tour No. 1 title

The inaugural World Golf Championships - American Express Championship, held on the immaculate Valderrama course on Spain's Costa del Sol, provided spectators with not only the opportunity to watch an enthralling contest unfold, featuring the indomitable Tiger Woods and the phlegmatic Miguel Angel Jiménez, but also the chance to monitor a tournament within a tournament.

As the final day of the 1999 European Tour dawned, Colin Montgomerie knew that either Sergio Garcia or Lee Westwood could still thwart his determined effort to win the Volvo Order of Merit title for a record seventh successive time.

In the end, Montgomerie was home and hosed. If Frankie Dettori was in seventh heaven when he went through the card at Ascot in one day, then Montgomerie had good reason to feel like doing a flying dismount similar to that perfected by the Italian. The Scot, of course, was a touch less theatrical although clearly delighted about finishing

TIGER WOODS and HARVEY GOLUB, Chairman and CEO, American Express: sharing inaugural success

MIGUEL ANGEL JIMÉNEZ: sportsmanship and good grace of the highest order

VIJAY SINGH: "You need to be on your toes out there"

the millennium as the European Tour number one. His sequence might never be beaten, and will certainly remain in the record books, as will the memory of the incredible duel between Woods and Jiménez that decided the outcome of this fascinating Championship.

Fresh from his superb triumph in the Volvo Masters, and enjoying the finest year of his career, Jiménez was followed by thousands of enthusiastic supporters, who greeted every birdie made by their compatriot with Augusta-like fervour that echoed through the pine and cork trees of the undulating Valderrama course. Jiménez repaid them all with a performance that was quite magnificent, and if he was to lose at the end in a play-off then he did so with sportsmanship and good grace of the highest order.

All of this was to come. Blustery conditions, with the wind blowing from off the sea, provided a stiff, first day examination paper for the 62 World Golf Championship graduates. Woods felt that it was very important not only to put the ball on the fairway, but in a position from where it was possible to "leave an uphill putt." Vijay Singh passed the test, scoring 67 to lead by one from Jim Furyk, but admitted: "You need to be on your toes out there." Singh was asked whether he liked the course. He replied: "When you

DOUBLE TOP: Tiger Woods and Colin Montgomerie, Tour No.1s across the Atlantic, flanked by Edward L. Moorhouse, Executive Vice President and Chief Legal Officer, US PGA Tour, and Kenneth D Schofield CBE, Executive Director, European Tour

play well, you like it. I liked it today!"

Mark James also found the course to his liking on the first day, being one of five players to score 69, and with typical resilience he remained in the hunt at the halfway stage. Tim Herron and Chris Perry scored 66 and 67 respectively to share the lead on 137, five under par, one ahead of Justin Leonard (67) and Singh (71), with James, following a 70, tied for fifth place one, shot further back.

James admitted to not playing as well in the second round as he did in the first, although his putter was hotter. He revealed that when he turned professional in 1976 he was dreaming of a four-figure cheque, not a million dollar first prize. "This is a good tournament," he stressed. "And it's on a course similar to that which you would play in a major."

Those words were well supported by the leaderboard at the end of the third round. Then Jiménez, with a 69, and Perry, with a 72, shared the lead with four under par totals of 209. In other words, they were one shot closer to par than Singh was after the first round. It is a scenario familiar to major championships, when the name of the game is to just stay in touch which, quite frequently, means being little more than one or two under par. If that sounds easy, then it is not on a course such as Valderrama where any excursion from the fairways usually leads to a shot being dropped.

Fifteen players were under par following the third round, but they were separated by only four shots. Woods had done

LEE WESTWOOD: Volvo Order of Merit runner-up

SHOT OF THE WEEK

Miguel Angel Jiménez had only seconds earlier holed from 40 feet from off the green for a birdie at the tenth to tie the lead with Tiger Woods, as ahead of him the American faced a chip from behind the 11th for an eagle three. Woods duly holed, moved two ahead and then birdied the next. The eagle had given The Tiger the cushion that became vital in keeping his challenge for a second 1999 World Golf Championship victory alive when he tumbled to a triple-bogey eight at the 17th hole.

an admirable job of "hanging around" with scores of 71-69-70, enabling him to be tied third with Tom Lehman, Justin Leonard and Nick Price, all former Open Championship winners, and Hal Sutton. In fact, Woods birdied the last two holes, and declared: "Level par would have been

SERGIO GARCIA: two successive 69s

KEN SCHOFIELD, Executive Director of the European Tour (far left), unveiled the Gene Sarazen Cup at the opening ceremony with (left to right): TIM FINCHEM, Commissioner PGA Tour, JON LINEN, Vice Chairman of American Express, ARTHUR SANDERSON, Executive Director, PGA Tour of Australasia, KOSAKU SHIMADA, Executive Director, Japan Golf Tour, and LOUIS MARTIN, Chief Executive, Southern Africa Tour

THE COURSE

Robert Trent Jones enhanced the shot-making values of Valderrama when in 1975 he remodelled the course, which is spectacular for both its beauty and difficulty. The American influence of this steeply undulating panoramic course is clearly visible: long, elevated, tree-framed tees; huge, contoured greens; and cavernous, white sand traps that dazzle in the sun. The wind will always play a significant role, and this was most certainly the case on the final day of the World Golf Championships – American Express Championship.

MARK JAMES: end-of-season flourish for Europe's outstanding Ryder Cup team captain

The International Federation of PGA Tours announced that the WGC – American Express Championship would donate $250,000 to charities in the region of Andalucia with The First Tee initiative at La Cañada Golf Club, a few kilometres from Valderrama, being the principal recipient. The First Tee is dedicated to providing affordable golf access to those who otherwise might not have the opportunity to play the game, with a special emphasis on junior golfers.

a good score today, but I messed up and went one better!"

José Maria Olazábal had moved into the fray with a 69 to be on 211 with, among others, Westwood, and Garcia, with a second successive 69 following an opening 74, was at 212. James had retreated with a 74 for 213 – he was one of six players on level par – and Colin Montgomerie, despite being tied 22nd, was only five behind. All to play for, so to speak, with not only that one million dollar first prize at stake, but the Volvo Order of Merit winner to be decided.

The final twist, however, was to see two players, Woods and Jiménez, move away from their rivals at such a pace that with nine holes to play there was no other player pressing them. There is always talk of the major championships coming down to the final stretch, those emotional last nine holes, and so it came to pass at Valderrama as the wind blew hard under a

hot sun. Woods, out in 33, had moved alongside Jiménez at the top of the leader board. The American was motoring. He birdied the tenth, but then so did Jiménez, playing two matches behind him. The Spaniard contrived to hole a putt of 40 feet from off the green but, little more than 30 seconds later, Woods chipped in from behind the 11th for an eagle three to move two ahead.

Woods made a two at the downhill 12th, but then Jiménez made a birdie at the 11th. Woods birdied the 14th, but bogeyed the 16th. So when Jiménez birdied the 14th, they were separated by only one shot. Then, at the 17th, Woods must have felt that it was not going to be his day. He struck what appeared to be an excellent third shot, the ball backed up from beyond the pin, rolled ever so slowly back past the pin and eventually disappeared into a watery grave. He marked an eight on his card. Jiménez bogeyed the

16th, but even so he now needed two pars to win. He made one at the 17th, ever so bravely, but at the 18th he took five. Now the hole needed to be played again for the play-off, and, with the light failing, Jiménez once more failed to negotiate those 454 yards in par.

So Woods claimed his second World Golf Championship of 1999. He became the first player to win eight official PGA Tour events in a single season since Johnny Miller in 1974 and the first player to win four consecutive starts on the PGA Tour since Ben Hogan in 1953. Yet, as Woods received the Gene Sarazen Cup, so one man moved away from centre stage into the Media Centre to be interviewed by all of Spain's leading golf writers. Miguel Angel Jiménez had not won the title but he had earned the applause of a nation.

Mitchell Platts

CLUB DE GOLF, VALDERRAMA, SPAIN, NOVEMBER 4–7, 1999 • PAR 71 • YARDS 6830

Pos	Name & Country	Rnd 1	Rnd 2	Rnd 3	Rnd 4	Total	Prize Money €	£
1	Tiger WOODS (USA)	71	69	70	68	278	853190.32	609421.66
2	Miguel Angel JIMÉNEZ (Sp)	72	68	69	69	278	341276.12	243768.66
3	Dudley HART (USA)	75	68	70	70	283	255957.10	182826.50
4	Lee WESTWOOD (Eng)	73	67	71	73	284	150730.29	107664.49
	Nick PRICE (Zim)	69	71	70	74	284	150730.29	107664.49
	Stewart CINK (USA)	75	65	71	73	284	150730.29	107664.49
7	Chris PERRY (USA)	70	67	72	76	285	115180.70	82271.93
	Sergio GARCIA (Sp)	74	69	69	73	285	115180.70	82271.93
	Fred FUNK (USA)	71	68	74	72	285	115180.70	82271.93
	Scott HOCH (USA)	69	70	72	74	285	115180.70	82271.93
11	David TOMS (USA)	72	68	71	75	286	79346.70	56676.21
	José Maria OLAZABAL (Sp)	73	69	69	75	286	79346.70	56676.21
	Bob ESTES (USA)	69	72	72	73	286	79346.70	56676.21
	Justin LEONARD (USA)	71	67	72	76	286	79346.70	56676.21
	Jim FURYK (USA)	68	73	71	74	286	79346.70	56676.21
16	Tim HERRON (USA)	71	66	75	75	287	59723.32	42659.51
	Vijay SINGH (Fiji)	67	71	75	74	287	59723.32	42659.51
	Davis LOVE III (USA)	74	70	73	70	287	59723.32	42659.51
19	Hal SUTTON (USA)	75	66	69	78	288	52897.80	37784.14
20	Bob MAY (USA)	77	69	74	69	289	45048.45	32177.46
	Dennis PAULSON (USA)	76	71	68	74	289	45048.45	32177.46
	Jarmo SANDELIN (Swe)	70	74	75	70	289	45048.45	32177.46
	Craig PARRY (Aus)	72	73	71	73	289	45048.45	32177.46
	Colin MONTGOMERIE (Scot)	70	72	72	75	289	45048.45	32177.46
25	Mark JAMES (Eng)	69	70	74	77	290	35620.70	25443.36
	Jarrod MOSELEY (Aus)	76	69	72	73	290	35620.70	25443.36
	Angel CABRERA (Arg)	74	74	70	72	290	35620.70	25443.36
	Retief GOOSEN (SA)	75	69	74	72	290	35620.70	25443.36
	Tom LEHMAN (USA)	72	67	71	80	290	35620.70	25443.36
30	Stuart APPLEBY (Aus)	76	66	74	75	291	32207.93	23005.66
	Jean VAN DE VELDE (Fr)	72	73	70	76	291	32207.93	23005.66
	Mike WEIR (Can)	73	68	72	78	291	32207.93	23005.66
	Padraig HARRINGTON (Ire)	76	74	70	71	291	32207.93	23005.66
34	John HUSTON (USA)	72	74	72	74	292	30714.85	21939.18
	Jeff SLUMAN (USA)	77	70	69	76	292	30714.85	21939.18
	Steve ELKINGTON (Aus)	74	72	71	75	292	30714.85	21939.18
37	Rodney PAMPLING (Aus)	71	74	69	79	293	29435.07	21025.05
	Paul LAWRIE (Scot)	76	68	76	73	293	29435.07	21025.05
	Bob TWAY (USA)	75	72	71	75	293	29435.07	21025.05
40	Loren ROBERTS (USA)	72	72	71	80	295	27515.39	19653.85
	Naomichi "Joe" OZAKI (Jpn)	76	71	69	79	295	27515.39	19653.85
	Darren CLARKE (N.Ire)	79	67	71	78	295	27515.39	19653.85
	Phil MICKELSON (USA)	69	71	77	78	295	27515.39	19653.85
	Duffy WALDORF (USA)	74	77	73	71	295	27515.39	19653.85
	Ernie ELS (SA)	74	75	71	75	295	27515.39	19653.85
46	Notah BEGAY III (USA)	77	71	73	75	296	25809.01	18435.01
	Steve PATE (USA)	72	74	72	78	296	25809.01	18435.01
48	Jeff MAGGERT (USA)	70	74	79	74	297	24315.93	17368.52
	Bernhard LANGER (Ger)	71	70	80	76	297	24315.93	17368.52
	Carlos FRANCO (Par)	75	73	74	75	297	24315.93	17368.52
	Scott DUNLAP (USA)	74	71	75	77	297	24315.93	17368.52
	Ted TRYBA (USA)	77	71	70	79	297	24315.93	17368.52
53	Kazuhiko HOSOKAWA (Jpn)	73	73	72	80	298	23142.79	16530.56
	Robert KARLSSON (Swe)	74	68	74	82	298	23142.79	16530.56
55	Brent GEIBERGER (USA)	75	71	68	85	299	22609.54	16149.67
	Alex CEJKA (Ger)	79	76	72	72	299	22609.54	16149.67
	Brian WATTS (USA)	75	74	79	71	299	22609.54	16149.67
58	Craig SPENCE (Aus)	72	73	75	80	300	22182.94	15844.96
59	David FROST (SA)	76	73	74	81	304	21863.00	15616.43
	Thomas BJÖRN (Den)	72	81	74	77	304	21863.00	15616.43
61	Richard KAPLAN (SA)	78	75	73	80	306	21543.06	15387.90
62	Glen DAY (USA)	78	67	81	DQ	226	21329.76	15235.54

Opportunity and incentive

The way David Park used his chance

to become a European Tour winner

encourages the hopefuls he left behind

*I*f there was a defining moment in 1999 that underlined the reason and purpose of the European Challenge Tour, it was when David Park used both opportunity and incentive to become a European Tour champion. The Welshman's meteoric rise from being comparatively little known to headline-maker took less than a fortnight, but underlined just what can be achieved if you seize the chance when it comes along.

A professional since late 1997 after playing in the Walker Cup, the amiable Park spent 1998 learning his trade on the European Challenge Tour, winning the Rolex Trophy in Switzerland on the way and eventually finishing ranked 29th. Here was a star in the making, someone who was ready for the big arena.

The man from Hereford was fast out of the blocks in 1999, winning the OKI Telepizza Challenge in Spain, the second tournament of the European Challenge Tour season. But his sights were focused on a big future and when his ranking secured an entry into the European Tour's Moroccan Open in June he didn't waste it. Indeed, Park made a huge impact, and it was only after six holes of an absorbing play-off that he lost the opportunity of victory to Miguel Angel Martin. And only one week later, Park was in the winner's enclosure. Victory in the Compaq European Grand Prix at Slaley Hall in Northumberland, just two days after his 25th birthday, enabled him to equal Greg Norman's 22-year-old record of winning on only his second start on the European Tour.

As the golfing world marvelled that the European Tour had found a new star, Park's success wasn't lost on the many European Challenge Tour colleagues he left behind. They took heart in what he had achieved, believing they, too, might take a similar route whenever the chance came along. It was a time when the game in Europe realised the talent that exists within the ranks of the European Challenge Tour, which nurtures more David Parks.

The year of 1999 also presented another avenue for European Challenge Tour players to exploit. The first Double-Badge event, one involving players from both the European Challenge Tour and the European Tour, came with the West of Ireland Classic in Galway. Encouragingly, it was won by Costantino Rocca, a European Challenge Tour graduate in 1989, and there will be more opportunities of this nature in the future.

So it is not surprising that as the European Challenge Tour rings down the curtain on the 20th Century it is in buoyant mood and, as its name implies, ready to face whatever challenges the new millenium is likely to present.

Park's success was one highlight of the 1999 season, which was not marked by a plethora of records. No one approached the heights – five victories and over £81,000 in winnings – set by Warren Bennett in the previous year and who

prospered further on his promotion to the European Tour by winning the Scottish PGA Championship. But it was still a year to remember.

In essence, you need to shoot lower scores to win on the European Challenge Tour. In recent years the average cut figure has been steadily falling. In 1998 it was around one over par. In 1999 it had dropped again by half a stroke. "The strength of the game on the European Challenge Tour is improving every year," says Alain de Soultrait, the Tour's Director. "You will always get the cream of good players, but now our strength in depth is getting deeper and it is getting harder and harder to win tournaments."

A few years ago you could pick a winner from a select band of players whose skills stood them apart from the rest. Now, after 11 years, any one of 50 players could mount the winner's rostrum.

The nature of the European Challenge Tour and its raison d'être is as a stepping stone to the European Tour as well as a way back for those who lose their playing privileges. It is a learning process as well as a rehabilitation, with the leading 15 ranked players at the end of the season gaining automatic promotion to the European Tour.

Over the years, the European Challenge Tour has produced an ever-growing list of champions who have gone on to become household names as far as European golf is concerned. Costantino Rocca, Thomas Björn, Ignacio Garrido, Jarmo Sandelin, Michael Campbell, and now Warren Bennett, have all graduated through the European Challenge Tour since its inception in 1989 and more will follow.

There is no doubt that the European

CARL SUNESON: three victories to head Rankings

IAIN PYMAN: Moscow and Paris winning connection

HENNIE OTTO: sixth among successful graduates

Challenge Tour is now the finest proving ground, a fact underlined by the number of players who have retained their cards on the European Tour.

These numbers have been growing to such an extent that of the Class of 1998, those who graduated to the all-demanding, world-class European Tour last season, 13, or 87%, kept their cards. That wasn't easily accomplished in a Ryder Cup year when competition was fierce.

Another factor, as with the European Tour, is the cosmopolitan nature of the European Challenge Tour. Most golf-playing nations of the world are represented in its ranks while a glance at the 1999 Roll of Honour shows that there were 24 winners representing 13 different nationalities.

The Tour again visited many countries, 17 in all, from Kenya and the Ivory Coast in Africa, through Europe and finishing with the Grand Final in Cuba. "There are no barriers in golf," says de Soultrait. "We will continue to increase the number of countries where we can play as long as they have good courses.

MARKUS BRIER: first Austrian to graduate to European Tour

We should not be afraid to do this."

The Tour began in March in familiar surroundings at Muthaiga in Nairobi, Kenya, for the Tusker Kenya Open, one of the oldest tournaments on the Challenge Tour schedule. Dutchman Maarten Lafeber got his season off to a flier with a 19 under par victory, followed two weeks later by Park's initial success of 1999 in Spain.

England's Ian Poulter edged home when the Tour retraced its steps to Africa in April for the Ivory Coast Open, before Carl Suneson secured the first of his win-treble on home soil in the Comunidad Valenciana Challenge de España at El Saler.

In May, French Riviera-based American, Kevin Carissimi, Gustavo Rojas, an experienced campaigner from Argentina, and Australian Lucas Parsons took the honours in Luxembourg, Italy and France respectively. In June more names were added to the Tour's ever-lengthening list of new champions with Per G Nyman – no relation to the European Tour's Swede of the same name – and Swiss Juan Ciola entering the winner's circle, the latter triumphing after a play-off in the Diners Club Austrian Open against New Zealand's Elliott Boult.

The Challenge Tour then entered its busiest spell, moving to Italy, France, Switzerland (twice), Finland (twice) and Slovenia in successive weeks, before England again staged the Challenge Tour Championship, under new sponsors Beazer Homes, at a splendid new venue –

Bowood Golf and Country Club near Calne, in Wiltshire. However, there was nothing new about the winner, Suneson, securing his third victory of the season – his second had come in the Rolex Trophy in Geneva – in true champion fashion, a closing 66 giving the Spaniard an eight-shot winning margin.

If there is one player who represents the multi-national aspect of the Challenge Tour, it is Suneson. He has an English mother and was born in Las Palmas, Canary Islands, where his Swedish father, Gunnar, is a restaurateur.

His victory at Bowood secured his European Tour card for the year 2000, and he did it in front of four generations of the Suneson family – his grandparents, his father, wife Elena, and son, Carl Junior. "I think I had my card before this week, but this confirms it," he said. "I played well and putted well, but patience and experience were the keys. Now I want to go on and win the Rankings." Prophetic words, as it turned out.

The 32-year-old, who took Spanish citizenship three years ago after representing England as an amateur, discovered in 1995 that he was diabetic. Two years ago he underwent surgery on a hand, while a troublesome thyroid added to his problems. "It has been a nightmare," he added. "The thyroid problem meant I couldn't control my hands, and I used to flare up on the golf course for no apparent reason. But, hopefully, that is all behind me now and the future is looking much rosier."

It certainly seems that way, as it does for England's Iain Pyman. The 26-year-old Yorkshireman, who lost his card on the European Tour in 1998 and failed to regain it at the European Tour Qualifying School, came up trumps in the BMW Russian Open at the Moscow Golf and Country Club in August, despite a couple of late scares. Pyman, who was Amateur champion in 1993 and won the silver medal in that year's Open Championship at Royal St Geroge's, felt his best way back to the top level was through the European Challenge Tour. He confirmed it by storming through the Challenge de France Bayer at Golf Disneyland near

LUCAS PARSONS: Australian with a liking for France

MAARTEN LAFEBER: 19 under par win to start season

Paris in October, despite opening with a 76, but he had to shake off Rojas at the sixth extra hole of a marathon play-off.

Rojas, who won the Open dei Tessali in May, also lost a play-off for the Volvo Finnish Open to Paul Nilbrink of Sweden, at Espoo in July. But he was a consistent performer and deserved to secure his playing rights for the European Tour in 2000.

The same could be said of Markus Brier, from Austria, who finished third in the Challenge Tour Rankings without winning a tournament. Again, consistency was the key, finishing runner-up twice and third three times. He is looking forward to being the first Austrian member of the European Tour and hopes his success will boost golf in his homeland and encourage some young Austrians to follow in his footsteps.

The longest play-off, certainly in terms of time, was reserved for the Formby Hall Challenge in August. Two Scots, Greig Hutcheon and Alastair Forsyth, tied after 72 holes, but weather delays on the final day meant that the play-off couldn't go beyond one hole before darkness fell. The two players agreed to share the victory, but this wasn't allowed under Challenge Tour regulations. A result must be achieved for category and ranking purposes. So, the players returned to the Lancashire club 18 days later and Hutcheon triumphed with a birdie at the second extra hole.

It hoisted him into the top 15 of the Challenge Tour Rankings, a position he managed to retain by just 80 euro (£57), after a dramatic Grand Final, for which the Tour broke new ground by travelling to the Caribbean and the island of Cuba. In Suneson's absence, Pyman knew he had to win to overtake the Spaniard, but it was not to be.

So, all the attention was focussed on who would clinch a place in the season's end top 15. What transpired in a week of high winds, some torrential rain but soaring temperatures, was a dramatic victory for New Zealand's Stephen Scahill, who birdied the final two holes for a closing 70 and an 11 under par 277, shaking off playing partner, José Manuel Lara, from Spain.

Scahill's success saw him leap from 16th to fifth in the rankings, while Lara, who needed to finish alone in second place to secure his top 15 rankings spot, finished tied with Swede, Henrik Stenson. It meant that Lara finished ranked 19th, a touch of *déjà vu*, as he had written a similar story in the previous year's Grand Final in Portugal.

Lara was philosophical about his luck. "I knew I needed a birdie on the last to perhaps force a play-off, but it wasn't to be," he said. "But that's golf. I played well and now I have to look to the future." In fact, Lara had a putt of eight feet for a

339

birdie, but failed to hole out.

Scahill described his birdie-birdie finish as: "That is my whole season wrapped up in those two putts. The one at 17 had a six-foot swing, while I knew I could afford to bogey the last and still get into the top 15. So the one at 18 was a bonus. I'm pleased to be back on the European Tour after losing my card two years ago."

Lara's missed putt was a huge bonus for Hutcheon, as it kept the Scot in the 15th and final European Tour card-winning slot. Others wearing broad smiles were Denmark's Knud Storgaard, who had a closing 68, and Sweden's Johan Skold, with a 66. Missing out were three other Swedes, Raimo Sjöberg, Klas Eriksson and Eric Carlberg, who were all pushed out of the top 15.

So, when the dust settled, Suneson topped the European Challenge Tour Rankings with three victories, ahead of Pyman, who had two. Of the top 15, two were from England, while the other 13 were from different nations, eight regaining membership to the European Tour, while seven will be newcomers. It was a season for new faces, with 13 first-time winners from eight different countries.

The shot of the year undoubtedly came during the BMW Russian Open at the splendid Moscow Country Club, about 40 minutes drive from the centre of the city. The Robert Trent Jones Junior-designed layout situated in the middle of a forest, is one of the finest venues on the European Challenge Tour schedule and all of its winners have gone on to secure their cards for the European Tour. That was the case again in 1999 when Pyman triumphed, but Niels Kraay, a 27-year-old Dutchman, landed the biggest prize when he fired a four iron shot into the cup at the 197-yard eighth hole in the final round to win a BMW Five-Series car worth in excess of £40,000. Like every hole-in-one, it was a shot in a million but it could prove to be the turning point as far as Kraay is concerned, just as Morocco was for David Park.

David Hamilton

CHALLENGE TOUR RANKINGS

		€	£
1	Carl SUNESON (Sp)	69,641.80	49,744.14
2	Iain PYMAN (Eng)	56,993.00	40,709.29
3	Markus BRIER (Aus)	50,184.34	35,845.96
4	Gustavo ROJAS (Arg)	47,953.00	34,252.14
5	Stephen SCAHILL (NZ)	47,583.25	33,988.04
6	Hennie OTTO (SA)	44,023.07	31,445.05
7	Maarten LAFEBER (Hol)	39,190.45	27,993.18
8	Bradley DREDGE (Wal)	36,606.39	26,147.42
9	Benoit TEILLERIA (Fr)	34,619.74	24,728.39
10	Lucas PARSONS (Aus)	34,521.66	24,658.33
11	Didier DE VOOGHT (Bel)	33,732.65	24,094.75
12	Knud STORGAARD (Den)	33,560.94	23,972.10
13	Philip GOLDING (Eng)	32,896.79	23,497.71
14	Johan SKOLD (Swe)	31,424.13	22,445.81
15	Greig HUTCHEON (Scot)	31,027.28	22,162.34
16	Klas ERIKSSON (Swe)	30,947.63	22,105.45
17	Eric CARLBERG (Swe)	30,908.98	22,077.84
18	Raimo SJÖBERG (Swe)	30,865.87	22,047.05
19	Jose Manuel LARA (Sp)	29,030.10	20,735.79
20	Mattias ELIASSON (Swe)	27,958.09	19,970.06
21	Henrik STENSON (Swe)	27,356.47	19,540.34
22	Elliot BOULT (NZ)	26,223.25	18,730.89
23	Nils RORBAEK (Den)	24,947.40	17,819.57
24	Marc PENDARIES (Fr)	24,915.83	17,797.02
25	Thomas NORRET (Den)	23,946.70	17,104.79
26	Adam MEDNICK (Swe)	23,888.76	17,063.40
27	Patrik GOTTFRIDSON (Swe)	23,176.05	16,554.32
28	Niclas FASTH (Swe)	22,328.99	15,949.28
29	Matthew BLACKEY (Eng)	21,473.23	15,338.02
30	Ian POULTER (Eng)	21,428.10	15,305.79
31	Per G NYMAN (Swe)	21,333.03	15,237.88
32	Erol SIMSEK (Ger)	21,139.31	15,099.51
33	Kalle BRINK (Swe)	21,116.12	15,082.94
34	Andrew BUTTERFIELD (Eng)	20,735.64	14,811.17
35	Pehr MAGNEBRANT (Swe)	20,674.20	14,767.29
36	Simon HURD (Eng)	20,671.98	14,765.70
37	Ola ELIASSON (Swe)	19,390.45	13,850.32
38	David HIGGINS (Ire)	18,387.28	13,133.77
39	Fredrik HENGE (Swe)	17,912.65	12,794.75
40	Simon D. HURLEY (Eng)	17,670.74	12,621.96
41	Mikael PILTZ (Fin)	17,371.71	12,408.36
42	Martin ERLANDSSON (Swe)	16,974.73	12,124.81
43	Leif WESTERBERG (Swe)	16,429.52	11,735.37
44	Paul NILBRINK (Swe)	15,859.70	11,328.36
45	Kevin CARISSIMI (USA)	15,376.64	10,983.31
46	Grant DODD (Aus)	14,430.38	10,307.41
47	Juan CIOLA (Swi)	14,074.50	10,053.21
48	Simon WAKEFIELD (Eng)	13,998.82	9,999.16
49	David LYNN (Eng)	13,972.99	9,980.71
50	Brian NELSON (USA)	13,502.61	9,644.72
51	Dominique NOUAILHAC (Fr)	13,449.47	9,606.76
52	Gary MURPHY (Ire)	13,358.88	9,542.06
53	Richard S JOHNSON (Swe)	13,210.25	9,435.89
54	Mikael LUNDBERG (Swe)	13,020.31	9,300.22
55	Mårten OLANDER (Swe)	12,826.76	9,161.97
56	Erik ANDERSSON (Swe)	12,674.21	9,053.01
57	Sebastien DELAGRANGE (Fr)	12,380.87	8,843.48
58	Fredrik LARSSON (Swe)	12,082.87	8,630.62
59	José Manuel CARRILES (Sp)	12,079.96	8,628.54
60	Justin ROSE (Eng)	11,473.85	8,195.61
61	Daniel WESTERMARK (Swe)	11,027.72	7,876.94
62	Peter HEDBLOM (Swe)	10,584.42	7,560.30
63	Andrew CLAPP (Eng)	10,357.91	7,398.51
64	Frédéric CUPILLARD (Fr)	9,463.11	6,759.36
65	Richard BLAND (Eng)	9,405.02	6,717.87
66	Robert COLES (Eng)	9,148.92	6,534.94
67	Euan LITTLE (Scot)	9,084.45	6,488.89
68	Marcus WHEELHOUSE (NZ)	8,965.37	6,403.84
69	Ulrik GUSTAFSSON (Swe)	8,938.11	6,384.36
70	Morten BACKHAUSEN (Den)	8,831.26	6,308.04
71	Bjorn PETTERSSON (Swe)	8,793.07	6,280.76
72	Ivo GINER (Sp)	8,671.52	6,193.94
73	Grant HAMERTON (Eng)	8,562.89	6,116.35
74	Pascal EDMOND (Fra)	8,449.37	6,035.26
75	Scott WATSON (Eng)	8,309.72	5,935.51
76	Fredrik ANDERSSON (Swe)	7,915.53	5,653.95
77	Francesco GUERMANI (It)	7,825.82	5,589.87
78	Peter LAWRIE (Ire)	7,744.93	5,532.09
79	Morten HAGEN (Nor)	7,546.83	5,390.59
80	Jean Marie KULA (Fr)	7,530.56	5,378.97
81	Juan NUTT (Ven)	7,326.46	5,233.19
82	Rudi SAILER (Aus)	7,231.69	5,165.49
83	Gianluca BARUFFALDI (It)	7,225.95	5,161.39
84	Victor CASADO (Sp)	7,190.46	5,136.04
85	Marcello SANTI (It)	7,077.76	5,055.54
86	Andrew BARNETT (Wal)	7,051.00	5,036.43
87	Mark LITTON (Wal)	6,865.94	4,904.24
88	Carl WATTS (Eng)	6,545.54	4,675.39
89	Nick LUDWELL (Eng)	6,509.90	4,649.93
90	Nicolas VANHOOTEGEM (Bel)	6,395.22	4,568.01
91	Luis CLAVERIE (Sp)	6,343.69	4,531.21
92	Andrew SANDYWELL (Eng)	6,342.64	4,530.46
93	Sam LITTLE (Eng)	6,237.78	4,455.56
94	Christophe POTTIER (Fr)	5,844.74	4,174.81
95	Gary MARKS (Eng)	5,820.54	4,157.53
96	Jorgen AKER (Swe)	5,786.75	4,133.39
97	Gianluca PIETROBONO (It)	5,713.45	4,081.04
98	Jesper KJAERBYE (Den)	5,703.74	4,074.10
99	Gary CLARK (Eng)	5,675.14	4,053.67
100	Federico BISAZZA (It)	5,663.91	4,045.65

The toughest of proving grounds for new talent

Opportunity and Incentive have been the twin driving forces for all who have put their ambitions and talent to the test on the toughest of proving grounds, the European Challenge Tour, over the past 11 years.

In 1999 the opportunity factor amounted to the staging of 28 tournaments covering 17 countries, from Kenya to Cuba. And the incentive to be among the best 15 challengers went far beyond prize money. They gained promotion to the European Tour for coveted places alongside Colin Montgomerie, Open Championship winner Paul Lawrie, Masters champion José Maria Olazábal, Lee Westwood, Sergio Garcia and the many more world-class stars who will head the 2000 action.

Life on the European Challenge Tour is as hard as it gets with young hopefuls from all corners of the globe turning their make-or-break tournament career dreams into the most intense form of competition. Those who have fulfilled their dreams include Thomas Björn, the 1999 Sarazen World Open winner, Costantino Rocca and Ignacio Garrido, who graduated from the European Challenge Tour to reach the heights of Ryder Cup team selection and share ten European Tour victories to date.

But for sheer human drama, and proof positive that the European Challenge Tour is a fabulous conveyor belt of new talent, the 1999 adventures of Welshman David Park take a lot of beating. After winning the OKI Telepizza Challenge in Spain he seized the opportunity to experience the European Tour for a week through an invitation to compete in the Moroccan Open. He finished second after a play-off.

Then, as his deserved reward, came the incentive of a place in the following week's European Tour event, the Compaq European Grand Prix, and this time he captured the title to equal superstar Greg Norman's 22-year-old record of winning on only his second European Tour appearance. And there on the European Tour he now remains with his place guaranteed up to the end of the year 2001.

The tremendous progress of the European Challenge Tour, its dramas, and the achievements of its stars-of-tomorrow players are all charted, with updated biographies, records, statistics, and everything else worth knowing, in the fact-packed and illustrated **2000 European Challenge Tour Guide**. It's a must for the library of every golf follower.

Ordering a copy is simple: send a cheque for £12.50 (which includes postage and packing), made payable to the PGA European Tour, to Frances Jennings, Communications Division, European Tour, Wentworth Drive, Virginia Water, Surrey GU25 4LX - or telephone 01344 840446 with credit card details.

Year of memorable progress

Tommy Horton rules again

but he sees his dominance

coming under serious threat

The year of 1999 witnessed the moment when the European Seniors Tour's image and tone became truly universal. All 18 events were enriched by the sheer quality of performance and depth of international talent.

Andy Stubbs, Managing Director of the European Seniors Tour, said: "We have created what has become a substantial platform on which to move into the new millennium, and build for the future. Sponsors are impressed by the improved scoring on the Tour. The standard of play is getting better and better. We are benefiting from the good players coming through the European Seniors Tour Qualifying School, boosting our quality level all through the ranks.

"Our future expansion is aimed at the Continent of Europe with, for example, new events in Spain and Portugal, where we did not have one in 1999.

"Our immediate objective is to top 20 tournaments and exceed £2.5 million prize money in 2000 and, eventually, to reach our goal of filling all 24 weeks between May and the end of October."

Tommy Horton, again presented with the John Jacobs Trophy by the "Father" of the European Tour, John Jacobs OBE, for heading the European Seniors Tour Order of Merit for a record fourth successive year, and for the fifth time in all, is the first to admit that the all-round improvement in playing standards really is making it tough to stay at the top. Having retired from his long-serving role as club professional at Royal Jersey, Horton missed only one tournament on his way to 138,943 euro (£99,245) in prize money. After earning nearly one million euro (£714,000) in nine seasons with the over-50s – three times his winnings from a successful European Tour career spanning more than 30 years – he is beginning to feel the rest of the field closing up on him.

He said: "There are so many solid, experienced players coming into the Tour now, especially from America and Australia, that only the best possible golf has a chance of winning anything. We have seen that happen week after week. Just look at the low scoring again this year."

Horton's two victories – one less than the previous year – were matched by two Australians, Bob Shearer and senior rookie Ross Metherell, England's Neil Coles and Northern Ireland's Eddie Polland. Two Americans, David Oakley and another first-year senior Alan Tapie, along with Italian Alberto Croce were also among the winners.

JOHN JACOBS and **TOMMY HORTON:** *handover habit*

TOMMY HORTON: European Seniors Tour has trebled his career winnings

NEIL COLES: multiple winner commands respect of the whole golf world

For Coles, in particular, it was the further extension of an enduring talent and truly remarkable career. The European Tour pioneer, long-serving chairman of the Board of Directors, and eight-times Ryder Cup player, stretched his collection of tournament titles to a total of 44. Astonishingly, too, at the age of 65, his 98,345 euro (£70,246) for fourth place in the European Seniors Tour Order of Merit, was his most rewarding season ever. It is a record that deservedly earns him the respect of the whole golf world.

The strong American presence was underlined by the fact that four from across the Atlantic climbed into the top ten in the Seniors Tour Order of Merit. One in particular caught the eye as a challenger for most of the campaign. Jerry Bruner, who qualified in tenth spot at the Seniors Tour Qualifying School at Hardelot in 1998, was a snack food distributor until two years ago when he was persuaded to have a crack at Seniors golf. The Californian was a revelation during the summer, gaining four second place finishes and was outside the top ten only six

CHRISTY O'CONNOR JUNIOR: Senior British Open champion

ROSS METHERELL: won The Belfry PGA Seniors Championship

EDDIE POLLAND: two titles and Order of Merit runner-up

times in his 17 starts. It all added up to third spot behind Horton in the rankings with 105,243 euro (£75,173) in prize money.

Bernard Gallacher was the summer's high-profile newcomer and although he failed to make it a winning Seniors debut, the former Ryder Cup captain just about achieved his expectations.

"Not having played for a number of years I did not set my sights too high," he said. "The competition was tougher than I expected. There's a lot of travelling involved so you have to be fit to stay in control of your game. I was pleased to have made six top ten finishes."

Gallacher's best title chance came in the Greek Seniors Open in Glyfada where he shared the lead with four holes to play, before missing out on a play-off won by

Croce after four extra holes with Spain's Antonio Garrido. "I look forward to playing a lot of golf in Europe," said Gallacher. "I am a bit of a home bird and have no plans to try for a playing ticket in America. The European Seniors Tour is still growing, and I want to do all I can to help that development."

Over the past five years the Seniors Tour's flagship event, the Senior British Open at Royal Portrush, has developed a habit of creating its own special drama and storybook winners. Brian Barnes won the title twice over the famous Dunluce links, where his father-in-law Max Faulkner won the Open Championship in 1951. Two years ago, Gary Player, in his 62nd year, made it his ninth senior major title in a play-off with fellow South African, John Bland.

In 1998 Brian Huggett, at 61, scored once more for the super seniors with victory over Eddie Polland in a sudden-death play-off. But if Polland just failed to realise his dream of winning on Irish soil in front of his own people, Christy O'Connor Junior made sure he would achieve just that.

He took a break from amassing dollars on the Seniors Tour in America to clinch the famous trophy at his first attempt, less than a year after his son Darren died in a car crash. "Part of this Championship is for him," declared an emotional O'Connor. His total of six under par 282 was three better than Bland, again settling for the runners-up cheque.

For the second successive year, Horton launched the campaign with a victory. This time it was the Beko Classic

DAVID JONES: two years of consistency led to victory

in Turkey where he finished on five under par 211, three better than American newcomer Alan Tapie. For the second time in a year, John Morgan crossed the Atlantic to plunder an Irish title when he picked up the AIB Irish Seniors Open at Mount Juliet with a one-shot victory. American David Oakley, who shouldered into the European senior scene by claiming second place in the 1996 Senior British Open, finally collected a winner's cheque in the MDIS and Partners Festival of Golf at Mill Ride.

BOB SHEARER: Down Under winner of two top titles

Bob Shearer, one of a posse of formidable Australians now enjoying the Tour, collected the first of his two titles in the Philips PFA Classic at Marriott Meon Valley. He was later to win again against the beautiful backdrop of the Bad Ragaz resort in Switzerland, this time with a commanding 12 under par 198 victory in the PGA Seniors Open. One of the year's most popular winners was David Jones, the Northern Ireland professional, whose consistent form over two years had brought him three runners-up spots. He pulled off the Jersey Seniors Open at La Moye with a two-shot margin.

Eddie Polland also finally broke his winning duck at the Lawrence Batley Seniors in Huddersfield, where he built a winning total of 204 on the back of a pair of 66s in the first two rounds. The jovial Irishman rounded off the year with a two-shot victory in the prestigious Senior Tournament of Champions at the Buckinghamshire.

Alan Tapie moved into the top five in the rankings with a total of ten under par 200 for victory in the Elf Seniors Open in France and his form for the rest of the Seniors season ensured he held on to that position in the final Order of Merit.

Neil Coles proved the star turn in front of live television cameras and a huge gallery in the Energis Senior Masters at Wentworth Club. His swing was as silky as ever on the way to a winning 11 under par 205. A month later the Tour's super senior was making another winner's speech, this time at the famous Dalmahoy course where he compiled three sub-70 scores to win the Dalmahoy Scottish Seniors Open.

Senior rookie Ross Metherell, a coach of repute in Australia, took some of his own advice in assembling a 13 under par winning 200 in the De Vere Hotels Seniors Classic at Ferndown. He kept his head down again at The Belfry's PGA National course just two weeks later, winning The Belfry PGA Seniors Championship by a shot from American Bill Brask.

Horton effectively made it tough for his challengers to catch him in the rankings when he won the Monte Carlo Invitational at Mont Agel, and Warrington club professional Mike Slater, previously a breaker of three course records, realised his considerable potential with victory in the Ordina Legends in Golf in Holland.

For them individually, and for the growing European Seniors Tour as a whole, it was a memorable year of progress.

Bryan Potter

SENIORS MONEY LIST

		€	£
1	Tommy HORTON (Eng)	138,943.95	99,245.68
2	Eddie POLLAND (N. Ire)	106,977.81	76,412.72
3	Jerry BRUNER (USA)	105,243.40	75,173.86
4	Neil COLES (Eng)	98,345.15	70,246.54
5	Alan TAPIE (USA)	91,648.66	65,463.33
6	Antonio GARRIDO (Sp)	89,141.69	63,672.64
7	Bill BRASK (USA)	87,371.15	62,407.96
8	Ross METHERELL (Aus)	85,817.01	61,297.86
9	David JONES (N. Ire)	84,347.52	60,248.23
10	David OAKLEY (USA)	82,745.55	59,103.96
11	David HUISH (Scot)	79,197.50	56,569.64
12	Bob SHEARER (Aus)	75,585.17	53,989.41
13	John MORGAN (Eng)	71,996.50	51,426.07
14	Bernard GALLACHER (Scot)	71,541.33	51,100.95
15	Jim RHODES (Eng)	70,900.59	50,643.28
16	Ray CARRASCO (USA)	68,474.32	48,910.23
17	Michael SLATER (Eng)	65,433.99	46,738.56
18	Alberto CROCE (It)	65,266.47	46,618.91
19	Terry GALE (Aus)	62,627.29	44,733.78
20	Liam HIGGINS (Ire)	54,226.89	38,733.49
21	Ian STANLEY (Aus)	53,881.78	38,486.99
22	Craig DEFOY (Wal)	50,082.52	35,773.23
23	Norman WOOD (Scot)	49,977.84	35,698.46
24	Brian WAITES (Eng)	45,042.05	32,172.89
25	Agim BARDHA (Alb)	43,540.35	31,100.25
26	Brian HUGGETT (Wal)	42,091.86	30,065.61
27	Malcolm GREGSON (Eng)	38,615.78	27,582.70
28	Bob LENDZION (USA)	38,028.72	27,163.37
29	Bobby VERWEY (SA)	37,531.86	26,808.47
30	David CREAMER (Eng)	37,353.73	26,681.24
31	J.R. DELICH (USA)	36,339.16	25,956.54
32	Fritz GAMBETTA (USA)	35,845.06	25,603.61
33	Denis O'SULLIVAN (Ire)	32,598.00	23,284.29
34	Joe MCDERMOTT (Ire)	31,342.86	22,387.76
35	Noel RATCLIFFE (Aus)	30,215.94	21,582.81
36	Paul LEONARD (N. Ire)	28,302.36	20,215.97
37	Maurice BEMBRIDGE (Eng)	28,231.11	20,165.08
38	John MCTEAR (Scot)	27,134.98	19,382.13
39	Geoff PARSLOW (Aus)	26,610.17	19,007.26
40	Stewart GINN (Aus)	25,763.33	18,402.38
41	Bill HARDWICK (Can)	21,588.35	15,420.25
42	*John GRACE (USA)	21,428.13	15,305.81
43	Barry SANDRY (Eng)	21,383.02	15,273.59
44	Joe CARR (USA)	21,331.08	15,236.49
45	Bob MENNE (USA)	20,344.79	14,531.99
46	John GARNER (Eng)	20,309.03	14,506.45
47	Gordon MACDONALD (Scot)	19,999.68	14,285.49
48	Jay DOLAN III (USA)	18,671.68	13,336.91
49	Tony JACKLIN (Eng)	18,651.38	13,322.41
50	John FOURIE (SA)	17,354.85	12,396.32

Where prospects start to thrive at 50 and over

While Tommy Horton and Christy O'Connor Junior keep winning, and Neil Coles, at 65, continues to add year after year to his great collection of titles, who can deny that the most enduring talents in golf are to be found on the ever-expanding European Seniors Tour.

The pioneering spirit thrives and prospers on the over-50s Tour where the rejuvenated ambitions of stars in the past have created a fresh and exciting future for them all.

And their enthusiasm, linked to old-fashioned grace and respect for the game of golf, guarantees the friendliest but still intensely competitive tournaments to be enjoyed by increasing galleries and growing TV audiences.

The proud progress of the European Seniors Tour, and the achievements of its international force of challengers, right to the finish of the 1999 season, are fully chronicled in the sixth edition of the **European Seniors Tour Official Guide**.

Packed with updated biographies, records, statistics adding up to thousands of facts, the illustrated guide makes an invaluable work of reference to enhance any golf library.

Ordering a copy of the **2000 European Seniors Tour Official Guide** is simple.

Send a cheque for £12.50 (which includes postage and packing), made payable to the PGA European Tour, to Frances Jennings, Communications Division, European Tour, Wentworth Drive, Virginia Water, Surrey GU25 4LX, or telephone 01344 840446 with credit card details.

Young shoulders, wise heads

The mixture that makes
MacGregor Week an
Academy of Excellence

The truly admirable trait among devotees of the royal and ancient game is their constant eagerness to help others who wish to improve. It is a self-less disposition that can be perceived among weekend golfers as well as the greatest exponents of the sport.

When such willingness is backed by almost 100 years of collective experience of those passing on that wisdom, the results can be compelling. This, then, is

TOMMY HORTON: gifting experience to Max Anglert and Mårten Olander

JOHN PARAMOR: so you want a free drop?

JOHN ENNISLAND (MACGREGOR) AND DARREN CLARKE: building relationships

the significance of the MacGregor Week (The European Tour Training School) at San Roque in southern Spain in which some extremely wise old heads meet up with some very willing and eager young shoulders.

It has been described as the ultimate basic training for aspiring tournament professionals because all aspects of their chosen career as well as their own abilities – strengths and weaknesses – are assessed and analysed by the most distinguished and accomplished experts in each field.

And it works supremely well because past graduates of the week include Thomas Björn, David Carter, Andrew Coltart, Mathias Grönberg, Vijay Singh, Sven Strüver, Lee Westwood and many

HAROLD SWASH, TOMMY HORTON, JOHN JACOBS, DENIS PUGH: making the jigsaw fit

PER NYMAN: warning of things to come

1998 Volvo Masters winner Darren Clarke as well as 1996 Peugeot Open de España champion Padraig Harrington.

The great strength of the week is that every piece of the jigsaw that goes to making a complete golfer is scrutinised fully from basic technique to general fitness, psychology, rules procedures, media interviews and business deals. Moreover, the new candidates are able to meet the proven experts in these skills in a completely informal and, if required, confidential atmosphere.

others who have all moved on to make considerable impact on the international golf arena.

More than this, the expertise available is of such high quality that even established stars slip back for a pre-season check-up during MacGregor Week and indeed the 20 aspirants who made their way via the European Tour Qualifying School and the European Challenge Tour to a much-sought-after place at this elite academy of excellence in January found themselves in the company of the Masters Tournament winner José Maria Olazábal,

Olazábal reflected: "The general assistance to the young players here is crucial in the sense they will learn a lot of things that I did not have the chance to learn when I started. It would have made life much easier for my generation if we could have done this."

But just as important as the instruction is the demonstration of skills that accompanies it. Tommy Horton, who introduced the concept of a school for young professionals back in 1977, is acknowledged to be one of the game's great exponents of the short game and left his pupils at the San Roque Suites Hotel complex wide-eyed in wonderment at some of the strokes he fashioned for them.

Andrew Raitt, an Anglo-Scot who graduated from the University of Nevada and was the 1998 British Assistants' champion, said: "You reach this level and think you know a fair bit about it. Then you see Tommy pitch off a bare lie with a six iron and see what a different game they play. It is quite fantastic."

Certainly, it would be difficult to come away from the MacGregor Week without acquiring some broader knowledge and development of skills, particularly after working in the close company of the venerable John Jacobs, unquestionably the most influential golfing tutor of

ROB NOTHMAN: welcome to BBC 5 Live

his generation who has guided many careers including that of Olazábal.

The list of distinguished experts also included Denis Pugh, who has worked with Colin Montgomerie and Frank Nobilo; sports psychologist Alan Fine, who has helped Montgomerie and David Feherty; Guy Delacave, Head Physiotherapist for the European Tour; Harold Swash, the game's foremost expert on putting techniques, as well as sports scientist Helen Lennon. Add to that an on-the-spot rules quiz by European Tour Chief Referee John Paramor plus an exhaustive grilling from press, radio and television reporters and it was clear the new candidates were left in little doubt what to expect when they emerged on Tour.

Sweden's Per Nyman gave early warning of things to come when he produced a superlative 65 over the neighbouring Valderrama course, venue of the 1997 Ryder Cup, and covered the closing six holes in six under par to take the £1,500 top prize in the MacGregor Challenge and collect an invitation from the Japanese owners of San Roque to compete in the Acom International Open later in the season.

Each player also received a complete analysis of his round from the Axa Performance Data statistics system and was therefore able to assess which areas of his game needed improvement, although Nyman, with 24 putts in his round after a lesson from Swash, must have been well aware of one particular strength.

For the newcomers, the MacGregor Week offers a priceless insight into the world they are about to join. George O'Grady, Deputy Executive Director of the European Tour, told them they were about to become members of a "family" in which everyone shares a sense of involvement in the week-to-week pursuit of success.

William Marsh, President and Chief Executive Officer of MacGregor Golf which sponsors the venture, defined the unique value of the week thus: "It gives us an opportunity to build relationships with the Tour, the players and people who manage the Tour. It gives us direct feedback to continuously enhance our performance as a company. Through this week we can add something to the game of golf." So, too, can the Class of '99 as they add to the list of honours already achieved.

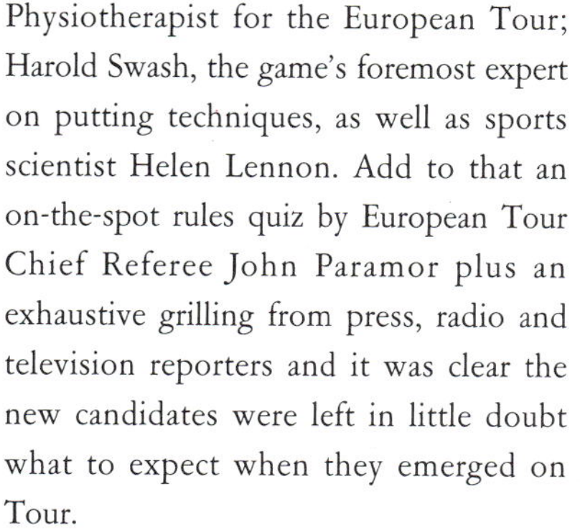

JOSÉ MARIA OLAZÁBAL: a classroom tip from the Master

Michael McDonnell

Friendship in faraway places

The "Olympics of Golf" unites nations
and spreads increasing goodwill
with a wonderful history of tradition

The World Cup of Golf, first played as the Canada Cup in 1953, attained the proud tradition of being hosted by no fewer than 23 different countries when in 1999 it was played on the exclusive Mines Resort City course, in Kuala Lumpur, Malaysia.

This continued at the end of the millennium the fine record of the World Cup being taken to faraway places. The event was the brainchild of John Jay Hopkins, a wealthy Canadian industrialist, visionary and keen golfer. He was appalled by the atrocities and horrors of the Second World War. He felt there had to be a way to unite nations in friendship, and decided on golf being the best vehicle. He formed the International Golf Association and decided that his new tournament would be called the Canada Cup. It was changed to the World Cup of Golf in 1967, some 11 years after his death.

It has been stated that no tournament has done more to popularise the game internationally than the World Cup. The participation of lesser golfing nations has always been of paramount importance. Only seven nations competed in the first championship, won by the Argentinean team of Roberto de Vicenzo and Antonio Cerda, but from that moment the competition began to spread the gospel of the game to all corners of the globe. Gary Player, who has represented South Africa 16 times in the World Cup, said: "I have

phenomenal memories of the World Cup. It has taken great players to places where they wouldn't have gone otherwise. Today, golf is big in many of these

NICK FALDO and DAVID CARTER: 1998 winners for England

MINES RESORT & GOLF CLUB: spectacular 1999 host venue in Malaysia

countries and a lot of credit for that must go to the World Cup."

During its history, the World Cup has been played in countries like China, Venezuela, Thailand and Indonesia with remarkable success, and in 1999 the International Golf Association chose Malaysia, a bustling and industrious nation, to host the competition. Malaysia and golf go back a long way. One of its most famous clubs, Royal Selangor, recently celebrated its centenary, and its players have performed regularly in the World Cup since 1969.

The Mines Resort City course, designed by Robert Trent Jones Junior, followed on as host venue from Gulf Harbour, Auckland, New Zealand, where in 1998 David Carter and Nick Faldo made history when they won the World Cup of Golf for England for the first time since the competition began. Faldo, winner of three Open Championships and three Masters Tournaments, posted a superb eight under par total of 280, and Carter concluded an outstanding World Cup by holing a birdie putt of 18 feet on the 18th green. Faldo said: "When you look at the great names on the trophy then you know this is something special

COLIN MONTGOMERIE: International Trophy winner 1997

PAUL McGINLEY and PADRAIG HARRINGTON: 1997 winners for Ireland

Americans dominated the event in the 1960s when Nicklaus and Palmer reigned supreme and, more recently, following such successes as those by Spain (1976, 1977, 1982, and 1984), Canada (1980 and 1985), Wales (1987), Australia (1989), Germany (1990) and Sweden (1991), Fred Couples and Davis Love III teamed to provide glory for the United States again in 1992, 1993, 1994, and 1995. In fact, in 1995 the World Cup of Golf took a huge step forward when it went to the People's Republic of China, so becoming the first major international golfing event to be held in mainland China, and it was there that Couples and Love established a notable record by becoming the first partnership in the history of the event to win four years in succession. This historic moment was sealed at Mission Hills, on the outskirts of Shenzhen, and history was made again a year later in 1996 when 80,000 people saw local heroes Ernie Els and Wayne Westner storm to a landslide victory for South Africa at Erinvale on the outskirts of Cape Town.

The Kiawah Island Resort, host to the 1991 Ryder Cup, in South Carolina, provided the setting for Padraig Harrington and Paul McGinley to capture the 1997 World Cup of Golf for Ireland, ahead of Scotland, for whom Colin Montgomerie was in majestic form. He put together scores of 68-66-66-66 to win the International Trophy for the individual low scorer.

to win. We are talking of great eras from Ben Hogan and Sam Snead to Jack Nicklaus and Arnold Palmer and so on."

During its glittering history the World Cup of Golf has been won by the United States on 21 occasions, the first time being 1955 when Chick Harbert and Ed Furgol triumphed by nine shots. The

The World Cup of Golf has a wonderful history of tradition, and in the last decade or so the European Tour has been directly involved with the competition. During that time, Burch Riber, as Executive Director of the International Golf Association, has seen that the tradition has been continued and in addition David Ciclitira, Chairman and Chief Executive of the Parallel Media Group, has successfully and innovatively promoted the event.

Now the World Cup of Golf advances with the game of golf into the new millennium, and it does so with a special foundation shaped in 1953 with such vision that the competition has earned the title of "The Olympics of Golf".

FRED COUPLES and DAVIS LOVE III: America's record holders

Mitchell Platts

ERNIE ELS and WAYNE WESTNER: 1996 winners watched by 80,000 spectators

Asprey & Garrard
Golfer of the Month
Awards 1999

Colin Montgomerie, Golfer of the Month in May and September, receives a silver salver from
Edward Asprey, Corporate Director of Asprey & Garrard

The Asprey & Garrard Golfer of the Year Award comprises ten monthly awards and an annual award which is to be announced.
Previous winners have been:

1998 Lee Westwood	1993 Bernhard Langer	1988 Severiano Ballesteros
1997 Colin Montgomerie	1992 Nick Faldo	1987 Ian Woosnam
1996 Colin Montgomerie	1991 Severiano Ballesteros	1986 Severiano Ballesteros
1995 Colin Montgomerie	1990 Nick Faldo	1985 Bernhard Langer
1994 Ernie Els	1989 Nick Faldo	

Ernie Els
(above left)
JANUARY

David Howell
(above)
FEBRUARY

Miguel Angel Jiménez
(above right)
MARCH and OCTOBER

José Maria Olazábal
(centre left)
APRIL

Colin Montgomerie
MAY and SEPTEMBER

David Park
(centre right)
JUNE

Paul Lawrie
(below left)
JULY

Sergio Garcia
(below right)
AUGUST

Quality guides expansion

The new Marquess Course at Woburn
and PGA Golf de Catalunya
signpost the exciting way ahead

Record crowds, basking in the sunshine, enjoyed an outstanding Victor Chandler British Masters when the tournament returned to The Duke's Course at Woburn Golf and Country Club in August. American Bob May captured his maiden professional title, edging out Colin Montgomerie, in a week which provided PGA European Tour Courses with good cause to celebrate.

It was in April, 1997, that PGA European Tour Courses entered into a joint venture with Woburn Golf and Country Club. The British Masters had not been played on the superb Duke's Course since 1994 but now, with a new sponsor, Victor Chandler, at the helm for a minimum of five years, the Championship returned to Woburn where it will remain long into the millennium.

What is more, the return to Woburn provided the professionals, some of whom played the course, with an opportunity to take a first look at the new Marquess Course which sits just across the lane from the Duke's and Duchess courses.

The Duke's and Duchess courses are well established, and with the Marquess Course, which will be officially opened in June, 2000, will make Woburn Golf and Country Club, one of the most famous names in British golf,

also one of the few 54-hole venues in England.

The Marquess Course has been designed by Ross McMurray, of European Golf Design, in association with Peter Alliss, Clive Clark and Alex Hay. Measuring 7,223 yards, the undulating fairways thread their way through magnificent pines, chestnuts and oaks. The greenside bunkers place the premium on accuracy, and the rolling greens provide a variety of pin positions.

BBC television commentator Alex Hay, former Club Professional and then Managing Director of Woburn, says: "For the last 12 years I have believed that this Estate hid what could surely be one of golf's finest gems. Now with the creation of the Marquess Course, so named after Lord Tavistock who first brought golf to Woburn, I can sit back and say 'I told you so', for without doubt the magnificent course being constructed is destined to become one of the finest, not just in Europe, but anywhere."

Some observers who have walked the course regard The Marquess as the "Augusta National of England", and there can be no question that PGA European

Tour Courses have seriously added to their portfolio with the growth of Woburn Golf and Country Club in addition to the arrival of PGA Golf de Catalunya in Spain.

The Sarazen World Open provided a wonderful start for PGA Golf de Catalunya as a venue for European Tour events when it unfolded there in October with Denmark's Thomas Björn taking the title. PGA Golf de Catalunya, lying 45 minutes north east of Barcelona in the La Selva region, close to Girona, is the newest facility to be opened for play. It was designed by Angel Gallardo and Neil Coles, two men with illustrious playing careers on the European Tour and with equally illustrious credentials as golf course architects. Between them they have created a very special golfers' haven on land dense with cork, oak and pine trees, with the mountains of Montseny to the west and vistas of the Pyrenees to the north. Overall, the course measures 7,204 yards from the back tees.

Gallardo, who is Vice-chairman of the PGA European Tour Board of Directors, first set eyes on the land ten years ago when he was approached by the Royal Automobile Club of Catalunya to assess its feasibility as a golf course. "When I first visited the site," says Gallardo, "the sheer size of the land was staggering. It was dense

PGA European Tour Courses PLC

with vegetation and it was difficult to visualise anything. I spoke to Neil Coles and we eventually arrived at our preferred clubhouse position and were able to route the holes to return to the clubhouse. Before the course was finished I had already played each hole in my mind, analysed each drive and approach shot, how the greens should slope, the reward for a good shot and the penalty for a bad one."

Neil Coles, MBE, who is Chairman of the PGA European Tour Board of Directors, and whose playing career stretches back over 40 years, concurs with Gallardo to say: "The site is very attractive

Courses continues to expand and is in discussion with a number of UK and European projects. The first of these to come to fruition will be the opening of a new resort in Germany in May 2000. "Fleesensee Hotels and Sports" will be a resort that encompasses over 600 rooms, four golf courses, 17 tennis courts, and a state-of-the-art "Wellness" centre. The hotels involved include a luxury Radisson Hotel, a Robinson family hotel and the Dorfhotel group. PGA European Tour Courses will manage the sports facilities. The golf courses will offer different types of challenges for different standards of play. There will be two tournament

opment and management of golf courses that can host professional tournaments under the auspices of the European Tour. The aim of the Company is to expand and develop golf facilities throughout Europe that not only provide a championship test for professionals but also offer outstanding amenities for the visiting golfer. This philosophy is implemented at their four flagship courses, Kungsängen in Sweden, Quinta do Lago in Portugal, Woburn Golf and Country Club and PGA Golf de Catalunya.

The policy of expansion and development that underlines PGA European Tour Courses's approach has been further

Quinta do Lago

THE MARQUESS COURSE: destined to become one of the finest anywhere

PGA GOLF DE CATALUNYA

with mature cork, oak trees, firs and heathers and the undulating terrain offered some interesting hole options. We designed the course with a number of elevated tee positions which provide some spectacular views. With most courses you have to create spectator mounding, the setting of this course gave us all the viewing locations that are needed for a major tournament."

PGA Golf de Catalunya is destined to take its place as one of the finest golf resorts in Europe. It has full clubhouse facilities, bars and restaurants, a driving range, putting greens and a golf academy. The opening last June marked the completion of the first stage of the plan which incorporates a second golf course, a 200-room hotel, and residential villas.

Meanwhile, PGA European Tour

courses with short game areas, putting greens and a Golfodrom driving range. There will also be a par 67 academy course, and 18 holes of "short golf" aimed at beginners, juniors and families.

Racquet sports will also be well represented with eight indoor and nine outdoor courts and three squash courts. All the facilities will share common telecommunications equipment allowing the visitor to travel freely around the resort, charging their room with any on-site goods or service. The resort is located between Berlin and Hamburg, close to the Müritz National Park. This area is already popular with tourists and Fleesensee will help attract even more visitors to the region.

PGA European Tour Courses is uniquely placed for the ownership, devel-

emphasised by Ken Schofield, Executive Director of the PGA European Tour. He summarises: "The development of European Tour Courses signifies not only our desire to enter the 21st Century with a strong portfolio of courses, but also to design and refine our own courses for Tour competition. This will support our policy to provide the best possible courses for play on the European Tour, the European Seniors Tour and the European Challenge Tour. PGA Golf de Catalunya is a case in point; the newest course in the portfolio, designed by Neil Coles and Angel Gallardo, and set on undulating land. We feel confident it challenges the best players in the world and we feel the same about The Marquess Course at Woburn Golf and Country Club."

Mitchell Platts   361

AXA
PERFORMANCE DATA[SM]

FOR THE 1999 EUROPEAN TOUR SEASON

STROKE AVERAGE

1	Colin MONTGOMERIE (Scot)	(76)	69.59
2	Sergio GARCIA (Sp)	(46)	70.28
3	Miguel Angel JIMÉNEZ (Sp)	(80)	70.30
4	Lee WESTWOOD (Eng)	(68)	70.44
5	Retief GOOSEN (SA)	(101)	70.49
	Bob MAY (USA)	(88)	70.49
7	Eduardo ROMERO (Arg)	(59)	70.85
	Gary ORR (Scot)	(107)	70.85
9	Padraig HARRINGTON (Ire)	(94)	70.88
10	Mark MCNULTY (Zim)	(66)	70.91
11	Angel CABRERA (Arg)	(84)	70.92
12	Peter O'MALLEY (Aus)	(72)	70.99
13	Michael CAMPBELL (NZ)	(78)	71.01
14	Alex CEJKA (Ger)	(110)	71.04
15	Ernie ELS (SA)	(41)	71.05
16	Robert KARLSSON (Swe)	(80)	71.11
17	Darren CLARKE (N.Ire)	(74)	71.12
	Greg TURNER (NZ)	(74)	71.12
	Jamie SPENCE (Eng)	(89)	71.12
20	Bernhard LANGER (Ger)	(78)	71.14
21	Paul LAWRIE (Scot)	(88)	71.15
22	Ian WOOSNAM (Wal)	(72)	71.19
23	Ian GARBUTT (Eng)	(98)	71.22
24	Emanuele CANONICA (It)	(76)	71.25
25	Gary EVANS (Eng)	(98)	71.26
	Jean VAN DE VELDE (Fr)	(100)	71.26
27	Stephen LEANEY (Aus)	(72)	71.28
	John BICKERTON (Eng)	(102)	71.28
29	Peter MITCHELL (Eng)	(95)	71.29
30	Thomas BJÖRN (Den)	(77)	71.31
31	Jarmo SANDELIN (Swe)	(86)	71.35
32	Mark ROE (Eng)	(59)	71.36
	Jeev Milkha SINGH (Ind)	(78)	71.36
34	Russell CLAYDON (Eng)	(74)	71.38
35	Ignacio GARRIDO (Sp)	(96)	71.43
	David CARTER (Eng)	(93)	71.43
	Paul MCGINLEY (Ire)	(92)	71.43
38	Steve WEBSTER (Eng)	(85)	71.46
39	Diego BORREGO (Sp)	(64)	71.48
	Andrew COLTART (Scot)	(99)	71.48
41	Paul BROADHURST (Eng)	(94)	71.50
42	Costantino ROCCA (It)	(100)	71.51
43	Jarrod MOSELEY (Aus)	(68)	71.54
44	Peter BAKER (Eng)	(98)	71.59
45	Ricardo GONZALEZ (Arg)	(80)	71.60
46	Steen TINNING (Den)	(76)	71.61
	Peter SENIOR (Aus)	(36)	71.61
48	Miguel Angel MARTIN (Sp)	(83)	71.63
	Anthony WALL (Eng)	(101)	71.63
50	Francisco CEA (Sp)	(88)	71.65
51	David GILFORD (Eng)	(78)	71.67
52	John SENDEN (Aus)	(70)	71.69
53	Peter LONARD (Aus)	(48)	71.71
54	Nick O'HERN (Aus)	(60)	71.72
	Roger WINCHESTER (Eng)	(82)	71.72
56	Jean-Francois REMESY (Fr)	(66)	71.73
57	José Maria OLAZABAL (Sp)	(48)	71.75
58	Santiago LUNA (Sp)	(84)	71.76
59	Phillip PRICE (Wal)	(87)	71.77
60	Christopher HANELL (Swe)	(86)	71.79
	Dean ROBERTSON (Scot)	(97)	71.79
62	David PARK (Wal)	(48)	71.81
63	Pierre FULKE (Swe)	(84)	71.82
64	Des SMYTH (Ire)	(77)	71.83
65	Mark JAMES (Eng)	(76)	71.84
66	Lian-Wei ZHANG (PRC)	(26)	71.85
	Marc FARRY (Fr)	(95)	71.85
68	Per-Ulrik JOHANSSON (Swe)	(64)	71.86
69	José COCERES (Arg)	(68)	71.87
70	David HOWELL (Eng)	(96)	71.91
	Gary EMERSON (Eng)	(57)	71.91
72	Massimo SCARPA (It)	(82)	71.96
73	Geoff OGILVY (Aus)	(60)	71.97
	Thomas LEVET (Fr)	(96)	71.97
	Patrik SJÖLAND (Swe)	(72)	71.97
76	Mathias GRÖNBERG (Swe)	(73)	71.99
	Roger WESSELS (SA)	(82)	71.99
78	Søren KJELDSEN (Den)	(98)	72.00
	José RIVERO (Sp)	(72)	72.00
	Barry LANE (Eng)	(85)	72.00
81	Craig HAINLINE (USA)	(66)	72.02
82	Andrew MCLARDY (SA)	(78)	72.04
83	Paul EALES (Eng)	(84)	72.05
84	Katsuyoshi TOMORI (Jpn)	(60)	72.07
85	Anders HANSEN (Den)	(90)	72.09
86	Domingo HOSPITAL (Sp)	(67)	72.10
87	Paolo QUIRICI (Swi)	(84)	72.12
	Stephen GALLACHER (Scot)	(84)	72.12
89	Andrew OLDCORN (Scot)	(86)	72.22
90	Thomas GÖGELE (Ger)	(84)	72.23
91	Stephen FIELD (Eng)	(72)	72.24
	Daren LEE (Eng)	(74)	72.24
	Miles TUNNICLIFF (Eng)	(86)	72.24
94	Fredrik LINDGREN (Swe)	(70)	72.26
	Lucas PARSONS (Aus)	(27)	72.26
96	Andrew RAITT (Eng)	(76)	72.29
97	Mats LANNER (Swe)	(71)	72.30
98	Sven STRÜVER (Ger)	(90)	72.31
	Joakim HAEGGMAN (Swe)	(70)	72.31
100	Jorge BERENDT (Arg)	(60)	72.33

( ) = rounds played

DRIVING ACCURACY (%)

1	Francisco CEA (Sp)	(88)	80.1
2	Richard GREEN (Aus)	(62)	79.9
3	Miguel Angel JIMÉNEZ (Sp)	(80)	76.9
4	Pierre FULKE (Swe)	(84)	76.6
5	Ian HUTCHINGS (SA)	(68)	76.4
	Stephen BENNETT (Eng)	(48)	76.4
7	Mark MCNULTY (Zim)	(66)	75.8
8	Jean-Francois REMESY (Fr)	(66)	74.7
9	Andrew OLDCORN (Scot)	(86)	74.5
10	Lee WESTWOOD (Eng)	(68)	74.0
11	Des SMYTH (Ire)	(77)	73.9
12	Daren LEE (Eng)	(74)	73.7
13	Pedro LINHART (Sp)	(59)	73.6
14	Tony JOHNSTONE (Zim)	(56)	73.2
15	Anders HANSEN (Den)	(90)	73.1
	Phillip PRICE (Wal)	(87)	73.1
	Henrik NYSTROM (Swe)	(56)	73.1
18	Peter O'MALLEY (Aus)	(72)	72.6
19	Warren BENNETT (Eng)	(63)	72.4
20	Gary ORR (Scot)	(107)	72.3

DRIVING DISTANCE (YDS)

1	Emanuele CANONICA (It)	(76)	295.5
2	Geoff OGILVY (Aus)	(60)	292.4
3	Angel CABRERA (Arg)	(84)	287.2
4	Alberto BINAGHI (It)	(66)	286.3
5	Ernie ELS (SA)	(41)	286.2
6	Sergio GARCIA (Sp)	(46)	285.8
7	Ricardo GONZALEZ (Arg)	(80)	282.2
8	Marcello SANTI (It)	(52)	282.1
9	Stephen ALLAN (Aus)	(64)	281.8
10	Jarmo SANDELIN (Swe)	(86)	281.6
11	Stephen GALLACHER (Scot)	(84)	281.3
12	Santiago LUNA (Sp)	(84)	280.9
13	Mark PILKINGTON (Wal)	(44)	280.8
14	Darren CLARKE (N.Ire)	(74)	280.1
15	Ignacio GARRIDO (Sp)	(96)	279.9
16	Andrew RAITT (Eng)	(76)	279.8
17	Retief GOOSEN (SA)	(101)	279.5
18	Per HAUGSRUD (Nor)	(52)	279.4
19	Paolo QUIRICI (Swi)	(84)	279.2
20	Marc FARRY (Fr)	(95)	278.3

Sand Saves (%)

1	Tony JOHNSTONE (Zim)	(56)	80.7
2	Stephen BENNETT (Eng)	(48)	78.0
3	Severiano BALLESTEROS (Sp)	(50)	75.4
4	Bernhard LANGER (Ger)	(78)	73.5
5	Trevor IMMELMAN (SA)	(30)	72.0
6	Olle KARLSSON (Swe)	(56)	70.8
7	Sergio GARCIA (Sp)	(46)	70.7
8	Miguel Angel JIMÉNEZ (Sp)	(80)	68.5
	Ricardo GONZALEZ (Arg)	(80)	68.5
10	Costantino ROCCA (It)	(100)	68.3
11	Justin ROSE (Eng)	(38)	67.4
12	Colin MONTGOMERIE (Scot)	(76)	66.7
13	Pedro LINHART (Sp)	(59)	66.3
14	Jean-Francois REMESY (Fr)	(66)	66.2
15	Greg TURNER (NZ)	(74)	65.9
16	John BICKERTON (Eng)	(102)	64.8
17	Peter SENIOR (Aus)	(36)	63.2
18	Per NYMAN (Swe)	(80)	63.0
19	José COCERES (Arg)	(68)	62.8
20	Gary EVANS (Eng)	(98)	62.7
	Christian CÉVAER (Fr)	(47)	62.7
22	Ignacio GARRIDO (Sp)	(96)	62.6
23	Peter LONARD (Aus)	(48)	61.6
	Alberto BINAGHI (It)	(66)	61.6
25	John SENDEN (Aus)	(70)	61.5
	Francis VALERA (Sp)	(46)	61.5
27	Des SMYTH (Ire)	(77)	61.2
28	José Maria OLAZABAL (Sp)	(48)	61.1
29	Steve WEBSTER (Eng)	(85)	60.0
30	Mark MOULAND (Wal)	(82)	59.7

Greens in Regulation (%)

1	Colin MONTGOMERIE (Scot)	(76)	79.3
2	Lee WESTWOOD (Eng)	(68)	76.2
3	Miguel Angel JIMÉNEZ (Sp)	(80)	75.9
4	Peter BAKER (Eng)	(98)	75.7
5	Ian GARBUTT (Eng)	(98)	75.6
	Ernie ELS (SA)	(41)	75.6
7	Bernhard LANGER (Ger)	(78)	74.2
8	Francisco CEA (Sp)	(88)	74.1
9	Bob MAY (USA)	(88)	74.0
10	Angel CABRERA (Arg)	(84)	73.7
11	Sergio GARCIA (Sp)	(46)	73.3
	Emanuele CANONICA (It)	(76)	73.3
	Gary ORR (Scot)	(107)	73.3
14	Padraig HARRINGTON (Ire)	(94)	72.6
	Pierre FULKE (Swe)	(84)	72.6
16	Costantino ROCCA (It)	(100)	72.3
17	Steve WEBSTER (Eng)	(85)	72.1
18	Peter O'MALLEY (Aus)	(72)	72.0
	Mark MCNULTY (Zim)	(66)	72.0
20	Per-Ulrik JOHANSSON (Swe)	(64)	71.9
	Jesus Maria ARRUTI (Sp)	(54)	71.9
22	Peter MITCHELL (Eng)	(95)	71.7
	Eduardo ROMERO (Arg)	(59)	71.7
	Per HAUGSRUD (Nor)	(52)	71.7
25	David CARTER (Eng)	(93)	71.3
	John SENDEN (Aus)	(70)	71.3
27	Paul MCGINLEY (Ire)	(92)	71.1
	Mark JAMES (Eng)	(76)	71.1
29	Ian WOOSNAM (Wal)	(72)	71.0
30	Thomas BJÖRN (Den)	(77)	70.9

Colin Montgomerie

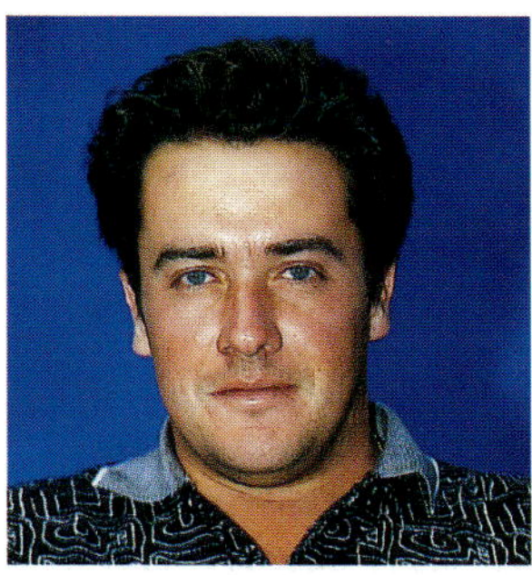

Francisco Cea

Emanuele Canonica

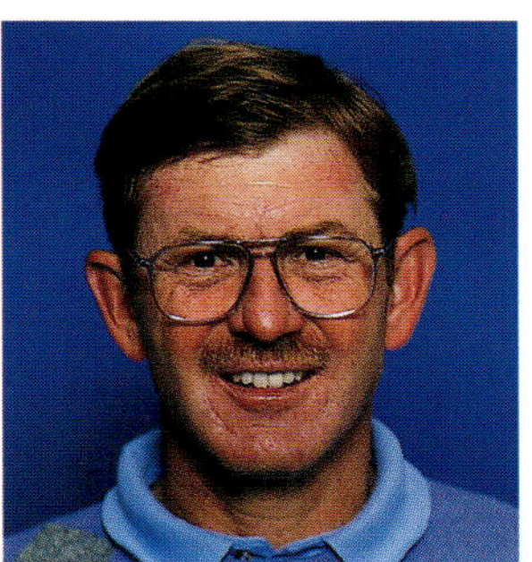

Tony Johnstone

Severiano Ballesteros

Average Putts Per Round

1	Severiano BALLESTEROS (Sp)	(50)	28.1
2	Gary EVANS (Eng)	(98)	28.4
3	Pedro LINHART (Sp)	(59)	28.6
4	Per NYMAN (Swe)	(80)	28.7
	Jarmo SANDELIN (Swe)	(86)	28.7
	Mark ROE (Eng)	(59)	28.7
	Dean ROBERTSON (Scot)	(97)	28.7
8	Henrik BJORNSTAD (Nor)	(51)	28.8
	Paul BROADHURST (Eng)	(94)	28.8
	David HOWELL (Eng)	(96)	28.8
11	Jarrod MOSELEY (Aus)	(68)	29.0
	Jamie SPENCE (Eng)	(89)	29.0
13	Roger WESSELS (SA)	(82)	29.1
14	David PARK (Wal)	(48)	29.2
	Retief GOOSEN (SA)	(101)	29.2
	Christopher HANELL (Swe)	(86)	29.2
	Mats HALLBERG (Swe)	(54)	29.2
	Greg TURNER (NZ)	(74)	29.2
19	Robert LEE (Eng)	(34)	29.3
	Paul LAWRIE (Scot)	(88)	29.3
	Russell CLAYDON (Eng)	(74)	29.3
	Robert KARLSSON (Swe)	(80)	29.3
	John MELLOR (Eng)	(85)	29.3
	Stephen BENNETT (Eng)	(48)	29.3
	Olle KARLSSON (Swe)	(56)	29.3
	Daniel CHOPRA (Swe)	(86)	29.3
	Andrew COLTART (Scot)	(99)	29.3
28	Jean VAN DE VELDE (Fr)	(100)	29.4
	Patrik SJÖLAND (Swe)	(72)	29.4
	José Maria OLAZABAL (Sp)	(48)	29.4
	Marc FARRY (Fr)	(95)	29.4

Putts Per Green in Regulation

1	Severiano BALLESTEROS (Sp)	(50)	1.724
2	Jamie SPENCE (Eng)	(89)	1.747
3	Robert KARLSSON (Swe)	(80)	1.750
4	Gary EVANS (Eng)	(98)	1.752
5	Miguel Angel JIMÉNEZ (Sp)	(80)	1.753
	Mark ROE (Eng)	(59)	1.753
7	David HOWELL (Eng)	(96)	1.754
8	Jarmo SANDELIN (Swe)	(86)	1.755
9	Darren CLARKE (N.Ire)	(74)	1.756
	Russell CLAYDON (Eng)	(74)	1.756
11	Paul BROADHURST (Eng)	(94)	1.757
	Thomas BJÖRN (Den)	(77)	1.757
13	Retief GOOSEN (SA)	(101)	1.758
14	Jarrod MOSELEY (Aus)	(68)	1.759
15	Per NYMAN (Swe)	(80)	1.760
16	Ernie ELS (SA)	(41)	1.762
17	Patrik SJÖLAND (Swe)	(72)	1.763
	Colin MONTGOMERIE (Scot)	(76)	1.763
	Mark MCNULTY (Zim)	(66)	1.763
20	Paul LAWRIE (Scot)	(88)	1.764
	Ian WOOSNAM (Wal)	(72)	1.764
22	Wayne WESTNER (SA)	(35)	1.765
23	Bernhard LANGER (Ger)	(78)	1.766
24	David PARK (Wal)	(48)	1.768
25	Dean ROBERTSON (Scot)	(97)	1.769
26	Diego BORREGO (Sp)	(64)	1.770
27	Alex CEJKA (Ger)	(110)	1.772
	Roger WESSELS (SA)	(82)	1.772
	Paul MCGINLEY (Ire)	(92)	1.772
	Henrik BJORNSTAD (Nor)	(51)	1.772

Volvo Order of Merit 1999

Pos	Name & Country		Total Prize Money €	£
1	Colin MONTGOMERIE (Scot)	(21)	1822880.08	1302057.20
2	Lee WESTWOOD (Eng)	(21)	1320804.83	943432.02
3	Sergio GARCIA (Sp)	(12)	1317693.32	941209.51
4	Miguel Angel JIMÉNEZ (Sp)	(23)	1148289.78	820206.99
5	Retief GOOSEN (SA)	(28)	1059984.62	757131.87
6	Paul LAWRIE (Scot)	(26)	901452.75	643894.82
7	Padraig HARRINGTON (Ire)	(25)	855162.96	610830.69
8	Darren CLARKE (N.Ire)	(22)	731290.71	522350.51
9	Jarmo SANDELIN (Swe)	(24)	629131.97	449379.98
10	Angel CABRERA (Arg)	(22)	622852.05	444894.32

Lee Westwood

Colin Montgomerie

Pos	Name & Country		€	£
11	Bob MAY (USA)	(24)	609662.45	435473.18
12	Ernie ELS (SA)	(13)	588359.51	420256.79
13	Jean VAN DE VELDE (Fr)	(27)	583087.01	416490.72
14	Thomas BJÖRN (Den)	(24)	546934.90	390667.79
15	Bernhard LANGER (Ger)	(24)	496607.92	354719.94
16	Jarrod MOSELEY (Aus)	(21)	493939.62	352814.01
17	Alex CEJKA (Ger)	(29)	490493.41	350352.44
18	Mark JAMES (Eng)	(23)	474199.20	338713.71
19	Robert KARLSSON (Swe)	(23)	465674.20	332624.43
# 20	John BICKERTON (Eng)	(31)	426404.15	304574.39
21	Gary ORR (Scot)	(28)	414865.58	296332.56
22	David HOWELL (Eng)	(29)	414275.14	295910.81
23	Peter O'MALLEY (Aus)	(21)	392585.85	280418.46
24	Andrew COLTART (Scot)	(28)	382227.03	273019.31
25	Dean ROBERTSON (Scot)	(31)	379255.06	270896.47
26	Ian WOOSNAM (Wal)	(23)	377113.53	269366.81
27	David CARTER (Eng)	(28)	376754.05	269110.04
28	Pierre FULKE (Swe)	(26)	371304.05	265217.18
29	Eduardo ROMERO (Arg)	(18)	369795.54	264139.67
30	Greg TURNER (NZ)	(20)	369278.47	263770.34
31	Ignacio GARRIDO (Sp)	(27)	346157.87	247255.62
32	José Maria OLAZÁBAL (Sp)	(18)	338359.97	241685.69
33	Stephen LEANEY (Aus)	(23)	326681.73	233344.09
34	Peter BAKER (Eng)	(29)	321412.00	229580.00
35	Costantino ROCCA (It)	(29)	314416.99	224583.56
36	Phil PRICE (Wal)	(25)	303428.65	216734.75

Pos	Name & Country		€	£
37	Paul MCGINLEY (Ire)	(26)	295125.53	210803.95
38	Miguel Angel MARTIN (Sp)	(26)	288596.97	206140.69
39	Jamie SPENCE (Eng)	(26)	280484.65	200346.18
40	David PARK (Wal)	(15)	274076.00	195768.57
41	Michael CAMPBELL (NZ)	(22)	269688.00	192634.29
42	Gary EVANS (Eng)	(28)	257396.46	183854.61
43	Patrik SJÖLAND (Swe)	(25)	252344.47	180246.05
44	Per-Ulrik JOHANSSON (Swe)	(21)	249650.40	178321.71
45	Santiago LUNA (Sp)	(26)	248879.11	177770.79
46	Sven STRÜVER (Ger)	(28)	245728.69	175520.49
47	Paul BROADHURST (Eng)	(31)	245579.43	175413.88
48	Steve WEBSTER (Eng)	(25)	244620.69	174729.06
49	Marc FARRY (Fr)	(29)	236366.05	168832.89
50	Jeev Milkha SINGH (Ind)	(24)	222783.29	159130.92
51	Ian GARBUTT (Eng)	(28)	222624.84	159017.74
52	Peter MITCHELL (Eng)	(28)	217733.13	155523.66
53	Russell CLAYDON (Eng)	(23)	214975.75	153554.11
54	Paul EALES (Eng)	(25)	214340.29	153100.21
55	José COCERES (Arg)	(23)	203213.09	145152.21
56	Søren KJELDSEN (Den)	(30)	202869.66	144906.90
57	Jean-Francois REMESY (Fr)	(20)	201512.98	143937.84
58	Francisco CEA (Sp)	(26)	201416.12	143868.66
59	Anthony WALL (Eng)	(29)	197568.12	141120.09
60	Van PHILLIPS (Eng)	(31)	195132.24	139380.17
# 61	Ricardo GONZALEZ (Arg)	(23)	189085.98	135061.41
# 62	Christopher HANELL (Swe)	(26)	184782.04	131987.17
63	Mark MCNULTY (Zim)	(18)	183239.88	130885.63
64	Greg OWEN (Eng)	(30)	177032.90	126452.07
$ 65	Geoff OGILVY (Aus)	(20)	175149.58	125106.84
66	Katsuyoshi TOMORI (Jpn)	(19)	175050.40	125036.00
67	Mats LANNER (Swe)	(25)	170516.06	121797.19
68	Michael JONZON (Swe)	(26)	167310.14	119507.24
# 69	John SENDEN (Aus)	(22)	164158.32	117255.94
$ 70	Emanuele CANONICA (It)	(22)	163590.57	116850.41
71	Roger WESSELS (SA)	(26)	162628.31	116163.08
$ 72	Diego BORREGO (Sp)	(20)	161642.55	115458.96
73	Mathias GRÖNBERG (Swe)	(23)	160604.30	114717.36
74	Brian DAVIS (Eng)	(26)	159428.40	113877.43
75	Peter LONARD (Aus)	(15)	158172.40	112980.29

Sergio Garcia

Miguel Angel Jiménez

76	Eamonn DARCY (Ire)	(23)	158003.29	112859.49
77	Steen TINNING (Den)	(23)	156799.98	111999.99
78	Scott DUNLAP (USA)	(6)	154857.12	110612.23
79	José RIVERO (Sp)	(24)	151415.15	108153.68
80	Paolo QUIRICI (Swi)	(26)	146248.17	104462.98
# 81	Warren BENNETT (Eng)	(21)	145933.38	104238.13
# 82	Roger WINCHESTER (Eng)	(26)	145227.43	103733.88
83	Thomas LEVET (Fr)	(29)	140785.24	100560.89
$ 84	Andrew MCLARDY (SA)	(25)	138974.64	99267.60
85	Barry LANE (Eng)	(25)	133651.38	95465.27
86	Des SMYTH (Ire)	(24)	131949.43	94249.59
87	Craig HAINLINE (USA)	(21)	129948.76	92820.54
88	Gerry NORQUIST (USA)	(16)	129467.51	92476.79
89	Thomas GÖGELE (Ger)	(26)	128747.43	91962.45
90	David GILFORD (Eng)	(23)	128432.25	91737.32
91	Pedro LINHART (Sp)	(21)	123913.50	88509.64
92	Stephen ALLAN (Aus)	(21)	123553.76	88252.69
93	Sam TORRANCE (Scot)	(22)	123356.17	88111.55
94	Raymond RUSSELL (Scot)	(28)	122790.80	87707.71
95	Nick FALDO (Eng)	(17)	122004.18	87145.84
96	Mark ROE (Eng)	(18)	118226.50	84447.50
$ 97	Gary EMERSON (Eng)	(20)	112142.24	80101.60
# 98	Per NYMAN (Swe)	(27)	111584.75	79703.39
# 99	Massimo SCARPA (It)	(25)	111156.79	79397.71
100	Rolf MUNTZ (Hol)	(27)	109326.62	78090.44
#101	Stephen GALLACHER (Scot)	(26)	108955.42	77825.30
102	Richard GREEN (Aus)	(22)	107156.48	76540.34
103	Wayne RILEY (Aus)	(20)	106838.09	76312.92
104	Raphaël JACQUELIN (Fr)	(29)	106523.80	76088.43
105	Jonathan LOMAS (Eng)	(29)	106084.48	75774.63
#106	John MELLOR (Eng)	(29)	105242.18	75172.99
$107	Anders HANSEN (Den)	(26)	105206.17	75147.26
$108	Nick O'HERN (Aus)	(18)	104080.76	74343.40
#109	Jorge BERENDT (Arg)	(18)	102788.07	73420.05
110	Andrew OLDCORN (Scot)	(25)	100470.75	71764.82

#111	Fredrik LINDGREN (Swe)	(24)	98099.26	70070.90
#112	Soren HANSEN (Den)	(28)	95002.76	67859.11
113	Domingo HOSPITAL (Sp)	(23)	93608.87	66863.48
114	Paul AFFLECK (Wal)	(26)	93293.44	66638.17
$115	Jeremy ROBINSON (Eng)	(19)	91745.74	65532.67
116	Miles TUNNICLIFF (Eng)	(27)	90666.63	64761.88
117	Peter SENIOR (Aus)	(11)	89009.18	63577.99
118	Massimo FLORIOLI (It)	(32)	87427.37	62448.12
119	Malcolm MACKENZIE (Eng)	(30)	87356.09	62397.21
120	Joakim HAEGGMAN (Swe)	(25)	83853.03	59895.02
121	Mark MOULAND (Wal)	(30)	82619.72	59014.09
#122	Daren LEE (Eng)	(25)	81332.37	58094.55
123	Stephen FIELD (Eng)	(25)	80899.59	57785.42
$124	Andrew RAITT (Eng)	(24)	78164.14	55831.53
125	Roger CHAPMAN (Eng)	(25)	77176.86	55126.33
126	Andrew SHERBORNE (Eng)	(33)	77035.85	55025.61
^127	Fredrik JACOBSON (Swe)	(30)	76433.72	54595.51
128	Tony JOHNSTONE (Zim)	(18)	76271.75	54479.82
$129	Richard BOXALL (Eng)	(26)	71842.30	51315.93
130	Derrick COOPER (Eng)	(29)	66775.03	47696.45
131	Michael LONG (NZ)	(24)	63566.46	45404.61
$132	Ian HUTCHINGS (SA)	(21)	61984.62	44274.73
133	Silvio GRAPPASONNI (It)	(19)	60925.00	43517.86
134	Klas ERIKSSON (Swe)	(6)	58754.00	41967.14
135	Tom GILLIS (USA)	(23)	52702.10	37644.36
136	Daniel CHOPRA (Swe)	(33)	52047.34	37176.67
137	Andrew BEAL (Eng)	(29)	51642.25	36887.32
$138	Johan RYSTRÖM (Swe)	(16)	51488.40	36777.43
139	Ross MCFARLANE (Eng)	(26)	50114.00	35795.71
140	Olle KARLSSON (Swe)	(21)	50054.83	35753.45
$141	Alberto BINAGHI (It)	(23)	49363.17	35259.41
$142	Robert Jan DERKSEN (Hol)	(24)	48916.16	34940.11
143	Severiano BALLESTEROS (Sp)	(20)	46119.50	32942.50
^144	Maarten LAFEBER (Hol)	(5)	45008.34	32148.81
145	Fabrice TARNAUD (Fr)	(28)	44267.83	31619.88
*146	Lian-Wei ZHANG (Chi)	(8)	43538.68	31099.06
147	Rodger DAVIS (Aus)	(16)	42932.00	30665.71
148	Jim PAYNE (Eng)	(20)	39998.59	28570.42
$149	Henrik BJORNSTAD (Nor)	(20)	38488.99	27492.14
150	Dennis EDLUND (Swe)	(27)	38137.77	27241.26

Retief Goosen

\#   Denotes 1998 Challenge Tour Graduate

\$ Denotes 1998 Qualifying School Graduate

*   Denotes Affiliate Member

•   Figures in parentheses indicate number of events played

365

The PGA European Tour

(A COMPANY LIMITED BY GUARANTEE)

BOARD OF DIRECTORS

N C Coles, MBE *Chairman*

A Gallardo, *Vice Chairman*	M H James (alternate K J Brown)	J E O'Leary
D Cooper	D Jones	R Rafferty
B Gallacher, OBE	T A Horton	D J Russell

P A T Davidson *(non Executive Tour Group Director)*
K S Owen *(non Executive Tour Group Director)*

TOURNAMENT COMMITTEE

M H James (Eng), *Chairman*
M Lanner (Swe), *Vice Chairman*
A Binaghi (It)
R Chapman (Eng)
R Claydon (Eng)
D Cooper (Eng)
P Eales (Eng)
A Forsbrand (Swe)
B Langer (Ger)
R Lee (Eng)
C Montgomerie, MBE (Scot)
O Sellberg (Swe)
J Spence (Eng)
S Torrance, MBE (Scot)
J Van de Velde (Fr)

EXECUTIVE MANAGEMENT

Executive Director	K D Schofield CBE
Deputy Executive Director	G C O'Grady
General Counsel	M D Friend
Assistant to Executive Director and Ryder Cup Director	R G Hills
Group Marketing Director	S F Kelly
Director of Communications and Public Relations	M S Platts
Director of Tour Operations	D W Garland
Assistant Director of Tour Operations	D A Probyn
Chief Referee	J N Paramor
Senior Referee and Qualifying School Director	A N McFee
Managing Director, European Seniors Tour	K A Stubbs
Deputy Managing Director, European Seniors Tour	P Adams
Director of International Policy	K Waters
European Challenge Tour Director	A de Soultrait
Group Company Secretary	M Bray
Senior Tournament Director	M R Stewart
Director of Tournament Services	E Kitson
Director of Tournament Development	J Birkmyre
Group Finance Planner	J Orr

The Contributors

Mike Aitken *(The Scotsman)*
Scottish PGA Championship

Mike Britten
Peugeot Open de España
Moroccan Open
The Sarazen World Open

Jeremy Chapman *(Racing Post)*
Victor Chandler British Masters

Bruce Critchley *(Sky Sports)*
The Compass Group English Open

Norman Dabell
Algarve Portuguese Open
Madeira Island Open
Belgacom Open

Bill Elliott *(The Observer/Today's Golfer)*
The 33rd Ryder Cup Matches

Andy Farrell *(The Independent)*
US PGA Championship

Alan Fraser *(Daily Mail)*
WGC – NEC Invitational

Sergio Garcia
My 1999 Canon Shot of the Year

Mark Garrod *(Press Association)*
Heineken Classic
Qatar Masters
Volvo Masters

David Hamilton
European Challenge Tour

Martin Hardy *(The Express)*
Benson and Hedges Malaysian Open

Alan Hedley *(The Journal)*
Compaq European Grand Prix

Peter Higgs *(Mail on Sunday)*
Deutsche Bank – SAP Open TPC of Europe

John Hopkins *(The Times)*
US Open

John Huggan *(Golf World US)*
BMW International Open
Alfred Dunhill Cup

Renton Laidlaw *(The Golf Channel)*
TNT Dutch Open
Volvo Scandinavian Masters

Jock MacVicar *(Scottish Daily Express)*
Dubai Desert Classic
The Standard Life Loch Lomond

Michael McDonnell
MacGregor Week
Volvo PGA Championship
Murphy's Irish Open
128th Open Golf Championship
The Year in Retrospect

Colin Montgomerie MBE
A Golden Decade

James Mossop *(Sunday Telegraph)*
Alfred Dunhill South African PGA
Championship
Mercedes-Benz – Vodacom South African
Open Championship

Rob Nothman *(BBC Radio Five Live)*
Benson and Hedges International Open

Mitchell Platts *(European Tour)*
Masters Tournament
WGC – American Express Championship
World Cup of Golf
European Tour Courses

Bryan Potter
European Seniors Tour

Gordon Richardson
Fiat & Fila Italian Open
Novotel Perrier Open de France
Canon European Masters
Linde German Masters

Colm Smith *(Irish Independent)*
Smurfit European Open
West of Ireland Golf Classic

Art Spander
WGC – Andersen Consulting Match Play

Mel Webb *(The Times)*
Turespaña Masters – Open Andalucia
Estoril Open
German Open
Trophée Lancôme

John Whitbread *(Surrey Herald)*
Cisco World Match Play Championship

The Photographers

Tom Able-Green/Allsport
68 top, 73, 74 bottom

AGJ Golf Library
35 top centre, 89 top left

Chris Buchanan/Allsport
213

David Cannon/Allsport
1, 7 top, 9 bottom, 10 top left, 11 bottom, 14 top, 15 top centre, top right & bottom, 21 top, 24 top, 26, 32 bottom, 33, 37 bottom, 66, 69 top left, 88 top, 104, 107 top, 109, 110 bottom left, 111, 148, 151 top right & bottom, 152 bottom, 155 bottom, 156 top, 158, 180-182, 184 bottom, 186 left, 208 bottom, 209 top right, 210 bottom, 266-270, 290, 292, 293 bottom left

Phil Cole/Allsport
165 top, 216-220, 308-313

J.D. Cuban/Allsport
81 bottom

Jon Ferrey/Allsport
256 bottom, 257 left, 258 bottom, 260

John Gichigi/Allsport
164 top left, 346 top left

Michael S. Green/AP
40-41, 243 top left

Jim Gund/Sports Illustrated
243 bottom left

Harry How/Allsport
24 bottom, 28 bottom right, 80, 83, 183, 241, 244 top

Phil Inglis Photography
4, 191 top

Rusty Jarrett/Allsport
8, 22, 23 top left

Craig Jones/Allsport
12, 13, 20, 21 bottom, 25, 28 bottom centre, 31, 38, 81 top, 82, 84 top & bottom left, 108 bottom, 184-185, 186 right, 187, 240, 244 bottom, 254-255, 256 top, 257 right, 258 top right, 259 top, 261, 367

Ross Kinnaird/Allsport
202 top right, 206-207, 208 top centre, 209 bottom, 211 bottom, 212 bottom, 359 bottom right

Warren Little/Allsport
137, 344

Tim Matthews/Allsport
86, 87, 88 bottom, 89 top right, 89 bottom left, 90, 171 top

Donald Miralle/Allsport
78, 79

Stephen Munday/Allsport
7 bottom, 10 top right, 11 top, 14 bottom, 15 top left, 16, 23 bottom, 30, 32 top, 34, 35 bottom, 36 top, 37 top, 54, 56-65, 105, 106, 107 bottom, 108 top, 110 top left, 118-122, 132 top left, 139 top, 149, 151 top left, 154, 155 top left, 156 bottom, 157 top left, 200-204, 209 top left, 212 top, 214, 248-253, 272-277, 291, 293 top & bottom left, 297-301, 337, 342, 346 top right, 354, 355 top, 356 bottom, 358, 359 top right, 361, 368

Scott Olson/Reuters
243 right

Andrew Redington/Allsport
17, 23 top right, 28 top & bottom left, 29, 67, 68 bottom, 69 top right/bottom, 70, 72, 74 top, 75-77, 112-117, 136, 138, 139 bottom left, 150, 152 top, 157 top left (1&2) & bottom left, 162 top, 168-172, 194-198, 208 top left & top right, 210 top left & right, 211 top, 212 centre, 236-239, 314, 316-317, 320, 323-324, 326, 328-329, 330 top, 332-333, 334-336, 338-339, 343, 350-353, 355 bottom, 356 top, 358 top left, centre left, bottom left, 366

Paul Severn/Allsport
6, 9 top, 35 top left & top right, 36 bottom, 42, 43 bottom, 44-46, 48-53, 92-103, 124-135, 142-146, 160-161, 162 bottom, 164 top right & bottom, 165 bottom, 166, 174-178, 188-192, 222-228, 230-234, 262-265, 278-282, 284-288, 302-307, 315, 318-319, 321-322, 327, 330 bottom, 331, 345, 347-348, 359 top centre & centre right

Roberto Schmidt/AFP
242

Jamie Squire/Allsport
245, 246

Matthew Stockman/Allsport
258 top left, 259 bottom

Duif du Toit/Touchline Picture Agency
43 top

Ian Walton/Allsport
296

Nick Wilson/Allsport
55